Emotion and Motivation

Perspectives on Social Psychology

The four volumes in this series collect readings from the *Blackwell Handbooks of Social Psychology* and present them thematically. The results are course-friendly texts in key areas of social psychology – *Social Cognition*, *Self and Social Identity*, *Emotion and Motivation*, and *Applied Social Psychology*. Each volume provides a representative sample of exciting research and theory that is both comprehensive and current and cross-cuts the levels of analysis from intrapersonal to intergroup.

Social Cognition, edited by Marilynn B. Brewer and Miles Hewstone
Self and Social Identity, edited by Marilynn B. Brewer and Miles Hewstone
Applied Social Psychology, edited by Marilynn B. Brewer and Miles Hewstone
Emotion and Motivation, edited by Marilynn B. Brewer and Miles Hewstone

Emotion and Motivation

Edited by

Marilynn B. Brewer
and
Miles Hewstone

Blackwell Publishing

350 Main Street, Malden, MA 02148-5020, USA
108 Cowley Road, Oxford OX4 1JF, UK
550 Swanston Street, Carlton, Victoria 3053, Australia

First published 2004 by Blackwell Publishing Ltd.

Library of Congress Cataloging-in-Publication Data

Emotion and motivation / edited by Marilynn B. Brewer and Miles Hewstone.
p.   cm.
Includes bibliographical references and index.
ISBN 1-4051-1068-6 (pbk. : alk. paper)
1. Emotions–Social aspects.   2. Motivation (Psychology)–Social aspects.
I. Brewer, Marilynn B., 1942–   II. Hewstone, Miles.

BF531.E4826 2004
152.4–dc21
2003011036

A catalogue record for this title is available from the British Library.

Set in 10/12^{1}/2pt Adobe Garamond
by Graphicraft Limited, Hong Kong
Printed and bound in the United Kingdom
by MPG Books, Bodmin, Cornwall

For further information on
Blackwell Publishing, visit our website:
http://www.blackwellpublishing.com

Contents

Part II: Social Motivation

Preface

When the *Blackwell Handbooks of Social Psychology* project was conceived, we sought to go beyond a simple topical structure for the content of the volumes in order to reflect more closely the complex pattern of cross-cutting theoretical perspectives and research agendas that comprise social psychology as a dynamic enterprise. The idea we developed was to represent the discipline in a kind of matrix structure, crossing levels of analysis with topics, processes, and functions that recur at all of these levels in social psychological theory and research. Taking inspiration from Willem Doise's 1986 book (*Levels of Explanation in Social Psychology*) four levels of analysis – intrapersonal, interpersonal, intragroup, and intergroup – provided the basis for organizing the Handbook series into four volumes. The two co-editors responsible for developing each of these volumes selected content chapters on the basis of cross-cutting themes represented by basic social psychological processes of social cognition, attribution, social motivation, affect and emotion, social influence, social comparison, and self and identity.

The four-volume *Handbook* that resulted from this organizational framework represents the collective efforts of two series editors, eight volume editors, and 191 contributing authors. The *Intraindividual Processes* volume, edited by Abraham Tesser and Norbert Schwarz, provides a comprehensive selection of work on social cognition, affect, and motivation, which focuses on the individual as the unit of analysis. The *Interpersonal Processes* volume, edited by Garth Fletcher and Margaret Clark, also covers the cognition, affect, and motivation themes as they are played out in the context of close interpersonal relationships and dyadic exchanges. Again in the volume on *Group Processes*, edited by Michael Hogg and Scott Tindale, the themes of cognition, affect, and motivation are well represented in work on collective behavior in small groups and social organizations. Finally, the volume on *Intergroup Processes*, edited by Rupert Brown and Samuel Gaertner, covers work that links cognitive, affective, and motivational processes to relationships between social groups and large collectives.

In all four volumes of the *Handbook*, the concepts of emotion and motivation occupy a prominent position, featuring as key aspects of many of the central theories of social psychology and the phenomena they seek to explain. Because of the matrix structure of the four volumes of the *Blackell Handbooks of Social Psychology*, it is possible to draw from all four volumes to create a selection of readings on emotion and motivation that cross-cuts the levels of analysis from intrapersonal to intergroup. This volume contains a set of such readings, which we have selected for the purpose of providing a representative sampling of vibrant research and theory in this area that is both comprehensive and current.

Marilynn Brewer and Miles Hewstone

Acknowledgments

The editor and publishers gratefully acknowledge the following for permission to reproduce copyright material:

Brown, Rupert and Gaertner, Sam (Eds.) (2001). *Blackwell Handbook of Social Psychology: Intergroup Processes.* Oxford: Blackwell Publishing. Reprinted with permission.

Fletcher, Garth J. O. and Clark, Margaret S. (Eds.) (2001). *Blackwell Handbook of Social Psychology: Interpersonal Processes.* Oxford: Blackwell Publishing. Reprinted with permission.

Hogg, Michael A. and Tindale, Scott (Eds.) (2001). *Blackwell Handbook of Social Psychology: Group Processes.* Oxford: Blackwell Publishing. Reprinted with permission.

Tesser, Abraham and Schwarz, Norbert (Eds.) (2001). *Blackwell Handbook of Social Psychology: Intraindividual Processes.* Oxford: Blackwell Publishing. Reprinted with permission.

The publishers apologize for any errors or omissions in the above list and would be grateful to be notified of any corrections that should be incorporated in the next edition or reprint of this book.

Introduction

Although modern social psychology is thought of as a largely cognitive discipline, both emotion and motivation are key components of an overall approach, not least because of their interplay with cognition.

Research on emotion is difficult to characterize (see Frijda, 1986), but there is fairly general agreement that *emotions* are valenced reactions to personally significant events. There is also agreement that emotional processes unfold in time, and involve a variety of components (physiological, behavioral, and cognitive). The broad importance of emotion in social psychology is evidenced from the fact that emotion spans all three of the main levels of analysis that psychologists apply to their subject matter – cognitive, physiological, and social-cultural. Insights have been gained from all three levels – best thought of as complementary, rather than competing – and many of the benefits of this approach for social psychology are contained in this volume.

Like emotions, motivations also occupy a central role in classic and contemporary theories of social psychology (see Weiner, 1992). Broadly speaking, research on *motivation* focuses on the determinants of what type of goals people choose, and how they go about implementing those goals; thus any field in social psychology could, in principle, be analyzed from a motivational perspective. A motivational approach helps us to understand *why* we make some of the social judgments we do, and why we behave socially in some of the ways we do. As such, it complements a cognitive approach that focuses on *how* we process social information and make decisions.

Taken as a set, these 14 readings underline the importance of emotion and motivation in contemporary social psychology. Although it is true that from the 1980s onwards social psychology became a predominantly cognitive discipline, and much was learned by this focus, the field today is much better balanced. Many of the most fascinating research questions are not susceptible to a purely cognitive analysis, and are only likely to be fully understood by a tripartite approach in terms of cognition, emotion and motivation.

REFERENCES

Frijda, N. (1986). *The Emotions*. Cambridge, UK: Cambridge University Press.
Weiner, B. (1992). *Human Motivation*. Newbury Park, CA: Sage Publications.

PART I

Affect and Emotions

Introduction

The readings in this Part are representative of current theory and research on affect and emotions in social psychology, and they illustrate the insights of an approach highlighting affect and emotions across some of the different levels of analysis within social psychology. A review of perspectives on the nature of this field is given in the first reading (Parrott), which provides a perfect orientation point, with its clarification of definition, functions of emotions, and the general approaches that have been taken in studying emotion in social psychology.

The next two readings explore emotions in interpersonal settings, where people frequently experience intense emotions. Clark, Fitness and Brissette are interested in the degree to which partners in a relationship feel responsibility for one another's needs. They propose that more emotion is shown in relationships when people expect their needs to be met; and some people are more emotionally expressive generally, because they are more confident that their needs will be met by others, and/or are more willing to meet the needs of others. Berscheid and Ammazzalorso are concerned with a different variable, which can also only be understood in relationship terms, the degree of interdependence between two people. They argue for a strong connection between close relationships and emotional experience, and explore some of the conditions that appear to trigger intense emotions.

In contrast to the close relationships of interest to the previous two readings, emotions are also of interest at the intra-group level. Thompson, Husted Medvec, Seiden and Kopelman review evidence of three distinct perspectives on emotions in negotiation – the rational negotiator, the positive negotiator, and the irrational negotiator; they both sift the sometimes competing advice and explore common misconceptions about emotions in negotiations. In the following reading, Kelly explores affective processes at the more general level of the group. She examines how group moods and emotions influence group-level judgments and information processing.

The final reading in this Part moves to a different level, that of intergroup relations. Wilder and Simon review theory and research on how affective states influence the display of intergroup bias, including prejudice, stereotyping and discrimination.

CHAPTER ONE

The Nature of Emotion

W. Gerrod Parrott

Most topics studied by social psychologists involve emotion in some way. Consider how cognitive dissonance is motivated by anxiety about self-esteem, or how conformity is influenced by the embarrassment of conspicuous deviation and the contentment of belonging. The list is impressively long: social comparisons generate envy, dejection, and pride; social anxiety underlies many group processes; romantic relationships have their love and jealousy, aggression its anger, altruism its sympathy, and persuasive communications almost any emotion one can name. Emotions, then, are at the heart of many social psychological phenomena.

This chapter presents an overview of perspectives on the nature of emotion. The first section discusses foundational issues in the study of emotion, including its definitions, the functions of emotion, and the general approaches that have been taken in studying it. The general thesis is that emotion spans all of the levels of analysis that psychologists apply to their subject matter: to reduce them to three, these are the social and cultural, the cognitive, and the physiological. The remainder of this chapter describes emotion at each of these three levels and presents some of the most important issues and findings that may be gleaned from each.

Definitions, Conceptions, and Basic Issues

Defining emotion

Although there is no single, agreed-upon definition of emotion, there is considerable consensus that emotional states are best thought of as processes that unfold in time, involving a variety of components. Whether these components are necessarily or only typically part of emotions is a matter of some debate. The beginning of an emotional episode typically includes an evaluative perception of the nature of the situation, known as an *appraisal* (Lazarus, 1991). An emotional appraisal evaluates events or objects as significantly affecting a person's concerns, goals, or values in a positive or negative way. The presence of appraisals is one reason why many theorists have argued that emotions have a cognitive aspect (e.g. Solomon, 1976), although, as I will discuss later, not all theorists are persuaded that appraisals are necessary.

Emotional reactions can involve changes in thinking, behavior, physiology, and expression. The effects of these changes may influence readiness to think and act in certain ways, as well as signal this readiness to others, thereby affecting social interaction and relationships. The development of an emotion over time depends on how the situation is evaluated and coped with. In a narrow sense, an emotional state ends when attention is drawn to another issue, but, in a larger sense, the emotional episode may be said to continue until such point as the evaluation of the event changes significantly (Frijda, Mesquita, Sonnemans, & Van Goozen, 1991). In summary, then, an emotion can be loosely defined as a reaction to personally significant events, where "reaction" is taken to include biological, cognitive, and behavioral reactions, as well as subjective feelings of pleasure or displeasure. The issues surrounding the definition of emotion have been reviewed in several recent volumes (e.g. Ekman & Davidson, 1994; Russell, Fernández-Dols, Manstead, & Wellenkamp, 1995).

Even with such a loose definition it is important to realize that the meaning of "emotion" in academic psychology often differs somewhat from that in ordinary language. First of all, the general term "emotion" plus the terms for specific emotions such as "sadness" and "shame" are all words in the English language, and these words often have no precise equivalents in other languages (Wierzbicka, 1992). Whether psychologists can or should strive for definitions that span cultural and linguistic boundaries is unclear (Russell, et al., 1995). Second, the everyday connotation of "emotion" often includes the judgment that the response is in some way exceptional, such as by being excessive, inappropriate, dysfunctional, immoral, or praiseworthy. Emotion terms have developed for the purposes of everyday speakers of the language; these purposes often include judgments of the appropriateness of a person's actions, but social psychologists do not necessarily share those purposes. Finally, in everyday usage, the term "emotion" refers to a wide range of phenomena that have little in common. The concept of emotion is fuzzy around the edges. For example, there is little doubt that anger and sadness are emotions, but there is less agreement about whether to include moods (depression, irritability), long-term emotions (love that continues for years), dispositions (benevolence, cantankerousness), motivational feelings (hunger, sexual arousal), cognitive feelings (confusion, *deja vu*), and "calm" emotions (sympathy, satisfaction).

If the goals of research require fidelity to everyday usage, loose definitions of emotion appear to be the best that are possible. In order to be true to the everyday usage of the word "emotion," many investigators have proposed that its meaning be represented as a "fuzzy category" with no precise definition (Fehr & Russell, 1984). This representation is often proposed to have the structure of a script or narrative (Shaver, Schwartz, Kirson, & O'Connor, 1987). On the other hand, if the goals of research are to develop objective understanding of aspects of emotion independent of folk conceptions, the preferred strategy may be to develop more precise definitions independent of everyday usage (Clore & Ortony, 1991). For example, for purposes of research it may be helpful to postulate attributes that will be considered necessary and sufficient for a psychological event to be considered an emotion. Researchers seeking this latter goal must be careful to distinguish their concepts from everyday conceptions that may bear the same labels.

Relation of emotions to other aspects of mind

For centuries, philosophers and psychologists have found it convenient to distinguish between different aspects of the mind. Plato, in *The Republic*, has Socrates argue that the soul can be divided into three parts: an appetitive part that produces various irrational desires, a spirited part that produces anger and other feelings, and a reasoning part that permits reflection and rationality. This tricotomy shows similarity to one expressed in contemporary psychology between *conation*, the aspect of mind directed toward action, *affect*, the aspect of mind involving subjective feeling, and *cognition*, the aspect of mind involving thought.

It is certainly legitimate to observe that mental activity involves these aspects, and there is no doubt that a valid conceptual distinction can be made between them. Nevertheless, disagreement and confusion has resulted from these distinctions because some psychologists have treated these *aspects* of the mind as if they were *distinct parts* of the mind, whereas others have not. The rationale for separating these aspects of mind is usually based on the fact that people sometimes feel an emotion that they believe to be irrational, or fail to feel an emotion they believe to be warranted. Such conflicts can make it appear that motivation, emotion, and cognition can act as independent entities, and some theorists have been persuaded to adopt such a view, although it then becomes necessary to account for the many ways that these entities influence one another (see Bless, 2001). Other theorists, however, stress that emotions have both cognitive and motivational qualities, and therefore think of these elements as referring to different *aspects* of mental events, not as corresponding to actual separations within the mind (e.g. Peters, 1958).

Level of analysis

In any science, phenomena can be studied at any of several levels of analysis. For example, in the physical sciences water can be considered from the points of view of the elementary particles and forces of physics, or of the atoms and molecules of chemistry. In the biological sciences evolution can likewise be studied at a variety of levels, ranging from molecular genetics to ecology. The same is true in psychology, with emotion serving as a good example. Emotion can be studied in terms of biology, of thinking, and of the social context. The choice of level of analysis determines a number of important aspects of research, including the choice of measures. On the biological level, emotions are measured in terms of activity in the nervous system and in terms of changes in the periphery of the body (e.g. sweaty palms, muscle tension). On the cognitive level, measures might include people's ratings of their beliefs about the cause of a certain event, their expectations that a certain action will bring about a certain end, or their attention toward or away from certain classes of stimuli. On the social level, measures might include the amount of time people spend making eye contact, changes in how people are perceived, or changes in interpersonal relationships. Other levels of analysis could be distinguished from these, but these three are sufficient to illustrate the basic point, which is that no one level of analysis is more central or more "scientific" than any other. Each addresses important aspects of emotion, and a complete understanding of emotional phenomena often requires that insights from all three be combined.

Function

What is the function of the emotions? Some have construed emotions as either dysfunctional or, at best, as lacking function. For example, the Stoics, such as Epictetus and Marcus Aurelius, believed that (most) emotions were the result of erroneous thought and should be avoided. More recently, Charles Darwin (1872/1955) understood emotional expressions as vestigial movements that formerly had functions in our evolutionary past but are now mostly useless, and philosopher Jean-Paul Sartre (1948) characterized emotions as ways of avoiding responsibility and truth. Arguments for the dysfunctionality of emotions thus encompass the biological, cognitive, and social levels of analysis.

Others, however, have maintained that emotions serve a variety of useful functions, and their functionalist approaches to emotions can be found at all levels of analysis, too. Ironically, the theory that has been most influential in this regard is that of Darwin, whose theory of natural selection, not his theory of vestigial emotional expression, has formed the basis of post-Darwinian evolutionary biology. Evolutionists use the theory of natural selection to understand emotions as adaptations that often serve useful functions. They argue that, although emotions can sometimes be maladaptive or inappropriate, anything as common and significant as emotions must have been subject to evolutionary pressures, so animals possessing emotions must have had some advantages over animals that did not. This argument, of course, leaves open the possibility that emotions were advantageous to our ancestors in their habitats but are no longer useful to us in ours. There are some emotions that seem to be of this latter type: some of our reactions to stress, such as increases of heart rate and of certain hormone levels, seem much more useful in fleeing from predators than in preparing for presentations, and these responses may be responsible for such stress-related illnesses as heart attacks and stomach ulcers (Selye, 1976). But, on the whole, it is generally thought that emotions serve useful roles of various sorts. At the biological level, they can be viewed as preparing the body for actions that are usually adaptive in the situations that produce the emotion (Frijda, 1986). Functionalism may be found at the cognitive level of analysis as well. The theory of Oatley & Johnson-Laird (1987) finds functionality in the way that emotions alter a person's priorities, thereby serving to allocate limited resources among multiple plans and goals. At the social level, emotions' functions have been examined in units as small as the interactive dyad (e.g. communication of social intentions: Fridlund, 1994) and as large as an entire culture (e.g. to express and fortify cultural values and social structures: Lutz, 1988). For a thorough review of functionalist perspectives see Gross & Keltner (in press).

This range of opinions about the functionality of emotions can be rather confusing. It may be that it results in part from confusions between the academic and everyday meanings of "emotion." Theorists using the everyday sense may be more likely than theorists using an academic definition to consider cases that are irrational, that result from ulterior motives such as the need for self-esteem, or that are otherwise especially likely to be maladaptive. Yet the disagreements are not only definitional. Another problem is that emotions do not have fixed effects; any given category of emotion, such as anger or happiness, can motivate a variety of expressions and actions, and socialization and choice of self-regulation strategies can have an enormous effect on whether a particular emotion is adaptive or maladaptive (Parrott, in press). Perhaps a reasonable compromise position is that emotions have the potential to be functional and adaptive, but only if socialized and regulated to be appropriate for the particular context in which they occur. Further research on the ways in which emotions may be functional or dysfunctional would be helpful in improving understanding of this issue.

Social and Cultural Approaches to Emotion

To take a social approach to emotion is to focus on how emotion pertains to social situations and relationships. Many emotions have to do with our appearance to others, our relationships with others, our duties toward others, and our expectations of others. Communication, culture, and the social functions of individual emotions thus form the main emphases of the social approach.

Communication

The social nature of emotion is apparent when considering how people communicate their emotions to others and how they recognize others' emotions. Considerable research has investigated the ways in which such communication takes place in humans and animals. Charles Darwin (1872/1955) is the person most responsible for directing attention to expressions of emotion. Research by Ekman (1973) and others has extended Darwin's work, suggesting that there exists a set of human facial expressions that are universally recognizable and innate. These facial expressions include those of sadness, fear, joy, anger, disgust, and surprise.

Certain limitations to the research paradigms employed to date have led some to question the validity of this conclusion. The use of still photographs of posed facial expressions and of forced-choice response formats, for example, might compromise the validity and ecological relevance of the findings (Russell, 1994). Moreover, controversy exists about how to interpret the meaning of facial expressions. According to Ekman, facial expressions of emotion automatically occur when emotions are experienced. To some extent, they may be suppressed, modified, or exaggerated to conform with social conventions, known as *display rules*, but there nevertheless exists an innate connection between facial expressions and emotional experience. This theory has been challenged by Fridlund (1994), who argues that facial expressions of emotion do not so much express an inner emotional state as they communicate intentions and wishes to others. At present there does not seem to be decisive evidence favoring either approach. The disagreement has spurred a new wave of theory and research on nonverbal expressions (see Russell & Fernández-Dols, 1997). Future theoretical developments may well involve a combination of current theories.

Social constructionism

The current debate about facial expressions addresses a second issue as well, the question of whether emotions are universal or differ across cultures. The position that emotions are universal is well represented by Ekman's approach, and is usually justified in terms of the genetic basis of human emotionality, which is approached at the biological level of analysis described later in this chapter. The position that human emotions are shaped by particular cultures is necessarily approached at the social and cultural level of analysis. *Social constructionism* is the thesis that, to some extent, emotions are the products of culture. (See Harré, 1986, and Harré & Parrott, 1996, for collections of articles reflecting this approach.)

According to social constructionists, human cultures influence the emotions by influencing the beliefs, values, and social environment that members of the culture possess. The emotions may be understood as being enmeshed within an entire system of beliefs and values, so an emotion can hardly be said to exist independent of the culture of which it is a part. Consider, for example, an emotion that existed in Western cultures in medieval times but seems to have become extinct by the year 1400 or so: *accidie*. Accidie occurred when one was bored with one's religious duties and procrastinated in carrying them out; one felt both bored and also sad about one's religious failings and the loss of one's former enthusiasm for religious devotions. The cure for accidie was to resume one's religious duties and to feel joyful in doing so. The emotion was intimately tied to a set of moral values concerning one's religious duties; to feel it at all was a sin. The emotion faded from existence when values changed during the Renaissance. Now, when people in Western cultures are bored and procrastinate, they feel guilt, an emotion that is related to a culture based on individual responsibility, not one of spiritual duty (Harré & Finlay-Jones, 1986). The implication is that cultural beliefs and values make certain emotions possible, and that the same culture may permit a somewhat different set of emotions at one time than at another.

A similar point can be made about two different cultures existing at the same time. The anthropologist Lutz (1988) argues that the emphasis on social relationships and sharing that exists in the South Pacific atoll of Ifaluk gives rise to emotions that are not equivalent to any Western emotion. *Fago*, for example, is something like our sadness, but it differs by being specific to a close relationship toward a less fortunate person – a person in need – to whom one feels compassion. This point has been made by studying a culture in depth, as Lutz did, and also by comparing multiple cultures. For example, Markus & Kitayama (1991) have argued that cultures may be plotted along a dimension of self-construal that ranges from being relatively independent with others at one extreme to being relatively interdependent of others at the other. They argue that "ego-focused" emotions such as anger, frustration, and pride will be experienced more by people with relatively independent selves, whereas "other-focused" emotions such as shame, belongingness, and sympathy will be experienced more by people with relatively interdependent selves. (For a review of cultural perspectives in social psychology, see Miller, 2001.)

Social functions of emotions

Regardless of whether emotions are considered to be universal or culturally relative, the social level of analysis is characterized by attention to the ways that emotions function in social situations. This attention is often best directed to particular emotions rather than to the broad category of emotion in general. For example, anger has been found to play important roles in the regulation of interpersonal behavior in many North American cultures. Anger is part of a system that enforces normative standards, arising when a person interprets another's actions as a voluntary, unjustified transgression, and often functioning to repair the relationship between the angry person and the target of the anger (Averill, 1982).

Studies of shame, guilt, and embarrassment have suggested that these emotions can function to motivate behavior that conforms to social and moral norms and that makes restitution for past misdeeds. Shame is generally found to focus on the adequacy of a person's self, or on the exposure of that self to public disapproval; guilt, in contrast, is generally found to focus more on particular misdeeds and to be more the result of a person's private conscience than of public exposure (for a comprehensive review, see Tangney & Fischer, 1995). Embarrassment is in some ways similar to shame, in that it is linked to public exposure, but may be distinguished from it in several ways: unlike shame, it does not require belief that one is immoral or defective, and it is not experienced in private. Embarrassment results from the perception that the present social situation is socially awkward, often (but not necessarily) because others perceive the self in some negative way. Embarrassment thus motivates people to mind how they are perceived by others, to behave in role-consistent ways, and generally to conform (for a review, see Miller, 1996).

Envy and jealousy may also be considered from the standpoint of their social functions. "Envy" refers to the painful or negative emotion experienced toward a person who has what oneself wants but lacks. It typically includes a mix of hostility and inferiority. The emotion can motivate achievement and innovation to catch up with the rival, or hostility to undercut the rival's advantage. There is wide variation in the extent to which expression of envy is tolerated in different cultures, and thus in the extent to which it is necessary for those with enviable qualities to fear the envy of others (Schoeck, 1969). Because of fear of envy, self-presentations often conceal or downplay a person's successes and advantages. The word "jealousy" can be used to refer to envy, but it can also be used to refer to a quite different type of emotional reaction, one that requires a more complex set of relationships among three people rather than just two. Jealousy, in this sense, is an emotion that occurs when one person perceives that his or her relationship with another person is threatened by a rival who could take the jealous person's place. Like envy, jealousy comes in a variety of forms, but these generally may be seen as motivating a person to protect and nurture the threatened relationship or, if it is too late for that, to cope with its loss. Salovey (1991) provides a good collection of articles on envy and jealousy.

There are, of course, many more emotions that can be studied at the social level of analysis, but this sample will serve to illustrate the approach.

Cognitive Approaches to Emotion

The way people think is clearly related to their emotions. This is not to say, of course, that the social or the biological approach is "wrong," only that it is often helpful to talk about emotions as a set of beliefs or a mode of information processing rather than as a social role or a set of events in the brain (even though the cognitions are socialized by culture and require brain activity). On the cognitive level of analysis certain truths about emotion are more readily apparent than at other levels of analysis.

One clear advantage of the cognitive level is that it facilitates discussion of a person's beliefs. Emotions usually occur because events have been interpreted in a certain way, and, once emotions occur, people often think in a somewhat altered manner. Thus, certain types of thinking characteristically precede emotion, and emotions themselves involve ways of thinking as well as social functions and bodily responses. Each of these cognitive aspects of emotion has been the topic of investigation by psychologists.

Appraisal

The thinking that leads to emotion is usually called the *appraisal*. It is characterized by an assessment of the current situation and its implications for the well-being of oneself and the things that one cares about. The classic experiments demonstrating the importance of appraisals in emotions were performed by Richard Lazarus, who asked people to watch movies showing extremely unpleasant scenes of people being mutilated in primitive rites or in woodworking accidents. Before viewing the films, some of the people were encouraged to interpret the filmed events as harmful and painful, whereas others were encouraged to deny the extent of the harm and interpret them as benign, and still others were encouraged to distance themselves from the victims and view the scenes in a more detached, intellectual manner. All of the people then viewed the same films, yet the first group experienced more stress and more intense, negative emotions than did the other two groups. After the film Lazarus asked the viewers to describe how they were feeling, and he also measured certain physiological symptoms of autonomic nervous system activity; the groups differed on both the self-report and the physiological measures. These experiments demonstrated how changes in cognitive appraisal could produce differences in the intensity of emotions that occur (Lazarus, 1966).

There is controversy over the type of judgments that should be included in the concept of "appraisal." Some appraisals are quite careful and deliberate, as when one thinks through a remark one heard and only gradually realizes that it was inconsiderate and derogatory to oneself – and then one becomes angry. Many times, however, it seems that appraisals, if they indeed play a role in producing emotions, must be very quick, outside conscious awareness, and independent of our rational faculties.

There are two ways to resolve this dilemma, and a lively debate over which alternative is better occurred in the pages of *American Psychologist* (Lazarus, 1982, 1984; Zajonc, 1980, 1984). One resolution was advocated by Robert Zajonc (1980), who proposed that cognition and emotion may be conceived as two independent systems, often working together, but capable of being at odds. Zajonc's theory can account for discrepancies between emotion and reason, but it does so in a manner that creates many problems. Why is it possible to call certain emotions "irrational" if emotions do not intrinsically entail beliefs? Why does emotional development seem to require cognitive development (e.g. children don't get embarrassed until they know about social roles and appearances)? Most emotions are "about" something, such as "not studying for the test," but it seems necessary to be cognitive to be "about" something. In short, there is a host of problems with proposing a separation between emotion and cognition (Lazarus, 1982; Solomon, 1976). The most important problem is the fact that the way in which a person thinks about a situation obviously affects how he or she feels. If one becomes angry when one discovers that one's friend has once again left a pile of dirty dishes in the sink, and then discovers that the friend had been about to do the dishes when he received news about the death of his father, one's anger goes away and different emotions (surprise at the news, feeling sorry for your friend) take its place. The dual system account appears to deal only awkwardly with such an ordinary case.

A different alternative to Zajonc's "dual system" solution is suggested by such theorists as Lazarus (1982) and Beck (1976), both of whom view emotion as always linked to cognition. The key to their solutions is a claim that is routinely made about non-emotional cognition as well, namely, that there are *different types* of cognition, and that not all cognition is conscious, deliberate, or verbal (Parrott & Sabini, 1989).

Recognizing that cognition can be difficult to control and that people can perseverate in beliefs that they recognize to be undesirable permits one to account for conflicts between emotion and reason in a manner that nevertheless conceives of emotion as involving cognition, and many psychologists prefer this solution for this reason. Other psychologists prefer Zajonc's dual systems solution. More recent criticisms of research on appraisal have focused on whether appraisals are necessary causes of emotion. Critics contend that appraisals are but one of many causes of emotions, some of which are best understood at the social or physiological levels of analysis (Parkinson, 1997). Continuing debate over this issue can be expected in years to come.

Regardless of the outcome of this debate, it is clear that in most cases there is a good deal of agreement between a person's way of thinking and the emotions that person feels, and much research has been directed at characterizing the types of assessment that are associated with different emotions. That is, what thoughts lead to what emotions? Logical and experimental analysis suggests that emotions can be classified according to the type of beliefs that underlie them (Ortony, Clore, & Collins, 1988). Many emotions have to do with reactions to events, and these emotions can be subcategorized according to whether the event is judged simply according to desirability (joy) or undesirability (distress), or whether further judgments are also involved. For example, if the event is desirable for *another* person, one may be pleased about this (happy-for) or displeased (resentment). And if one is anticipating a future event, one may have an emotion if this event would be desirable (hope) or undesirable (fear). And if one has pleasant anticipations, they may later be dashed (disappointment) or confirmed (satisfaction), and if one has unpleasant anticipations, they too may later go unrealized (relief), or be confirmed ("fear confirmed"). For other emotions the cognitive focus is less on the event itself than it is on the people who are *responsible* for the event. If other people are believed to be the agents responsible for the event, then one may find their actions praiseworthy (admiration) or blameworthy (contempt). If one believes oneself to be responsible for the event, then one may find one's own actions to be praiseworthy (pride) or blameworthy (shame). Some emotions seem to combine assessments of responsibility with assessments of the consequences of the events for oneself or for others; emotions such as anger, gratitude, remorse, and gratification are of this hybrid type. Anger, for example, combines distress over an undesired event with reproach of an agent responsible for producing it (Ortony, Clore, & Collins, 1988). Still other emotions seem related not to events or agents, but to our overall liking or disliking of a person or object: love and hate are common examples of this class.

A variety of schemes for representing the appraisals associated with various emotions have been proposed, such as appraisal components or themes (for a review, see Smith & Pope, 1992).

Several conclusions may be drawn from these attempts at classification. First, not all emotion words correspond to a single, simple appraisal as do the ones mentioned above. Jealousy, for example, refers not so much to a single appraisal as to an entire syndrome of appraisals and emotions that are likely to occur in a certain situation, namely, when one faces the threat of losing a valued relationship to a rival. Envy (as used in modern English) similarly can refer to anything from longing or admiration of someone who has something desired by oneself to hatred of that person for being superior. It is therefore possible to distinguish single emotions from what might be called emotional *episodes* (Parrott, 1991).

It also becomes clear that the *concepts* of emotions that are being developed by researchers are not identical with the *emotion words* used in everyday language. For example, in the classification described above there is clearly a logical place for an emotion in which a person is pleased that an undesirable event has happened to another person – and, in fact, most people have experienced such pleasure at another's misfortune. The English language, however, does not have a good word for such an emotion. German does, though: they call it *Schadenfreude*. This example illustrates that the correspondence between our language and our experience is imperfect.

Finally, analysis of emotional appraisals suggests the sort of things that determine what people get emotional about and thus, in a sense, what people care about. They care about their goals, plans, and values; they care about social relationships; they care about duties and responsibilities; they care about the good and evil in people's characters. It is assessments along these lines that define and distinguish the various emotions. There is no one perfect classification scheme for emotions. Which classification is best depends on one's purposes.

Emotion's effects on cognition

Given that cognition leads to emotion in these ways, what can be learned about how people think once they are emotional? Answers to this question tend to be of two types. Some accounts depict emotional thought as being biased by a person's *motivation*. Because it is often possible to construe events in more than one way, people may have a tendency to select interpretations that are most consistent with the way they wish the world to be. (See Dunning, 2001, for a review of motivated biases.)

Not all accounts of emotional bias invoke motivation, however; some emotional biases can be explained as the result of normal judgmental or memory processes. Being in an emotional state, say, of anger, may provide information about one's present situation (Schwarz, 1990), or may tend to remind one of previous times when one has been angry and of beliefs that are consistent with being angry (Blaney, 1986). (See Bless, 2001, for more detail about the ways in which emotions affect people's thinking.)

Two-factor theory

One application of the cognitive approach to emotion has come from investigating people's understanding of the causes of their own emotional feelings. Studies conducted in 1924 by the Spanish physician Gregorio Marañon suggested that most people injected with adrenalin reported feeling no emotion at all, or felt "as if" they were emotional but only in a cold or empty way. A very few people felt a genuine emotion, and these appeared to be people who had been thinking about emotional situations in their present lives. These findings led Stanley Schachter to propose that emotions consist of two components: physiological arousal *plus* cognitive attributions linking the arousal with emotional circumstances believed to have caused it (Schachter & Singer, 1962). This theory gave rise to an enormous amount of research over the following two decades in which researchers investigated its implications.

The one implication that has received consistent experimental support is that arousal from one source can intensify an emotion unrelated to the true source of the arousal. For example, people who are aroused because they have recently gotten off an exercise bicycle may feel angrier and act more aggressively after being insulted than do people lacking arousal. The people apparently feel angrier because they attribute their arousal to having been insulted. Evidence supporting this claim comes from findings that there is no increase in anger immediately after getting off the bicycle – at this point people have plenty of arousal, but they are aware that exercise caused it so do not attribute it to anger. Six minutes after getting off the bicycle there again is no increase in anger – at this point there is no more arousal. Two minutes after getting off the bicycle, however, people do feel more anger, apparently because they no longer attribute their lingering arousal to bike riding and instead misattribute it to having been insulted (Zillmann, 1979). Such findings, plus the original Marañon experiment, support the idea that Schachter's two-factor theory describes a genuine phenomenon, but this theory cannot seriously be considered as a general account of emotions. As will be described later, arousal is not necessary for emotional experience. Furthermore, the support for most other predictions of the theory is lacking (Reisenzein, 1983).

Physiological Approaches to Emotion

Physiological approaches to emotion may be divided into two types. The first type emphasizes the bodily symptoms of emotions: the pounding heart, dry mouth, sweaty palms, and "butterflies in the stomach" that are characteristic of many powerful emotions. This approach emphasizes regions of the body that lie beyond the brain and spinal cord in the periphery of the nervous system, and for this reason it may be termed the *peripheral approach* to emotion. The second physiological approach to emotion has the opposite emphasis, on brain activities that appear to be responsible for emotions. It may be termed the *central approach* to emotion.

The peripheral approach

The most influential statement of the peripheral approach was made by William James (1884), who tried to account for why emotions have the feeling qualities that they do. James proposed what he intended to be a very counterintuitive theory, namely, that emotional feelings are simply the awareness of various bodily changes. If one encounters a ferocious bear, James said, one first perceives the bear, and then one's body responds to this perception with increased heart rate, greater blood flow to the leg muscles, deeper breathing, widening of the eyes, and so forth. Emotions, James claimed, are nothing other than the awareness of such bodily changes – there is no "emotion" that precedes such changes.

The strength of James's theory is that it attempts to account for the "feel" of emotions, a task that most psychologists have shied away from despite its centrality to many conceptions of emotion. But there are many problems with James's view, some factual and some conceptual. One central prediction of the theory must be recognized in order to understand its problems. If we allow that there can be more than one type of emotion, and if emotions are simply our awareness of bodily changes, then it follows that different emotions must be characterized by different patterns of bodily changes and that these changes are what distinguish the emotions for us. This prediction has not fared well.

The most famous of the many attacks on James's theory was made by Walter Cannon (1927), who was an expert on the autonomic nervous system. One of the two parts of the autonomic nervous system, the sympathetic nervous system (SNS), is closely associated with many of the bodily responses characteristic of powerful emotions: it produces the "arousal" that formed part of Schachter's two-factor theory. The SNS controls a variety of responses that may be easily understood in terms of a scheme invented by Cannon himself: the SNS produces changes in the body that are needed for the *fight-or-flight response*. That is, in many emergency situations it is adaptive for animals to be able to mobilize all of the energy they can muster for a relatively short, intense burst of life-saving activity – to fight for its life or to flee from a predator or to escape from some catastrophe. The SNS affects the body so that adrenalin is produced, oxygen is absorbed, blood is pumped, energy is burned, and muscles work at their peak capacity. Cannon's research led him to conclude that the fight-or-flight response is almost always the same for such intense but otherwise different-seeming emotions as rage and fear. He also knew that the full SNS response often takes a second or more to occur, whereas people seem to experience emotions without such a delay. Furthermore, such non-emotional causes as exercise and fevers produce SNS arousal without emotional experience, and injections of adrenalin do not cause most people to feel an emotion. These and other facts persuaded Cannon that emotion could not be equated with the awareness of emotion-like changes in the body.

Subsequent investigations have supported most of Cannon's criticisms of James. Consider recent research on people who have suffered spinal cord injuries. Some spinal cord injuries not only confine people to wheelchairs, but also prevent them from receiving sensations from much of their bodies. If emotional feeling were dependent on sensations from the body, one would expect such people to experience emotions less strongly, but this is not the case – they experience emotions as intensely as they did before their injuries, as intensely as do people without injuries, and as intensely as people who have spinal cord injuries that do not block feelings from the body (Chwalisz, Diener, & Gallagher, 1988).

A conceptual problem also exists for James's theory. His claim – that people first perceive an event and then their bodies respond – appears to beg a crucial question: how does the body know how to respond appropriately? Clearly, what James called "perception" must involve more than just that. The event must be interpreted and evaluated for significance to some extent before an appropriate response can be made. The need for such an evaluation

– an appraisal – is one of the main reasons that the physiological approach to emotion can be usefully supplemented by cognitive and social approaches.

But just because SNS arousal is not necessary for our emotional feelings it does not mean that this activity cannot contribute to our emotional experience or that it is not an important part of an emotional response. There is some evidence that bodily feelings contribute somewhat to emotional experience – smiling does seem to make people feel a bit happier than they do when not smiling, for example – but the contribution to emotional intensity seems fairly small compared to other factors such as the significance of the event (Laird, 1984). Emotional bodily changes evolved because they prepare the body to function in adaptive ways. Powerful emotions are characterized by a preparedness for emergency activity, and bodily changes are part of this preparation. Not all emotions are like this, however – consider sadness. Autonomic changes can also function as signs that a person is emotional; sometimes people recognize emotion in themselves and in others by noting the presence of SNS arousal, and the detection of such activity is the basis of so-called "lie detector" testing. A review of the peripheral approach to emotion may be found in Cornelius (1996).

The central approach

In response to Cannon's critique of James in the 1920s, researchers taking a physiological approach to emotion increasingly began to adopt what may be termed the *central approach*. Other researchers joined Cannon in proposing that there exist structures in the brain that are responsible for controlling many aspects of emotions, including the SNS. Papez (1937) and MacLean (1970) proposed that an interconnected set of structures located near the middle of the brain – called the *limbic system* – produced emotional feelings and responses.

Evidence for this claim is of several types. It is possible to stimulate activity in nerves by applying small amounts of electrical current to them, and stimulation of parts of the limbic system can produce emotional behavior. Damage to parts of the limbic system alters emotional behavior. Humans with epilepsy that alters the activity of the limbic system can undergo dramatic changes in emotion. Drugs that alter moods are known to work on the nerves in the limbic system. Diseases that damage parts of the nervous system produce changes in mood and emotional behavior. For example, one part of the limbic system is a structure called the *amygdala*. Stimulation of regions of the amygdala can produce aggressive behavior, whereas damage to it can result in the reduction of aggression. Epileptic seizures focused on the amygdala can cause humans to go into a rage and violently attack others, and surgical removal of these regions (as last-resort treatment of epilepsy) can end these episodes of rage. Rabies is known to produce violent behavior, and it causes damage to the nervous system, particularly in the region around the amygdala. A few violent criminals have been found to have had brain tumors near the amygdala. Although there are good reasons to be cautious in interpreting these types of evidence, there does appear to be a general trend across many types of evidence linking structures in the limbic system to emotional thinking, feelings, and behavior (Frijda, 1986). A well-known synthesis of research in the centralist tradition would be that of LeDoux (1993).

Certain assumptions of the central approach do seem valid, then. It is possible to learn about emotions by studying the brain structures and processes that are associated with them. It is important to understand that the discovery of physiological processes linked with emotion does not mean that emotions are "just physiological," however. The functions of the limbic areas appear to be linked to the evaluations, judgments, and feelings that go into emotion and to a variety of social and sexual functions. Emotions' cognitive and social aspects require brain processes to occur and emotions can be studied on that level, but they cannot be understood completely without considering all three levels of explanation.

Conclusion

In this chapter we have seen how emotion has been studied in psychology at three different levels of analysis: the physiological, the cognitive, and the social and cultural. Insights have been gained from all three levels, and it should now be clear that the levels are complementary, not contradictory. The fact that different cultures can have somewhat different emotions in no way implies that these emotions do not have cognitive or physiological aspects as well, nor does the fact that modern antidepressant medications might have "cured" accidie imply that this emotion did not require a certain set of beliefs and institutions. One of the most important tasks of psychology is to understand the interrelations between these different aspects of emotion, and social psychologists are well-positioned to contribute to that understanding.

REFERENCES

Averill, J. R. (1982). *Anger and aggression: An essay on emotion.* New York: Springer.

Beck, A. T. (1976). *Cognitive therapy and the emotional disorders.* New York: Meridian.

Blaney, P. H. (1986). Affect and memory: A review. *Psychological Bulletin, 99,* 229–246.

Bless, H. (2001). The consequences of mood on the processing of social information. In Tesser, A. & Schwarz, N. (Eds.), *Blackwell handbook of social psychology: Intraindividual processes* (pp. 391–412). Oxford: Blackwell Publishing.

Cannon, W. B. (1927). The James–Lange theory of emotions: A critical examination and an alternative theory. *American Journal of Psychology, 39,* 106–124.

Chwalisz, K., Diener, E., & Gallagher, D. (1988). Autonomic arousal feedback and emotional experience: Evidence from the spinal cord injured. *Journal of Personality and Social Psychology, 54,* 820–828.

Clore, G. L., & Ortony, A. (1991). What more is there to emotion concepts than prototypes? *Journal of Personality and Social Psychology, 60,* 48–50.

Cornelius, R. R. (1996). *The science of emotion: Research and tradition in the psychology of emotions.* Upper Saddle River, NJ: Prentice Hall.

Darwin, C. (1872/1955). *The expression of the emotions in man and animals.* New York: Greenwood Press.

Dunning, D. (2001). On the motives underlying social cognition. In A. Tesser & N. Schwarz (Eds.), *Blackwell handbook of social psychology* (pp. 348–374). Oxford: Blackwell Publishing.

Ekman, P. (1973). Cross-cultural studies of facial expression. In P. Ekman (Ed.), *Darwin and facial expression: A century of research in review* (pp. 169–229). New York: Academic Press.

Ekman, P., & Davidson, R. J. (1994). *The nature of emotion: Fundamental questions.* New York: Oxford University Press.

Fehr, B., & Russell, J. A. (1984). Concept of emotion viewed from a prototype perspective. *Journal of Experimental Psychology: General, 113,* 474–486.

Fridlund, A. J. (1994). *Human facial expression: An evolutionary view.* San Diego, CA: Academic Press.

Frijda, N. H. (1986). *The emotions.* Cambridge, UK: Cambridge University Press.

Frijda, N. H., Mesquita, B., Sonnemans, J., & Van Goozen, S. (1991). The duration of affective phenomena or emotions, sentimenta and passions. In K. T. Strongman (Ed.), *International review of emotion* Vol. 1 (pp. 187–255). Chichester, UK: Wiley.

Gross, J., & Keltner, D. (in press). *The functions of emotion: A special issue of Cognition and Emotion.* Hove, UK: Psychology Press.

Harré, R. (Ed.) (1986). *The social construction of emotions.* Oxford: Blackwell Publishers.

Harré, R., & Finlay-Jones, R. (1986). Emotion talk across times. In R. Harré (Ed.), *The social construction of emotions* (pp. 220–233). Oxford: Blackwell Publishers.

Harré, R., & Parrott, W. G. (1996). *The emotions: Social, cultural and biological dimensions.* London: Sage Publications.

James, W. (1884). What is an emotion? *Mind, 9,* 188–205.

Laird, J. D. (1984). The real role of facial response in the experience of emotion: A reply to Tourangeau and Ellsworth, and others. *Journal of Personality and Social Psychology, 47,* 909–917.

Lazarus, R. S. (1966). *Psychological stress and the coping process.* New York: McGraw-Hill.

Lazarus, R. S. (1982). Thoughts on the relations between emotion and cognition. *American Psychologist, 37,* 1019–1024.

Lazarus, R. S. (1984). On the primacy of cognition. *American Psychologist, 39,* 124–129.

Lazarus, R. S. (1991). *Emotion and adaptation.* New York: Oxford University Press.

LeDoux, J. E. (1993). Emotional networks in the brain. In M. Lewis, & J. M. Haviland (Eds.), *Handbook of emotions* (pp. 109–118). New York: Guilford Press.

Lutz, C. A. (1988). *Unnatural emotions: Everyday sentiments on a Micronesian atoll and their challenge to Western theory.* Chicago: University of Chicago Press.

MacLean, P. D. (1970). The triune brain, emotion, and scientific bias. In F. O. Schmitt (Ed.), *The neurosciences: Second study program* (pp. 336–349). New York: Rockefeller University Press.

Markus, H. R., & Kitayama, S. (1991). Culture and the self: Implications for cognition, emotion, and motivation. *Psychological Review, 98,* 224–253.

Miller, J. G. (2001). The cultural grounding of social psychology theory. In A. Tesser & N. Schwarz (Eds.), *Blackwell handbook of social psychology: Intraindividual processes* (pp. 22–43). Oxford: Blackwell Publishing.

Miller, R. S. (1996). *Embarrassment: Poise and peril in everyday life.* New York: Guilford Press.

Oatley, K., & Johnson-Laird, P. N. (1987). Towards a cognitive theory of emotions. *Cognition and Emotion, 1,* 29–50.

Ortony, A., Clore, G. L., & Collins, A. (1988). *The cognitive structure of emotions.* New York: Cambridge University Press.

Papez, J. (1937). A proposed mechanism of emotion. *Archives of Neurology and Psychology, 38,* 725–744.

Parkinson, B. (1997). Untangling the appraisal–emotion connection. *Personality and Social Psychology Review, 1,* 62–79.

Parrott, W. G. (1991). The emotional experiences of envy and jealousy. In P. Salovey (Ed.), *The psychology of jealousy and envy* (pp. 3–30). New York: Guilford Press.

Parrott, W. G. (in press). Multiple goals, self-regulation, and functionalism. In A. Fischer (Ed.), *Proceedings of the Xth Conference of the International Society for Research on Emotions*. Amsterdam: ISRE Publications.

Parrott, W. G., & Sabini, J. (1989). On the "emotional" qualities of certain types of cognition: A reply to arguments for the independence of cognition and affect. *Cognitive Therapy and Research, 13,* 49–65.

Peters, R. S. (1958). *The concept of motivation*. London: Routledge & Kegan Paul.

Reisenzein, R. (1983). The Schachter theory of emotion: Two decades later. *Psychological Bulletin, 94,* 239–264.

Russell, J. A. (1994). Is there universal recognition of emotion from facial expression? A review of methods and studies. *Psychological Bulletin, 115,* 102–141.

Russell, J. A., & Fernández-Dols, J.-M. (Eds.) (1997). *The psychology of facial expression*. Cambridge, UK: Cambridge University Press.

Russell, J. A., Fernández-Dols, J.-M., Manstead, A. S. R., & Wellenkamp, J. (Eds.) (1995). *Everyday concepts of emotion*. NATO ASI series D, Vol. 81. Dordrecht: Kluwer.

Salovey, P. (1991). *The psychology of jealousy and envy*. New York: Guilford Press.

Sartre, J.-P. (1948). *The emotions: Outline of a theory*. New York: Philosophical Library.

Schachter, S., & Singer, J. E. (1962). Cognitive, social, and physiological determinants of emotional state. *Psychological Review, 69,* 379–399.

Schoeck, H. (1969). *Envy: A theory of social behaviour*. Indianapolis, IN: Liberty Press.

Schwarz, N. (1990). Feelings as information: Informational and motivational functions of affective states. In R. Sorrentino, & E. T. Higgins (Eds.), *Handbook of motivation and cognition* Vol. 2 (pp. 527–561). New York: Guilford Press.

Selye, H. (1976). *The stress of life*. 2nd edn. New York: McGraw-Hill.

Shaver, P., Schwartz, J., Kirson, D., & O'Connor, C. (1987). Emotion knowledge: Further exploration of a prototype approach. *Journal of Personality and Social Psychology, 52,* 1061–1086.

Smith, C. A., & Pope, L. K. (1992). Appraisal and emotion: The interactional contributions of dispositional and situational factors. In M. S. Clark (Ed.), *Review of Personality and Social Psychology, Vol. 14: Emotion and social behavior* (pp. 32–62). Newbury Park, CA: Sage.

Solomon, R. C. (1976). *The passions*. Notre Dame: University of Notre Dame Press.

Tangney, J. P., & Fischer, K. W. (Eds.) (1995). *Self-conscious emotions: The psychology of shame, guilt, embarrassment, and pride*. New York: Guilford Press.

Wierzbicka, A. (1992). Talking about emotions: Semantics, culture and cognition. *Cognition and Emotion, 6,* 285–319.

Zajonc, R. B. (1980). Feeling and thinking: Preferences need no inferences. *American Psychologist, 35,* 151–175.

Zajonc, R. B. (1984). On the primacy of affect. *American Psychologist, 39,* 117–123.

Zillman, D. (1979). *Hostility and aggression*. Hillsdale, NJ: Erlbaum.

CHAPTER TWO

Understanding People's Perceptions of Relationships is Crucial to Understanding their Emotional Lives

Margaret S. Clark, Julie Fitness, and Ian Brissette

Psychological research on emotion has been flourishing. However, as relationship theorists, we find something strikingly odd about the resulting literature. What is striking is that this literature almost all focuses on the experience and expression of emotions *within a single individual*. We know much about how our moods and emotions influence our processing of information, how we represent our own emotional experiences in our minds, what causes our own experiences of emotion, what our facial expressions of emotion look like, how our temperaments contribute to our emotional experiences, and how our emotions drive our liking for and behavior toward others. The list of work focusing squarely on individuals could go on. This work does have relevance to understanding relationships. However, as Ekman and Davidson (1994) have aptly noted, the interpersonal aspects of emotion have been given "short shrift" by psychologists.

Is there anything about the nature of relationships that can inform our understanding of people's emotional lives? We along with Berscheid and Ammazzalorso (chapter 3, this volume) would respond with a resounding, yes. Berscheid and Ammazzalorso make a case for one variable that can only be understood in relationship terms, that is, the degree of interdependence between two people, being a variable which is crucial for purposes of understanding people's emotional lives. We make a case for a different variable that also can only be understood in relationship terms as being crucial for understanding people's emotional lives. This variable is relationship members' felt responsibility (or lack thereof) for one another's needs.

Our arguments will be based upon four straightforward assumptions. The first is that emotions function not only to communicate one's own needs to oneself (Frijda, 1993;

We acknowledge NSF grant SBR9630898 and a grant from the Fetzer Foundation which supported Margaret Clark's participation in this project. We also acknowledge graduate training grant T32MH19953 which supported Ian Brissette's participation in this project.

Simon, 1967), but also to communicate one's needs to others in one's social environment (Fridlund, 1991; Jones, Collins, & Hong, 1991; Levenson, 1994; Miller & Leary, 1992). This helps others to address our needs and helps us to mobilize external resources (Buck, 1984, 1989; Clark & Watson, 1994; Scott, 1958, 1980). The second assumption is that our emotions communicate both to ourselves and to others the extent to which we care about the needs of those others. The third assumption is that any one person's social relationships can be distinguished from one another on the basis of the extent to which members feel responsible for one another's needs. Sometimes we feel very little responsibility for another's needs. Sometimes we feel a moderate amount. Sometimes we feel a great deal of responsibility. The fourth and final assumption is that there are chronic individual differences in terms of the extent to which people feel responsible for other people's needs and in terms of the extent to which people believe others feel responsible for their own needs. For instance, attachment researchers would argue that insecure/avoidant people have enduring models of other people as being unresponsive to their needs. Or, to give another example, Clark, Ouellette, Powell, and Milberg (1987) have noted that there exist individual differences in communal orientation such that people differ in their tendencies to be responsive to others' needs and to expect others to be responsive to their own needs.

Putting the assumptions together leads us to the simple prediction that, to the extent to which people believe others will be responsive to their needs and to the extent to which they, themselves, feel responsible for their partner's needs, more emotion will be expressed. In some cases, we will argue, more emotion will be experienced in the first place. Moreover, what emotion is expressed will be reacted to more favorably.

Although there is considerable evidence for all these assertions, to our knowledge this evidence has not been pulled together in a single place. The evidence is of two broad types. First, there is what we would call "within" person evidence. That is, it appears that any given person will be more emotional (and will react more positively to partners' expressions of emotion) when the emotion occurs within the context of relationships in which that person expects his or her needs to be met than with in the context of other relationships in which that person does not hold such expectations. Second, there is much, quite parallel, "between" person evidence for our propositions. That is, it appears that some people are more emotionally expressive (and react more positively to partners' expressions of emotion) than are other people *because* they are more confident in general that their needs will be met by others and/or more willing to meet the needs of others. In other words, some types of relationships seem to be characterized by more emotionality than others and some types of people seem to be characterized by more emotionality than others.

Consider the "within" person evidence first. This is evidence that beliefs about responsiveness to needs vary by type of relationship and that emotions covary with those beliefs.

Types of Relationships and Emotion

Clark, Mills, and their colleagues (Clark & Mills, 1979, 1993; Mills & Clark, 1982) have drawn distinctions between social relationships based upon the implicit rules governing the distribution of benefits in relationships. In most of their papers they have distinguished between communal relationships and exchange relationships. In communal relationships members feel an obligation to demonstrate concern for the other's welfare. Thus benefits are given to fulfill the other person's needs or simply to signal or express a general concern for the other person. In these relationships when a benefit is given to a person, that person does not incur a specific debt which must be repaid with a comparable benefit. Clark and Mills point to friendships, romantic relationships and family relationships as relationships which often exemplify communal relationships.

Clark and Mills have distinguished communal relationships from other relationships in which members feel no special sense of responsibility for the other's welfare. Their most frequently used example of such other relationships are exchange relationships in which benefits are given on the basis of comparable benefits received in the past or with the expectation of being repaid with comparable benefits in the future. Exchange relationships are often exemplified by relationships between people who do business with one another (e.g., a store owner and a customer), and by acquaintances (e.g., parents who work out a car pool to transport their respective children to and from soccer practices). However, exchange relationships are not the only example of non-communal relationships. Exploitative relationships in which the members are primarily concerned with their own needs, and are willing to act in unjust ways so as to extract benefits for themselves, are another kind of non-communal relationship.

Distinctions between social relationships based upon whether or not members feel responsible for the other's needs are important to understanding emotion because emotional expression carries information about needs. Sad people have generally lost something. They may need help in regaining it or help in coping with the loss. Angry people feel unjustly treated. They may need help in ascertaining whether their feelings are justified or help in figuring out a way to rectify the situation. Happy people generally are not needy. Those who feel responsible for them may help them celebrate whatever made them happy but need not address any particular need beyond that. As a consequence of people feeling a special responsibility to meet the other's needs, expressing emotions should be more important to communication within the context of communal relationships than to communication in other types of relationships. Therefore, we would expect emotions to be expressed more frequently within communal than within other, non-communal, relationships.

Expressing emotions more frequently or more intensely when one believes the other feels responsible for one's needs

That emotions are, indeed, expressed more often in communal than in other relationships is supported by the results of at least two studies (Clark & Taraban, 1991, Study 2; Barrett, Robin, Pietromonaco, & Eyssell, 1998). Pairs of same-sex friends were recruited for the Clark and Taraban (1991) study. They were told they would have a discussion with their friend or with a member of a different pair of friends who was a stranger to the participants. The experimenter commented that when people are told to talk, they sometimes have a problem finding something to talk about. To make things easier, a form suggesting conversation topics was being handed out. Each participant was to rank-order the topics in terms of his or her preferences and the experimenter would then pick a topic both partners seemed to like. The form listed fifteen topics. Five were intrinsically emotional in nature (i.e., "times you have felt especially serene," "your fears," "things that make you sad," "things that make you angry," and "what makes you happy"). The rest were not (e.g., "your future plans," "your favorite restaurants," "your opinions of Carnegie Mellon"). Topics were ordered randomly on the form. After all four participants completed the topic choice forms, the study was complete. The results were clear. All five emotional topics were ranked as more preferable in the Friends than in the Strangers condition with four of those differences reaching traditional levels of significance and one being marginally significant.

Barrett, Robin, Pietromonaco, and Eyssell (1998) also report data linking the existence and strength of communal relationships with emotion expression. They had college students, both males and females, keep daily diaries of happiness, sadness, nervousness, surprise, anger, embarrassment, and shame experienced and expressed within the context of any interaction lasting for ten minutes or longer. They did this for seven days. Participants also indicated the closeness of their ongoing relationships with other people. (Barrett et al. did not define closeness for their participants, but we would argue that most people interpret that term in a communal sense, that is, in terms of mutual caring). The intensity of participants' emotional experiences and the degree to which they expressed those emotions was positively and significantly associated with the rated closeness of their relationship with the other person. Interestingly, Barrett et al. also had participants rate the closeness they felt with the other *within* each individual interaction. This measure also was associated with greater experience and expression of emotion overall. Shimanoff (1988) has reported similar findings.

Although Clark and Mills began their theoretical work with a simple, qualitative, distinction between communal and non-communal relationships, they have also described a quantitative dimension to communal relationships (Mills & Clark, 1982). Specifically, communal relationships vary in the degree to which members feel responsible for the other person's needs – a dimension Clark and Mills refer to as the strength of the communal relationship. In weak communal relationships members feel a small amount of responsibility for the other person's needs and will give some benefits (i.e., those that are not very costly to them) on a communal basis. An example of a low-strength communal relationship would be the relationship a person has with a stranger whom the person is meeting for the very first time. If that stranger asked for the time, the person probably would give it, thereby meeting a need of the stranger undoubtedly without expecting anything in return. However, the person would be unwilling to provide benefits on a communal basis that were much more costly or effortful than telling the time.[1] In increasingly stronger communal relationships members feel greater amounts of responsibility for the other's needs. Communal relationships with friends are stronger. Most people would not only give their friend the time, but also would do such things as treat the friend to lunch, run an errand for the friend, and comfort the friend if he or she was feeling down. Most people have even stronger, indeed very strong, communal relationships with their children. Many parents would do almost anything to meet their children's needs.

The implications of the strength dimension of communal relationships for emotional expression are straightforward. As a result of emotions very often signaling one's own needs or one's concern for one's partner's needs, the expression of one's own emotions and emotional experience and expression in response to one's partner's needs ought to increase in close conjunction with the strength of communal relationships. Thus people presumably express more emotion to spouses than to casual friends and more emotion to casual friends than to mere acquaintances.

A questionnaire study recently conducted by Brissette and Clark (1999) provides evidence that more emotion is expressed as communal relationships grow stronger. Forty-two people in this study rated the communal strength of a number of their existing relationships, as well as the likelihood that they would express a variety of emotions in each of those relationships. To measure communal strength, a communal relationship was first defined as one in which the other responds to the participant's needs without requiring or expecting a comparable benefit in return. We added that, in these relationships, people do not keep track of who has provided what to whom, but they do keep track of who needs what. Then we asked each person to rate eighteen relationships on nine-point Likert scales anchored by −4 (indicating that the relationship was "Not at all communal") to +4 (indicating that the relationship was "Very strongly communal"). Participants rated their relationships with: a stranger, their mother, a casual friend, a sister or brother, their boss at work, their professor, a neighbor, a close friend, a member of a sports team (along with them), a classmate, their cousin, a member of their church or temple, their priest, minister, or rabbi, a fellow employee at work, their father, a member of their fraternity or sorority, and their roommate.[2]

All participants received instructions for rating their emotions on a separate sheet. The instructions began with the statement that, "We experience many, many emotions from day to day. Sometimes we freely express the emotions we are feeling to others; sometimes we do not – choosing to suppress them instead." Then the participants were asked to rate their willingness to express happiness, contentment, hurt, sadness, anger, disgust, guilt, and fear (both when each emotion was caused by the person to whom the emotion would be expressed and when it was caused by someone or something else). They used seven-point Likert scales to do this. The scales ranged from −3 (indicating that they would be very likely to suppress the emotion) to +3 (indicating that they would be very likely to express the emotion).

As expected, there were positive, within-subject correlations between each person's rating of how communal a particular relationship was and that person's rating of willingness to express each of the emotions within their relationship. When the emotions were caused by the other those correlations were .23 for anger, .27 for disgust, .40 for fear, .39 for guilt, .39 for hurt, .43 for sadness, .43 for contentment, and .48 for happiness. When the emotions were caused by someone or something else the correlations were .45 for anger, .48 for disgust, .57 for fear, .45 for guilt, .54 for hurt, .51 for sadness, .43 for contentment, and .49 for happiness. All reached statistical significance with the exception of the correlations between how communal one's relationship was and willingness to express anger and disgust when those emotions were caused by one's partner.[3]

The means for willingness to express the various emotions across relationships clearly indicated that although people were willing to express positive emotions to some extent in almost all relationships, they were more willing to do so the stronger the communal nature of the relationship. Moreover, although people were willing to express negative emotions within moderately strong to quite strong communal relationships, they reported being likely to *suppress* negative emotions in relationships low in communal strength. Other findings, consistent with the idea that more emotion will be expressed the stronger the communal nature of a relationship, have been reported by Fitness (in press), Pennebaker (1995), and Rime (1995). Rime and Pennebaker have found that when people experience emotional events, they seek support from their friends and families. Fitness (in press) found that 83 percent of people who reported experiencing an angry incident at work also reported having expressed those feelings to their close friends and family members not only to "let off steam" but also for purposes of reassurance.

In sum, there is clear evidence that the more concerned people are with one another's needs, the more likely they are to express emotions. We turn now to a related point. That is, not only does it appear that more emotion will be expressed the more communal a relationship is, it is also apparent that expressing emotion will be *viewed as more appropriate* and will be *reacted to more positively* to the extent that the relationship in question is communal. We review evidence supporting this next.

Reacting positively to others' emotional expressions when one feels responsible for those others' needs

Two studies support the contention that expressions of emotion will be reacted to more positively when one is oriented toward meeting the other's needs than when one is not. In the first (Clark & Taraban, 1991, Study 1), the impact of expressing irritability, happiness, and sadness on liking for another person, with whom one had been led to desire a communal or a non-communal relationship, was examined. Students participated in this study one at a time, but were led to believe another participant was involved in the study at the same time. When the participant arrived, he or she was seated in front of a monitor and could see another participant (his or her supposed partner) seated at a similar desk. In fact, the monitor showed a videotape of a male or female, attractive, undergraduate confederate. At this point the experimenter turned off the monitor and told the participant the study actually dealt with impression formation. The experimenter went on to explain that the first person to arrive (i.e., the one shown on the monitor) was always designated as the stimulus person and that that person continued to believe the study was about word games. However, the second person to arrive, the actual participant, (being addressed) was to form an impression of the stimulus person – first on the basis of a background information sheet, supposedly filled out by that other person, and later on the basis of a brief interaction.

A manipulation of desire for a communal as opposed to an exchange or no particular relationship was included on this form. In the communal condition, the partner was described as new to the university and quite interested in meeting new people. In the exchange condition, the other was described as married and busy. This person was obviously unavailable for new friendships or romantic relationships. Most importantly for the present point, a manipulation of the partner's expressed emotion appeared on the bottom half of the form. There, the other person indicated either that he or she currently was in no particular mood (the control condition) or that he or she was currently feeling happy, sad, or angry. Finally, the participant rated the other on a number of dimensions (e.g., agreeableness, pleasantness, likeability). These ratings were summed to form an overall measure of likeability. The results were clear.

When no emotion was expressed, liking ratings in the communal and in the non-communal condition were identical. However, when happiness, sadness, or irritability was expressed, liking was greater when participants had been led to desire a communal relationship with the other than when they had not. It appears that expressions of emotion are more appropriate in communal than in other relationships. Moreover, it is notable that within the communal conditions, expression of emotions, *even* negative emotions did not cause significant drops in liking. In contrast, within the non-communal condition, expressing irritability did decrease liking. Why might negative emotions be reacted to more negatively within non-communal than within communal relationships? We think the answer is that negative emotions indicate some level of neediness on the part of the other person. When our sense of obligation for the other's needs and desire to respond to those needs is low, we do not want to deal with the other's irritability or sadness. We may even be irritated ourselves at being forced to witness the emotion. To the extent to which we do feel responsible for the other's needs, or desire the opportunity to assume such responsibility, expressions of the same emotions will be less off-putting. Indeed, if such expressions open up a chance to respond to the other's needs and build a desired relationship, these expressions may even be welcomed.

The second study supporting the idea that expressions of emotion will be reacted to more positively in the context of a communal than in the context of a non-communal relationship has been reported by Clark, Ouellette, Powell, and Milberg (1987). In this study people were recruited for an investigation of links between moods and creativity. Participants were informally told there was another person participating at the same time. However, that person supposedly had left the room briefly. Then the participant filled out a questionnaire which asked, among other things, why he or she had signed up for the study and also what his or her current mood was. The participant's picture was also taken – supposedly as another way to judge mood. The participant was given instructions for his or her painting task and it was casually mentioned that the other person had filled out his or her questionnaire, had had his or her picture taken, and would be returning shortly to complete a balloon sculpture task. In preparation for the other's task, the experimenter casually commented, that other would have to blow up balloons. The actual participant could help if he or she wished but did not have to do so and could just begin painting. Then the experimenter left the room telling the participant to place his or her picture and questionnaire on top of the other participant's materials.

As hoped, the participants looked at the other's completed materials and, depending upon their experimental condition, found out that the other either was feeling no particular mood or sad. They also found out the other was available and anxious to form new communal relationships (e.g., a friendship or romantic relationship), or was quite busy, occupied in other communal relationships, and presumably not interested in forming new communal relationships. The dependent variable was helping. Our question was, how long would the participant spend (if any time) helping the other person to blow up balloons? The results, shown in figure 2.1, were clear.

As expected, participants helped more in the communal than in the non-communal condition. Most interesting for present purposes, though, is the fact that the impact of the other's sadness depended upon the nature of the desired relationship. When a communal relationship was desired, the other's sadness significantly increased the time participants

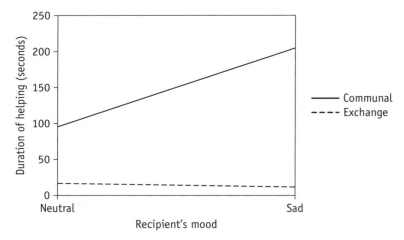

Figure 2.1 Mean duration of helping as a function of relationship manipulation and recipient mood

spent helping. When no communal relationship was desired, the other's sadness had no impact on the time participants spent helping.

We actually suspect that, had scores on the measure of helping not been so low in the non-communal condition in the absence of the sadness cue (leaving no room on our measure of helping for them to drop further), they may have dropped when the non-communal other expressed sadness. Fitting with our own speculation that expressions of sadness may be reacted to negatively in non-communal settings are some comments by Hoover-Dempsey, Plas, and Strudler-Wallston (1986). They argue that a woman weeping in work settings results in embarrassment for the woman and confusion and even anger on the part of others around her. However, they not, such negative reactions to weeping do *not* occur in what they call "intimate" or "personal" relationships (and what we might characterize as communal relationships). Miss Manners (aka Judith Martin) (1982) also provides an example of expressing sadness in non-communal relationships leading to annoyance. She reports a boss's reaction to his employees expressing sadness generated by their personal problems. This man says, "I consider myself a reasonable boss. I know that people might have down cycles in their work, and I try to allow for that." However, he adds, he really does not want them expressing their sadness to him saying, "Frankly, it just makes me angry when they try to enlist my sympathies about how they feel bad . . ." (p. 244). Miss Manners agrees with him and also with us when she notes that such expressions should be reserved for "people with whom they have close ties of blood or affection," or, as we would put it, people who feel responsibility for our personal needs.

The view that negative emotions will be reacted to more positively in more communal relationships also helps to explain some otherwise seemingly discrepant findings in the literature. Specifically, when researchers have asked people to evaluate a person *whom they have never met* (and thus with whom they do not have a communal relationship), finding out that that person is feeling a negative emotion (irritated, angry, gloomy, frustrated) causes the person to be judged to be unsociable, unpopular, and non-conventional (Sommers, 1984, Study 3). In contrast, when *spouses* (who typically show a strong desire to follow communal norms in their relationship, cf. Grote & Clark, 1998), have been asked to evaluate messages from their mates, messages that include unpleasant emotions, disclosures of vulnerabilities, and hostilities toward persons other than the spouse often prompt more positive responses and attitudes than do messages devoid of such negative elements (Shimanoff, 1988).

In sum, it is evident that expressing emotion is more commonplace within the context of communal relationships, and is very often reacted to with more liking and more responsiveness in communal than in non-communal relationships. We think expressions of emotion lie at the very heart of communal relationships. They communicate our needs to others. They allow others to be responsive to our needs. Being willing to express emotions indicates that we trust the other with information about our vulnerabilities – that is, we trust the perseon to use that information to support us rather than to take advantage of our weaknesses. On the other hand, emotions are not central to interacting with another on an exchange or economic basis. Indeed, to the extent to which they do reveal our weaknesses and neediness, expressing emotions in non-communal interactions makes us vulnerable and easy to exploit.

Experiencing more emotion in response to others' needs the more one feels responsible for those needs

To this point, we have argued that people are more willing to express emotion the more they feel they are in a relationship in which the partner feels responsible for their needs. Moreover, we have argued, emotional expressions generally are reacted to more positively in such relationships. Going beyond this, it is important to note that most communal relationships are mutual – not only do we assume the other cares about our needs and should and will respond to those needs on a communal basis, so too do we care about that other's needs and feel we should respond to those needs on a communal basis. In addition, there are certain asymmetric communal relationships in which one feels greater responsibility for the welfare of the other than one expects the other to feel for the self (e.g., a mother's relationship with her own young child). Feelings of responsibility for the *other's* welfare not only have clear implications for expressing certain emotions (i.e., those experienced in response to the other's needs – emotions such as guilt, empathic sadness, and empathic happiness), they also have implications for experiencing these emotions in the first place.

Consider the experience of these emotions first. An example is empathic sadness. One should feel this emotion when one's partner has experienced a loss and, holding the loss constant, one should feel more sadness the more responsibility one feels for the welfare of the other. Is there any evidence for this? Yes. In two separate studies Batson, Duncan, Ackerman, Buckley, and Birch (1981) manipulated how similar college females felt to another college female by providing feedback that the other had answered a personal profile and interest inventory either in very much the same way as the participant or in quite a different way. Later on participants in the highly similar conditions reported feeling more similar to the other and also, importantly for our present arguments, feeling that they valued the other's welfare (on an index that included ratings of valuing the other's welfare, wanting the other to be happy, and not wanting the other to suffer). Following the similarity manipulation, Batson et al. exposed all participants to a person in need and measured the extent to which participants reported feeling sympathetic, compassionate, softhearted, and tender. As they expected, and fitting with our current arguments, people in the high similarity conditions who reported caring more about the other's welfare also experienced more empathic compassion than did those in the low similarity conditions. Analogous results have been reported by Batson, Turk, Shaw, and Klein (1995) and by Krebs (1975). What is important here for our purposes is the clear link between feelings of responsibility for another and the experience of empathic compassion. The fact that similarity was an important elicitor not only of a sense of communal responsibility but also of feelings of communal compassion is intriguing and fits well with the well-established links between similarity and the formation of friendships (Byrne & Nelson, 1965; Newcomb, 1961).

Next consider empathic happiness. There is evidence that this too is experienced more frequently within the context of relationships in which we feel responsible for our partner's needs than in other relationships. Specifically, Williamson and Clark (1989, Study 3; 1992) reported two studies in which they measured positive and negative moods at the beginning of the studies, then manipulated desire for a communal versus an exchange relationship with another "participant." Later, the true participants were either induced to help (or were not induced to help) the other "participant." Finally the experimenters measured mood again. In both studies helping the other was associated with improvements in mood *only* when a communal relationship was desired. Moreover, in the 1992 study, participants were led to feel that they had to help the other or that they had chosen to help the other. The improvement in mood when a communal, but not when an exchange, relationship was desired occurred whether or not the help was freely given or was required. This suggests that the fact that the needy other was benefited was key to the improvement in mood rather than the improvement in mood being dependent upon the helper seeing him or herself as a good person for having chosen to help the other (as might be suggested by Bem's self-perception theory, 1972).[4]

Finally, consider guilt. Guilt usually implies that one feels badly about having not met another's needs or that one has harmed the other's welfare in some way. It is straightforward to argue that this should occur primarily within the context of relationships in which one feels responsible for the other person's needs.[5] It is also straightforward to argue that the stronger one's feelings of responsibility for the other's welfare, the more guilt should be felt for the same neglectful behavior. For example, one should feel more guilty if one forgets one's mother's birthday than if one forgets a friend's birthday and more guilty if one forgets a friend's birthday than if one forgets an acquaintance's birthday.

There is evidence to support the idea that guilt is, indeed, an emotion that is closely associated with communal relationships – work by Baumeister, Stillwell, and Heatherton (1994, 1995). Baumeister et al. had college students describe, in writing, two situations in which they had angered someone. The situations were to be important and memorable, and preferably chosen from the past two or three years. Participants described the incident taking care to include the background, the incident itself, and the consequences. One of the descriptions was to be of an incident after which the student "felt bad or suffered from a feeling of having done something wrong." The other description was to be of an incident after which the participant "did not feel bad or suffer from a feeling of having done some-thing wrong." After collecting the stories, the researchers coded them "for whether the victim was depicted as someone with whom the subject had a communal relationship (defined as involving norms of mutual concern for each other's welfare, such as in family or romantic relationships)" or not (Baumeister et al., 1995, p. 181).

As the investigators predicted, the incidents chosen as examples of times the participants had felt bad, or suffered from feelings of having done something wrong, were more likely to have taken place in the context of a communal relationship than were the incidents chosen to represent times participants did not feel bad or suffer from a feeling of having done something wrong (see also Baumeister et al., 1995, Study 2; Vangelisti, Daly, & Rudnick, 1991). Thus, guilt seems to have been experienced more often in the context of communal than non-communal relationships.

The evidence on empathic sadness, happiness, and guilt taken together suggests that any emotion that indicates to oneself that one cares about the welfare of another person should occur more frequently and more intensely the more communal in nature one's relationship with another person. Asch (1952) noted that "Emotions are our ways of representing to ourselves the fate of our goals" (p. 110). Emotion researchers have long acknowledged the truth of this statement when the goals relate to our personal welfare (Frijda, 1993; Simon, 1967). What this research suggests is that our goals sometimes include other people's welfare as well. Thus we would argue that our emotions also represent to us the fate of the goals of others about whose welfare we care.

Interestingly this evidence also suggests that experiencing emotion in response to the need states of another may be taken as a signal to oneself that the relationship is a communal one (if one feels good when another's needs are met or bad when they are not) or, indeed, that the relationship is not a communal one (if one feels bad when another's needs have been met or good when they have not been met). That people do, indeed, infer that they care about another person when they feel good upon the other's needs being met, and bad upon the other's needs not being met or upon the other actually being harmed, is supported by a number of studies (Aderman, Brehm, & Katz, 1974; Batson, Turk, Shaw, & Klein, 1995; Mills, Jellison, & Kennedy, 1976; Zillmann & Cantor, 1977).

Expressing more emotion when another has a need the more one feels responsible for those needs

Our theoretical position also suggests, of course, that not only should one experience more guilt, empathic compassion, and empathic happiness within the context of relationships in which one feels responsible for a partner's needs, one also should express these emotions more often within such relationships. The experience of these emotions communicates to oneself that one cares about the other; but it is the expression of these emotions that is important to communicating this caring to the other. There is less empirical data to back up this idea. However, we would note that Baumeister et al. (1995) found that not only was guilt experienced more often in the context of communal relationships, it was expressed more often within those relationships as well. Of course, these results could be accounted for by simply arguing that one must experience an emotion before it can be expressed. In fact, in our own study, described above in connection with expressing emotions conveying one's own needs, we did include one emotion indicating concern for the other's welfare – namely, guilt. Within that study, we asked our participants to tell us, when they did experience guilt, the extent to which they expressed it to others. The results for guilt caused by neglecting that other's needs were clear. Our participants said they would be far less likely to express guilt feelings to others with whom they had weak communal relationships (e.g., strangers, coworkers, neighbors, professors, and classmates) than they would be to express their guilt to those with whom they had stronger communal relationships (e.g., roommates, siblings, close friends, mothers, and fathers).

Summing up our points thus far

We have argued that, to predict and to understand the expression of emotions conveying information about one's needs, it is crucial to take relationship context into account. Just as experiencing our own emotions alerts us to our own needs and the necessity of doing something about those needs (Frijda, 1986, 1993; Simon, 1967), so too can emotional expression alert our relationship partners about our needs and the necessity of responding to those needs (Buck, 1984, 1989). However, whereas we are all presumably concerned about our own needs (one could say we have a communal relationship with ourselves), not everyone else is concerned about our needs and those who are concerned about them are concerned to differing degrees. This suggests that we will be selective in expressing emotions to others – choosing to express more emotions conveying our needs to those who care most about our welfare. Existing research supports these claims.

Moreover, we have argued, to understand fully the experience and expression of emotions which we experience in response to other people's need states (empathic happiness and sadness as well as guilt), one also must take relationship context into account. Our feelings of responsibility for the needs of others differs dramatically from relationship to relationship. We should experience more empathic emotions and guilt the more we care for another. We should also choose to express these emotions more the more we care for the other. Existing research supports these contentions as well.

At this point we would like to add a caveat to our arguments. We have suggested that the existence (or lack thereof) of communal relationships makes a difference to experiencing guilt and empathic emotions but not to experiencing our own happiness, sadness, anger, and so forth. We have said this because we assume everyone feels responsible for attending to their own needs whereas people are selective in feeling responsible for other people's needs. However, we do not wish to suggest that being in the presence of others who feel responsible for our own needs is completely irrelevant to the experience of our own emotions. Here is why. As we have argued, people should express more emotions conveying their own needs in communal than in other relationships. Others have argued that the very act of expressing emotion provides feedback that intensifies that emotion (Laird, 1974; Laird & Bresler, 1992; Riskind & Gotay, 1982; Riskind, 1984). By choosing to express more emotion in communal relationships we may experience feedback which causes us to actually experience more emotion in those relationships as well. Moreover, not only may expression of emotion intensify that emotion through intrapersonal feedback, it may also influence the experience of the emotion through interpersonal feedback. In some cases such interpersonal feedback may intensify the emotion. For example, when we express emotion our relationship partners may encourage us to express more emotion or to talk more about the emotional experience thereby intensifying or prolonging the experience of emotion. In other cases interpersonal feedback may diminish the experience. When we express emotion our relationship partner may calm us down, reassure us, or redirect our attention elsewhere. When our partner is living up to the norms of a communal relationship, which type of interpersonal strategy he or she chooses should be determined by what that partner believes to be in our best interests.

Types of People and Emotion

To this point we have argued that emotional expression will occur primarily within the context of relationships in which one believes the other feels a responsibility for one's needs and/or in which one feels a responsibility for the other's needs. To some extent we have also argued that emotional experience will follow the same pattern. We have further argued that everyone has a variety of relationships which vary in the extent to which such responsibilities are felt and that those felt responsibilities modulate their emotional lives. Moving ahead in our analysis it is also important to point out that beliefs that others will be responsive to one's own needs and feelings of responsiveness to other's needs vary not just by relationship context. There are also chronic individual differences in such beliefs. Some people are chronically high in the tendency to believe that others will be responsive to their needs and in the tendency to turn to others for help. Others are chronically more cynical. They do not believe others will "be there" for them and they do not tend to turn to others for help. The positions we have taken thus far in this chapter carry the further implication that our emotional lives also will vary according to these chronic individual differences.

Differences in beliefs that others care about one's welfare are captured in a variety of concepts in the extant literature – secure versus insecure attachment styles (Hazan & Shaver, 1987; Bartholomew & Horowitz, 1991), high communal versus low communal orientation (Clark et al., 1987), and chronic tendencies to perceive that one does have social support available to one versus perceptions that one does not have such support available (Cohen & Hoberman, 1983; Cutrona & Russell, 1987). Thus, we would expect people's emotional lives to covary with such established individual differences between people. Existing literature suggests that they do.

Expressing more emotions when one has a chronic tendency to believe partners feel responsible for one's needs

In discussing relationship types we noted that studies by Clark & Taraban (1991), Barrett, Robin, Pietromonaco, and Eyssell, 1998, and Brissette and Clark (1999) all support the idea that people express more emotion in the context of relationships in which they believe the other bears a special responsibility for their needs. Is there parallel evidence that people who are chronically high in the belief that others will be responsive to their needs also express more emotion to their relationship partners? The answer, drawn from the attachment literature, is yes (Feeney, 1995, 1999).

In one study Feeney (1995) examined emotional expression within young adults' dating relationships. Dating couples completed a 15-item measure of attachment based on Hazan and Shaver's (1987) original measure. From this, measures of Comfort (Secure to Avoidant) and Anxiety were extracted. In addition members of the couple completed a measure of emotional control based on the Courtauld Emotional Control Scale (Watson & Greer, 1983). They completed this with regard to emotions experienced in relation to their current dating partner. The scale tapped willingness to express/suppress feelings of anger, sadness, and anxiety.

For our purposes the interesting question is whether secure people, who tend to believe that others will be responsive to their needs, were *less* likely to suppress expressions of these negative feelings to their partners than were insecure people. The results were clear. The more securely attached members of the couples were, the less likely they reported they were to suppress expressions of anxiety (−.31 for females; −.44 for males) and to suppress expressions of sadness (−.38 for females, −.26 for males). In addition, the more securely attached females were, the less likely they were to suppress anger (−.29), but this effect was not obtained for males. All the reported correlations reached significance. Importantly, they remained significant after the researchers controlled for the reported frequency of the emotion in question being experienced. Thus, chronic individual differences in tendencies to perceive that one's partner will be responsive to one's needs do parallel situational/relationship differences in tendencies to believe the other should be responsive to one's needs.[6]

In her later, 1999, study, Feeney again linked Comfort (indicative of security as opposed to avoidance) with willingness to express emotion. This time members of married couples were asked about their willingness to express anger, sadness, anxiety, happiness, love, and pride to their partner when those emotions were caused by their partners, as well as when these emotions were caused by something not involving the partner. As in the 1995 study, feelings of security (comfort in her terms) were negatively linked with controlling/suppressing each of these emotions both when the emotion had been caused by the partner and when it had not. For husbands, the relevant correlations were −.19 and −.22 for anger (partner-related first, other second), −.27 and −.22 for sadness, −.20 and −.26 for anxiety, −.36 and −.28 for happiness, −.35 and −.23 for love, and −.33 and −.31 for pride. All were significant and remained significant after the reported frequency and intensity of experiencing each of these emotions were partialled out. For wives, the correlations were −.29 and −.17 for anger, −.24 and −.22 for sadness, −.31 and −.22 for anxiety, −.14 and −.15 for happiness, −.21 and −.21 for love, and −.12 and −.17 for pride. All correlations except the correlation of Comfort with willingness to express partner-related pride were significant. Importantly, all those correlations that were significant remained significant after the reported frequency and intensity of experiencing each of these emotions were partialled out (except for the negative correlation between Comfort and control of expressing partner-related love.)

Other work supporting the notion that people's perceptions that their partner cares for them will be associated with greater expressions of emotions has been reported by Collins

(Collins, 1994; Collins & Di Paula, 1997). These researchers interviewed 92 HIV-infected men. During the interview the men filled out Sarason, Sarason, Shearin, & Pierce's (1987) Social Support Questionnaire (short form) with regard to up to five members of their close social network.[7] They also filled out a ways of coping index (Folkman, Lazarus, Dunkel-Schetter, DeLongis, & Gruen, 1986). For our purposes, what is important about the latter index taps the tendency to suppress expressing distress when in the presence of others. (This scale includes items such as, "I tried to avoid letting others know how bad my situation was," and "I tried to put up a happy front when around others.") Consistent with our current theoretical analysis, the authors observed a negative relationship between the average level of receipt of support their participants perceived, and suppression of distress ($r = -.21$, $p < .07$), a relationship that, while marginal in significance, became significant when they controlled for physical health in the analyses ($r = -.24$, $p < .05$).[8]

Reacting more positively to others' emotional expressions when one feels responsible for those others' needs

In discussing how relationship type influences reactions to others' expressions of emotions, we noted evidence that the more people desire a communal relationship with the other the more positively they react to the other's expression of emotion (Clark & Taraban, 1991; Clark et al., 1987). This effect, too, has a parallel in the individual difference literature.

In particular, Clark et al. (1987) have developed a measure of communal orientation which taps chronic individual differences in people's tendencies to feel responsible for others' needs. It includes such items as "When making a decision, I take other people's needs and feelings into account," and "I believe it's best not to get involved taking care of other people's personal needs" (reverse scored). Clark et al. (1987, Study 1) administered this scale to a group of college students at the beginning of a semester. Later on in the same semester, some of these students were recruited to participate in a study ostensibly on creativity. Each participant arrived individually at a psychology faculty member's office. The faculty member greeted the participant and said a research assistant actually would conduct the study. She would take the participant to the relevant lab.

On the way, the faculty member led some participants to believe the research assistant was feeling sad whereas other participants were given no information about the assistant's emotional state. Next they encountered the research assistant, seated at a cluttered desk and the faculty member left. The research assistant, who was unaware of her own alleged mood, was obviously not only not ready to run the study but also clearly worried about her own work. She told the participant she had to get some materials for the creativity study and, as she left the room to get them, she asked the participant for some personal help. Specifically, she asked the participant to alphabetize a stack of 116 index cards with references written on them. The measure of interest was the amount of help, if any, the participants would give the "research assistant" and whether responsiveness to her sadness would depend upon the potential helper's level of communal orientation (a variable which was unknown to both the experimenter and "research assistant" at the time the study was run). The pattern of results is shown in figure 2.2.

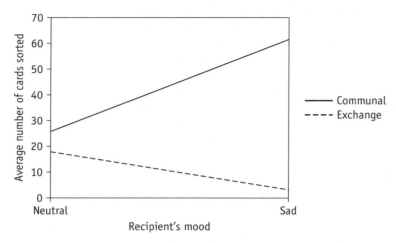

Figure 2.2   Number of cards sorted as a function of donor relationship orientation and recipient mood

As can be seen, people high in communal orientation helped more than those low in communal orientation. More importantly for the present point, though, communal orientation appears to have an impact on reactions to sadness, with the research assistant's sadness garnering increased help from high communal persons but actually resulting in less help from those low in communal orientation. The interaction only approached significance in this case. However, the parallel between the observed pattern found in this study and that in Figure 2.1 (obtained when desire for a communal relationship was manipulated) is striking and the marginal interaction is clearly consistent with the thesis of the present chapter.

Believing others will be responsive to one's needs and coping with one's own emotional states

An important part of one's emotional life, particularly when dealing with negative emotions such as distress, fear, anxiety, and anger is how one reacts to one's own emotional states. Such reactions are a part of the knowledge structures regarding emotions that people have stored in memory. For instance, prototypes of sadness aggregated across people include reacting in the following ways: "talking to someone about sadness," "crying, tears, whimpering," and "saying sad things" as well as "suppressing feelings," "acting happy," "withdrawing from social contact," "talking little or not at all." Their prototypes of fear include: "crying, whimpering," "screaming, yelling" and "pleading, crying for help" as well as "acting unafraid, hiding the fear," "comforting self, trying to keep calm" (Shaver, Schwartz, Kirson, & O'Connor, 1987). But what determines whether one really does talk to someone else about one's sadness as opposed to withdrawing from social contact? Again, we would argue, an important determinant will be one's judgment that the person with whom one is with holds a positive attitude regarding being responsive to one's needs. To the extent to which one perceives that the other does hold such a positive view, emotion will be expressed; to the extent to which one does not, emotion will be suppressed.

Several studies offer support for this contention. Some have come out of the attachment literature, some from work on communal orientation and coping with stress. They all support the idea that people who hold a chronically higher tendency to believe others will be responsive to their needs will react to emotion by seeking others out; whereas those who do not hold such beliefs will not seek others out.

Simpson, Rholes, and Nelligan (1992) report one study supporting these ideas. In their study dating couples filled out an attachment style questionnaire and then the female member of each couple was exposed to an anxiety induction procedure. Specifically, an experimenter took her pulse and said, "In the next few minutes, you are going to be exposed to a situation and set of experimental procedures that arouse considerable anxiety and distress in most people. Due to the nature of these procedures, I cannot tell you any more at the moment." The experimenter also casually showed the woman the room that would be used for the study. It was dark, windowless, and contained what appeared to be psychophysiological equipment. Then the woman was led back to a waiting room where her partner (who did not undergo the anxiety provoking situation) was seated. The couple was left alone for five minutes and their interactions were videotaped.

Individual differences in security versus avoidance were not related to the levels of anxiety which observers rated the women as showing. However, how women reacted to their anxiety was dependent upon whether they were secure or not. Secure women, who presumably had high expectations of their partner's responsiveness to their needs, sought more comfort and support from their partners. Insecure women, who presumably had low expectations of their partner's responsiveness to their needs, reacted in a very different fashion. They did not seek much support from their partners. Instead they did such things as trying to distract themselves by thumbing through magazines in the waiting room.

Three additional studies supporting the idea that beliefs about the responsiveness of others to one's needs influence one's own reactions to distress have been reported recently by Brissette and his colleagues (Clark, Brissette, & Grote, 1998; Brissette, Clark, & Scheier, 1999). In all three studies, participants filled out the communal orientation scale (Clark et al., 1987). In two studies people were simply asked the extent to which they tended to react to being in need by seeking out support from close others versus coping with the problem themselves. Then they were asked how becoming especially distressed when they had a need for help influenced these tendencies. In both studies, those high in communal orientation (i.e., those who presumably feel others are responsive to their needs) said they responded to especially high distress by being more likely to rely on others for help and by seeking out more help from others. This is not surprising. After all, when one is especially distressed one is likely to be especially in need of help. What is more surprising is that people low in communal orientation not only reported being less likely to seek out help from others in general but also reported reacting to feeling especially distressed by becoming less likely to seek help. In other words, they reported reacting to their negative emotions by withdrawing from others. The third study was a longitudinal study. College students filled out measures of communal orientation, perceived stress, and perceived support at the beginning of a semester and then again at the end of the semester. Increases in stress led to declines in perceived support among those low in communal orientation, but were not associated with perceptions of support among those who were high in communal orientation.

The overall point of describing these studies is to suggest that the importance of differences in perceived responsiveness to needs for understanding people's emotional lives appears to extend beyond the experience and expression of emotion to styles of coping with emotion as well. Those who view others as responsive to needs not only freely express more emotion and, as a result, probably experience more emotion, they also react to emotional experiences by seeking others out. Those who view others as low in responsiveness to needs are less likely to express emotion, may experience more pallid emotions, and they appear to react to aversive emotional experiences by withdrawing from others.

Possible Interactions between Types of People and Types of Relationships

To this point, we have argued that two very important relationship variables are crucial to understanding individuals' experiences and expressions of emotions: (1) the degree to which one believes one's relationship partner cares about one's own welfare, and (2) the degree to which one cares about one's relationship partner's welfare. We began making a case for this thesis by using data suggesting that people's emotional experiences and expressions vary according to relationship context. More emotion and more intense emotions are experienced and expressed within communal than within other relationship contexts. Then we made a case for the same thesis using data suggesting that people's emotional experiences and expressions vary according to individual differences in the extent to which they expect others to be responsive to their needs. However, relationship context and individual differences are unlikely to have entirely independent effects on people's emotional lives. Rather, we hypothesize that relationship context and individual differences interact (even though we know of no relevant empirical evidence).

First, we suspect that almost everyone, regardless of attachment style, communal orientation, or chronic individual differences in perceived social support, understands (implicitly) and draws distinctions between stronger, weaker communal relationships and non-communal relationships. Moreover, we believe that almost everyone, no matter how secure, or how communally oriented, or how much perceived support they believe they have, suppresses emotional expression when they are in non-communal relationships. For example, people on the whole simply do not go around expressing their fears, sadness, and happiness when in formal business settings. Moreover, on the rare occasions when they do, other people, on the whole, view their behavior as inappropriate. To put it another way, individual differences in both the tendencies to view others as responsive to one's needs and to feel responsible for other's needs probably make little difference to people's emotional lives within the context of clear-cut, non-communal relationships.

Instead, we suspect the individual differences that we have discussed as being relevant to people's emotional lives are going to have their biggest impact within the context of relationships that our culture dictates ought to be communal and intimate in nature – relationships with friends, family, and romantic relationships. Indeed, it is within the actual (or imagined) context of such relationships that the effects cited above have been observed. It may also be the case that chronic individual differences in beliefs about responsiveness to needs make a difference within relationships in which norms regarding such responsiveness are not clearly set by the culture – for instance, in relationships with people one has just met who *might* become friends or romantic partners.

Responsiveness to Needs and Expression of Emotion: Reciprocal Effects

To this point we have emphasized how perceiving that another person will be responsive to one's needs will influence expression and, to some extent, experiences of emotion. We have also emphasized how feeling responsible for another person's needs will influence the experience and expression of certain emotions. However, to talk of perceptions of responsibility for needs driving emotional experience and expression is too simple. Just as perceptions of responsiveness to needs are likely to have an impact on experiences and expressions of emotion so too, we believe, does emotional expression have an impact on the quality of relationships, on responsiveness to needs and, eventually, on perceptions of responsiveness to needs.

Why? There are many reasons. First, the expression of emotions enables others to better meet our needs, which in turn should enhance positive feelings and the communal nature of the relationship. Beyond this, the communication function of emotions goes beyond just conveying information about needs. When emotions are expressed to a person, not only does the person to whom they are expressed learn something about the needs of the person expressing them, he or she also learns that the other is willing to communicate those needs. Expressions of emotion should indicate that the emotional person is open to the formation, maintenance, or deepening of a communal relationship. In turn, this may strengthen the communal relationship not only through enhanced responsiveness to the emotional person's needs but also by enhancing liking, willingness to express emotions in return, and comfort with the relationship. Moreover, when one experiences empathic happiness, sadness, or guilt in response to another person's needs, one may infer from those experiences and expressions that one really does care for the other person. This too may result in the creation or the strengthening of a communal relationship.

The idea that expressing emotion in relationships may strengthen those relationships is supported by some recent findings reported by Feeney (1999) linking willingness to express emotion with marital satisfaction. As we have described already, she measured the extent to which married couples reported suppressing anger, sadness, anxiety, happiness, love, and pride in their relationships, and she linked insecure attachment to greater control of all these emotions. Relevant to the present point is the fact that she also measured marital satisfaction in her study using Norton's (1983) measure. Regression analyses revealed that, *after* controlling for own attachment styles, control of one's own negative and positive emotions and one's partner's control of negative and positive emotions were all negatively associated with marital satisfaction. Moreover, these negative associations reached statistical significance in five of the eight cases.[9] Some similar findings have been reported by Feeney, Noller, & Roberts (1998) and by Laurenceau et al. (1998, Study 2).

In addition, several studies support the idea that experiencing emotion in response to another person's need states (or lack thereof) may strengthen communal relationships. For instance, long ago Mills, Jellison, and Kennedy (1976) reported two studies in which participants received feedback via a meter regarding their feelings when another person experienced good or bad fortune. Those people receiving feedback that they felt badly when another experienced a negative outcome, or that they felt positively when another experienced a good outcome, inferred that they liked that other more.[10]

More recently, Batson, Turk, Shaw, and Klein (1995) have provided another demonstration that if one feels badly when another is feeling needy one may infer that one cares about that person. In two studies Batson and his colleagues directly manipulated the extent to which participants felt empathy for a confederate in need. Then they measured the inferences these people drew about the nature of their relationship with the needy person. In the first study females either were assigned: (1) to a control condition in which they neither heard about another participant's troubles nor were induced to feel empathy for that participant, (2) to a high empathy condition in which they imagined how another participant (who had just been dropped by a boyfriend) felt, or (3) to a low empathy condition in which participants were exposed to the same information about the other person's troubles but were instructed to take an objective perspective and not to get caught up in how the other felt. A manipulation check on empathic feelings supported the effectiveness of the manipulation. More importantly for the point we are making, participants also inferred that they had a stronger communal relationship with the other after they had experienced enhanced empathy with that person. Specifically, participants were given the following instructions: "Think of someone whose welfare you value highly (e.g., a best friend or favorite family member). Now think of someone whose welfare you do not value highly (e.g., someone you know nothing about at all). Compared to these two extremes, how much do you value the welfare of (the other participant)." Mean responses to this question were lowest in the control condition, medium high in the low empathy condition and highest, by a significant amount relative to the low empathy condition, in the high empathy condition. Analogous findings were obtained in a second study in which the perception that participants were feeling empathy with another person in need were manipulated by providing participants in the high empathy condition with false physiological feedback indicating that they had (or had not) experienced arousal upon hearing of another's plight. Again, those participants believing that they had experienced empathy upon hearing of another's plight were especially likely to infer that they had a communal relationship with the other.

As Martin and his colleagues have pointed out, we appear to use our moods and emotions as inputs in processing information (Martin, Ward, Achee, & Wyer, 1993; Martin & Stoner, 1996; Martin & Davies, 1998). Here we emphasize that, as a result of experiencing and expressing emotion in response to another's needs we may strengthen the communal nature of the relationship through coming to care for that person more and, to the extent to which the other notices our empathic reactions, communicating that care to the other. Since liking begets liking (Kenny & LaVoie, 1982; Curtis & Miller, 1986) and, we presume, since caring begets caring, we would expect the expression of empathic emotions to one's relationship partner to feed back and to strengthen communal relationships.

Concluding Comments

We noted at the outset of this chapter that, although psychological research on emotion has been flourishing, most of it has focused on intrapersonal aspects of emotion. In this chapter we have tried to make a case that a variable that can *only* be understood in relationship terms, perceptions of relationship members' responsiveness to one another's needs, is crucial to fully understand people's emotional lives. This is a factor that varies as a function of relationship type and by person. It is also a factor that is central to relationship research although its importance even in that domain is often obscured by the fact that it comes cloaked in different terminologies in different investigators' research programs (e.g., communal versus exchange relationships, communal orientation, perceived social support, secure versus insecure attachment styles). It is the fact that perceptions of responsiveness to needs varies by relationship and *in combination with* the fact that expressing emotions carries information about our need states to others that makes perceptions of responsiveness to needs a crucial factor for emotion researchers to consider. We hope we have convinced the reader of this point.

There is another point we hope we have conveyed to our readers, one that is more relevant to the domain of relationship research than to the domain of emotions research. It is, simply, that our research tends to be fragmented by research groups and theory – there's attachment research, social support research, emotions research, communal/exchange research, and so forth. Each such program of research is valuable in its own right. Yet sometimes it is well worth while to take a step back and see the common themes and sets of findings that run through different, apparently independent, programs of research. In this case, the common theme we have pointed to is that perceptions of responsiveness to needs are closely linked with people's emotional lives.

NOTES

1 Exceptions may occur in emergency situations in which another person's need is very great relative to the cost a person would incur to help the other, and in which help from someone with stronger communal ties is unavailable. For instance, a person might call an ambulance for a stranger who has collapsed in front of that person's house and even wait outside with the person until the ambulance arrives.

2 Participants had most of these relationships, but not every one in every case. Thus, a few ratings made by participants were hypothetical and participants were told that this was OK in the initial instructions.

3 We believe the correlations for anger and disgust caused by the other were smaller than the remaining correlations because, as a mutual communal relationship grows in strength, *both* members' responsibilities for one another's needs grow. Thus, when another with whom one has a mutual communal relationship causes one to feel disgust or anger, one must be concerned not only with one's own needs but also with those of one's partner. As a result of the latter concern, one may suppress expressions of disgust and anger when those emotions have been elicited by one's partner so as not to hurt the partner's feelings.

4   The Williamson and Clark (1989, 1992) results also can be explained in terms of participants feeling good about promoting the development of communal relationships. Even so, the results are consistent with our overall arguments that feeling positive emotions in response to improving another's welfare is something that occurs primarily when we care about the other's needs. Moreover, experiencing empathic happiness when benefiting another and being pleased to have promoted the relationship are not incompatible processes.

5   One may also feel guilt in a non-communal relationship if one has broken the norms for that relationship. For instance, one may feel guilt in an exchange relationship for having not paid back a debt. However, we believe the primary source of guilt for most people is failure to demonstrate adequate concern about the welfare of those with whom they have communal relationships.

6   The dimension of anxious attachment was not associated with significant tendencies to suppress versus express emotion.

7   We are choosing to report this study on perceived support in the section of our chapter dealing with individual differences. We do this despite the fact that some researchers feel that perceptions of social support are determined primarily by support that is currently and objectively available in one's enviroment whereas others believe perceptions of support are determined by personality. In fact, our belief is that perceived social support is determined by both factors. Thus our placement of this study in the individual differences section of the chapter is somewhat arbitrary.

8   Although we are choosing to emphasize the support this finding provides for perceptions of another's responsiveness to needs resulting in greater tendencies to express emotion, it is, of course, possible that the effects go in the opposite direction. That is, it may be that expressing distress elicits support which, in turn, causes perceived support to rise. Our actual belief is that both effects occur.

9   Interestingly, the effects of attachment styles and of emotional control on marital satisfaction appeared to be largely independent in this study with the exception of some evidence that the negative relationship between husbands' security and satisfaction did seem to be mediated by suppression of emotional expression.

10 Interestingly, the same set of studies also demonstrated that feeling badly when another experiences good outcomes and good when another experiences bad outcomes can lead to an inference that one does not like that other.

REFERENCES

Aderman, D., Brehm, S. S., & Katz, L. B. (1974). Empathic observation of an innocent victim: The just world revisited. *Journal of Personality and Social Psychology, 29*, 342–347.

Andersen, P. A., & Guerrero, L. K. (1998). Principles of communication and emotion in social interaction. *Handbook of Communication and Emotion: Research, Theory, Applications, and Contexts* (pp. 49–96). San Diego, CA: Academic Press.

Asch, S. (1952). *Social psychology*. Englewood Cliffs, NJ: Prentice Hall.

Balswick, J., & Avertt, C. P. (1977). Differences in expressiveness: Gender, interpersonal orientation, and perceived parental expressiveness as contributing factors. *Journal of Marriage and the Family, 39*, 121–127.

Barrett, L. F., Robin, L., Pietromonaco, P. R., & Eyssell, K. M. (1998). Are women the "more emotional" sex? Evidence from emotional experiences in social context. *Cognition and emotion, 12*, 555–578.

Bartholomew, K., & Horowitz, L. M. (1991). Attachment styles among young adults: A test of a four-category model. *Journal of Personality and Social Psychology, 61*, 226–244.

Batson, C. D., Duncan, B. D., Ackermann, P., Buckley, T., & Birch, K. (1981). Is empathic emotion a source of altruistic motivation? *Journal of Personality and Social Psychology, 40,* 290–302.

Batson, C. D., Turk, C. L., Shaw, L. L., & Klein, T. R. (1995). Information function of empathic emotion: Learning that we value the other's welfare. *Journal of Personality and Social Psychology, 68,* 300–313.

Baumeister, R. F., Stillwell, A. M., & Heatherton, T. F. (1994). Guilt: An interpersonal approach. *Psychological Bulletin, 115,* 243–267.

Baumeister, R. F., Stillwell, A. M., & Heatherton, T. F. (1995). Personal narratives about guilt: Role in action control and interpersonal relationships. *Basic and Applied Social Psychology, 17,* 173–198.

Bem, D. J. (1972). Self-perception theory. In L. Berkowitz (Ed.), *Advances in experimental social psychology* (Vol. 6, pp. 1–62). New York: Academic Press.

Brissette, I., & Clark, M. S. (1999). *Emotional expression in social relationships: The type of relationship matters.* Unpublished manuscript.

Brissette, I., Clark, M. S., & Scheier, M. (1999). *Heightened stress as a determinant of perceptions of social support: The moderating role of communal orientation.* Unpublished manuscript.

Buck, R. (1984). *The communication of emotion.* New York: Guilford Press.

Buck, R. (1989). Emotional communication in personal relationships: A developmental-interactionist view. In C. Hendrick (Ed.), *Review of personality and social psychology: Vol. 10. Close relationships* (pp. 144–163). Beverly Hills, CA: Sage.

Byrne, D., & Nelson, D. (1965). Attraction as a linear function of positive reinforcement. *Journal of Personality and Social Psychology, 1,* 659–663.

Clark, L., & Watson, D. (1994). Distinguishing functional from dysfunctional affective responses. In P. Ekman & R. J. Davidson (Eds.), *The Nature of Emotion: Fundamental Questions* (pp. 131–136). New York: Oxford University Press.

Clark, M. S., Brissette, I., & Grote, N. (1998, June). *Perceptions of social support as a function of relationship orientation and arousal.* Paper presented at the meetings of the International Society for the Study of Personal Relationships, Skidmore College, Saratoga, New York.

Clark, M. S., & Mills, J. (1979). Interpersonal attraction in exchange and communal relationships. *Journal of Personality and Social Psychology, 36,* 1–12.

Clark, M. S., & Mills, J. (1993). The difference between communal and exchange relationships: What it is and is not. *Personality and Social Psychology Bulletin, 19,* 684–691.

Clark, M. S., Ouellette, R., Powell, M., & Milberg, S. (1978). Recipient's mood, relationship type, and helping. *Journal of Personality and Social Psychology, 53,* 94–103.

Clark, M. S., & Taraban, C. B. (1991). Reactions to and willingness to express emotion in two types of relationships. *Journal of Experimental Social Psychology, 27,* 324–336.

Cohen, S., & Hoberman, H. M. (1983). Positive events and social supports as buffers of life change stress. *Journal of Applied Social Psychology, 13,* 99–125.

Collins, R. L. (1994). Social support provision to HIV-infected gay men. *Journal of Applied Social Psychology, 24,* 1848–1869.

Collins, R. L., & Di Paula, A. (1997). Personality and the provision of support: Emotions felt and signaled. In G. R. Pierce, B. Lakey, I. G. Sarason, & B. R. Sarason (Eds.), *Sourcebook of social support and personality* (pp. 429–443). New York: Plenum.

Curtis, R. C., & Miller, K. (1986). Believing another likes or dislikes you: Behaviors making the beliefs come true. *Journal of Personality and Social Psychology, 51,* 284–290.

Cutrona, C. E., & Russell, D. W. (1987). The provisions of social relationships and adaptation to stress. In W. H. Jones & D. Perlman (Eds.), *Advances in personal relationships* (Vol. 1, pp. 37–67). Greenwich, CT: JAI Press.

Ekman, P., & Davidson, R. J. (1994). Afterword: What is the function of emotions? In P. Ekman & R. J. Davidson (Eds.), *The Nature of Emotion: Fundamental Questions* (pp. 137–139). New York: Oxford University Press.

Feeney, J. A. (1995). Adult attachment and emotional control. *Personal Relationships, 2,* 143–159.

Feeney, J. A. (1999). Adult attachment, emotional control, and marital satisfaction. *Personal Relationships, 6,* 169–185.

Feeney, J. A., Noller, P., & Roberts, N. (1998). Emotion, attachment, and satisfaction in close relationships. In P. A. Andersen & L. K. Guerrero (Eds.), *The handbook of communication and emotion* (pp. 473–505). San Diego, CA: Academic Press.

Fitness, J. (in press). Anger in the workplace: An emotion script approach to anger between workers and their superiors, co-workers, and subordinates. *Journal of Organizational Behavior.*

Folkman, S., Lazarus, R., Dunkel-Schetter, C., DeLongis, A., & Gruen, R. (1986). Dynamics of a stressful encounter. Cognitive appraisal, coping, and encounter outcomes. *Journal of Personality and Social Psychology, 50,* 992–1003.

Fridlund, A. J. (1991). Sociality of solitary smiling: Potentiation by an implicit audience. *Journal of Personality and Social Psychology, 60,* 229–240.

Frijda, N. H. (1986). *The emotions.* Cambridge, England: Cambridge University Press.

Frijda, N. H. (1993). Moods, emotion episodes, and emotions. In M. Lewis and J. M. Haviland (Eds.), *Handbook of emotions* (pp. 381–404). New York: Guilford Press.

Goldberg, S., MacKay-Soroka, S., & Rochester, M. (1994). Affect, attachment, and maternal responsiveness. *Infant Behavior and Development, 17,* 335–339.

Grote, N. K., & Clark, M. S. (1998). Distributive justice norms and family work: What is perceived as ideal, what is applied and what predicts perceived fairness? *Social Justice Research, 11,* 243–269.

Hazan, C., & Shaver, P. (1987). Romantic love conceptualized as an attachment process. *Journal of Personality and Social Psychology, 52,* 511–524.

Hoover-Dempsey, K. V., Plas, J. M., & Strudler-Wallston, B. (1986). Tears and weeping among professional women: In search of new understanding. *Psychology of Women Quarterly, 10,* 19–34.

Jones, S. S., Collins, K., & Hong, H. (1991). An audience effect on smile production in 10-month-old infants. *Psychological Science, 2,* 45–49.

Kenny, D. A., & LaVoie, L. (1982). Reciprocity of interpersonal attraction: A confirmed hypothesis. *Social Psychology Quarterly, 45,* 54–58.

Krebs, D. (1975). Empathy and altruism. *Journal of Personality and Social Psychology, 32,* 1134–1146.

Laird, J. D. (1974). Self-attribution of emotion: The effects of expressive behavior on the quality of emotional experience. *Journal of Personality and Social Psychology, 29,* 475–486.

Laird, J. D., & Bresler, C. (1992). The process of emotional experience: A self-perception theory. In M. S. Clark (Ed.), *Emotion* (pp. 213–234). Newbury Park, CA: Sage.

Laurenceau, J., Barrett, L. F., & Pietromonaco, P. R. (1998). Intimacy as an interpersonal process: The importance of self-disclosure, partner disclosure, and perceived partner responsiveness in interpersonal exchanges. *Journal of Personality and Social Psychology, 74,* 1238–1251.

Levenson, R. W. (1994). Human emotion: A functional view. In P. Ekman & R. J. Davidson (Eds.), *The nature of emotion: Fundamental questions* (pp. 123–126). New York: Oxford University Press.

Martin, J. (1982). *Miss Manners' guide to excruciatingly correct behavior.* New York: Atheneum.

Martin, L. I., Achee, J. W., Ward, D. W., & Harlow, T. F. (1993). The role of cognition and effort in the use of emotions to guide behavior. In R. S. Wyer, Jr., & T. K. Srull (Eds.), *Perspectives on anger and emotion* (pp. 147–157). Hillsdale, NJ: Lawrence Erlbaum.

Martin, L. L., & Davies, B. (1998). Beyond hedonism and associationism: A configural view of the role of affect in evaluation, processing, and self-regulation. *Motivation and Emotion, 22*(1), 33–51.

Martin, L. L., & Stoner, P. (1996). Mood as input: What people think about how they feel moods determines how they think. In L. L. Martin & A. Tesser (Eds.), *Striving and feelings: Interactions between goals, affect, and self-regulation* (pp. 279–301). Hillsdale, NJ: Erlbaum.

Martin, L. L., Ward, D. W., Achee, J. W., & Wyer, R. S. (1993). Mood as input: People have to interpret the motivational implications of their moods. *Journal of Personality and Social Psychology, 64*, 317–326.

Miller, R. S., & Leary, M. R. (1992). Social sources and interactive functions of emotion: The case of embarrassment. In M. S. Clark (Ed.), *Emotion and social behavior* (pp. 202–221). Newbury Park, CA: Sage.

Mills, J., & Clark, M. S. (1982). Exchange and communal relationships. In L. Wheeler (Ed.), *Review of Personality and Social Psychology* (Vol. 3, pp. 121–144). Beverly Hills, CA: Sage.

Mills, J., Jellison, J. M., & Kennedy, J. (1976). Attribution of attitudes from feelings: Effect of positive or negative feelings when the attitude object is benefited or harmed. In J. Harvey, W. Ickes, & R. Kidd (Eds.), *New Directions in Attribution Research* (Vol. 1, pp. 271–289). Hillsdale, N. J.: Erlbaum.

Newcomb, T. M. (1961). *The acquaintance process.* New York: Holt, Rinehart, & Winston.

Norton, R. (1983). Measuring marital quality: A critical look at the dependent variable. *Journal of Marriage and the Family, 45*, 141–151.

Pennebaker, J. (1995). Emotion, disclosure, and health: An overview. In J. Pennebaker (Ed.), *Emotion, disclosure, and health* (pp. 3–10). Washington, DC: American Psychological Association.

Rime, B. (1995). The social sharing of emotion as a source for the social knowledge of emotion. In J. Russell & J. Fernandez-Dols. (Eds.), *Everyday conceptions of emotions* (pp. 475–489). Dordrecht: Kluwer Academic.

Riskind, J. H. (1984). They stoop to conquer: Guiding and self-regulatory functions of physical posture after success and failure. *Journal of Personality and Social Psychology, 47*, 479–493.

Riskind, J. H., & Gotay, C. C. (1982). Physical posture: Could it have regulatory or feedback effects on motivation and emotion? *Motivation and Emotion, 6*, 273–298.

Sarason, I. G., Sarason, B. R., Shearin, E. N., & Pierce, G. R. (1987). A brief measure of social support: Practical and theoretical implications. *Journal of Social and Personal Relationships, 4*, 497–510.

Scott, J. P. (1958). *Animal behavior.* Chicago: University of Chicago Press.

Scott, J. P. (1980). The function of emotions in behavioral systems: A systems theory analysis. In *Emotion: Theory, Research, and Experience: Vol. 1. Theories of Emotion* (pp. 35–56). New York: Academic Press.

Shaver, P., Schwartz, J., Kirson, D., & O'Connor, C. (1987). Emotion knowledge: Further exploration of a prototype approach. *Journal of Personality and Social Psychology, 52*, 1061–1086.

Shimanoff, S. B. (1988). Degree of emotional expressiveness as a function of face-needs, gender, and interpersonal relationship. *Communication Reports, 1*, 43–59.

Simon, H. A. (1967). Motivational and emotional controls of cognition. *Psychological Review, 74*, 29–39.

Simpson, J. A., Rholes, W. S., & Nelligan, J. S. (1992). Support seeking and support giving within couples in an anxiety-provoking situation: The role of attachment styles. *Journal of Personality and Social Psychology, 62*, 434–446.

Sommers, S. (1984). Reported emotions and conventions of emotionality among college students. *Journal of Personality and Social Psychology, 46*, 207–215.

Sroufe, L. A., & Waters, E. (1977). Attachment as an organizational construct. *Child Development, 48*, 1184–1199.

Thoits, P. A. (1989). The sociology of emotions. *Annual Review of Sociology, 15*, 317–342.

Timmers, M., Fischer, A. H., & Manstead, A. S. R. (1998). Gender differences in motives for regulating emotions. *Personality and Social Psychology Bulletin, 24,* 974–985.

Vangelisti, A. L., Daly, J. A., & Rudnick, J. R. (1991). Making people feel guilty in conversations: Techniques and correlates. *Human Communication Research, 18,* 3–39.

Watson, M., & Greer, S. (1983). Development of a questionnaire measure of emotional control *Journal of Psychosomatic Research, 27,* 299–305.

Wessman, A. E., & Ricks, D. F. (1966). Mood and personality. New York: Holt, Rinehart, & Winston.

Williamson, G. M., & Clark, M. S. (1989). Providing help and desired relationship type as determinants of changes in moods and self-evaluations. *Journal of Personality and Social Psychology, 56,* 722–734.

Williamson, G. M., & Clark, M. S. (1992). Impact of desired relationship type on affective reactions to choosing and being required to help. *Personality and Social Psychology Bulletin, 18,* 10–18.

Zillmann, D., & Cantor, J. R. (1977). Affective responses to the emotions of a protagonist. *Journal of Experimental Social Psychology, 13,* 155–165.

CHAPTER THREE

Emotional Experience in Close Relationships

Ellen Berscheid and Hilary Ammazzalorso

Close interpersonal relationships are the setting in which people most frequently experience intense emotions, both the positive emotions, such as joy and love, and the negative emotions, such as anger and fear. No other context in which people customarily live their lives appears to be as fertile a breeding ground for emotional experience as close relationships are. Most emotion theorists recognize that emotions are most frequently and intensely experienced in the context of close relationships (see Ekman & Davidson, 1994). Lazarus, for example, states that "most emotions involve two people who are experiencing either a transient or stable interpersonal relationship of significance" (1994, p. 209).

It is not surprising, therefore, that many of the questions people ask about close relationships concern the emotions they experience in them. When young adults are asked to list the things they wish to understand about close relationships, for example, emotional phenomena invariably figure high on their lists (Berscheid, 1998). They often ask: "Can you both love and hate your partner?"; "Is it abnormal to feel jealous?"; "How can one prevent anger at outside sources from carrying over into anger at a relationship partner?"; "How can I get my partner to feel more passion?"; "Does separation increase passion and love?"; "Can the butterflies in the stomach and other feelings of love reoccur throughout the relationship, 10 or 20 years later?"

Overview of Chapter

This chapter addresses the strong connection between close relationships and emotional experience from the perspective of the Emotion-in-Relationships Model (ERM) (Berscheid, 1983, 1986, 1991; Berscheid, Gangestad, & Kulakowski, 1984). We begin by outlining how the infrastructure of a close relationship differs from that of casual and superficial relationships. Following a brief discussion of the nature of emotional experience and the conditions that appear to trigger intense emotion, we discuss why these emotion triggers are often present in the infrastructure of close relationships but tend to be absent in superficial relationships. Evidence supporting ERM from a study of the emotional effects of separation of close romantic partners is presented next. Then, we differentiate between emotional experiences whose origins lie entirely within the relationship as opposed to emotional experiences occurring in association with the partner but whose precipitating sources lie outside the relationship; the latter is commonly referred to as "emotion spillover." Finally, we discuss some implications of ERM for the experience of jealousy and other negative emotions in the relationship, as well as its implications for current therapeutic approaches to the treatment of negative emotions that dissatisfied relationship partners frequently experience.

The Infrastructure of a Close Relationship

People sometimes wonder if their relationship with another is a close one. At times, they even wonder if they have any relationship at all. Unable to answer this question themselves, some turn to their partner and ask, "Do we still have a relationship?" Other people simply assume that their relationships are close but later events force recognition that their partners did not share their view. As Weber observes in her analysis of breakups of non-marital romantic relationships: "Indeed, one partner's 'breakup' is the other partner's dead end: The latter may reasonably claim that, in his or her mind, there was no 'breakup' because there was no relationship to break up!" (1998, p. 272). Still other people assume their relationship is not close but when the relationship dissolves, they experience surprisingly intense emotions, causing them to wonder if the relationship wasn't much closer than they ever realized.

Relationship scholars, too, have questioned what relationship closeness means. Their efforts to conceptualize the construct of closeness resulted from their intuitive belief that differences in closeness would help explain many important relationship phenomena (see Clark & Reis, 1988), a belief now confirmed. Relationship scholars initially approached their task by recognizing that the term "close" is a descriptive adjective that modifies the noun "relationship"; that is, "closeness" simply refers to a property of a relationship. Thus before addressing the question of closeness, they first had to confront the even more basic question, "What is a relationship?"

Relationship

Most relationship scholars view the *interaction* that takes place between two people to be the living tissue of an interpersonal relationship (see Berscheid & Reis, 1998). Two people are "interacting" when the behavior of one influences the behavior of the other and vice versa. As this implies, the essence of a relationship is the oscillating rhythm of influence that appears in the partners' interactions. If two people have never interacted, they do not have a relationship; if they seldom interact, they probably do not have much of a relationship; but if they often interact, and if each partner's behavior is influenced by the other partner's behavior, then, from the perspective of most relationship scholars, they are in a relationship with each other. The concept of relationship thus refers to two people whose behavior is *interdependent* in that a change in behavior of one is likely to produce a change in behavior of the other.

The relationship scholar's view may not agree with the views of the relationship partners. One or both partners may believe that a close relationship exists when, from the relationship scholar's perspective, it does not; that is, neither has appreciable influence on the other's activities. "Parallel" or "empty-shell" marriages, where the partners move through time and space together but have little or no impact on the other, are an example. Conversely, some partners may believe that they do not have a relationship with another although they do; that is, there exists a strong pattern of mutual influence in the partners' activities. Partners who are in a relationship are most likely to believe they are not when they dislike each other (see Berscheid, Snyder, & Omoto, 1989).

Closeness

If the essence of a relationship lies in the partners' interaction pattern, then it follows that the descriptor "close" must refer to some property, or collection of properties, of their interaction pattern. Most relationship scholars use the adjective "close" to refer to an interaction pattern in which each partner's behavior is highly dependent on the other partner's behavior. Thus a *close* relationship usually is viewed as one in which the partners are *highly interdependent*.

Although the partners may be highly interdependent, it is unlikely that their degree of dependence on each other is equal. Most relationships, even close relationships, are somewhat asymmetrical in that one partner's activities are more influenced by the other partner's activities than vice versa. A parent–child relationship is an example of an asymmetrical relationship because the child is more influenced by the parent's activities than the parent is influenced by the child's activities (although mothers of "colicky" infants might disagree).

Assessment of the closeness of a relationship, then, requires an assessment of the degree of dependence the partners exhibit in their interaction with each other. Kelley et al. (1983) observe that most relationship scholars regard at least four properties of the partners' interaction pattern to be indicative of high interdependence and thus closeness. First, the interaction pattern reveals that the partners *frequently* influence each other's behaviors; second, they influence a *diversity* of each other's behaviors (i.e., they influence many different kinds of their partner's activities, not simply their leisure activities, for example); third, the magnitude of influence they exert on their partner on each occasion observed is *strong*; and, finally, these three properties have characterized the couple's interaction pattern for a relatively *long duration* of time.

In sum, the infrastructure of a relationship refers to the recurrent patterns of influence that the partners exert on each other's behavior, whether deliberately or unintentionally. The kinds of behaviors the partners influence may include: cognitive behaviors, such as thoughts and feelings; physiological behaviors, such as heart rate and blood pressure; as well as more easily observable motor and verbal behaviors. Examination of the infrastructure of a close relationship, as opposed to a less close or superficial relationship, will reveal that one partner's behavior can be reliably predicted from the other partner's behavior. It is this highly interconnected behavioral infrastructure that appears to be the soil in which the experience of intense emotion flourishes.

Intense ("Hot") Emotion

In the early 1960s, Stanley Schachter and his associates experimentally demonstrated that emotional experience has both a physiological component and a cognitive component (e.g., Schachter & Singer, 1962). The physiological component refers to visceral arousal and the cognitive component refers to the individual's cognitive interpretation of the internal event of arousal and the external circumstances in which it occurs as an "emotional" experience. Schachter demonstrated that people are unlikely to report that they are experiencing an emotion unless they also perceive that they are experiencing peripheral physiological arousal (e.g., a pounding heart, sweaty palms, and other physiological events usually associated with autonomic nervous system [ANS] discharge) and also have cognitively interpreted both the internal event of arousal and the external context in which it has occurred to mean that they are experiencing an emotion.

Following Schachter's studies, the topic of emotion experienced a renaissance in psychology (see Lewis & Haviland, 1993). In fact, since Schachter presented evidence supporting his "two-component" theory of emotion, the task of answering the many questions associated with human emotional experience seems to have attracted as many workers as the task of constructing the Tower of Babel did – and with much the same result: emotion theorists and researchers have had a great deal of trouble communicating with each other. Controversy clouds the answers to even the most fundamental questions about the antecedents and consequences of emotional phenomena (see Ekman & Davidson, 1994). Few emotion theorists and researchers even agree on just exactly what an emotion is (see Berscheid, 1990; Plutchik, 1994). As a result, those who wish to pursue a better understanding of emotional experience in close relationships must choose among a bewildering variety of theoretical approaches to emotion but they have few guideposts to make their choice.

Differing views of emotion

Some theorists contend that there are certain "basic" emotions, whereas others, "constructionists," repudiate that notion and believe that each emotional experience is formed afresh, or "on-line," from the elements present in a particular situation. Because no situation is ever likely to repeat itself in all its particulars, constructionists thus take the position that there are innumerable emotional states which, although they bear similarities to each other, are never precisely the same from one occasion to the next.

Even within these two opposing camps, there is disagreement. For example, those who argue that some emotions are basic – and thus that other emotions are simply a "blend" of a smaller number of basic emotions – do not agree on precisely which emotions are basic nor, as this suggests, do they agree on how many basic emotions there are. Ortony and Turner (1990), for example, estimate that the number of basic emotions currently proposed by theorists who take the position that some emotions are more basic than others ranges from 2 to 18.

Adding to the confusion is the fact that emotion theories frequently have different foci. For example, some theories focus on the expression of emotion once it is experienced (e.g., Ekman, 1982); some theories attempt to describe the neurological circuitry associated with emotional experience (e.g., Panksepp, 1994); some emphasize the coping behavior often associated with emotional experience (e.g., Lazarus, 1991); some emphasize the cognitive circuitry of emotion (e.g., Oatley & Johnson-Laird, 1987); and others highlight still other facets of emotion (e.g., its evolutionary history; Plutchik, 1980).

Because emotion theories differ widely in the phenomena they address, and thus in many of their particulars, it is not surprising that they differ also in their definitions of emotion. When one attempts to impose some order on the plethora of views of what an emotion is, it becomes clear that they can be arrayed along a dimension of inclusiveness – or the range of events the theorist regards as instances of emotional experience.

Inclusiveness. At the highly inclusive end of the dimension are those emotion theorists who regard an emotion to be any experienced state that carries *positive or negative valence.* For these emotion theorists, preferences (e.g., for vanilla over chocolate), values (e.g., liberal vs. conservative), as well as attitudes, appraisals, evaluations, and other cognitive states that carry positive or negative valence, are viewed as "emotional" states. Even boredom, lassitude, or ennui – usually regarded as negative states by the individual experiencing them – are regarded as emotional states by some theorists.

At the other, more restricted, end of the spectrum are those theorists who argue that such inclusive definitions of emotion include far too much to be useful. They contend that by defining emotional events so broadly, virtually all of human experience becomes defined as "emotional" experience, a far too large and unwieldy array to provide special insight into the kinds of emotional events in which most people are interested (for a discussion of this point, see Mandler, 1997). Supporting their argument are the results of factor analytic studies of human language, which consistently reveal that affective valence (positive–negative) is the primary dimension underlying people's symbolic representations of the external world, including representation of animate and inanimate objects, events, and experiences (Osgood, Suci, & Tannenbaum, 1957). These theorists argue, then, that if the cognitive evaluations of all the objects, persons, and events that people typically encounter carry some degree of positive or negative valence, then people are always in some sort of "emotional" state.

Thus, some theorists of emotion restrict the kinds of events they are willing to call an emotion. Many, for example, restrict emotion to events that are accompanied by ANS arousal. Although they recognize that several other physiological systems are involved in emotional experience, they believe that the experience of ANS arousal is a necessary condition for people to perceive that they are experiencing an emotion (e.g., Schachter & Singer, 1962; Mandler, 1997).

Arousal as a component of emotional experience. When people talk about the intense emotions they experience in their close relationships, they usually are not talking about states of boredom, or even mildly favorable or unfavorable appraisals of their partner's behavior or attributes. To the contrary, laypersons appear to be Schachterians: when they talk about the emotions they experience in their close relationships, they usually are talking about experiences in which their knees tremble, their faces flush, their heart pounds, and – as will be recalled from one person's question about close relationships – they feel "butterflies" in their stomachs. In other words, they are usually talking about states in which they experience the symptoms of peripheral physiological arousal. It is experiences such as these – often termed "hot" emotions by emotion theorists and researchers, as opposed to milder feelings, attitudes, and appraisals – that many relationship partners say they wish to better understand.

It is, in fact, precisely this kind of experience that Aristotle, the first theorist to treat the subject of emotion, wished to know more about; that William James (e.g., 1884), who introduced the topic of emotion to psychology, wished to know more about; that Stanley Schachter, whose demonstrations that physiologically unaroused individuals are unlikely to report that they are experiencing an emotion, wanted to know more about; and what such contemporary theorists as George Mandler (e.g., 1997) wish to know more about. These theorists view peripheral (ANS) arousal as an essential component of emotional experience and thus they exclude positively or negatively valenced states unaccompanied by such arousal from the realm of their theories of emotion. They also often argue that ANS arousal is in itself – and apart from its contribution to self-reports of emotional experience – an import-ant event for the human. Mandler (e.g., 1975), for example, argues that it is such an important event that the individual is likely to be aware of it – that the perception that one is experienc-ing the internal event of arousal has high priority status for representation in consciousness.

Relatedly, those emotion theorists who restrict their definitions of emotion to experiences that carry *both* arousal and valence, as opposed to those who define emotion inclusively *only* with respect to valence, believe that the antecedents and consequences of the former events are different from the latter and, thus, that these two types of experiences demand different theoretical approaches. They also argue that the consequences of experiences that involve both arousal and valence, and lead to people's reports that they are experiencing an emotion, more frequently make a significant difference to the people experiencing them, as well as to those who interact with those people, than do experiences that involve valence alone (see Berscheid, 1990).

The thesis that arousal is an important event for the human, and that arousal states differ in their consequences from non-arousal states, has been supported by recent neuroscientific findings. Arnsten (1998), for example, has reviewed neurobiological evidence suggesting that during stressful experiences often associated with self-reports of emotion, catecholamine neuromodulators released in the peripheral and central nervous systems activate opposing actions in the brain – actions that turn on the amygdala (long associated with the expression of emotion) and turn off the prefrontal cortex (associated with working memory and also with the inhibition of inappropriate responses and distractions, both of which contribute to effective problem solving). Moreover, it long has been observed that emotional events are better remembered than valenced events unaccompanied by arousal. Gold (e.g., 1992) has identified one possible mediator of improved memory for emotional events. He finds that the arousal accompanying emotional states may affect neuroendocrine processes regulating memory storage; specifically, Gold has demonstrated that epinephrine release appears to modify brain function and enhance memory storage through an increase in blood glucose level. These recent findings at the neurophysiological level of analysis are consistent with previous findings of relationship researchers at the psychological level of analysis. For ex-ample, Knapp and Clark (1991) have shown that people interacting in bad moods make poor problem-solvers whereas good moods do not have a commensurate beneficial effect.

The Emotion-in-Relationships Model (ERM)

The view of emotional experience taken by ERM is consistent with that taken by most laypersons and those emotion theorists who view peripheral arousal as an essential component of emotional experience. ERM thus addresses "hot," or intense, emotions rather than cooler, or milder, valenced feelings, appraisals, and evaluations. Moreover, it adopts the general position taken by Mandler on the antecedents and consequences of such emotions.

ERM adopts Mandler's theory of emotion for two reasons: First, the aim of ERM is to better understand *why* intense emotions more frequently occur in the context of close relationships than in other contexts and, second, it attempts to predict *when* such emotions are likely to occur in relationships. What makes Mandler's theory of emotion especially useful for thinking about the experience of emotion in the context of close relationships, is that, unlike most other theories of emotion, it attempts to identify the precipitating conditions of emotional experience. Most other theorists pick up the thread of emotional experience *after* it has been precipitated by some event. For example, William James's examination of emotional experience began after the individual perceived the "exciting fact" (as he termed it) – the barrel of a gun, a snake in the path, or a threatening husband. In contrast, Mandler directly confronts the question of the nature of the "exciting fact," or the nature of events that are likely to cause emotion. Moreover, in addition to addressing the question of *when* an emotion will be experienced, Mandler also considers the question of the probable intensity of the emotional experience and its duration.

Mandler's theory of emotion

Mandler begins by observing that one of the human's most important evolutionary inheritances – one that has been essential to the survival of *Homo sapiens* – is our innate ability to detect whether the state of the world around us is the "same" as before or "different" from before. If our world has changed – if it is unfamiliar and different from that we expected and have adapted to – it is potentially dangerous and thus we may need to take action to protect our well-being. Our changed environment, however, may also present us with new opportunities to enhance our well-being; if so, action also may be required to take advantage of those opportunities. In either case, the detection of a discrepancy between the world as we currently perceive it and the world as we have known it in the past signals that new ways of living, adapting, and behaving may be required to protect or to enhance our welfare.

Mandler thus believes that humans have evolved in such a way as to be cognitively sensitive to the *detection of a discrepancy* between the world as we expected it to be and the world as we currently perceive it to be, and to automatically undergo bodily changes to help us take survival-promoting actions when a discrepancy is detected. In sum, Mandler theorizes that the detection of a discrepancy provides the occasion for arousal (the initiation of "excitation") that combines with a positive or negative valenced cognitive evaluation of the situation (e.g., as one that presents a threat to well-being or an opportunity to enhance well-being) to produce emotional experience. Thus, in Mandler's theory of emotion, discrepancy detection fulfills a necessary condition for the experience of "hot" emotion.

The arousal-producing and attention-orienting nature of unexpected events has been demonstrated by Stiensmeier-Pelster, Martini, and Reisenzein (1995), who found that expectancy-disconfirming events were more likely to elicit intense feelings of surprise and lead to causal thinking to resolve the discrepancy than events that did not violate prior expectations. Similarly, Gendolla (1997) found that it is unexpected events, rather than attributions of luck, that lead to feelings of surprise in the context of achievement situations. Moreover, Meyer, Reisenzein, and Schutzwohl (1997) demonstrated that schema-discrepant events lead to delayed execution of a simple action previously routinely performed after the event, as well as to subjective feelings of surprise and involuntary attention to the event. In yet another study, when MacDowell and Mandler (1989) experimentally manipulated degree of cognitive discrepancy, they found that heart rate showed larger increases after unexpected events than after expected, and that ANS arousal and subjective reports of emotion were most highly correlated when their respondents had experienced a discrepant event.

Cognitive expectancies about the nature of our social and physical environments have appeared in at least some theories of emotion since Hebb (1946) published his influential theoretical analysis of fear. As a consequence of his experiments with monkeys, Hebb declared, in opposition to conventional psychological wisdom at the time, that "no amount of analysis of the stimulating conditions alone can be expected to elucidate the nature of fear, or lead to any useful generalization concerning its causes . . ." (1946, p. 274). Fear, rather than being generated by the properties of the stimulus alone (e.g., a snake), was theorized to be a joint product of the nature of the stimulus and what Hebb called "autonomous" central processes. Specifically, Hebb proposed that "fear originates in the disruption of temporally and spatially organized cerebral activities" (1946, p. 274). Violation of cognitive expectancies, of course, is a large and important subset of events that disrupt "organized cerebral activities."

Currently, expectancies play a central role not only in Mandler's theory but also in Gray's (e.g., 1994) theoretical analysis of emotion. Gray postulates three emotion systems: a behavioral approach system, a fight/flight system, and a behavioral inhibition system, each of which can be described on the behavioral level, the neural level, and the cognitive level. Gray's analysis of the cognitive level, which has focused primarily on the behavioral inhibition system, importantly includes a hypothetical construct he calls "the comparator." The comparator function is a continuous monitoring of whether the current state of the world is the same as, or different from, the expected state of the world.

Neurophysiologists attempting to understand the interplay between emotional and cognitive processes in infant brain development also highlight the role of cognitive expectancies (e.g., Blakemore, 1998; Greenough, Black, & Wallace, 1987). Siegel, in fact, comments that "*The brain can be called an 'anticipation machine,' constantly scanning the environment and trying to determine what will come next*" (1999, p. 30 [emphasis in the original]).

There is extensive evidence that humans do react quickly and automatically to unexpected changes in their environment. Any unexpected disruption or interruption in the individual's customary behavioral routines, progress toward current goals and plans, and cognitive/perceptual beliefs and expectations about people and events appears to produce activation of the sympathetic nervous system (SNS; which, together with the parasympathetic nervous system, comprises the ANS). Since the work of the physiologist Walter Cannon (1929), the SNS has been viewed as a "fight or flight" emergency action system that reacts to potential danger by channeling blood supply to the muscles and brain, increasing heart rate and rate of metabolism, and raising the sugar content of the blood to provide a boost of energy – all symptoms associated with physiological arousal and the experience of emotion.

Mandler theorizes that activation of SNS arousal not only prepares the individual to *physically* respond to the changed environment but the individual's conscious perception of the internal event of SNS arousal may act as a *cognitive* "back-up" signal that alerts the individual that something is different in his or her world and thus that action may need to be taken to protect or enhance well-being. This view assumes that perceptions of environmental change may be processed by the mind and result in SNS activation and the perception of SNS symptoms before the perceptions of change in the external environment reach conscious awareness. This assumption has experimental support (e.g., Ohman & Soares, 1994; Kunst-Wilson & Zajonc, 1980); that is, people may react autonomically to stimuli they do not consciously perceive and cannot report. Thus, the perception that one is experiencing the symptoms of internal physiological arousal, symptoms that Mandler believes have priority status for representation in consciousness, may precipitate scanning of the environment to locate the cause of the arousal. In this way, if the individual is not immediately conscious of the environmental change, perception of the internal event of arousal helps ensure that changes in the environment will be noticed.

In sum, Mandler concludes that discrepancies are the major occasions for emotions to occur and that "the construction of emotion consists of the concatenation in consciousness of some cognitive evaluative schema together with the perception of visceral arousal" (1997, p. 71). Moreover, Mandler theorizes that the longer the discrepancy exists without resolution, the more intense the arousal should be and thus the more intense the emotion. Successful adaptation to the change is theorized to terminate emotional experience. Successful adaptation is marked by the individual's resumption of previously disrupted behavioral routines and progress toward his or her plans and goals, and/or by cognitive resolution of the violated expectations (e.g., by determination of their meaning, particularly their meaning for the individual's welfare, and by determination of whether action is required and, if so, what action will maximally protect or increase well-being).

Relationship infrastructure and emotion: ERM

It now can be seen why the infrastructure of a close relationship, where the two partners' activities are highly interdependent, would be an especially fertile ground for the experience of intense emotion as contrasted to less close relationships. As a relationship develops, the partners come to know each other increasingly well. "Knowing" the partner means being able to accurately predict how the partner will behave in many different situations, especially those in which the partner's behavior has positive or negative implications for the individual's own welfare. Each prediction, or expectation, about the partner's behavior guides the individual's own behavior in interaction with the partner. Knowing how their partners will behave under a variety of conditions thus allows people to plan and act in such a way as to protect and enhance their own welfare in interaction with the partner.

As the partners learn more about each other and move toward closeness by becoming increasingly dependent on each other's activities for the performance of their daily behavioral routines and the fulfillment of their plans and goals, the number and strength of their expectancies about each other increase. As a result, their opportunities for expectancy violation, and for emotional experience, also increase. When important expectancies about a close relationship partner are violated – when our partners turn out not to be the persons we thought they were – we truly are endangered. The partner has become unfamiliar and, thus, possibly unsafe. He or she has become a stranger; hence, the word "estranged" is often used to describe once-close partners. We no longer know how to act in interaction with the partner in ways that will protect and enhance our well-being. Moreover, all of our customary behaviors and plans and goals that depend on the partner's behavioral contributions may be threatened.

In brief, violation of expectancies about a close relationship partner should satisfy the conditions for the experience of emotion. Sometimes, of course, the violation does not jeopardize our well-being but, rather, it enhances it and so provides the occasion for the experience of positive emotion. For example, violation of a wife's expectation that her husband would forget their wedding anniversary for the eighteenth time by his gift of a diamond necklace and a trip to Paris should be greeted not only with surprise but with positive, rather than negative, emotion. On the other hand, the husband who has faithfully observed every previous anniversary with extravagant gifts and who delivers as expected for the eighteenth time is unlikely to precipitate as strong an emotional experience. Mild positive feeling, or even "ho-hum," is more likely this dutiful husband's reward, an observation made by many relationship therapists, who have termed this effect "reinforcement erosion": events that were initially rewarding often lose their reward power over time (e.g., Jacobson & Margolin, 1979). Of course, if the faithfully observant spouse should *fail* to perform as expected – if he unexpectedly sneaks away on a fishing trip without leaving a card, much less a gift – one suspects the wife would experience emotion.

Relationship expectancies.   As the relationship develops, then, the partners are developing expectancies about each other's habits, attitudes, personality, character, and other behavioral dispositions. Social psychologists working in the areas of person perception and cognition have been particularly interested in unraveling the processes by which people attribute dispositions to another from observing the other's behavior and noting the conditions under which it occurred. Each dispositional attribution we make to our partner represents an expectation of how he or she will behave in a variety of situations.

But many of our expectancies about our partner are not constructed through actual interaction with the partner and observance of his or her behavior. Rather than being custom-tailored to the partner's actual behavior, many of our expectancies about our partner are of the ready-made, "one size fits all," variety, and we bring them to the relationship from the start. Some of these pre-formed expectancies we immediately drape over our unsuspecting partner have their source in our past relationships. Hence, the interest relationship scholars have shown in "relationship schemas" and the history of their development (see Berscheid & Reis, 1998). For example, adults with a "secure" adult attachment style and relationship schema have been shown to have different expectations for their partner's behavior in romantic relationships than those with an "insecure" attachment style (e.g., Hazan & Shaver, 1987; Shaver, Collins, & Clark, 1996).

In addition to our own past relationship experiences, many of our pre-formed expectancies about our partner derive from our past observations of other people's relationships or from relationships we have read or heard about. Most of us have expectancies, for example, about how a husband – or wife – is supposed to look, feel, and act, or how a friend, or a coworker, or a neighbor is likely to behave under a variety of conditions. Thus, cultural norms, customs, and understandings are another source of many of our expectations about our partner's behavior.

Our partners may be aware of some of the contents of the extensive baggage of expectancies we bring to our relationships with them. In particular, they are most likely to be aware of the expectancies concerning relationships that the culture instills, for they often share such expectations. But it is unlikely that they are aware of all our expectancies, especially those that are idiosyncratic to us and to our past relationship experiences. Moreover, they are likely to remain unaware of our idiosyncratic expectancies until they inadvertently violate one of them and become the target of our emotional outburst. Such outbursts are likely to come as a surprise to them. Our bewildered partner asks, "What did I do?" But when we are experiencing emotion and the reason is not apparent to our partners, the question they should be asking us is "What did you expect?" It is likely that we expected them to do something that they failed to do or we did not expect them to do something that they did do.

It is sometimes difficult for us to answer the question, "What did you expect?" We are not always fully aware of what we expect. In fact, most of us would have a hard time articulating all the expectations we have of our relationship partners, especially when those expectations have become so entrenched that they operate outside of conscious awareness (e.g., see Fletcher & Fincham, 1991, for a discussion of "automatic" processing in the context of close relationships). Hence, our experience of emotion in relationships is not infrequently a learning experience for us as well as for our partner. It is an opportunity to get to know ourselves better, to become acquainted or reacquainted with the assumptions and expectations we hold about the world in general and our partner and the relationship in particular. That wisdom and self-knowledge is often gained from observing our own emotional reactions to events is sometimes reflected in our emotional post-mortems – often by statements prefaced with such phrases as, "I guess I thought you . . ."; "I just didn't know I wouldn't like. . . ."

In short, beneath the surface of every relationship is a web of expectancies the partners hold for each other's behavior. These expectancies allow the partners to coordinate their actions and plans to maximize their own and the other's welfare. When repeatedly confirmed, these expectancies allow interactions to run smoothly (see Snyder & Stukas, 1999). In fact, the closer and more enduring the relationship, the more likely it is that these expectancies are not only numerous but strongly held because they have been repeatedly confirmed.

Expectancies we hold about our partner and the relationship may be viewed as the emotional hostage the individual has given to the relationship – or, as Berscheid (1983) puts it, they represent the individual's "emotional investment" in the relationship because each expectancy represents the potential for violation of the expectation and, thus, discrepancy detection. The greater the number of expectancies, and the more strongly they are held, the greater the potential for emotion, although that potential may never be realized during the life of a relationship because those expectancies may never be disconfirmed. In contrast, those who expect little from the partner or from the relationship have little potential to experience emotion in the relationship because holding an expectation about the partner or the relationship is a necessary condition for discrepancy detection.

Disruption of behavioral activities.   Simply being in close proximity to another person much of the time gives that person the opportunity to perform actions that unexpectedly *facilitate* the achievement of our plans and goals. Such facilitation, and the resultant enhancement of our welfare, is, in fact, the *raison d'être* of most close relationships, especially romantic and marital relationships. The validity of this premise is confirmed by many studies showing that human happiness and physical and mental health are strongly associated with satisfying close relationships. The beginnings of such relationships are often marked by such intense positive emotions as "joy" and "elation" (see Baumeister & Leary, 1995), which, as Mandler notes, usually contain a strong element of happy surprise. For example, people who have fallen in love often express wonder that their world has dramatically changed, often overnight, in such a felicitous way. They say such things as "I can't believe this is happening to me!" or "It's hard to believe that someone as wonderful as you could care for a wretch like me!"

But extended close proximity and interaction with anyone not only provides the opportunity for that person to unexpectedly facilitate our aims and goals to better our life, and thus to precipitate the experience of positive emotion in our relationship with him or her, but it also gives that person the opportunity to unexpectedly *interfere* with the performance of our usual activities and with the achievement of valued goals. This would be true of virtually anyone in close physical proximity to us, whether a close relationship existed or not (hence the popular saying that "Houseguests and dead fish start to stink after three days"). Thus, most relationship scholars believe that conflict is inevitable in all relationships moving toward closeness. Some theorists, in fact, mark conflict as a relationship "stage," a period that all close relationships must pass through (e.g., Scanzoni, 1979). For this reason, many marital therapists view the probable success of a marriage to be determined not by whether the couple experiences conflict (because all do) but, rather, by whether the couple can resolve their conflicts.

Over time, if the relationship is to survive, the partners will learn to coordinate their daily activities and reconcile their individual plans and goals in such a way as to protect and enhance, rather than threaten and diminish, each other's well-being. In doing so, they are likely to develop what Berscheid (1983) terms highly "meshed interaction sequences" of behavior, or interaction routines in which each partner's influence takes the form of facilitating and augmenting the other partner's actions as the sequence or plan unfolds. In many close marital relationships, such well-meshed sequences often include shopping and preparing meals, getting the kids off to school in the morning, and entertaining guests. Sexual interactions, too, are usually highly dependent on the partner not only performing the appropriate and expected actions but performing them at the appropriate and expected time in the behavioral sequence.

If many of the individual's daily and routinely performed behavioral sequences are meshed to the partner's, and if the partner fails to perform as expected, then the individual's expectancies are violated, his or her customary performance of the sequence is disrupted, and, unless some substitute for the partner's failed actions is quickly found, arousal should occur, a negative cognitive valence should be attached to the failure, and a negative emotional experience should result. People who unexpectedly lose their long-term close relationship partners, whether through their partner's rejection of the relationship or through the partner's death, are likely to experience great disruption. Enormous "grief" – and even sometimes "anger" at the loved one who was so inconsiderate as to die and leave the individual bereft – are not unusual. In superficial relationships, however, there is much less to be disrupted and the emotional reaction to dissolution of the relationship should be less intense.

It will be recalled that Mandler theorizes that the intensity and duration of emotion is a function of the degree of disruption and its duration. In the case where the relationship is dissolved through the voluntary action of one of the partners, one can predict that the other's emotional reaction to dissolution will be a function of two variables: (1) the degree of interdependence characteristic of the relationship (i.e., the closer the relationship, the more the disruption upon dissolution); and (2) the speed with which the disrupted individual is able to find the means to resume those disrupted behavioral activities and progress toward those plans and goals and thus restore his or her well-being. The latter suggests that the intensity and duration of an individual's emotional reaction to relationship dissolution often depends on the speed with which a "substitute" partner can be found – one who can step into the role the absent partner once played in the individual's life and who can facilitate the individual as well as the former partner did.

Thus, the prediction of emotional reaction to relationship dissolution requires not only assessment of the closeness of the relationship, but also assessment of the likelihood that the individual will be able to quickly obtain an alternative partner. Many individuals who voluntarily terminate a relationship, of course, do so only after they themselves have secured an alternative partner – a third person with whom they have already established a relationship and who can provide the same facilitation, or even greater facilitation, of their welfare than their former partner did. Such individuals are unlikely to experience much negative emotion upon dissolving their previous relationship; indeed, they may experience happiness and relief if their former relationship was interfering with the further development of their new relationship.

In brief, ERM predicts that because people in close relationships are highly interdependent on each other, they have developed, whether consciously or unconsciously, many strong expectations about the partner and his or her behaviors that, when violated, provide the occasion for the experience of emotion because those interdependencies usually have implications for the individual's welfare. In contrast, people in superficial relationships, where each partner lives his or her life largely independently of the other person's activities, have fewer opportunities for expectancy violation and, even when such expectancies do exist and are violated, their consequences are likely to be much less severe in terms of threat to the individual's well-being.

Most long-term partners' expectancies are not violated, of course. As previously noted, their behaviors, plans, and goals have become well coordinated over time and there are few occasions of "discrepancy detection" in the relationship and thus little occasion for intense emotion. It is for this reason that the *current* emotional surface of a relationship may be misleading of its *potential* to cause the partners' intense emotion. A relationship may appear to be emotionally "dead" because the partners hold few expectancies about each other and those they do hold have few implications for the individual's well-being. But other relationships, especially very close relationships, may appear to be emotionally moribund because, although the partners are highly interdependent on each other, they have learned to smoothly coordinate their activities with each other and thus they never disconfirm each other's expectancies.

Berscheid describes the interdependencies characteristic of close relationships as "hidden ticking emotional bombs" because they will explode and cause great disruption when the relationship is dissolved. And all relationships dissolve. It is one of the saddest facts of the human condition that even the closest and happiest of relationships end – if not by some circumstance of fate that causes separation, then by the death of one of the partners. Upon dissolution, the individual's life circumstances will change so drastically, and his or her well-being is likely to be so threatened, that the loss of a close relationship partner is accompanied by the experience of the strongest negative emotions a human is capable of experiencing, often compromising the remaining partner's immunocompetence, and resulting in illness and even death (see Stroebe & Stroebe, 1993).

Separation from the Partner

Several investigators have examined hypotheses derived from ERM concerning the degree of emotional disruption an individual is likely to experience upon separation from the partner or dissolution of the relationship. In a prospective longitudinal study, for example, Simpson (1987) found that greater relationship closeness, as measured by the Relationship Closeness Inventory (RCI), which measures behavioral interdependence (Berscheid et al., 1989), and fewer alternative partners were associated with the experience of greater distress following relationship dissolution.

The results of a natural field experiment conducted by Attridge (1995) also confirm ERM predictions. Attridge examined the emotional reactions of women who were in serious dating relationships that had lasted for an average of one and a half years at the time of the study. Forty-two of the women experienced separation from their partner due to their own participation in an international "study abroad" program. Their emotional reactions were contrasted to 44 women who did not experience separation from their partners during the period of the study. Both the experimental "separated" couples and the control "non-separated" couples were assessed at three points: Time 1, prior to separation; Time 2, during separation; and Time 3, following separation. The assessments at Time 1 and Time 3 included Closeness (on the RCI, Berscheid et al., 1989), Relationship Longevity, Relationship Satisfaction (Hendrick, 1988), and Disruption Potential, a 5-item measure of the degree to which the partner's absence would lead to a disruption of the individual's normal activities and her likelihood of finding a substitute partner during the separation (internal reliability = .63; test-retest reliability = .69).

Table 3.1   Correlations of Mean Amounts of Negative Emotion with Time 1 Relationship
Closeness, Disruption Potential, Relationship Satisfaction, and Relationship Longevity as a Function
of Separation Status During the Separation Period (Time 2)

Measure	Condition	
	Long-distance	Stay-at-home
	Negative emotion	
Relationship Closeness	.33*	.09
Disruption Potential	.39**	.08
Relationship Satisfaction	−.05	−.28
Relationship Longevity	.14	−.21

* $p < .05$. ** $p < .01$.

In accord with ERM, Attridge predicted that the closer the relationship, the greater the
frequency and intensity of emotional experience upon separation. Emotion during separation
was assessed by giving respondents a list of positive and negative emotions and asking
them to indicate, "How frequently in the past week did you feel each emotion concerning
your partner and/or the relationship?" Attridge found that neither Relationship Longevity
nor Relationship Satisfaction predicted emotional experience for either Separated or Non-
separated partners. For Separated partners, however, both degree of Closeness and Disruption Potential were associated with the experience of negative emotion whereas no such effect
was found for Non-separated partners (see table 3.1). It should be emphasized that Closeness
and Disruption Potential did not by themselves lead to emotional experience; rather, they
interacted with the event of separation to produce the experience of emotion. Moreover,
neither the length of the relationship nor (perhaps surprisingly to some people) the individual's satisfaction with the relationship were associated with the experience of emotion,
whether the partners were separated or not.

Attridge's study confirms another ERM prediction: It will be recalled that ERM predicts
that an increase in the experience of "hot" emotion, rather than mild feelings or other
valenced states, should result from disruption of a close relationship. As table 3.2 illustrates,
Attridge found that only emotions characterized by high arousal – that is, the more intense
emotions – were significantly associated with increases in closeness for separated partners.
Separated couples who were close experienced increases in fear, jealousy, passion, and joy.
However, the milder feeling states characterized by less arousal (e.g., happy, needed, content,
sad, and lonely) showed no increases for anyone, not even close couples who were separated.

Emotion Spillover

Berscheid (1983) differentiates between emotion whose primary source lies *in* the relationship – by the partner's violation of the individual's expectancies, usually by unexpectedly

Table 3.2 Correlations of Intense and Weak Emotions with Time 1 Relationship Closeness/Disruption Potential Composite as a Function of Separation Status During the Separation Period

(Time 2) *Emotion Measure*	Condition	
	Long-distance	*Stay-at-home*
	Closeness/Disruption Potential	
"Hot" emotions		
Fear	.49*	.12
Jealousy	.53*	.14
Anger	.08	.10
Frustration	.15	.19
Passion	.40*	−.09
Joy	.47*	−.10
Excitement	−.11	−.21
Less Intense Feeling States		
Sad	.01	.07
Lonely	.15	.16
Happy	.10	.06
Needed	.15	.16
Content	.06	.02

* $p < .001$

facilitating or unexpectedly frustrating ongoing behavior sequences, plans, and goals – from emotion experienced in association with the partner but whose true source lies in an event *outside* the relationship. The partners' experiences of affective events outside the relationship have been shown to influence affective events inside the relationship. For example, relationship scholars have demonstrated that transient mood states generated by such events as watching a sad movie may influence what people remember about their relationship, what behaviors of the partner are likely to be noticed, and also, as Forgas, Levinger, and Moylan (1994) demonstrated, an individual's satisfaction with his or her partner and the relationship (satisfaction changing in such a way as to be congruent with the individual's mood at the time of the evaluation).

Emotional events whose origins are outside the relationship have great potential to create emotional storms within a close relationship, as the phrase "emotion spillover" suggests. Emotion spillover refers to an individual's experience of emotion caused by a non-relationship event (e.g., being fired from the job; falling ill) that interferes with the individual's customary interaction performance within the relationship. This, then, disrupts the partner and precipitates the partner's experience of emotion "in" the relationship (since it has been caused by the individual), which, in turn, is likely to disrupt the partner's usual interaction performance – a disruption whose effects are likely to reverberate back to the individual, further heightening that person's emotional experience.

Conger and his associates (1990) studied couples caught in the wave of farm fore-closures in the 1980s and found that economic strain not only promoted hostility in marital interaction but it reduced the frequency of supportive behaviors in the relationship – at the very time, of course, that supportive behaviors were especially needed. Job stress, too, has been shown to affect couple interaction. For example, Repetti (1989) found a significant association between an air traffic controller's exposure to job stressors and anger and aggression in the controller's family interactions.

Again, ERM predicts that emotion spillover, or the ricocheting of emotional consequences of events outside the relationship into the relationship, is more likely to occur in close relationships where the partners are highly interdependent and vulnerable to disruption than it is in less close relationships. Thus – and ironically – when an outside event produces negative emotion for an individual in a close relationship, the individual's partner may be *less* likely to remain tranquil and supportive than a superficial partner might be because the partner is likely to be experiencing emotion him- or herself; the partner's emotional state, in turn, may interfere with the partner's ability to perform as the individual expects, thus adding internal fuel to the individual's externally-generated emotional fire.

The tendency of emotion-precipitating events occurring outside the relationship to wreak disruption within a close relationship provides one more reason why close relationships, as opposed to superficial relationships, are the most frequent context for the experience of intense emotion. And there is yet another reason why close relationship partners, as contrasted to the less close, are more likely to experience intense emotion: they are more vulnerable than superficial partners are to the experience of jealousy – a highly negative emotion that has been the subject of much theory and research (see Berscheid, 1994).

Jealousy

Jealousy has been defined as ". . . the emotion that people experience when control over valued resources that flow through an attachment to another person is perceived to be in jeopardy because their partner might want or might actually give and/or receive some of these resources from a third party" (Ellis & Weinstein, 1986, p. 341). Not all individuals in such situations experience the emotion of jealousy, however, and, if they do, not all experience it with the same intensity. ERM predicts that it is individuals within close, as opposed to less close, relationships who are most likely to experience this emotion and, moreover, given high interdependence, it is those individuals who have available to them few substitute partners should the relationship dissolve who will most intensely experience jealousy when they perceive that a third party threatens the relationship.

These ERM predictions are consistent with the findings of many studies. For example, Buunk (1982) found that relationship partners who were highly dependent on their relationships expected to feel more jealousy when visualizing hypothetical third-party affairs, and White (1981) found that women's experiences of jealousy were significantly correlated with their inability to obtain an alternative relationship partner. Moreover, DeSteno and Salovey (1996) found that people were more likely to experience jealousy when a potential rival for their partner's attention was in a domain of "high self-relevance" (e.g., in areas important to the self such as the achievements shared by both self and rival). It is just this sort of rival, of course, who constitutes the greatest threat to the relationship because such persons can most easily replace the individual in facilitating the partner's interaction behaviors and current goals.

Another study that underscores the importance of the individual's ability to find a replacement partner should the third party succeed in breaking up the relationship is provided by Bringle (1995). Homosexual men, who had less exclusive relationships than the heterosexual men in this study, experienced less jealousy in their intimate relationships than did the heterosexual men. Heterosexual men may have been more dependent on their partners than the homosexual men were and they may have had fewer readily available partner substitutes. This interpretation of Bringle's finding is supported by his report that the incidence of jealousy increased in both groups between 1980 and 1992 and the increase was accompanied by an increase in the exclusiveness of both homosexuals' and heterosexuals' intimate relationships.

In sum, ERM predicts that the likelihood of an individual experiencing jealousy within a relationship is a function of three factors: the closeness of the relationship, the availability of substitute partners, and the degree to which the third party represents a threat to the continuance of the relationship.

Therapeutic Approaches to Negative Emotion in Relationships

Distressed relationships are the most common presenting problem of those who seek psychotherapy (e.g., Pinsker, Nepps, Redfield, & Winston, 1985). Distressed relationships, not surprisingly, are characterized by a great deal of negative affect and emotion (e.g., see Weiss & Heyman, 1990). Relationship therapists have long recognized the association between negative emotion and the disconfirmation of an expectancy about the partner or the relationship. Unrealistic expectations are doomed to be disconfirmed. Moreover, if the expectation is rigidly held even in the face of repeated disconfirmations, the individual is likely to chronically experience negative emotion in the relationship. Eidelson and Epstein (1982) developed the Relationship Belief Inventory to assess the degree to which relationship partners hold unrealistic beliefs and expectations about close relationships (e.g., the expectation that partners who care about each other should be able to sense each other's needs and preferences without overt communication). These investigators, as well as Fincham and Bradbury (1993), have found that holding such unrealistic beliefs is negatively associated with marital satisfaction. Moreover, Sabatelli (1988) has found that as contrasted to married partners, unmarried individuals hold significantly higher and more idealistic expectations about their prospective spouse and the relationship. Sabatelli concludes that unrealistic expectations may account for the reliable and significant drop in satisfaction in marital relationships during the first year of marriage (see Karney & Bradbury, 1995).

ERM suggests that if violated expectations are the most usual precipitating cause of intense emotion in close relationships, then the reduction of negative emotion in the relationship may be achieved primarily by two means. The first is to persuade the violating partner to bring his or her behavior in line with the individual's expectations. This is the "change the partner" approach that most people try first – with more or less success (usually less), depending on their communication, negotiation, and conflict resolution skills and the motivation and ability of the partner to change his or her behavior. This is one reason, of course, why improving communication and conflict resolution skills is a frequent objective of relationship therapy.

The second means by which the individual may reduce his or her experience of negative emotion in the relationship, however, is to change his or her own expectations to bring them in line with the partner's actual behavior. This is the "change myself (and accept the partner)" approach. Needless to say, most people find this second approach less desirable than the first because it not only requires them to change their *own* behavior but it not infrequently requires them to relinquish plans and goals they not only expected the partner *would* facilitate but believe the partner *should* facilitate. Moreover, the relinquishment of valued goals whose achievement is believed to enhance well-being should itself be accompanied by negative emotion (e.g., sadness). Thus, the task of revising our discrepant expectations to be congruent with the way the world *is* – rather than how we thought the world was or how we wish it to be – can be difficult and painful. But it may be less painful in the long run than retaining unrealistic relationship expectations that are doomed to be violated again and again and yet again, generating on each successive occasion the fresh experience of negative emotion. It should be noted that at least one individual therapy technique, Ellis's Rational-Emotive Therapy (e.g., Ellis & Dryden, 1997), directly seeks to ameliorate the negative emotions distressed individuals experience (whether in association with their interpersonal relationships or otherwise) by uncovering the individual's unrealistic expectations and directly attacking those that give rise to chronically experienced negative emotion.

With respect to distressed relationships (as opposed to distressed individuals), the traditional technique followed by many relationship therapists has been to teach partners compromise and accommodation strategies and skills to help them change those behaviors that are causing their partner to experience negative emotion and to manage their own negative emotions. For example, relationship therapists Notarius, Lashley, and Sullivan state that, "Anger is the fuel that fires relationship conflict, and its heat can either forge adaptive relationship change or melt down the foundation of the relationship" (1997, p. 219). These theorists advise their clients to "practice, practice, and practice alternative responses to anger" (1997, p. 245). Such alternative responses include replacing the "hot thoughts" that generate anger with "cool thoughts" that promote conversation and problem solving, quieting physiological arousal with relaxation techniques, and avoiding critical remarks that make the partner defensive (1997, p. 245). Unfortunately, outcome studies of relationship therapy often have been less favorable than for other kinds of therapy (see Berscheid & Reis, 1998). As a consequence, alternative approaches to traditional relationship therapy have been sought.

One promising new approach – Integrative Behavioral Couple Therapy (IBCT) – has been developed by Jacobson and Christensen (e.g., 1996), who have observed that many couples experience incompatibilities that cannot be resolved by compromise or accommodation. For example, a physical disability may preclude the husband from performing garbage and snow removal duties as his wife expects and his low intelligence may be an insurmountable obstacle to his learning to play a decent game of chess. To ameliorate negative emotion in close relationships, IBCT integrates the traditional technique intended to change both partners' behaviors with strategies that simply promote the partners' acceptance and tolerance of each other's unpleasant behaviors through coming to see those behaviors in the "larger context of the other and of their relationship together" (Christensen & Walczynski, 1997, p. 266). Jacobson and Christensen assume that a combination of change and acceptance will be more powerful than either alone (e.g., if partners receive acceptance from each other, they may be more willing to change their behavior if they possess the ability to do so). Although Jacobson and Christensen arrived at IBCT through their clinical experience and wisdom, it can be seen that their approach simultaneously utilizes both means implied by ERM for reducing negative emotion in close relationships; that is, both partners are encouraged to change their behavior to meet the other's expectations but they also are encouraged to change their own expectancies. So far, outcome studies of IBCT are showing good results in increasing marital satisfaction (see Christensen & Walczynski, 1997).

Summary

The now vast psychological literature on the subject of human emotion remains an almost impenetrable thicket to relationship scholars who hope to better understand the many emotional phenomena that occur in the context of close relationships. This chapter has sought to provide a brief reprise of the Emotion-in-Relationships Model (Berscheid, 1983), which attempts to explicate why close relationships are the most usual setting for the experience of intense emotions. In doing so, we have discussed the concept of relationship itself, the construct of closeness, the antecedents and consequences of emotional experience, and some emotional phenomena within relationships from the perspective of ERM. Given the important role that expectations about the partner and the relationship play in providing the conditions for the experience of emotion in close relationships, more research on the nature of such expectations held by different types of individuals for different types of relationships might prove fruitful for relationship scholars who seek to understand emotional phenomena within close relationships.

REFERENCES

Arnsten, A. F. T. (1998). The biology of being frazzled. *Science, 280,* 1711–1712.

Attridge, M. (1995). *Reactions of romantic partners to geographic separation: A natural experiment.* Unpublished doctoral dissertation, University of Minnesota.

Baumeister, R. F., & Leary, M. R. (1995). The need to belong: Desire for interpersonal attachments as a fundamental human motivation. *Psychological Bulletin, 117,* 497–529.

Berscheid, E. (1983). Emotion. In H. H. Kelley, E. Berscheid, A. Christensen, J. H. Harvey, T. L. Huston, G. Levinger, E. McClintock, L. A. Peplau, & D. R. Peterson, *Close relationships* (pp. 110–168). New York: W. H. Freeman.

Berscheid, E. (1986). Mea culpas and lamentations: Sir Francis, Sir Isaac, and "The slow progress of soft psychology." In S. Duck & R. Gilmour (Eds.), *The emerging field of personal relationships* (pp. 267–286). Hillsdale, NJ: Erlbaum.

Berscheid, E. (1990). Contemporary vocabularies of emotion. In B. S. Moore & A. M. Isen (Eds.), *Affect and social behavior.* New York: Cambridge University Press.

Berscheid, E. (1991). The emotion-in-relationships model: Reflections and update. In W. Kessen & A. Ortony (Eds.), *Memories, thoughts, and emotions: Essays in honor of George Mandler*. Hillsdale, NJ: Erlbaum.

Berscheid, E. (1994). Interpersonal relationships. *Annual Review of Psychology, 45*, 79–129.

Berscheid, E. (1998). A social psychological view of marital dysfunction and stability. In T. N. Bradbury (Ed.), *The developmental course of marital dysfunction*. New York: Cambridge University Press.

Berscheid, E., Gangestad, S. W., & Kulakowski, D. (1984). Emotion in close relationships: Implications for relationship counseling. In S. D. Brown & R. W. Lent (Eds.), *Handbook of counseling psychology* (pp. 435–476). New York: Wiley.

Berscheid, E., & Reis, H. T. (1998). Attraction and close relationships. In D. T. Gilbert, S. T. Fiske, & G. Lindzey (Eds.), *The handbook of social psychology* (4th ed.). Boston: McGraw-Hill.

Berscheid, E., Snyder, M., & Omoto, A. (1989). The relationship closeness inventory: Assessing the closeness of interpersonal relationships. *Journal of Personality and Social Psychology, 57*, 792–807.

Blakemore, C. (1998). How the environment helps to build the brain. In B. Cartledge (Ed.), *Mind, brain, and the environment: The Linacre lectures, 1995–6* (pp. 28–56). New York: Oxford University Press.

Bringle, R. (1995). Sexual jealousy in the relationships of homosexual and heterosexual men: 1980 and 1992. *Personal Relationships, 2*, 313–325.

Buunk, B. (1982). Anticipated sexual jealousy: Its relationship to self-esteem, dependency, and reciprocity. *Personality and Social Psychology Bulletin, 8*, 310–316.

Cannon, W. B. (1929). *Bodily changes in pain, hunger, fear, and rage*. New York: Appleton.

Christensen, A., & Walczynski, P. T. (1997). Conflict and satisfaction in couples. In R. J. Sternberg & M. Hojjat (Eds.), *Satisfaction in close relationships*. New York: Guilford Press.

Clark, M. S., & Reis, H. T. (1988). Interpersonal processes in close relationships. *Annual Review of Psychology, 39*, 609–672.

Conger, R. D., Elder, G. H., Jr., Lorenz, F. O., Conger, K. J., Simons, R. L., Whitbeck, L. B., Huck, S., & Melby, J. N. (1990). Linking economic hardship to marital quality and instability. *Journal of Marriage and the Family, 52*, 643–656.

DeSteno, D., & Salovey, P. (1996). Jealousy and the characteristics of one's rival: A Self-evaluation Maintenance perspective. *Personality and Social Psychology Bulletin, 22*, 920–932.

Eidelson, R. J., & Epstein, N. (1982). Cognition and relationship maladjustment: Development of a measure of dysfunctional relationship beliefs. *Journal of Consulting and Clinical Psychology, 50*, 715–720.

Ekman, P. (Ed.). (1982). *Emotion in the human face* (2nd ed.). Cambridge, England: Cambridge University Press.

Ekman, P., & Davidson, R. J. (1994). *The nature of emotion: Fundamental questions*. New York: Oxford University Press.

Ellis, A., & Dryden, W. (1997). *The practice of rational emotive behavior therapy* (2nd ed.). New York: Springer.

Ellis, C., & Weinstein, E. (1986). Jealousy and the social psychology of emotional experience. *Journal of Social and Personal Relationships, 3*, 337–357.

Fincham, F. D., & Bradbury, T. N. (1993). Marital satisfaction, depression, and attributions: A longitudinal analysis. *Journal of Personality and Social Psychology, 64*, 442–452.

Fletcher, G. J. O., & Fincham, F. D. (1991). Attribution processes in close relationships. In G. J. O. Fletcher & F. D. Fincham (Eds.), *Cognition in close relationships* (pp. 7–35). Hillsdale, NJ: Erlbaum.

Forgas, J. P., Levinger, G., & Moylan, S. J. (1994). Feeling good and feeling close: Affective influences on the perception of intimate relationships. *Personal Relationships, 1*, 165–184.

Gendolla, G. H. E. (1997). Surprise in the context of achievement: The role of outcome valence and importance. *Motivation & Emotion, 21*, 165–193.

Gold, P. E. (1992). Modulation of memory processing: Enhancement of memory in rodents and humans. In L. R. Squire & N. Butters (Eds.), *Neuropsychology of memory* (pp. 402–412). New York: Guilford Press.

Gray, J. A. (1994). Three fundamental emotion systems. In P. Ekman & R. J. Davidson (Eds.), *The nature of emotion: Fundamental questions* (pp. 243–247). New York: Oxford University Press.

Greenough, W. T., Black, J. E., & Wallace, C. S. (1987). Experience and brain development. *Child Development, 58*, 539–559.

Hazan, C., & Shaver, P. R. (1987). Romantic love conceptualized as an attachment process. *Journal of Personality and Social Psychology, 52*, 511–524.

Hebb, D. O. (1946). On the nature of fear. *Psychological Review, 53*, 259–276.

Hendrick, S. S. (1988). A generic measure of relationship satisfaction. *Journal of Marriage and the Family, 50*, 93–98.

Jacobson, N. S., & Christensen, A. (1996). *Integrative couple therapy: Promoting acceptance and change.* New York: Norton.

Jacobson, N. S., & Margolin, G. (1979). *Marital therapy: Strategies based on social learning and behavior exchange principles.* New York: Brunner/Mazel.

James, W. (1884). What is emotion? *Mind, 9*, 188–205.

Karney, B. R., & Bradbury, T. N. (1995). The longitudinal course of marital quality and stability: A review of theory, method, and research. *Psychological Review, 118*, 3–34.

Kelley, H. H., Berscheid, E., Christensen, A., Harvey, J. H., Huston, T. L., Levinger, G., McClintock, E., Peplau, L. A., & Peterson, D. R. (1983). *Close relationships.* New York: W. H. Freeman.

Knapp, A., & Clark, M. S. (1991). Some detrimental effects of negative mood on individuals' ability to solve resource dilemmas. *Personality & Social Psychology Bulletin, 17*, 678–688.

Kunst-Wilson, W. R., & Zajonc, R. B. (1980). Affective discrimination of stimuli that cannot be recognized. *Science, 207*, 557–558.

Lazarus, R. S. (1991). *Emotion and adaptation.* New York: Oxford University Press.

Lazarus, R. S. (1994). Appraisal: The long and short of it. In P. Ekman & R. J. Davidson (Eds.), *The nature of emotion: Fundamental questions* (pp. 208–215). New York: Oxford University Press.

Lewis, M., & Haviland, J. M. (Eds.). (1993). *Handbook of emotions.* New York: Guilford Press.

MacDowell, K., & Mandler, G. (1989). Constructions of emotion: Discrepancy, arousal, and mood. *Motivation and Emotion, 13*, 105–124.

Mandler, G. (1975). *Mind and emotion.* New York: Wiley.

Mandler, G. (1997). *Human nature explored.* New York: Oxford University Press.

Meyer, W., Reisenzein, R., & Schutzwohl, A. (1997). Toward a process analysis of emotions: The case of surprise. *Motivation and Emotion, 21*, 251–274.

Notarius, C. I., Lashley, S. L., & Sullivan, D. J. (1997). Angry at your partner?: Think again. In R. J. Sternberg & M. Hojjat (Eds.), *Satisfaction in close relationships.* New York: Guilford Press.

Oatley, K., & Johnson-Laird, P. (1987). Towards a cognitive theory of emotion. *Cognition and Emotion, 1*, 51–58.

Ohman, A., & Soares, J. J. F. (1994). "Unconscious anxiety": Phobic responses to masked stimuli. *Journal of Abnormal Psychology, 103*, 231–240.

Ortony, A., & Turner, T. J. (1990). What's basic about basic emotions? *Psychological Review, 97*, 315–331.

Osgood, C. E., Suci, G. J., & Tannenbaum, P. H. (1957). *The measurement of meaning.* Urbana: University of Illinois Press.

Panksepp, J. (1994). The clearest physiological distinctions between emotions will be found among the circuits of the brain. In P. Ekman & R. J. Davidson (Eds.), *The nature of emotion: Fundamental questions* (pp. 258–269). New York: Oxford University Press.

Pinsker, H., Nepps, P., Redfield, J., & Winston, A. (1985). Applicants for short-term dynamic psycho-therapy. In A. Winston (Ed.), *Clinical and research issues in short-term dynamic psychotherapy* (pp. 104–116). Washington, DC: American Psychiatric Association.

Plutchik, R. (1980). *Emotion: A psychobioevolutionary synthesis.* New York: Harper & Row.

Plutchik, R. (1994). *The psychology and biology of emotion.* New York: HarperCollins.

Repetti, R. L. (1989). Effects of daily workload on subsequent behavior during marital interaction: The roles of social withdrawal and spouse support. *Journal of Personality and Social Psychology, 57,* 651–659.

Sabatelli, R. M. (1988). Exploring relationship satisfaction: A social exchange perspective on the interdependence between theory, research, and practice. *Family Relations, 37,* 217–222.

Scanzoni, J. (1979). Social exchange and behavioral interdependence. In R. Burgess & T. Huston (Eds.), *Social exchange in developing relationships* (pp. 61–98). New York: Academic Press.

Schachter, S., & Singer, J. E. (1962). Cognitive, social and physiological determinants of emotional state. *Psychological Review, 69,* 379–399.

Shaver, P. R., Collins, N., & Clark, C. L. (1996). Attachment styles and internal working models of self and relationship partners. In G. Fletcher & J. Fitness (Eds.), *Knowledge structures and interaction in close relationships: A social psychological approach* (pp. 25–61). Hillsdale, NJ: Erlbaum.

Siegel, D. J. (1999). *The developing mind: Toward a neurobiology of interpersonal experience.* New York: Guilford Press.

Simpson, J. (1987). The dissolution of romantic relationships: Factors involved in relationship stability and emotional distress. *Journal of Personality and Social Psychology, 53,* 683–692.

Snyder, M., & Stukas, A. A. (1999). Interpersonal processes: The interplay of cognitive, motivational, and behavioral activities in social interaction. *Annual Review of Psychology, 50,* 273–303.

Stiensmeier-Pelster, J., Martini, A., & Reisenzein, R. (1995). The role of surprise in the attribution process. *Cognition & Emotion, 9,* 5–31.

Stroebe, M. S., & Stroebe, W. (1993). The mortality of bereavement: A review. In M. S. Stroebe, W. Stroebe, & R. O. Hansson (Eds.), *Handbook of bereavement: Theory, research, and intervention* (pp. 175–195). Cambridge, England: Cambridge University Press.

Weber, A. L. (1998). Losing, leaving, and letting go: Coping with nonmarital breakups. In B. H. Spitzberg & W. R. Cupach (Eds.), *The dark side of close relationships* (pp. 267–306). Mahwah, NJ: Erlbaum.

Weiss, R. L., & Heyman, R. E. (1990). Observation of marital interaction. In F. D. Fincham & T. N. Bradbury (Eds.), *The psychology of marriage: Basic issues and applications* (pp. 87–117). New York: Guilford Press.

White, G. (1981). Some correlates of romantic jealousy. *Journal of Personality, 49,* 129–147.

CHAPTER FOUR

Poker Face, Smiley Face, and Rant 'n' Rave: Myths and Realities about Emotion in Negotiation

Leigh Thompson, Victoria Husted Medvec,
Vanessa Seiden, and Shirli Kopelman

There is a mix of advice concerning the role of emotion in negotiation. Both the prescriptive and descriptive negotiation literatures toil with the questions of whether it is advisable to be emotional in a negotiation, whether a negotiator should play on the opponent's emotions, and whether it is better to display positive or negative emotions throughout a negotiation. Our review of the research literature identifies three distinct perspectives on the role of emotion at the bargaining table. These perspectives, which we label the rational negotiator, the positive negotiator, and the irrational negotiator, give rise to very different prescriptive advice. First, we review these three perspectives on emotion and critically examine the prescriptive advice that flows from each of these perspectives. Subsequently, we expose the assumptions and biases that underlie this advice. Finally, we suggest directions for future research.

Three Perspectives on Emotion in Negotiations

The rational negotiator

According to this perspective, the negotiator is best advised to neither feel nor express emotion at the bargaining table, as emotion is a weakness. Emotion is a signal that one has departed from rational analysis and is vulnerable to losing one's power or share of the bargaining zone. According to the economic model of negotiations, a rational actor – unburdened by emotions – is considered to be in a better position at the negotiation table. There are few, if any, empirical investigations that explicitly test this assumption, as it arises primarily as an extension of normative bargaining axioms (Nash, 1950; Raiffa, 1982).

The view that emotion is a weakness, or the "Mr. Spock" perspective (Thompson, Nadler, & Kim, 1999) gives rise to the common expression (with which professional students are bombarded), "keep a poker face." Indeed popular literature derived from rational bargaining theory warns negotiators from being easily goaded into emotional bursts of anger, for example; being manipulated so you are "apt to be tricked into an unfavorable settlement because of your emotional state" (Nierenberg, 1968, p. 46). Despite the appeal of the rational model, keeping a cool head is, of course, easier said than done – emotions seem to have a life of their own, beyond the control of the rational actor. "It is important for disputants to recognize that emotions can overwhelm logic. In fact, people are sometimes trapped into acting against their own best interests, even when they recognize that they are doing so" (Susskind & Cruikshank, 1987, p. 89). However, there is little empirical evidence to support the assertion that emotion, felt or expressed, is a weakness. The most direct support comes from the risk literature, which clearly advises negotiators to adopt a risk-neutral attitude; risk seeking or risk aversion can lead to suboptimal decision making and negotiated outcomes (Bazerman & Neale, 1982). Indeed, departures from risk neutrality are associated with less-than-desirable bargaining outcomes (see Neale & Bazerman, 1991; Thompson, 1998 for reviews).

The positive negotiator

A quite different view about negotiation emerges from the social psychological literature on negotiation. Social psychologists argue that expression of positive emotion, in contrast to a poker face, can be an advantage at the negotiation table. In a number of empirical invest-igations, positive emotion enhanced the quality of negotiated agreements, as compared to the outcomes reached by "neutral" (poker-faced) negotiators. The advantages of positive emotion derive from a theory of information processing, which argues that people process informa-tion differently when in a positive mood as opposed to a negative or a neutral mood (Isen, 1987). In what has become the seminal study in positive affect and negotiation, Carnevale and Isen (1986) induced positive emotion in some negotiators by instructing them to per-form a seemingly unrelated task of sorting cartoons into two piles – those that were very funny, and those that were not as funny. Negotiators in the manipulated conditions were also told they could keep the scratch pad they used during the experiment as a gift; negotia-tors in a control condition did not see the cartoons, nor were they given a gift. Negotiators in the positive affect condition reported more positive moods and subsequently created more mutually beneficial bargaining outcomes than the control group. Carnevale and Isen (1986) concluded that, "the use of positive affect may be a very useful tactic that may help negotiators discover optimal solutions . . . The ability to integrate, to find creative ways of combining issues, and to develop novel solutions may be necessary for negotiators to achieve anything beyond obvious compromises" (p. 12).

In a complementary fashion, empirical studies support the intuition that negative emotion has a detrimental impact on negotiation. For example, in one empirical investigation, people participating in a job contract negotiation achieved lower joint gains when they experienced high levels of anger and low levels of compassion toward each other than when they experi-enced positive emotion toward each other (Allred et al., 1996). In addition, angry negotiators were less willing to work with each other in the future. Other studies suggest that angry nego-tiators are more likely to overtly retaliate (Allred, 1996), endangering the negotiation process.

Other investigations that have measured and manipulated emotion report similar findings (for reviews, see Allred, Mallozzi, Matsui, & Raia, 1996; Barry & Oliver, 1996; Forgas, 1998; Thompson, Nadler, & Kim, 1999). Negotiators in a good mood generally realize higher individual and joint gains on both integrative and distributive negotiation tasks than do people who are in a neutral or negative mood (Kramer, Pommerenke, & Newton, 1993; Kumar, 1997). Specifically, negotiators in positive moods plan to use more cooperative strategies, engage in more information exchange, propose more alternatives, and are less likely to engage in contentious tactics (Carnevale & Isen, 1986). According to this perspective, positive affect promotes creative thinking (Isen, Daubman, & Nowicki, 1987), which, in turn, makes negotiators more likely to engage in innovative problem solving (Carnevale & Isen, 1986). This is particularly advantageous in integrative tasks where innovative thinking helps negotiators overcome the faulty fixed-pie perception (Thompson & Hastie, 1990) and achieve better joint outcomes (Carnevale & Isen, 1986).

The affect infusion model (AIM) (Forgas, 1995) supports the view that positive emotions enhance negotiators' effectiveness. However, the underlying psychological process is different than that proposed by the creative information-processing account. The AIM model posits that people's moods influence their cognitive evaluations. Essentially, the AIM model suggests that negotiators adopt mood-congruent bargaining strategies; according to this theory, happy negotiators will develop more cooperative tactics than unhappy negotiators (Forgas & Moylan, 1996).

The positive emotion view of negotiation strictly cautions negotiators against the perils that befall negotiators who express negative emotion. Perhaps the most well-developed theory in this regard is Gresham's law of conflict, which basically states that conflict can either take a constructive or destructive course and that the negotiator's own actions determine which course is more likely (Deutsch, 1973). Deutsch (1973) views emotions as attitudes and proposes that "a cooperative process leads to a trusting, friendly attitude and it increases the willingness to respond helpfully to the other's needs and requests" (p. 30). In contrast, a "competitive process leads to a suspicious, hostile attitude, and it increases the readiness to exploit the other's needs and respond negatively to the other's requests" (p. 30). This destructive course is often described as a *conflict spiral*. The dynamics of escalation are difficult to defuse because the emotions of negotiators tend to rise exponentially. "It appears that we humans are good at escalating confrontations, but we are ill-equipped to promote de-escalation. . . . Like small boars on a rising river, it is easy for disputing parties to lose control of the circumstances" (Susskind & Cruikshank, 1987, p. 93).

The irrational negotiator

A quite different perspective argues that negotiators who show blatant negative emotion (e.g., anger, rage, indignation, impatience) can be extremely effective at the bargaining table. We label this perspective the irrational negotiator because the stance that these negotiators take at the bargaining table appears to be extreme, risky, reckless, and seemingly out of control. A constellation of theoretical treatments give rise to the "irrationality" approach;

most notable are the views expressed by Thomas Schelling (1960) and Robert Frank (1988). We will ultimately argue, as do these theorists, that the "irrational" negotiator is, in fact, highly rational. Yet, on a strictly behavioral level, in terms of emotional expression, this person *appears* irrational and unreasonable. Irrational negotiators are effective because their irrational behavior convinces the other party that they would be willing to take great risks that would hurt both parties if they do not get what they want. Irrational negotiators use wild displays of negative emotion to persuade the other party to meet their demands. By appearing unstable and irrational, the irrational negotiator convinces his opponent that he would sooner walk away from the table without having reached an agreement than settle for anything less than he desires.

The irrational negotiator is effective to the extent that he can convince the other party that he will follow through with what seems to be an extreme course of action – perhaps because he has nothing to lose. Grave examples of such tactics can be found throughout history, as well as in the game theory literature. For example, before the German annexation of Austria, Hitler met to negotiate with the Austrian Chancellor von Schuschnigg. At some point in this dark historical meeting, Hitler's mode of influence escalated to extreme coercive power: It "became more strident, more shrill. Hitler ranted like a maniac, waved his hands with excitement. At times he must have seemed completely out of control . . . Hitler may then have made his most extreme coercive threats seem credible . . . [He threatened to take von Schuschnigg into custody, an act unheard of in the context of diplomacy]. He insisted that von Schuschnigg sign an agreement to accept every one of his demands, or he would immediately order a march into Austria" (Raven, 1990, p. 515).

Game theorists stress that irrational behavior must be convincing to be effective. Schelling (1960) gives the example of two negotiators playing a game of "chicken" in their cars – a highly risky game. One person assumes an advantage if she rips the steering wheel out of her car and throws it out the window, as long as her opponent sees her doing this. The other parry is then forced into being the one who moves out of the way; in other words, she is forced to concede, if both are to survive the game. But not just any behavior will suffice in order to evoke such concessions from the other party; in his book *Passions within Reason*, Frank (1988) argues that "for a signal between adversaries to be credible, it must be costly (or, more generally, difficult) to fake" (p. 99). Frightened that the negotiation may end in an impasse, the other party may be pressured to concede to what would normally be considered outrageous demands. This type of negotiation strategy is best characterized by the expression "the squeaky wheel gets the grease," and can be highly effective. The negotiator who rants and raves is likely to get a large portion of the pie. The irrational negotiator is thus, synonymous to what we call the rant 'n' rave approach.

A close cousin of the irrational negotiator is the manipulative negotiator – the negotiator who controls emotion to his or her advantage. This approach is more popularly known as Machiavellianism. Similarly, Aristotle argued that "anyone can become angry – that is easy. But to be angry with the right person, to the right degree, at the right time, for the right purpose, and in the right way – this is not easy." The actor who is so keenly in control of his emotions that the way in which they are displayed can be so precisely manipulated uses emotions in a highly rational way. However, little empirical evidence has tested this assumption.

Review of Three Models of Emotion in Negotiation and Prescriptive Implications

In this section, we critically examine the prescriptive advice that stems from each of the above perspectives. Some of this advice seems to be little more than common sense, whereas other advice is more counter-intuitive. As we will see, most of the prescriptive maxims derived from these approaches lack direct empirical support short of armchair observation, but many maxims have nevertheless attained the status of conventional wisdom. However, taken together, the prescriptive advice regarding the role of emotion in negotiation is often contradictory and confusing. In our discussion of these views, we pay special attention to the *type* of bargaining situation that is used to model negotiator behavior. To anticipate one of our conclusions, we argue that fundamentally different bargaining situations (i.e., fixed sum vs. variable sum and cooperative vs. non-cooperative) largely influence which strategy is most effective. Stated simply, in highly competitive bargaining situations, poker face or "irrational" strategies may indeed be effective; in contrast, in mixed-motive situations, particularly those in which parties' interests are not common knowledge, positive affect is often an advantage.

The rational negotiator approach

Probably the largest body of prescriptive research and theory on negotiation exalts the negotiator as a rational actor (Nash, 1950; Raiffa, 1982). As a rational actor, the negotiator is expected to follow the axioms of normative bargaining theory. Within these axioms, there is little room for the expression of emotion. For example, in his book, *The Art and Science of Negotiation*, Raiffa (1982) lists "self control, especially of emotions and their visibility" as the thirteenth most important characteristic (out of 34 key characteristics) of highly effective negotiators (p. 120). Similarly, Nierenberg (1968) claims that ". . . people in an emotional state do not want to think, and they are particularly susceptible to the power of suggestion from a clever opponent . . . [an] excitable person is putty in the hands of a calm, even-tempered negotiator . . ." (p. 46). A common prescriptive maxim that emerges from the rational negotiator approach involves the "poker face" philosophy.

According to the rational negotiator approach, the negotiator is strictly advised to keep a poker face. Even though a negotiator may feel emotion, he or she dare not express it, lest it leads to less than desirable outcomes. According to economists, the negotiator who expresses relief, satisfaction, and approval risks settling for a worse outcome than does the poker face negotiator. For example, Raiffa (1982) strictly cautions negotiators from displaying emotion ". . . don't gloat about how well you have done . . ." (p. 130). Janis and Mann's (1977) model of decision making formalizes the injurious impact of emotion on decision-making quality. Specifically, they argue that decision-makers experiencing high levels of emotional stress often undergo incomplete search, appraisal, and contingency planning thought processes. As a result, they make defective decisions.

Although there may be benefits to "keeping a poker face," such rational behavior may not always be in a negotiator's best interest. The very act of trying to keep a poker face may have adverse effects, especially if this requires high levels of monitoring and control. When we tell ourselves not to conjure certain thoughts, we find that it is virtually impossible to refrain from thinking the exact thoughts that we did not wish to enter our minds. There can be a paradoxical effect of attempting to control thoughts and emotions. For example, when people are instructed to not think about white bears, they immediately gain a vivid image of white bears. This well-documented process of ironic monitoring (Wegner & Wenzlaff, 1996) which keeps people from successfully monitoring their cognitions, may also prevent negotiators from adequately monitoring their emotions. The more people try to block out unwanted emotions or mental states, the more accessible these very emotions may become. Indeed, people who spend more time trying to repair their negative moods are most likely to suffer from persistent emotional problems such as depression and anxiety (Wegner & Wenzlaff, 1996).

The self-monitoring effects of controlling emotion may also interfere with the mutual process of entrainment, whereby one person's internal process is captured and modified by another person – such as when one person in a positive mood "affects" the mood of the other person with whom she is interacting (Kelly, 1988; see also this volume, chapter 5). Entrainment refers to the observation that when people interact, each person synchronizes her behavior in accordance with the behavioral and emotional states of the other person. In time, people develop an interpersonal rhythm that reflects a shared emotional and behavioral state. Entrainment is a natural biological process that is conducive to social relations (Kelly, 1988). The negotiator who is deliberately focused on repressing emotion may interfere with this process and prevent negotiators from developing a naturally synchronized pattern of interacting. Specifically, the negotiator who deliberately adopts the "poker face" strategy may contribute to a more stilted and awkward interaction. Indeed, the creation of dyadic rapport facilitates the attainment of more mutually beneficial outcomes (Drolet & Morris, 1998; Moore, Kurtzberg, Thompson, & Morris, 1998).

Similarly, emotions can be contagious (Hatfield, Cacioppo, & Rapson, 1992). If one negotiator conveys positive emotion, the other negotiator is likely to "catch" this positive emotional state and convey positive emotion as well. Positive emotion promotes cooperative and integrative negotiating strategies (Forgas & Moylan, 1996), and facilitates, which in turn helps avoid impasse (Drolet & Morris, 1998; Moore et al., 1998; Thompson & Kim, in press). Positive emotions thus facilitate the negotiation process.

The concerns with the "poker face" advice are not meant to imply that we should never attempt to monitor our emotions; rather, they suggest that when it comes to a "poker face," the nature of the parties' interdependence is a critical issue, as well as the timing of the negotiation. According to Kelley (1979), people in a negotiation may be cooperatively or competitively interdependent. Walton and McKersie (1965) make the same point in their theory of bargaining. Namely, in some bargaining situations, people have perfectly opposing interests; in other bargaining situations, people's interests are not perfectly opposed, and in fact may be compatible – we call this mixed-motive interdependence. The "poker face" strategy would seem to be most advantageous when parties' interests are perfectly, negatively opposed – that is, there is no advantage to parties becoming mutually entrained. In contrast, in mixed-motive situations there is potential for integrative agreement, and in these instances, it would make sense for parties to attempt to build rapport with the other party, through displays of (genuine) positive emotion. Indeed, when parties' interests are purely opposed, negotiators display counter-contagion, taking pleasure when the opponent loses; when negotiators' interests are aligned, they show more sympathetic emotional contagion. In addition, timing may be key. At the beginning of a negotiation, "schmoozing" and conveying positive emotion can help build rapport and are conducive to more integrative outcomes (Moore et al., 1998). On the other hand, at other points of the negotiation, masking our true feelings could be beneficial. For example, conveying elation at the end of a negotiation makes our opponent feel less successful and less satisfied with the negotiation (Thompson, Valley, & Kramer, 1995).

In summary, the "poker face" strategy may be useful in situations of competitive interdependence. The logic of the rational, poker face negotiator is one that pertains most directly to situations in which negotiators' interests are directly opposed, such that a gain or an advantage for one party comes at the direct loss of the other party. In such situations, negotiators compete directly with one another – a situation known as distributive bargaining. Because every negotiation situation involves a distributive element, even mixed-motive negotiations (Lax & Sebenius, 1986), this is an argument for rationality. This assertion is true normatively; however, behaviorally, a more common road that negotiators take to reach settlement is to build rapport, and building rapport necessitates positive emotion (Moore et al., 1998).

The positive emotion approach

The positive emotion approach takes a completely different perspective on the role of emotion at the bargaining table. There are three critical processes in this regard: One involves *feeling* positive emotion; another involves *expressing* positive emotion; a third involves *engendering* positive emotion in the opponent. A constellation of social psychological mechanisms are involved in this approach, and quite frankly, the exact causal determinants surrounding the effectiveness of positive emotion have yet to be clearly identified. Our review of the literature reveals two psychological mechanisms that may underlie the powerful positive emotion effect. One relates to balance principles and the other to information processing.

One psychological mechanism that may underlie positive emotions relates to basic principles of balance and congruence, dating back to Heider (1958) and Newcomb (1961). At the bargaining table the negotiator reasons something like the following: If I like the other party and I am interacting with him/her, then I should expect a favorable outcome. Similarly: If I do not like the other party and I am interacting with him/her, then I should expect a negative outcome. Quite often, negotiations break down because negotiators assume the worst about each other and take offense even when none was intended. Negotiators form either positive or negative impressions of the other party early on in a negotiation. The balance principle suggests that parties at the bargaining table will interpret the opponent's statements and behaviors in a positive light if they like each other. Furthermore, it is parties' expectations that guide negotiators' subsequent behaviors, and according to Deutsch (1973), determine whether the negotiation takes a productive or destructive course. The balance principle is also consistent with the notion of entrainment. If two negotiators feel positively toward each other, they are likely to develop positive rapport that facilitates the mutually beneficial attainment of settlement.

A quite different theoretical perspective is related to positive emotion and information processing (Forgas, 1998; Isen, 1987). According to this theoretical perspective, effective negotiation requires creative information processing and it is positive, rather than negative emotion, that instigates such cognitive processing. Specifically, the instantiation of positive affect is associated with more creative and varied cognitions – precisely those that can facilitate integrative bargaining (Forgas, 1998; Isen, 1987). Corroborating evidence from examinations of positive affect on creative ability suggests that when people are experiencing a positive mood, they are more creative (Baron, 1990; Isen et al., 1987). One explanation for this is that positive emotions can affect cognitive processes such that people are better at integrating information and more flexible in conveying their thoughts (Isen et al., 1987; Isen, Niedenthal, & Cantor, 1992). For example, in one investigation, people experiencing positive affect were more likely to see relationships among ideas and to link non-typical category exemplars together (Isen et al., 1992). In negotiations, an increase in cognitive complexity and creativity can lead to higher joint gains (Carnevale & Isen, 1986). In contrast, some research suggests that positive mood can induce more heuristic, as opposed to thoughtful information processing. Under certain circumstances, one's own positive mood may reduce the motivation to systematically process message content (Bohner, Crow, Erb, & Schwarz, 1992; Schwarz & Bless, 1991), and the perception of a positive mood in another may prompt the use of heuristics in impression formation (Ottati, Terkildsen, & Hubbard, 1997). Although this would seem to lead to worse, rather than more effective negotiation performance, we believe that the heuristic processing instigated by positive moods differs from the cognitive biases revealed in the negotiation literature.

A number of prescriptive maxims derive from the positive emotion approach to negotiation. A common maxim deriving from this perspective is, "Do not sour the negotiation with an extreme opening offer." The common lore is that an extreme opening offer will anger the other party and cause him or her to retaliate with an extreme offer in return. An opening offer, in the case of two negotiators who do not know each other well, represents the first impression that they have of one another. In the long run, it is feared that feelings of anger arising from an extreme opening offer can cause the opponent to be less cooperative, strongly increasing the probability of an impasse. A variety of research suggests that negative information learned early on about a person can have a powerful effect on impression formation (Asch, 1946).

In fact, there is some evidence that extreme offers may actually be strategically advantageous (Siegel & Fouraker, 1960; Thompson, 1995). Thompson (1995) found that negotiators with higher aspirations tended to place greater demands on their opponents, and ultimately realized greater payoffs. Thus in contrast to intuition, extreme opening offers may result in more profitable outcomes for the negotiator who makes them. Thus, the widely held assumption that one should not sour the negotiation with an extreme opening offer is flanked by two opposing theoretical assumptions and bodies of research. Research that supports the maxim indicates that uncooperative and hostile negotiators realize fewer joint gains than cooperative negotiators. Research that challenges the maxim suggests that the anchor provided by an extreme offer can actually help the party who makes the initial offer obtain a greater ultimate profit.

A second prescriptive maxim deriving from the positive emotion in negotiation view is the advice to "leave the other party feeling good." This popular belief is based on the notion that engendering positive feelings in the other party benefits future negotiations. The assumption is that if an opponent leaves the negotiation feeling good about the process and the outcome, that person will be likely to engage in a cooperative fashion in subsequent negotiations and to fulfill the terms of the current contract. In addition, the way an opponent feels about the negotiation at its completion has implications for our reputation. An opponent who feels good about a negotiation may speak highly of us, thus enhancing our reputation. Thus, assuming that these positive feelings endure, we can build a positive reputation and enjoy success in our future negotiations. On the other hand, we may assume that an opponent who leaves the negotiation with negative feelings will be unlikely to want to cooperate with us in subsequent interactions. If our opponent has a negative experience with us, we may also fear gaining a reputation for being uncooperative.

One reason why negotiators may want to end the negotiation on a positive note is that people tend to place a great deal of emphasis on the end point of an event and on the event's peak moment in determining their overall evaluation of the event itself (Fredrickson & Kahneman, 1993; Kahneman, Fredrickson, Schreiber, & Redelmeier, 1993; Redelmeier & Kahneman, 1996). The maxim "leave your opponent feeling good" resonates with this idea that the end point has a large impact on the overall evaluation of an experience. This suggests that even if an opponent felt as though she were pressured to make concessions during a negotiation, she could remember the negotiation favorably if the last few minutes of the interaction were experienced positively. For example, when opponents end the negotiation on a humorous note (e.g., "I will throw in my pet frog") acceptance rates are higher than when they do not (O'Quin & Aronoff, 1981).

Whereas we may want to leave our *opponents* feeling good at the conclusion of a negotiation, we do not want to show our opponent that *we* feel good. Thompson et al. (1995) found that independent of the actual outcome, negotiators felt less satisfied (and presumably less positive) with the negotiation when they believed their opponents were happy with the final outcome. This research also indicates that negotiators who told their opponent they felt good at the end of a negotiation ended up getting fewer dollars from their opponent in a subsequent allocation decision. This suggests that one should always avoid gloating at the end of a negotiation, regardless of how pleased one may be with the outcome. In fact, it may be wise to end a negotiation by pretending to be unhappy, thus causing the opponent to feel guilty and indebted.

A third perspective, which derives from the positive emotion view, is that hostility is detrimental to negotiation. The assumption is that hostility in a negotiation may breed further hostility that will spiral out of control. "Once an attack–defense cycle gets going the parties queue up to get their thrust in. The faster the attacks, and their replies, the higher the emotional tension. People in an emotional state make threats, not necessarily intending to carry them out, but threats provoke counter-threats and the parties may end up in a mutual exchange of sanctions because they boxed themselves into corners from which a retreat would [seemingly] cost too much . . . The consequence is that parties get nowhere except further apart which is the antithesis of negotiating" (Kennedy, Benson, & McMillan, 1980, pp. 42–43). The conflict spiral derives from Gresham's law. Such destructive conflict tends to escalate and expand, often irrespective of the initial cause, due to competition, misperception, and commitment processes (Deutsch, 1973).

The conflict spiral, or interchange of mounting negative affect, leading to irrational behavior is a cornerstone principle of dyadic communication. Individuals organize the continuous flow of interaction into discrete causal chunks (Swann, Pelham, & Roberts, 1987; Whorf, 1956). When engaged in conflict, people interpret these sequences of communication differently. Each party parses, or "punctuates" the conflict situation differently (Kahn & Kramer, 1990). That is, each party sees their own negative behavior as a defensive reaction to the unprovoked negative behavior of the other side; and simultaneously perceives the other party as an aggressor. Indeed, negative conflict spirals have been cited as a cause of war and continuing conflict between nations (Deutsch, 1973).

Even in the absence of outside provocation, processes internal to conflict cause it to escalate and persist over time. Once a conflict is underway, changes occur in the relationship between the conflicting groups. Negotiations often collapse when one party becomes angry with the other and desires to hurt the other party, rather than satisfy itself (Bazerman & Neale, 1983). The conflict spiral may further be fueled by the fact that negative emotions may be contagious (Hatfield et al., 1992).

Does the conflict spiral stemming from hostility imply that negotiators should avoid displaying hostile attitudes and behavior altogether? Not necessarily. In some cases, expressing hostility may actually facilitate the negotiation by allowing parties to "vent" or express emotion. "Particularly in interpersonal disputes, hostility may diminish significantly if the aggrieved party vents her anger, resentment, and frustration in front of the blamed party, and the blamed party acknowledges the validity of such emotions or, going one step further, offers an apology. With hostility reduced, resolving the dispute on the basis of interests becomes easier" (Ury, Brett, & Goldberg, 1988, pp. 6–7).

The benefits of positive emotion have been empirically examined nearly exclusively in the context of mixed-motive or integrative bargaining situations. In mixed-motive negotiations, parties must *cooperate* with one another to maximize the size of the pie and reach mutual settlement, yet *compete* with each other so as to gain as much as they can for themselves. This is a challenging goal because negotiators do not have complete information about the other party's interests and so it is not obvious how the most joint gains can be attained. The pie can be enlarged in a number of ways, such as by trading issues on which parties preferences and priorities differ, adding new compatible issues, or capitalizing on differences in beliefs (see Thompson, 1998 for an overview). As indicated above, negotiators who are in a positive mood reach more mutually beneficial settlements than do those in neutral (or negative) moods. However, an obvious, but as yet, unanswered question concerns the impact of emotion on the distributive (or competitive) component. Generally, experimental studies have not examined this issue and therefore, our conclusions are that when both negotiators are in a positive mood, greater joint gains will be attained than when negotiators are in a negative, or neutral, mood; but it is unclear whether the positive emotion negotiator will gain significantly less of the total joint gain if paired with a negative or neutral opponent.

The "rant 'n' rave" approach

The irrational negotiator perspective, or "rant 'n' rave" approach, asserts that the expression of extreme negative – to the point of irrational – behavior can be highly effective. To the extent that a negotiator can convince the other party that he or she is just crazy enough to take outrageous risks, he or she can actually achieve a bargaining advantage (Schelling, 1960). A negotiator who is faced with an irate opponent may capitulate to the other party to end the interaction quickly (Frank, 1988). Although little or no empirical research has examined this strategy, there are four psychological explanations that may account for its effectiveness: perceptual contrast, negative reinforcement, self-regulation theory, and somewhat paradoxically, game theory.

The door-in-the-face technique (Cann, Sherman, & Elkes, 1975; Cialdini, 1975), most commonly investigated in the persuasion contexts, highlights the usefulness of perceptual contrast. The basic premise is that to the extent that a person makes what is perceived to be an outlandish, ridiculous request, he or she is more likely to secure agreement to a subsequent, smaller request. The fundamental principle involved is that of perceptual contrast (Cialdini, 1993). Quite simply, when we compare two different requests, one extreme and the other more modest, we perceive the second request to be much more reasonable than if we were to consider only the second request without having heard the first one. In the same way, perceptual contrast explains why, if we lift a heavy object, set it down, and then lift a light object, we perceive the light object to be much lighter than it actually is. Skilled negotiators have been profiting from perceptual contrast effects for years (Cialdini, 1993). Consider the savvy car salesperson who shows the potential buyer the most expensive models before showing her the model in which she is actually interested. Compared to the $40,000 price tag of the expensive model, the $20,000 price tag of the intended sale seems much more palatable. Thus, the negotiator who is aware of perceptual contrast effects can use them to her advantage. By making an outrageous initial request, one can increase the possibility that the second request will be accepted by one's opponent.

A second psychological explanation for the rant 'n' rave approach relates to basic principles of negative reinforcement (Skinner, 1938). Negative reinforcement, or escape behavior, explains the increased likelihood of behavior that eliminates or removes an aversive stimulus. If the radio is playing obnoxious music, the listener will turn it off, thus eliminating the unpleasant stimuli. In a similar vein, because most people find it unpleasant to be around hostile, negative, and demanding people, they may be willing to give the person what he or she wants just to make the other person be quiet. Ironically, this behavior operates as a positive reinforcement to the person displaying negative behavior. Conceding to an opponent's bursts of irrationality means rewarding their hostile behavior, and increases the likelihood of this behavior in the future. Thus, "squeaky wheel" negotiators may capitalize upon and be reinforced for their hostile behavior.

Similarly self-regulation theory (Baumeister, Leith, Muraven, & Bratslavsky, 1998) explains why people may give in to a hostile opponent. This theory proposes that most people like to prolong positive moods and exposure to positive stimuli and minimize negative moods. People self-regulate by actively working to maintain a desired positive mood; one way to achieve this is to avoid negative stimuli. Being around a "ranting and raving" negotiator is usually unpleasant, so much so that the negotiator will want to remove him or herself from the situation, which often means capitulating.

Paradoxically, game theory also helps understand a number of prescriptive maxims that derive from the irrational negotiator perspective. Probably the most well known is the *squeaky wheel principle* (Singelis, 1998). The squeaky wheel principle states that a negotiator should demonstrate an unwillingness to move away from a stated position, by escalating the level of hostility and using threats. Whereas little or no empirical research has examined the efficacy of this strategy, Schelling (1960) and Frank (1988) provide qualitative evidence that this strategy can be remarkably effective.

For example, a threat that compels rather than deters often takes the form of administering the punishment until the other acts, rather than if he acts. Schelling (1960) describes a situation with two people in a row boat. If one threatens the other that if he doesn't row the former will tip the boat over, that would not be as powerful as starting to rock the boat fervently while yelling at the other to row if he wants him to stop rocking. Thus, "initiating steady pain, even if the threatener shares the pain, may make sense as a threat, especially if the threatener can initiate it irreversibly so that only the other's compliance can relieve the pain they both share" (Schelling, 1960, p. 196).

Frank (1988) in his book, *Passions within Reason*, develops the idea that being motivated by emotion can be a competitive advantage, as long as one can stand up to the commitment made during an emotional outburst. An emotional negotiator is more likely to be able to make a credible threat of walking away from an offer she perceives as unfair, even if that offer would entail an objective gain for herself. This may allow the emotional negotiator to procure a better offer from her opponent, thus capturing a larger share of the bargaining zone.

A second maxim to be derived from this strategy is what we call the *tough strategy*, which involves signaling toughness throughout the negotiation so that the opponent will respect your position. Negotiators who make fewer concessions and make smaller concessions are indeed more effective in terms of maximizing individual gain compared to those who make larger and more frequent concessions (Siegel & Fouraker, 1960; Yukl, 1974).

The rant 'n' rave strategy has been modeled (but not empirically examined) primarily in the context of non-cooperative bargaining situations – situations in which each party makes a unilateral choice, not knowing at the time what the opponent will do, but knowing what the full range of outcomes will be. Thus, this bargaining situation differs significantly from the integrative bargaining situation used in the positive emotion literature, which nearly exclusively focuses on behavior in cooperative bargaining situations – that is, situations in which parties must mutually agree for any settlement to be binding. Another significant difference between the typical rant 'n' rave context and that of positive emotion has to do with how much information the parties have regarding what the possible outcomes might be. The positive emotion research has focused on situations in which negotiators have incomplete information about the other's interests and thus, the two of them need to cooperate in large measure so as to jointly determine the range of possibilities. In contrast, the irrational negotiator approach has been primarily studied in situations where the opponents have the same information; situations that have binary cooperate or deflect choices, such as the prisoners' dilemma or chicken game.

There are several ways in which signaling toughness can impede a negotiation. Whenever we try to convey an emotional position like toughness we run the risk that our opponent will either fail to receive our intended message, or will grossly misinterpret it. A staunch position can easily be misinterpreted as coercion or hostility rather than the respect and deference the tough party hopes to convey. This type of misinterpretation sets the stage for a conflict spiral (Rothbart & Hallmark, 1988) which is likely to lead to an impasse.

As a case in point, consider what happened during World War II (Rothbart & Hallmark, 1988). Shortly after the United States joined the allied forces in World War II, the Americans and British engaged in costly bombing raids over Germany aimed at decreasing the Germans' "will to resist." Although the allies would have expected to respond to the German's hostility by initiating a counter-attack, they expected that the Germans would respond to their displays of aggression by retreating in fear and intimidation. Participants on both sides predicted that they would retaliate against their opponent's coercive tactics while their opponents would retreat in response to their displays of aggression. In addition, negotiators often signal toughness by adopting a Boulware strategy (Walton & McKersie, 1965), wherein they make their position known and propose a first and final offer. Boulwarism is not very effective (Raiffa, 1982) and can instigate a conflict spiral (Thompson, 1998). Whereas signaling toughness may engender the respect of your opponent, it may also quickly escalate conflict and make reaching a settlement virtually impossible.

Misperceptions about Emotions in Negotiation

The most common prescriptive maxims regarding emotion that guide the behavior of negotiators at the bargaining table are hardly consistent and, in some cases, downright contradictory. The prescriptive literature advises negotiators to be simultaneously rational, positive, and irrational. We undertake an examination of psychology of emotions in negotiations to disentangle the conflicting aspects of the above strategies. This requires a careful analysis of how people perceive emotions. Most important, it requires an analysis of how emotions are often misperceived. Specifically, three misperceptions about emotions in negotiations permeate much of the prescriptive advice offered to negotiators in all three of the perspectives we have reviewed. These three common misperceptions are that: (1) people can accurately understand and read emotions in others; (2) emotional states endure over time; and (3) emotion predicts behavior. We argue that these misperceptions affect negotiators' ability to effectively negotiate, in terms of maximizing both joint gain and individual gain.

Misperception 1: People can accurately understand and read emotions in others

Much prescriptive advice assumes that people have near-perfect insight into the emotions of others. Consider, the "keep a poker face" maxim. The maxim assumes that if a negotiator were to display any emotion, the other party would be able to accurately state and correctly interpret its meaning, thus conferring him with information about the opponent's position.

In other words, the "keep a poker face" maxim presupposes that negotiators can accurately detect emotion in others.

People have limited access even to their own emotions (Loewenstein & Schkade, 1997), let alone to the emotions of those around them, and they often mispredict why others feel the way they do (Ekman, 1985; Keltner, 1994). In addition, people misjudge the intensity of their feelings (Keltner & Robinson, 1993) and are overconfident in their ability to predict others' emotions (Dunning, Griffin, Milojkovic, & Ross, 1990). Whether it is because people fail to account for situational factors (Dunning et al., 1990; Kulik, Sledge, & Mahler, 1986), or are unable to distinguish genuine from contrived emotions (Keltner, 1994), people are not as adept as they believe themselves to be at predicting how other people will feel or behave in different circumstances.

Complementing this bias is the fact that we believe that others can read our internal states more accurately than is actually the case. Most of us believe that other people can readily read what we are thinking and feeling (Gilovich, Savitsky, & Medvec, 1998) and fear that we let too much information about our emotional states leak out. We fall prey to an "illusion of transparency," overestimating the extent to which our emotions "leak out," and become detectable to others (Gilovich et al., 1998). Negotiators who fall victim to this bias may be convinced that their genuine feelings of joy, anger, or anxiety have seeped out, and may not believe they have successfully concealed their true attitudes. The illusion of transparency bias suggests that it is difficult to know if we have successfully maintained a poker face. We may think we are conveying too much or very little emotion, but our opponents may not notice it at all.

Misperception 2: Emotional states endure over time

Much prescriptive advice assumes that emotional states endure over time. We generally assume that a positive event, such as winning the lottery, getting a raise, and falling in love will have a long-lasting effect on our overall happiness. We also assume that intensely negative events, such as getting fired, being in an accident, or losing a loved one will leave us unhappy forever. Contrary to popular belief, the emotional effects of extremely negative events or extremely positive events do not last nearly as long as we would think (Gilbert, Wilson, Pinel, & Blumberg, 1998; Suh, Diener, & Fujita, 1996; Wortman & Silver, 1989). We do not sustain prolonged levels of intense distress or elation, but rather, adapt to these hedonic states and return to a more neutral level of functioning (Frederick & Loewenstein, 1998).

Because our intuition about the effects of highly emotional events is often incorrect, we have a tendency to over-predict how long we will feel sad in response to a tragedy, or happy in response to a joyous event. For example, when people predicted how they would feel several months after the termination of a romantic relationship, they over-predicted the duration of their negative affect (Gilbert et al., 1998). Additionally, when faculty members predicted how they would feel after failing to achieve tenure, after receiving negative personal feedback, and after being turned down from an attractive job, they consistently over-predicted how long their negative affect would last – that is in comparison to the reports of people who *did* endure these unfortunate events (Gilbert et al., 1998).

According to the durability bias (Gilbert et al., 1998) we do not adequately account for the ability of our psychological immune system to *adapt*. Through a variety of psychological mechanisms, we are able to reinterpret, reinvent, or altogether ignore negative events to reduce the consequences of such events on our subjective well-being. These defenses provide a psychological shield that protects us from deviating too far below our chronic levels of subjective well-being. For this reason, it is quite likely that negotiators overestimate the impact a particular negotiation will have on their own subjective wellbeing, and overestimate the effect that a negotiated outcome will have on how someone else feels.

Indeed, people's prospective expectations and retrospective evaluations of events are more positive than the actual experience of the events (Mitchell, Thompson, Peterson, & Cronk, 1997). For example, in one investigation people anticipated that they would enjoy events like a trip to Europe, a Thanksgiving vacation, and a bicycle trip more than they actually did (as indicated by journals that were kept during the events), and remembered the events as being more enjoyable than they actually experienced them at the time. Their in-the-moment negative evaluations tended to be short-lived, and were quickly replaced by positive memories of the experiences (Mitchell et al., 1997).

What specific psychological processes account for this relative immunity to negative events? One possibility is that individuals selectively remember only the most positive aspects of an event so that their enduring memory will be positive. Likewise, they may distort or transform experiences so that an in-the-moment disappointment becomes a much-cherished memory. Most of us interpret an aggravating experience as a "comedy of errors," emphasizing the comic element more and more over time (Mitchell et al., 1997). Additionally, a desire for cognitive consistency compels people to have memories of an event that match their expectations of that event. Thus, a highly anticipated event, despite its actual quality, is likely to be remembered well. Overall, it seems that people are motivated to gloss over negative details of an event, and reframe events into a positive experience that will serve a positive self-image. This psychological immune system is "invisible" (Gilbert et al., 1998) in that it is largely unknown to us until we are forced to utilize it, and, in fact its invisible nature is critical to its effectiveness. If we were made aware of the way in which we were distorting information to alleviate our negative affect, we would be unable to properly defend ourselves psychologically. The idea of a psychological immune system helps us understand why our negative affect dissipates rather quickly, but does not offer a compelling explanation as to why we often experience a similar dissipation of positive affect. Why is it that previous lottery winners have been found to be no happier than non-winners? (Brickman, Coates, & Janoff-Bulman, 1978).

One explanation is *focalism* – the tendency to focus on the precipitating event to the exclusion of all others (Gilbert et al. 1998). Events happen within the context of our lives yet we often ignore this context when estimating the impact that a particular event will have on us. Thus, if we are asked how we would feel six months after winning the lottery, we focus only on that winning event, ignoring all of the other events that may also impact our affective state. On the other hand, when we report our actual happiness six months later, the fight we had that morning with our spouse, the call from our child's teacher, and the hunger pangs we are experiencing because we skipped breakfast are all very salient and have a distinct influence on our reported level of happiness. Thus, the context surrounding the event is often overlooked in people's predictions, but this context plays a very significant role in actually determining people's happiness.

Just as we mispredict the duration of our affective responses, so too, do we misconstrue the way in which the duration of our experiences influences our retrospective evaluations of them. One of the more universal beliefs is that people seek to maximize pleasure and reduce pain. Likewise, most of us assume that, if given the choice, we would prolong pleasurable or hedonic experiences, and diminish unpleasant experiences.[1] Contrary to basic psychological intuition, our evaluations of episodes are often based on trends rather than duration (Varey & Kahneman, 1992). For example, an episode that is painful for ten minutes is considered worse than an episode that is equally painful for the first ten minutes, but is followed by five minutes of less intense pain (Redelmeier & Kahneman, 1996).

Rather than basing evaluations on the aggregate level of pleasure or pain, we often base our evaluations on the peak and end moments of the experience (Redelmeier & Kahneman, 1996). This effect has been predominantly studied in terms of unpleasant or painful experiences. People's evaluation of painful or unpleasant experiences is based on the level of discomfort at the most intense moment of the episode (the peak) and the level of discomfort during the final moments of the episode (the end) (Fredrickson & Kahneman, 1993; Kahneman et al., 1993; Redelmeier & Kahneman, 1996). Thus, episodes that end with intense pain, even if they are brief, are evaluated worse than episodes that begin with the same initial level of pain, but have additional moments of decreasing pain tacked onto their end. This phenomenon of duration neglect (Fredrickson & Kahneman, 1993) has been demonstrated with painful colonoscopy procedures (Redelmeier & Kahneman, 1996), aversive film clips, and the submersion of extremities (such as fingers) into painfully cold water (Kahneman et al., 1993), but not yet in negotiations. The duration of the episode, or its integrated utility, seems to have little, if any effect on the way we feel about the experience.

People also give disproportional weight to the final moments of an interaction when retrospectively evaluating social interactions (Fredrickson, 1991). Fredrickson (1991) showed that people who believed their social interactions would be terminated at the end of the experimental session judged the entire social relationship on the affect they were experiencing during the final moments of the interaction. There was no correlation, however, between the relationship evaluations and the affect experienced during the final conversation among people who believed that they would reconvene with their social partner the following day. This suggests that we base our social evaluations on the way we feel about the relationship at the perceived end of the encounter.

But what does all of this mean for the conduct of negotiations? Do we need to leave our opponent feeling good? The durability bias (Gilbert et al., 1998) suggests that we greatly overestimate how long we and others will feel strong emotions. Thus, although many negotiators assume that positive feelings in their opponent will last indefinitely, research suggests that such feelings may actually be fleeting. If this is the case, then leaving an opponent feeling good at the end of a negotiation will have little impact on future negotiations that are temporally distant. Leaving an opponent with negative feelings may also be relatively harmless if the durability bias is accurate and these feelings wear off before the next interaction. On the other hand, if the feeling at the end is the most prominent in defining the other person's evaluation of the interaction then leaving the opponent feeling good may be useful in terms of your general reputation with the other party. However, if it is only the feeling at the end of the negotiation that is key, this may mean that one can be demanding throughout the negotiation as long as at the end of the negotiation one makes a concession which is then highlighted to one's opponent to make him or her feel good.

Misperception 3: Emotion predicts behavior

Much prescriptive advice assumes a distinct causal relationship between emotion and behavior. Presumably, one reason why negotiators care about emotion in negotiation is because they believe that emotions predict behavior. Consider the maxim "do not sour the negotiation with an extreme opening offer." The assumption behind this belief is that an extreme opening offer will anger the opponent and cause him or her to behave in a hostile, unco-operative manner. However, people's access to their own internal states – namely their emotions – is relatively limited and often faulty (Wilson, 1985; Wilson & Dunn, 1986; Wilson & Schooler, 1991). As a result, people often mispredict what they are feeling, which leads to subsequent mispredictions: about their corresponding behavior. Furthermore, when people try to introspect and monitor their feelings, it often leads to inconsistent behavior (Wilson, 1985; Wilson & Dunn, 1986; Wilson, Dunn, Kraft, & Lisle, 1989; Wilson, Hodges, & LaFleur, 1995; Wilson & LaFleur, 1995; Wilson, Lisle, Schooler, Hodges, Klaaren, & LaFleur, 1993; Wilson & Schooler, 1991).

Focusing on feelings themselves presumably makes attitudes more salient, and is therefore thought to increase attitude–behavior consistency; however, analyzing the reasons for feelings reduces attitude–behavior consistency. For example, when students were simply asked to think about which beverages they preferred, there was increased attitude–behavior consistency in the beverages they chose at their subsequent meal (Wilson & Dunn, 1986). When asked their reasons for preferring certain beverages, attitude–behavior consistency decreased at their subsequent meal.

Why does introspecting about reasons for preferences negatively affect attitude–behavior consistency? According to Wilson (1985) when people are asked to analyze the reasons for their feelings, they construct a plausible explanation to account for what are often uncon-scious, preverbal feelings. The problem is that people are often unaware of why they feel the way they do. When asked to defend their feelings, they focus on the most salient, reasonable interpretations, even if these explanations are inaccurate, or misrepresent their initial atti-tude. People search for "factors that are plausible and easy to verbalize even if they conflict with how they originally felt" (Wilson & Schooler, 1991, p. 182). "To the extent that these cognitions have a different valence from one's affect, and to the extent that behavior remains affectively based, attitude–behavior consistency will suffer" (Wilson & Dunn, 1986, p. 251). This suggests that attitude–behavior inconsistency is due to the fact that once people have analyzed the reasons for their feelings, they adopt a new attitude; however, their behavior is still based upon their original attitude. The outcome is an apparent inconsistency between their newly formed attitude and their behavior. An alternative explanation suggests that people's behaviors are actually aligned with their newly formed attitudes, and are thus inconsistent with the way they originally (and presumably, genuinely) felt.

Given that our attitudes are often inconsistent with our behavior, it is not surprising that we are overconfident in our ability to accurately predict our own behavior (Osberg & Shrauger, 1986; Vallone, Griffin, Lin, & Ross, 1990). One reason for overconfident self-predictions may be self-reflection (Wilson & LaFleur, 1995). As discussed above, people who analyze the reasons for their feelings and preferences demonstrate increased attitude–behavior inconsistency. Along with attitude–behavior inconsistency, introspection of this nature can lead to inaccurate and overconfident predictions about our own future behavior. The fundamental attribution error (Griffin, Dunning, & Ross, 1990; Nisbett & Ross, 1980; Ross, 1977) also contributes to people's tendency to be overconfident in their self-predictions. Although most often understood as a social or interpersonal phenomenon, people also discount situational factors when making predictions about their own behavior. In other words, people fail to consider the uncertainty of situational construals in predicting their own future responses. For example, when participants in different situations were asked to predict how much money they would spend on certain events, and how much time they would spend engaged in certain activities, they did not consider the uncertainty of their situations when predicting their future behavior or their confidence in these predictions (Griffin et al., 1990). "To the extent that people naturally and habitually treat their situational construals as if they are error-free representations of reality, their predictions and assessments are bound to be overconfident" (Griffin et al., 1990, p. 1138).

People's overconfidence in their ability to predict future behaviors transcends the intrapersonal realm, and is also evidenced in people's predictions about the behaviors of others. Just as people discount the uncertainty of situational construal in predictions about themselves (Griffin et al., 1990), so too do they discount situational factors when making predictions about the future behavior of others.

Individuals often use misguided inferences about the role that other people's dispositions played in past behaviors, and are therefore likely to overestimate the role such dispositions will play in their future behaviors (Dunning et al., 1990). Furthermore, even when people predict the future behaviors of those with whom they are quite familiar, they tend to underestimate situational variables and mispredict these people's future behaviors. They also tend to be overconfident in the accuracy of these predictions.

It may be our failure to properly predict how others make sense of, or *feel* about, situations that limits our ability to predict their behavior. Consistent misprediction of other people's behavior suggests that we are unable to infer the thoughts and feelings of other people. Overconfident predictions suggest that we are not fully aware of how easily and how often we fail to understand the way in which other people are subjectively construing situations. If people are overconfident about their opponents' behaviors in a negotiation, it is likely that they are overconfident in their assessments about how their opponents are feeling about the negotiation.

The discontinuity between emotion and behavior is key to evaluating the maxim "do not sour the negotiation with an extreme opening offer." First, we must consider whether extreme offers arouse feelings of anger in our opponents. Whereas common sense may tell us they should, empirical evidence suggests the opposite. Even if an extreme offer does anger our opponent, it is not clear that our opponent's anger will impact his behavior in the negotiation since there is often a dissociation between our feelings and our subsequent behaviors (Wilson & Dunn, 1986; Wilson & Schooler, 1991). This suggests that feelings of anger may not necessarily lead to hostile or uncooperative behavior. Thus, we may be misguided in avoiding extreme opening offers. First, we may not be as accurate as we believe in assessing the emotional response that will be triggered by an extreme offer and second, we may be overestimating the relationship between individuals' emotional reactions and their subsequent behavior.

Conclusion

In this chapter, we have outlined three prescriptive approaches for negotiation: the rational strategy, the positive strategy, and the irrational strategy. At first glance, these three perspectives of negotiation appear to be in conflict, as it would seem impossible for a negotiator to simultaneously not show emotion, display positive emotion, and express extreme negative emotion. In addition, these three views give rise to prescriptive advice that is not only contradictory across perspectives, but also whose validity is often called into question by existing research. We argue that there are three common misperceptions about emotions in negotiations that permeate the strategies offered to negotiators. Recognizing these misperceptions does not eliminate contradictions in the prescriptive advice, but it may help negotiators understand when certain approaches may be better than others, and understand the limitations of all of the strategies.

It would seem natural to address the question of which strategy is indeed the most effective in negotiation. We have partially attempted to answer this question by concluding that the optimal strategy depends in large part on the type of bargaining situation. To this end, we drew a distinction between the type of bargaining game, cooperative or non-cooperative, and concluded that in many cooperative bargaining situations, positive, as well as rational, strategies can be highly effective; whereas in non-cooperative bargaining games (e.g., prisoner's dilemma, etc.) aggressive, and rational strategies can be effective. Thus, in our treatment of the negotiation literature, we distinguish two fundamental bargaining objectives that are related to outcomes: the creation of value (this is typically referred to as the win-win aspect of negotiating) and the distribution of value (this is typically referred to as the win-or-lose aspect of negotiating). The distinction between integrative and distributive aspects of negotiations is hardly new. Raiffa (1982), Lax and Sebenius (1986), and Bazerman, Mannix, and Thompson (1988) have argued that negotiators face a mixed-motive enterprise in that they must cooperate with the other party so as to ensure agreement and to find joint value but simultaneously compete with the other party concerning the distribution or allocation of the joint value. The contribution of this chapter lies in illustrating the interaction between these situations and emotional content and process of negotiations.

Certain prescriptive strategies regarding the use of emotion may apply to the value-creation process while others apply to the distributive process. The social psychological perspective that advances the "positive emotion" negotiator emphasizes joint or mutual outcomes in non-zero-sum and cooperative games, whereas the irrational negotiator perspective emphasizes individual outcomes in zero-sum and non-cooperative games. The rational approach and its prescriptive poker face pertain mostly to situations in which negotiators' interests are directly opposed – the distributive aspects of either type of zero-sum or non-zero-sum games.

The three approaches we identify can also be considered three distinct mental models. Mental models describe the ways in which people understand social and physical systems and often refer to the way they think about problem solving (Johnson-Laird, 1983; Rouse & Morris, 1986). Negotiators have different kinds of mental models that they can apply to a negotiation situation, such as a "fixed-pie" model versus a "creative problem-solving" model (Van Boven & Thompson, 2000). We argue that the rational, positive, and aggressive approaches represent three different mental models for approaching negotiation.

Applying the accurate mental model to the negotiating situation is key for successful outcomes. People often misapply mental models, for example, operating a home thermostat like a gas pedal (Gentner & Gentner, 1983). Imagine a person interested in heating his home views the thermostat as either that of a kitchen oven or a gas pedal in the car. The former assumes that, by turning on the heat to a higher temperature, like operating the gas pedal in the car, the house will reach a higher temperature at a faster pace. The latter, accurately realizes that the house, similar to a kitchen oven, will reach the temperature on the dial (either 375 degrees for baking a cake or 68 degrees for warming the house) at the same rate no matter whether the thermostat of either is initially set to the desired temperature or to a higher one. This analogy stresses the importance of having a mental model that is appropriate for the given situation. To the extent that their negotiating mental model – rational, positive, or aggressive – is appropriate for the particular type of negotiation, negotiators will be more successful.

While the three approaches seem to be very different, the prescriptive advice that flows from them shares a disconcerting commonality. Specifically, much of this advice is based on flawed assumptions about people's ability to perceive emotions, the durability of emotions, and the relationship between emotions and behavior.

Throughout this chapter, we have attempted to identify some of the most common misperceptions regarding emotion. A better understanding of the role emotion actually plays in a negotiation can lead to a more informed use of the maxims and perhaps an ultimate blending of the three approaches. For example, a negotiator who recognizes that the way one feels at the end of an interaction is most important in defining that person's evaluation of the event, can use an aggressive approach throughout the negotiation to capture more of the pie, and can conclude the negotiation with a positive approach to secure a good reputation for future interactions. In the end, we argue that negotiators need to fit their negotiation strategies with the given situation and understand and capitalize on the psychology of emotion that underlies these strategies.

NOTE

1   The value of an experience is known as its utility (Varey & Kahneman, 1992). When we evaluate our experiences, we think of highly pleasurable experiences as having high utility, while a disagreeable experience is said to have high disutility.

REFERENCES

Allred, K. (1996). *Judgment anger and retaliation: A new perspective on conflict in organizations*. Unpublished manuscript.

Allred, K., Mallozzi, J. S., Matsui, F., & Raia, C. P. (1996). The influence of anger and compassion in negotiation performance. *Organizational Behavior and Human Decision Processes, 70*(3), 175–187.

Asch, S. (1946). Forming impressions of personality. *Journal of Abnormal and Social Psychology, 41*, 258–290.

Baron, R. A. (1990). Environmentally induced positive affect: Its impact on self-efficacy, task performance, negotiation, and conflict. *Journal of Applied Social Psychology, 20*(5), 368–384.

Barry, B., & Oliver, R. L. (1996). Affect in dyadic negotiation: A model and propositions. *Organizational Behavior and Human Decision Processes, 67*(2), 127–143.

Baumeister, R., Leith, K. P., Muraven, M., Bratslavsky, E. (1998). Self-regulation as a key to success in life. In W. M. Bukoski (Ed.), *Improving confidence across the lifespan: Building interventions based on theory and research* (pp. 117–132). New York: Plenum Press.

Bazerman, M. H., Mannix, E., & Thompson, L. (1988). Groups as mixed-motive negotiations. In E. J. Lawler & B. Markovsky (Eds.), *Advances in group processes: Theory and research*. Greenwich, CT: JAI Press.

Bazerman, M. H., & Neale, M. A. (1982). Improving negotiation effectiveness under final offer arbitration: The role of selection and training. *Journal of Applied Psychology, 67*(5), 543–548.

Bazerman, M. H., & Neale, M. A. (1983). Heuristics in negotiation: Limitations to effective dispute resolution. In M. H. Bazerman & R. J. Lewicki (Eds.), *Negotiating in organizations* (pp. 51–67). Beverly Hills, CA: Sage.

Brickman, P., Coates, D., & Janoff-Bulman, R. (1978). Lottery winners and accident victims: Is happiness relative? *Journal of Personality and Social Psychology, 36*, 917–927.

Bohner, G., Crow, K., Erb, H. P., & Schwarz, N. (1992). Affect and persuasion: Mood effects on the processing of message content and context cues and on subsequent behavior. *European Journal of Social Psychology, 22*(6), 511–530.

Cann, A., Sherman, S. J., & Elkes, R. (1975). Effects of initial request size and timing of a second request on compliance: The foot in the door and the door in the face. *Journal of Personality and Social Psychology, 32*(5), 774–782.

Carnevale, P. J., & Isen, A. (1986). The influence of positive affect and visual access on the discovery of integrative solutions in bilateral negotiations. *Organizational Behavior and Human Decision Processes, 37*, 1–13.

Cialdini, R. B. (1975). Reciprocal concessions procedure for inducing compliance: The door-in-the-face technique. *Journal of Personality and Social Psychology, 31*(2), 206–215.

Cialdini, R. B. (1993). *Influence: Science and practice*. New York: Harper Collins.

Deutsch, M. (1973). *The resolution of conflict*. New Haven, CT: Yale University Press.

Drolet, A., & Morris, M. W. (1998). *Rapport in conflict resolution: Accounting for how nonverbal exchange fosters coordination on mutually beneficial settlements to mixed motive conflicts*. Unpublished manuscript.

Dunning, D., Griffin, D. W., Milojkovic, J. D., & Ross, L. (1990). The overconfidence effect in social prediction. *Journal of Personality and Social Psychology, 58*, 568–581.

Ekman, P. (1985). *Telling lies: Clues to deceit in the marketplace, marriage, and politics*. New York: W. W. Norton.

Forgas, J. P. (1995). Mood and judgment: The affect infusion model (AIM). *Psychological Bulletin, 117*(1), 39–66.

Forgas, J. P. (1998). On feeling good and getting your way: Mood effects on negotiator cognition and bargaining strategies. *Journal of Personality and Social Psychology, 74*, 565–577.

Forgas, J. P., & Moylan, S. J. (1996). *On feeling good and getting your way: Mood effects on expected and actual negotiation strategies and outcomes.* Unpublished manuscript.

Frank, R. H. (1988). *Passions within reason: The strategic role of the emotions.* New York: W.W. Norton.

Frederick, S., & Loewenstein, G. (1998). Hedonic adaptation. In E. Diener, N. Schwartz, & D. Kahneman (Eds.), *Hedonic psychology: Scientific approaches to enjoyment, suffering, and well-being.* New York: Russell Sage Foundation.

Fredrickson, B. L. (1991). Anticipated endings: An explanation for selective social interaction (Doctoral dissertation, Stanford University, 1990). *Dissertation Abstracts International, 3*, AAD91–00818.

Fredrickson, B. L., & Kahneman, D. (1993). Duration neglect in retrospective evaluations of affective episodes. *Journal of Personality and Social Psychology, 65*, 45–55.

Gentner, D., & Gentner, D. R. (1983). Flowing waters or teeming crowds: Mental models of electricity. In D. Gentner & A. Stevens (Eds.), *Mental models.* Hillsdale, NY: Erlbaum.

Gilbert, D. T., Wilson, T. D., Pinel, E. C., & Blumberg, S. J. (1998). Affective forecasting and durability bias: The problem of the invisible shield. *Journal of Personality and Social Psychology, 75*(3), 617–638.

Gilovich, T., Savitsky, K., & Medvec, V. H. (1998). The illusion of transparency: Biased assessments of others' ability to read our emotional states. *Journal of Personality and Social Psychology, 75*(2), 332–346.

Griffin, D., Dunning, D., & Ross, L. (1990). The role of construal processes in overconfident predictions about the self and others. *Journal of Personality and Social Psychology, 59*, 1128–1139.

Hatfield, E., Cacioppo, J. T., & Rapson, R. L. (1992). Primitive emotional contagion. In M. S. Clark (Ed.), *Emotion and social behavior: Review of personality and social psychology* (Vol. 14, pp. 151–177). Newbury Park, CA: Sage.

Heider, F. (1958). *The psychology of interpersonal relations.* New York: Wiley.

Isen, A. M. (1987). Positive affect, cognitive processes, and social behavior. In L. Berkowitz (Ed.), *Advances in experimental social psychology* (Vol. 20, pp. 203–253). New York: Academic Press.

Isen, A. M., Daubman, K. A., & Nowicki, G. P. (1987). Positive affect facilitates creative problem solving. *Journal of Personality and Social Psychology, 52*, 1122–1131.

Isen, A. M., Niedenthal, P. M., & Cantor, N. (1992). An influence of positive affect on social categorization. *Motivation and Emotion, 16*(1), 65–78.

Janis, I. L., & Mann, L. (1977). *Decision making.* New York: Free Press.

Johnson-Laird, P. N. (1983). *Mental models.* Cambridge, MA: Harvard University Press.

Kahn, R. L., & Kramer, R. M. (1990). *Untying the knot: De-escalatory processes in international conflict.* San Francisco, CA: Jossey-Bass.

Kahneman, D., Fredrickson, B. L., Schreiber, C. A., & Redelmeier, D. A. (1993). When more pain is preferred to less: Adding a better end. *Psychological Science, 4*, 401–405.

Kelley, H. (1979). *Personal relationships.* Hillsdale, NJ: Erlbaum.

Kelly, J. R. (1988). Entrainment in individual and group behavior. In J. McGrath (Ed.), *The social psychology of time: New perspectives* (Vol. 91, pp. 89–110). Newbury Park, CA: Sage.

Keltner, D. (1994). *Emotion, nonverbal behavior and social conflict.* Paper presented to the Harvard Project on Negotiation, May, 1994.

Keltner, D., & Robinson, R. J. (1993). Imagined ideological differences in conflict escalation and resolution. *International Journal of Conflict Management, 4*, 249–262.

Kennedy, G., Benson, J., & McMillan, J. (1980). *Managing negotiations.* Englewood Cliffs, NJ: Prentice-Hall.

Kramer, R., Pommerenke, P., & Newton, E. (1993). The social context of negotiation: Effects of social identity and accountability on negotiator judgment and decision making. *Journal of Conflict Resolution, 37,* 633–654.

Kulik, J. A., Sledge, P., & Mahler, H. I. (1986). Self-confirmatory attribution, egocentrism, and the perpetuation of self-beliefs. *Journal of Personality and Social Psychology, 50,* 587–594.

Kumar, R. (1997). The role of affect in negotiations: An integrative overview. *Journal of Applied Behavioral Science, 33*(1), 84–100.

Lax, D. A., & Sebenius, J. K. (1986). *The manager as negotiator.* New York: Free Press.

Loewenstein, G., & Schkade, D. (1997). Wouldn't it be nice? Predicting future feelings. In E. Deiner, N. Schwartz, & D. Kahneman (Eds.), *Hedonic psychology: Scientific approaches to enjoyment, suffering, and well-being.* New York: Russell Sage Foundation.

Mitchell, T. R., Thompson, L., Peterson, E., & Cronk, R. (1997). Temporal adjustments in the evaluation of events: The "rosy view." *Journal of Experimental Social Psychology, 33,* 421–448.

Moore, D. A., Kurtzberg, T. R., Thompson, L., & Morris, M. W. (1998). *Long and short routes to success in electronically mediated negotiations: Group affiliations and good vibrations.* Working paper.

Nash, J. (1950). The bargaining problem. *Econometrica, 18,* 155–162.

Neale, M. A., & Bazerman, M. H. (1991). *Cognition and rationality in negotiation.* New York: Free Press.

Newcomb, T. M. (1961). *The acquaintance process.* New York: Holt, Rinehart, & Winston.

Nierenberg, G. I. (1968). *The art of negotiating.* New York: Barnes & Noble Books.

Nisbett, R. E., & Ross, L. (1980). *Human inference: Strategies and shortcomings of social judgement.* Englewood Cliffs, NJ: Prentice-Hall.

O'Quin, K., & Aronoff, J. (1981). Humor as a technique of social influence. *Social Psychology Quarterly, 44*(4), 349–357.

Osberg, T. M., & Shrauger, J. S. (1986). Self-prediction: Exploring the parameters of accuracy. *Journal of Personality and Social Psychology, 51,* 1044–1057.

Ottati, V., Terkildsen, N., & Hubbard, C. (1997). Happy faces elicit heuristic processing in a televised impression formation task: A cognitive tuning account. *Personality and Social Psychology Bulletin, 23*(11), 1144–1156.

Raiffa, H. (1982). *The art and science of negotiation.* Cambridge, MA: Harvard University Press.

Raven, B. H. (1990). Political applications of the psychology of interpersonal influence and social power. *Political Psychology, 11*(3), 493–520.

Redelmeier, D. A., & Kahneman, D. (1996). Patients' memories of painful medical treatments: Real-time and retrospective evaluations of two minimally invasive procedures. *Pain, 66*(1), 3–8.

Ross, L. (1977). The intuitive psychologist and his shortcomings: Distortions in the attribution process. In L. Berkowitz (Ed.), *Advances in experimental social psychology* (Vol. 10, pp. 173–200). New York: Academic Press.

Rothbart, M., & Hallmark, W. (1988). Ingroup–outgroup differences in the perceived efficacy of coercion and conciliation in resolving social conflict. *Journal of Personality and Social Psychology, 55,* 248–257.

Rouse, W., & Morris, N. (1986). On looking into the black box: Prospects and limits in the search for mental models. *Psychological Bulletin, 100,* 359–363.

Schelling, T. (1960). *The strategy of conflict.* Cambridge, MA: Harvard University Press.

Schwarz, N., & Bless, H. (1991). Happy and mindless, but sad and smart? The impact of affective states on analytic reasoning. In J. P. Forgas (Ed.), *Emotion and social judgments. International Series in Experimental and Social Psychology* (pp. 55–71). Oxford, UK: Pergamon Press.

Singelis, T. M. (1998). *Teaching about culture, ethnicity, and diversity: Exercises and planned activities.* Thousand Oaks, CA: Sage.

Siegel, S., & Fouraker, L. E. (1960). *Bargaining and group decision making.* New York: McGraw-Hill.

Skinner, B. F. (1938). *The behavior of organisms.* New York: Appelton, Century-Crofts.

Suh, E., Diener, E., & Fujita, E. (1996). Events and subjective well-being: Only recent events matter. *Journal of Personality and Social Psychology, 70,* 1091–1102.

Susskind, L., & Cruikshank, J. (1987). *Breaking the impasse: Consensual approaches to resolving public disputes.* New York: Basic Books.

Swann, W. B., Pehlam, B. W., & Roberts, D. C. (1987). Causal chunking: Memory inference in ongoing interaction. *Journal of Personality and Social Psychology, 53*(5), 858–865.

Thompson, L. (1995). The impact of minimum goals and aspirations on judgments of success in negotiations. *Group Decision Making and Negotiation, 4,* 513–524.

Thompson, L. (1998). *The mind and heart of the negotiator.* Upper Saddle River, NJ: Prentice-Hall.

Thompson, L., & Hastie, R. (1990). Social perception in negotiation. *Organizational Behavior and Human Decision Processes, 47*(1), 98–123.

Thompson, L., & Kim, P. (in press). How the quality of third parties' settlement solutions are affected by the relationship between negotiators. *Journal of Experimental Psychology: Applied.*

Thompson, L., Nadler, J., & Kim, P. (1999). Some like it hot: The case for the emotional negotiator. In L. Thompson, J. Levine, & D. Messick (Eds.), *Shared cognition in organizations: The management of knowledge* (pp. 139–161). Mahwah, NJ: Erlbaum.

Thompson, L., Valley, K. L., & Kramer, R. M. (1995). The bittersweet feeling of success: An examination of social perception in negotiation. *Journal of Experimental and Social Psychology, 31*(6), 467–492.

Ury, W. L., Brett, J. M., & Goldberg, S. B. (1988). *Getting disputes resolved: Designing systems to cut the costs of conflict.* San Francisco, CA: Jossey-Bass.

Vallone, R., Griffin, D., Lin, S., & Ross, L. (1990). The overconfident prediction of future actions and outcomes by self and others. *Journal of Personality and Social Psychology, 58,* 582–592.

Van Boven, L., & Thompson, L. (2000). *A look into the mind of the negotiator.* Paper presented at the Academy of Management meetings, Cincinnati, Ohio.

Varey, C., & Kahneman, D. (1992). Experiences extended across time: Evaluations of moments and episodes. *Journal of Behavioral Decision Making, 5,* 169–195.

Walton, R. E., & McKersie, R. B. (1965). *A behavioral theory of labor relations.* New York: McGraw-Hill.

Wegner, D. M., & Wenzlaff, R. M. (1996). Mental control. In E. T. Higgins & A. W. Kruglanski (Eds.), *Social psychology: Handbook of basic principles.* New York: Guilford Press.

Whorf, B. L. (1956). Science and linguistics. In J. B. Carroll (Ed.), *Language, thought, and reality. Selected writings of Benjamin Whorf.* New York: Wiley.

Wilson, T. D. (1985). Strangers to ourselves: The origins and accuracy of beliefs about one's own mental states. In J. H. Harvey & G. Weary (Eds.), *Attribution: Basic issues and applications* (pp. 9–36). Orlando, FL: Academic Press.

Wilson, T. D., & Dunn, D. S. (1986). Effects of introspection on attitude-behavior consistency: Analyzing reasons versus focusing on feelings. *Journal of Personality and Social Psychology, 22,* 249–263.

Wilson, T. D., Dunn, D. S., Kraft, D., & Lisle, D. J. (1989). Introspection, attitude change, and attitude-behavior consistency: The disruptive effects of explaining why we feel the way we do. In L. Berkowitz (Ed.), *Advances in experimental social psychology* (Vol. 19, pp. 123–205). San Diego, CA: Academic Press.

Wilson, T. D., & LaFleur, S. J. (1995). Knowing what you'll do: Effects of analyzing reasons on self-prediction. *Journal of Personality and Social Psychology, 68,* 21–35.

Wilson, T. D., Lisle, D. J., Schooler, J., Hodges, S. D., Klaaren, K. J., & LaFleur, S. J. (1993). Introspecting about reasons can reduce post-choice satisfaction. *Personality and Social Psychology Bulletin, 19*, 331–339.

Wilson, T. D., Hodges, S. D., & LaFleur, S. J. (1995). Effects of introspecting about reasons: Inferring attitudes from accessible thoughts. *Journal of Personality and Social Psychology, 69*, 16–28.

Wilson, T. D., & Schooler, J. (1991). Thinking too much: Introspection can reduce the quality of preferences and decisions. *Journal of Personality and Social Psychology, 60*, 181–192.

Wortman, C. B., & Silver, R. C. (1989). The myths of coping with loss. *Journal of Consulting and Clinical Psychology, 57*, 349–357.

Yukl, G. (1974). Effects of the opponent's initial offer, concession magnitude and concession frequency on bargaining behavior. *Journal of Personality and Social Psychology, 30*(3), 323–335.

CHAPTER FIVE

Mood and Emotion in Groups

Janice R. Kelly

Speculation about how moods and emotions affect group life have been an important part of psychological inquiry for decades. The concept of emotional "contagion" has been with us since Le Bon's (1896) early writings on crowd behavior and McDougall's (1923) writings on the group mind. Patterns of emotional behavior were also an important part of group development theories since the writings of Bion (1961) and Tuckman (1965). In addition, the emotional strain involved in task performance was an integral part of Bales' (1950) theory of equilibrium processes and phase movement in groups.

Over the past few decades, individual-level researchers investigating social phenomena have acknowledged that moods and emotions have profound influences on many areas of cognitive functioning. For example, mood has been found to affect aspects of persuasion and person perception, and it appears to do so through influencing the processes of memory, attention, and type of information processing (Forgas, 1992). More recently, however, it has been acknowledged that many aspects of affective phenomena have interpersonal antecedents and consequences (Wallbott & Sherer, 1986), and that emotional expression has an important impact on social interaction. Thus research should logically be directed toward examining the effects of mood and emotion on interpersonal interaction among group members.

The purpose of this chapter is to briefly review some of the past and the present research on mood and emotion in groups by examining two broad categories of effects – affect as an index of group development, and affect as a compositional factor. A series of questions that may be useful in directing future research efforts are then presented.

Types of emotional experience

Although the concept of group emotional life has been central to many theories of group structure and development, precise definition and measurement of group mood or emotion has not received a great deal of attention. For example, group emotion has been measured by the number of socio-emotional communicative acts (Bales, 1950; Tuckman, 1965) or by questionnaire measures of affective ties between group members (Mudrack, 1989). Researchers have also defined a variety of types of emotional experiences that may occur primarily in group settings. For example, the concept of "group cohesiveness" refers to the affective ties that bind a group together, or to a sense of solidarity or esprit de corp that may develop over the course of group interaction (Hogg, 1992; 2001). More recently, George (1990) coined the term "group affective tone" to describe the characteristic level of positive or negative affect experienced by some groups. These varied definitions and measures of group emotion reflect large differences in the underlying type of affect experienced by the group, and this chapter will retain such a broad definition.

Individual-level researchers have also described a variety of different types of affective experiences. The term "affect" is a general term used to describe a variety of feeling states including mood, emotion, and dispositional affect. However, researchers have tended to make distinctions between "mood" and "emotion" along a number of different dimensions (Isen, 1984). Emotions tend to be more intense in nature than are moods and tend to be target specific – that is, they are often directed toward a specific provoking stimulus. Moods, on the other hand, are more diffuse, and can potentially affect a wider range of stimuli (Frijda, 1986). Finally, emotions tend to be labeled with specific emotions terms, such as anger, happiness, and sadness (Plutchik, 1980), whereas moods tend to be labeled simply along a positive-negative or pleasant-unpleasant dimension (Nowlis, 1960). In contrast to both mood and emotion, "dispositional affect" describes a generalized tendency on the part of an individual to react in characteristically positive or negative ways to a range of stimuli (Watson & Clark, 1984). Since individual-level affective experiences may combine to form a group-level affective experience, all of these different individual-level and group-level affective terms are important in the understanding of the effects of mood and emotion on group experience.

Group Development

This section examines emotional factors that are involved in studies of group development. In general, studies of group development try to account for regular patterns of emotional expression as groups progress toward group goals. That is, group development researchers try to account for patterns of growth and change that occur as a group moves from the beginning to the end of its life cycle. Most models of group development assume that groups pass through predictable stages or phases as they develop, with each stage characterized by particular socio-emotional challenges and outcomes.

Bales' research on phase movement in groups

Research on group development has been ongoing for nearly 50 years, beginning with Bales and Strodbeck's (1951) pioneering work on phases that occur in decision-making groups. A number of researchers have posited that group movement toward particular goal states involves both progress in group locomotion activities (Festinger, 1950) and progress in group maintenance activities (Thibaut & Kelley, 1959) or emotional repair and well-being. Bales and colleagues (Bales, 1950; Bales & Slater, 1955; Bales & Strodbeck, 1951) proposed that, in fact, group progress involved alternating attention devoted to two sets of concerns – instrumental, or task-related concerns and expressive, or socio-emotional concerns.

According to Bales (1950), these concerns manifest themselves in terms of a series of continual shifts to establish equilibrium between instrumental and expressive activities, both at a micro act-by-act level and a more macro or phase level throughout the problem-solving session. The micro-level shifts were predicted by the equilibrium hypothesis, which posited that action in one set of activities (e.g., instrumental activities) created tension in the other set of activities (e.g., expressive activities). When tension becomes too high, progress toward the group goal ceases until that tension is reduced by reparative action in the corresponding category. Thus, groups continually cycle between instrumental and expressive communicative acts.

Bales also described macro-level shifts that corresponded to phase movements in the group. On the instrumental side, groups engage in activities concerning first orientation, then evaluation, and then control as the group progresses from the beginning to the end of a problem-solving session. To reflect the idea of an equilibrium between instrumental and expressive concerns, Bales also proposed corresponding activity in expressive categories. Both positive and negative socio-emotional acts increase from the beginning to the end of a session, as groups move from the relatively unemotional orientation stage to the more controversial control stage. Thus, for Bales, emotional expression was a central part of group functioning and performance.

Bales' (1950) work also included the development of a structured set of categories for observing communicative acts within problem-solving groups in order to systematically document the idea of both phase movement and equilibrium processes in groups. A consistent finding was that two kinds of leaders tended to differentiate in groups – a task specialist and a socio-emotional specialist (Parsons & Bales, 1955). Bales and his colleagues speculated that this differentiation was one way of dealing with the equilibrium problem. The strain created by the task specialist was best handled by a second, more socio-emotional leader. Elements of these two styles or specialties can be seen in more modern leadership theories, including Fiedler's contingency model (1981), Blake and Mouton's leadership grid (1964), and Hersey and Blanchard's theory of situational leadership (1976).

Models of group development

Since that time, literally hundreds of group development studies have been conducted, and the majority of studies and theories about group development highlight the importance of the group dealing with emotional issues. For example, Bennis and Shepard (1956), through their observations of T-groups, proposed that groups pass through two major phases of development, the first including issues of authority and structure, and the second including issues of intimacy and interdependence. Bion (1961) suggested that groups must work on emotionality issues, expressed in terms of dependency, fight/flight, or pairing, in order for progress toward group goals to continue. Tuckman (1965), in reviewing and integrating the existing literature on group development, proposed that groups go through identifiable phases of forming, storming, norming, and performing, with a final stage of adjourning added later by Tuckman and Jensen (1977). The storming stage in particular is one that is fraught with conflict as group members vie for status and roles within the group.

Since those researchers were primarily interested in group development in therapy groups, the emotional importance of the group and resolving emotionally laden issues was obviously central. However, studies developed on laboratory groups also suggest similar emotionally laden stages. For example, Schutz's (1966) model of group development focused on member needs at various periods throughout the group's life cycle. The first need is for inclusion and a sense of belonging to the group. Need for control is reflected by a struggle to sort out power and authority issues among group members. Finally, an affection need is reflected in work on interpersonal relations within the group.

More recently, Wheelen (1990, 1994) has proposed a model of group development that integrates findings from both therapy and laboratory groups. She notes that there are commonalities among proposed models regardless of type of group to which the model has been applied, length of time that the group interacts, and other variations, and these commonalities are described in her five-stage model. Stage 1, *Dependency and Inclusion*, is characterized by member dependency on the group leader and by initial polite attempts at determining group structure. Thus, this stage is characterized by emotional control rather than emotional expression. Stage 2, *Counterdependency and Fight*, is characterized by conflict among members and leader. Similar to the "storming" phase in Tuckman's (1965) model, negative affect is most prevalent. However, this conflict is assumed to be essential to the development of cohesion and the establishment of shared values. Stage 3, *Trust and Structure*, is characterized by the more mature determination of the elements of group structure and performance norms. Stage 4, *Work*, is characterized by effective progress toward group goals. Finally, Stage 5, *Termination*, is reflected in evaluation of past work, feedback, and the expression of feelings about fellow group members. Thus, emotionality also characterizes the final stage of group development.

Many of the past models reviewed above make particular assumptions about both the universality of the proposed stages and the need for groups to pass through each phase in succession. Other models are more cyclical in nature, positing that certain stages may recur as group members confront similar issues at a later date (Arrow, 1997). Still other theorists propose that group development cannot be characterized by phases or stages, but rather that sets of activities, including activities devoted to both group locomotion and group maintenance, occur simultaneously. Poole's contingency model (1983), for example, suggests that groups engage in three intertwining sets of activities involving task, relational, and topical focuses. Thus, group emotional work occurs simultaneously with group task work. McGrath's (1991) TIP model also describes groups as simultaneously engaging in work devoted to satisfying production, well-being, and member support functions.

Summary of group development

Theories of group development view group emotions as being a necessary part of group progress. Group emotion is a part of or a reaction to instrumental group work, and thus is a necessary part of the pacing of the group as it progresses toward its group goal. Group stages or cycles are characterized or defined by different types of emotional activity, and thus can serve as an index of the group's maturity.

Group development theories therefore view group emotions as arising from the natural consequences of interaction between group members over time. That is, different emotions are evoked at different times and the emotions that arise stem from the activities of the group itself. The next section, involving affective group composition, examines mood and emotion more as a characteristic of the group as a whole.

Affect as a Factor in Group Composition

The term "group composition" is used here in a very broad sense and includes what other researchers may at times describe as input conditions or at times as consequences of group interaction. The focus of this section is on the affective experience of the group as a whole, both in terms of group-level emotional experience (cohesiveness) and in terms of individual-level emotional experiences that form the parts of a group (manipulated mood). A number of broad categories of effects are examined including emotional contagion, group affective tone, and mood as a manipulated input variable to the group experience.

Emotional contagion

"Emotional contagion" refers to the process whereby the moods and emotions of those around us influence our own emotional state. That is, it is the process through which we "catch" other people's emotions. Although originally theorized in the context of patholo-gical crowd behavior (Le Bon, 1896) or the "group mind" (McDougall, 1923), more recent research has focused on the more commonly occurring day-to-day forms of emotional con-tagion that can occur from mere exposure to others' emotional states. Hatfield, Cacioppo, and Rapson (1993, 1994) call this "primitive emotional contagion," a relatively automatic and unconscious tendency to "mimic and synchronize facial expressions, vocalizations, pos-tures, and movements with those of another person and, consequently, to converge emotion-ally" (Hatfield et al., 1992). Contagion in general is thought to be multiply determined by a package of psychophysiological, behavioral, and social phenomena. It can elicit similar responses in a target (smiling back at someone else's smile, Hinsz, 1991) or complementary responses (countercontagion, such as when a parent finds a child's anger to be amusing). Further, Hatfield et al. (1993) argue that emotional contagion produces the important consequence of synchrony or entrainment of attention, emotion, and behavior and argue that this synchrony has an adaptive function for social entities.

A number of basic processes have been proposed to account for emotional contagion. For example, emotional contagion may occur through basic learning processes. Emotional contagion can be a conditioned emotional response, such as when two people's affective experiences are habitually linked, or an unconditioned emotional response, such as when a loud voice causes momentary fear. Hatfield et al. (1993, 1994) focus on interactional mimicry and synchrony, the automatic imitation and coordination of facial features, movements, and vocal rhythms that can occur in interaction, as a potential process underlying emotional contagion. People seem to automatically mimic the facial, movement, and vocal rhythms of others, and, as a consequence of feedback from this mimicry, "catch" their emotions.

McIntosh, Druckman, and Zajonc (1994) use the somewhat more general term "socially induced affect" to refer to situations where one person's affect is induced or caused by another person's affect. They feel that the causal implications of the term "induction" are more appropriate than the transference implied by the term "contagion." Further, "induction" denotes that some kind of affective experience, although not necessarily an identical one, is induced in another person. In their review of the literature, McIntosh et al. (1994) find stronger evidence for concordant rather than discordant socially induced affect, and suggest that the strength of the affect induced may be a function of how similar or well liked the source is by the target. They also suggest that plausible mechanisms involved in socially induced affect involve contagion, conditioning, and mimicry.

A third, related concept that has received some research attention involves behavioral entrainment (Condon & Ogston, 1967; Kelly, 1988; McGrath & Kelly, 1986) or interaction synchrony (Warner, 1988). Behavioral entrainment refers to the processes whereby one person's behavior is adjusted or modified in order to coordinate or synchronize with another's behavior. Synchrony usually refers to the coordination of both micro- or macrobody movements, but has also been used more broadly to refer to the coordination of affect and attitudes between interacting partners (Siegman & Reynolds, 1982). The outcome of this synchrony, generally, is positive affect, which can take the form of liking for the partner (Kelly, 1987), satisfaction with the interaction (Bernieri, Reznich, & Rosenthal, 1988), or greater group rapport (Tickle-Degnen & Rosenthal, 1987). Thus, with behavioral entrainment, affect arises as a byproduct of smooth interaction rather than as the result of transference.

Evidence for emotional contagion.   There is very strong evidence for many of the processes that are proposed to underlie emotional contagion (and socially induced affect or behavioral entrainment as well). A number of researchers have found evidence for many forms of behavioral synchrony, including synchrony in conversational rhythms (Jaffe & Feldstein, 1970; Warner, 1988), nonverbal behavior (Tickle-Degnen & Rosenthal, 1987), and more general interaction behavior (Bernieri, 1988). Evidence for facial mimicry has also been identified (Bavelas, Black, Lemery, & Mullett, 1987). In sum, there is plentiful evidence that we mimic or synchronize with the emotional behavior of others (Hatfield et al., 1994).

Evidence is also found for the effect of facial, postural, and vocal feedback influencing our own emotional state. A number of researchers, drawing on the facial feedback hypothesis, have demonstrated that the manipulation of facial muscles involved in the expression of particular emotions influences the degree to which the model experiences those emotions (Duclos, Laird, Schneider, Sexter, Stern, & Van Lighten, 1989; Larsen, Kasimatis, & Frey, 1990; Strack, Martin, & Stepper, 1988). Duclos et al. (1989) report evidence that postural feedback may also intensify emotional experience.

Finally, evidence for the convergence of emotional experience can be found in many areas of research, including developmental, clinical, social, and psychophysiological areas (see

Hatfield et al., 1994, for a review). In addition, there is some evidence that such synchrony and convergence are an important component in group rapport (Tickle-Degnen & Rosenthal, 1987).

Individual differences in emotional contagion susceptibility or transmission. A variety of individual difference factors have been proposed that suggest that certain kinds of people may be more likely to "catch" the emotions of others and other kinds of people may be better at transferring their emotions. For example, people who are high in feelings of interrelatedness, who are good decoders of emotional expressions, and who score high on emotional contagion scales are more likely to catch the emotions of those around them (Hatfield et al., 1994). Women, perhaps by serving as a proxy variable for the factors listed above, may also be more likely than men to be susceptible to emotional contagion effects.

On the other hand, people who are high in nonverbal expressiveness seem to be better able to transmit their emotions to others (Sullins, 1989, 1991). Hatfield et al. (1993) also suggest that transmitters must be able to feel, or at least to express, strong emotions, and that they should be relatively insensitive to those who are experiencing incompatible emotions. Their recent work with the emotional contagion scale (Doherty, Orimoto, Hebb, & Hatfield, 1993) also supports the notion of individual differences.

Emotional contagion and group composition. The process of emotional contagion implies that group members, if composed of people who are at least somewhat susceptible to emotional contagion, will converge in affect over time leading to a more or less affectively homogeneous group composition. That is, unless, particular limiting conditions are in place that prevent emotional contagion, groups working together over time should come to display similar levels of positive or negative affect. Some recent research also suggests that a group leader, especially one who is high in expressiveness, may be particularly likely to influence the emotional characteristics of his or her group. Barsade and Gibson (1998) suggest that knowledge of the emotional state of highly influential people in groups, or knowledge of extremities of the emotion of influential persons in groups may be important in determining group affective composition.

In addition, it is plausible that pessimistic or negatively toned groups may dissolve over time, while optimistic or positively toned groups would be more likely to be maintained, especially when referring to voluntary groups. What is the evidence for affective convergence in groups and what are the consequences of such emotional homogeneity?

Group affective tone

George (1990, 1996) has recently proposed that, not only can many groups be characterized by a homogeneous or internally consistent level of affect or "group affective tone," but also that these characteristic levels of affect can affect a variety of responses or behaviors within the group (George, 1991, 1995; George & Brief, 1992). For example, in a study of sales teams, George (1990) found that group affective tone, as measured by aggregating the teams' dispositional positive and negative affect, predicted a number of important outcomes.

Mean positive dispositional affect levels were negatively correlated with absenteeism, while mean negative dispositional affect levels were negatively correlated with customer directed pro-social behavior. Later work showed important associations between group affective tone as measured by aggregating reports of team member mood state and team performance.

More generally, an optimistic or positive emotional or affective tone is often cited as an important factor in many successful groups. For example, cohesion is often implicated in successful performance of various types of groups (Evans & Dion, 1991; Mullen & Copper, 1994). Other studies have shown that a positive emotional character, or "internal group harmony" can be the most important component in determining the quality of group outcomes (Hackman, 1991; Williams & Sternberg, 1988).

George (1996) argues that, although not all groups may possess a group affective tone, a number of processes work toward producing consistent levels of affect within particular groups. For example, borrowing from Schneider's (1987) attraction–selection–attrition framework, George suggests that people with similar levels of dispositional affect may be attracted to and form particular groups, and those with a dissimilar dispositional affect may leave that particular group, leading to a group composed primarily of persons with similar levels of dispositional affect. She also suggests that group members are exposed to similar types of tasks and similar group outcomes which commonly influence their level of group affect. Furthermore, she suggests that group members may be actively socialized as to a group's affective tone, thus ensuring consistency in this measure across time.

George (1990, 1996) proposes that group affective tone is a distinctively group-level concept. Group affective tone only exists when a group demonstrates high levels of inter-member consistency with respect to reports of affect levels. If such consistency exists, then individual-level reports of affect may be combined into a group average which reflects the group's affective tone. If intermember consistency does not exist (George suggests using James, Denaree, & Wolf's, 1984, method of estimating within-group interrater reliability), then an affective tone does not exist for that particular group.

Homogeneity versus heterogeneity of group affect.   George's work suggests that important outcomes are associated with homogeneous levels of positive or negative affect within a group. However, Barsade and Gibson (1998) point out that gains or positive group outcomes are potentially associated with either homogeneity or heterogeneity in affective composition. With respect to the positive benefits of group affective homogeneity, they cite studies suggesting positive relationships between personality composition and performance in groups, noting that many personality variables (such as extroversion or neuroticism) have distinctively emotion-laden implications (Mann, 1959). Furthermore, they suggest that affect is a dimension upon which people judge similarity to one another, and that based upon the well-known similarity-attraction findings (Byrne, 1971), affective homogeneity or similarity should lead to higher levels of member attraction or cohesion. As a consequence, group members should feel more comfortable with each other, should engage in more cooperative behavior, and thus should attain more positive group outcomes.

It is also possible that particular levels of homogeneous affect may prove detrimental to group performance. For example, there is some evidence that cohesiveness has a curvilinear relationship to group creativity (Lott & Lott, 1965; Woodman, Sawyer, & Griffin, 1993).

That is, both very high and very low levels of interpersonal cohesiveness were detrimental to creative performance. Such a curvilinear relationship may also exist for the relationship between particular homogeneous mood states and performance. For example, it is possible that extremes of both positive and negative moods will be associated with poorer performance than more moderate levels.

Barsade and Gibson (1998), citing organizational evidence of the benefits of heterogeneity, also point out that affective similarity in particular circumstances may also lead to negative consequences. For example, a group composed of members with high negative dispositional affect may be unduly pessimistic and unproductive. Drawing from the need compatibility literature, they argue that diversity of affective types may also lead to positive group outcomes, especially when dealing with specific emotions, such as anger or euphoria, which may need to be tempered in order for progress to be made. Extreme heterogeneity of moods, however, may also be disruptive to the smooth flow and coordination of efforts necessary for effective performance.

Cohesiveness. Group cohesiveness might be considered to be a special type of group affective tone, although one that is more limited in range of emotional expression and perhaps more cognitively mediated. Group cohesiveness generally describes emotional attraction among group members, although other types or dimensions of cohesiveness, such as commitment to the task or group pride, have also been identified (Mullen & Copper, 1994).

The literature on cohesiveness is vast and has been well reviewed in previous literature (Evans & Dion, 1991; Hogg, 1992; Mudrack, 1989; Mullen & Copper, 1994). In general, however, studies have shown that cohesive groups are better able to place pressure on their members toward uniformity in behavior and conformity to group norms (Festinger, 1950; Hackman, 1991; Hogg, 1992). In addition, a recent review of the literature suggests that there is a positive relationship between cohesiveness and group performance (Mullen & Copper, 1994), although this relationship is small in magnitude. The cohesiveness–performance relationship is stronger when cohesiveness is defined in terms of commitment to the group task rather than as emotional attraction. In addition, there seems to be a more direct relationship from performance to cohesiveness than from cohesiveness to performance. Further, cohesiveness–performance relationships were stronger in small groups and real groups, and especially strong among intact sport teams. It may be interesting in the future to investigate whether the basic findings concerning cohesiveness generalize to other positive affective experiences in groups as well.

Manipulation of mood in groups

One way of creating affectively homogeneous or heterogeneous groups, of course, is to manipulate the mood of individuals coming together into a group situation. Research taking this approach, however, is in its infancy. Since the few studies conducted in this area draw on individual-level findings and theories in order to formulate their hypotheses, this section will start with a brief review of past individual-level findings with respect to mood and social judgments.

A number of researchers have reported results that suggest that mood states bias judgments in a manner that is consistent with the mood that was induced (Isen, 1975, 1984; Tversky & Kahneman, 1973). That is, positive moods bias judgments in a positive manner, whereas negative moods bias judgments in a negative manner. These findings are generally interpreted based on the concept that mood states are linked in memory with other associated concepts. Mood can then influence social judgments and evaluations through a number of different processes, such as the priming of mood-consistent associations that influence the interpretation of ambiguous information, and directing attention to mood-consistent information.

Other researchers have focused on the effect that mood states have on information processing (Forgas, 1992; Sinclair & Mark, 1992; Worth & Mackie, 1987). In their integrative model, for example, Sinclair and Mark (1992) argue that mood states lead to changes in cognitive capacity, mood maintenance/repair strategies, and/or the use of mood as information, and that these factors in turn account for the heuristic versus systematic processing differences found for positive versus negative mood states. Forgas's (1992) AIM model also assumes that affect can play dual roles in judgments in that it can affect both processing and informational influences.

Still other researchers have focused primarily on the information value that a mood state may have with respect to a given situation (Schwarz & Clore, 1988) and how that information value may impact information processing, in part to account for the often asymmetrical effects of positive and negative moods. This "mood-as-information" approach suggests that a positive mood signals that the situation is benign and not worthy of further attention. Therefore, people in happy moods tend to engage in less effortful or vigilant information processing. Negative moods, on the other hand, signal potential threat, and lead individuals in negative moods to engage in effortful and systematic processing of information. Although the mood-as-information approach may also sometimes predict mood consistent effects in judgments, it focuses more on the information-processing strategies that underlie mood effects.

All of these models may be important in predicting and explaining the effects of mood and emotion in group situations. However, only a handful of studies have actually examined the effects of induced mood on any type of group situation. Forgas (1990), for example, induced positive, negative, or neutral moods in individual or group participants and asked them to make ratings of nine person categories on a number of dimensions. Consistent with previous research, individual judgments were biased in a mood-consistent manner, such that happy individuals made more positive judgments, and sad individuals made more negative judgments, compared to controls. The effect of being in a group was to accentuate the bias of positive moods, with happy groups making even more positive judgments, but to attenuate the bias of negative moods, with sad groups making less extreme negative judgments. Presumably, group members in negative moods engaged in more controlled information processing, and thus were not as influenced by mood state. These results are somewhat consistent with work that examines groups under stress. For example, Staw, Sandelands, and Dutton (1981) have reported that stressful environments lead to more rigid information processing, similar to negative moods leading to more systematic processing of information.

A few studies have also examined the effect of mood states on cooperative behavior among small group members. For example, Hertel and Fiedler (1994) examined the effects of induced positive and negative moods on cooperative and competitive behavior in a four-person prisoner's dilemma game. They found that positive mood states did not directly increase cooperative behavior, but rather increased the variability of responses. Across blocks of trials, positive mood subjects' most cooperative responses were more cooperative, and their most competitive responses were more competitive, than negative mood subjects. In a more recent study (Hertel, Neuhof, Theurer, & Kerr, under review), the effects of positive and negative moods were examined in the context of a chicken dilemma game. The results here suggested that the reliance on heuristics exhibited by individuals in positive moods increased adherence to salient norms in the situation, such as imitation of partners' behavior. Negative moods induced more systematic processing of information and led to a more rational decision-making strategy, such that individuals defected when others' cooperation was high, but cooperated when others' cooperation was low.

Group researchers are beginning to examine more fully the meaning and the effects of information processing in groups (Hinsz, Tindale, & Vollrath, 1997). It is likely that such research will also begin to integrate the implications of affective influences on information processing as well. As it does, there are some important issues to consider. Some conceptual issues include: Is group information processing analogous to individual information processing? Is group mood or emotion something other than the sum of individual affective experiences? Methodological questions include: Is a group mood an emergent property of a group, or is it something that can be induced or produced from combining the moods of the individual group members? For example, if a group is successful at working on a task and comes to feel good, is that the same as grouping good-feeling individuals together into a group. In addition, can we develop a reliable group-level measure of group mood? These important methodological and conceptual issues will undoubtedly be explored in the near future.

Questions for Future Research

The bodies of literature reviewed above describe a variety of approaches to theorizing and investigating various affective phenomena in groups. These approaches differ greatly in how they treat emotional phenomena in groups. Some describe emotionality as a process of interpersonal interaction. Some treat emotionality as a group-level descriptor that sets the context for group performance. Others use emotionality to describe regularly appearing sequences of behavior. The following section suggests a useful model for integrating some of the past research on mood and emotion in groups and for suggesting new areas of investigation.

The input–process–outcome model presents a typical way of thinking about small groups (Hackman & Morris, 1975; McGrath, 1984). The input–process–outcome model assumes that various input characteristics, such as task type, group structure, and individual differences, have their impact on group performance through their effect on group process. Such a framework might be useful for framing questions concerning the impact of mood and emotion on small groups. In particular, the model suggests that mood may affect group performance directly or interactively as an input characteristic, as a context or component of group process, or as a consequence or outcome of group interaction. Possible effects of mood at these three points are suggested below.

Mood and emotion as an input characteristic

Mood or emotion may impact group performance either directly as an input characteristic, such as is suggested by the work of George (1990, 1996), or through interactive effects with other group input factors. For example, mood or emotion may interact with task characteristics or group structure to affect group performance.

A number of models of individual-level mood effects suggest that moods may impact the types of cognitive processing of information engaged in by individuals (Forgas, 1992; Schwarz & Clore, 1988; Sinclair & Mark, 1992). Specifically, positive moods seem to promote more heuristic processing of information, whereas negative moods seem to promote more systematic processing of information. If individual group members are engaging in these different types of processing modes, then group performance would seem to depend on the degree to which heuristic or systematic processing of information is appropriate for effective group performance on any particular task. For example, we might expect that positive moods and heuristic processing may facilitate performance on simple or routine tasks, or what have been referred to as "problems" (Katz & Kahn, 1978). On the other hand, more systematic processing of information prompted by negative moods may be more effective for complex or novel problems, or what have been referred to as "dilemmas" (Katz & Kahn, 1978).

Moods and emotions may also interact with aspects of group structure. For example, Ridgeway and Johnson (1990) describe how expressions of positive and negative affect in group interaction are tied to aspects of member status and group norms concerning the development of group solidarity. Norms operate, for example, to constrain the expression of negative socio-emotional behavior, whereas expressions of positive socio-emotional behavior are relatively uninhibited, especially with respect to low-status group members reacting to high-status group members. Norms for the expression of affect may differ from group to group (Hochschild, 1983). We might expect to find more homogeneity or regularity of expressions of affect in highly cohesive groups where norms for emotional expressions are likely to be more crystallized and enforced (Jackson, 1966).

Group size may moderate the effect of affect on group structure or performance. For example, as group size increases, cohesiveness decreases, norm enforcement decreases, and member participation rates become more disproportionate. As a consequence, one would expect less homogeneity of affect within these groups, and less crystallized norms for emotional expression. One might also find that, as group size increases, the emotional tone of a group is more heavily influenced by single individuals in higher status or more powerful positions in the group.

Leadership variables may also affect the affective structure of groups. For example, theories of transformational or charismatic leadership describe how a single particularly influential leader can profoundly shape the goals and the emotional character of groups (House &

Baetz, 1979). Charismatic leaders derive their influence in part by their ability as inspirational speakers, projecting an appealing and emotionally charged vision of the future. Followers in turn become highly emotionally attached to the group and expend great effort and sacrifice for the good of the group (Burns, 1978; House & Baetz, 1979).

Mood and emotion as a context or process of group interaction

Much of the group development literature focuses on how types of emotional expression are tied to fairly regular or consistent phases of group development. However, more recent work suggests that other temporal patterns of emotional expression may also exist. Gersick (1988), for example, has identified a midlife crisis for groups that is characterized by anxiety and worry about the group's current procedures for accomplishing its given task. Such an emotional crisis signals a change in group procedures to more effective strategies for continued progress toward group goals (Arrow, 1997; Gersick, 1988).

Recent literature also suggests that an emotional context may be dictated by aspects of organizational culture (Kunda, 1992; Van Maanen & Kunda, 1989). Specifically, organizations; may develop particular norms for emotional display that constrain the feelings and expression of emotion among organizational members (Hochschild, 1983; Van Maanen & Kunda, 1989). It is likely that such feeling and display norms also exist at the group level (Barsade & Gibson, 1998). We know, for example, that therapy groups attempt to establish norms encouraging the free expression of emotions (Stokes, 1983), whereas customer service personnel are encouraged to express only positive emotions (Hochschild, 1983). Further investigation of emotion norms in various contexts is warranted.

Mood and emotion as a consequence of group interaction

It, has already been suggested that a number of processes exist to push groups toward homogeneous levels of affect. For example, emotional contagion processes may cause group members to catch other group members' moods. Emotion norms may encourage only specific types of emotional expression. It therefore seems reasonable to assume that homogeneous levels of affect, or a group affective tone (George, 1990, 1996), will develop as a consequence of group interaction.

The particular character of this group affective tone, in turn, has implications for a number of different outcomes. For example, the positivity or negativity of affective expressions may have implications for the stability of the group. More negative or pessimistic groups may be more likely to have high member turnover rates and may be more likely to disband than groups that are more positive and optimistic in emotional tone.

More generally, however, the emotional consequence of a prior group interaction may serve as an input to a future group interaction (Levine & Moreland, 1990). In that way, the emotional life of a group takes on a more dynamic and cyclical character. In addition, all of the questions posed above may be qualified by consideration of more global issues, such as the stage of development the group is in or the physical and social environment surrounding the group interaction.

Conclusions

The importance of mood and emotion to group interaction and performance is once again becoming recognized. In the past, research attempting to document the emotional character of communication within the group, such as studies of group development and group interaction process analysis, proceeded somewhat independently of work on group outcome or performance. With our increased knowledge of affective influences on individual-level judgments and processing of information, and with the increased emphasis on teams and work groups in industrial and organizational settings, the importance of examining how group moods and emotions influence group-level judgments and information processing is now being recognized. The possible ways that mood and emotion can affect group interaction and performance noted above are only a partial list of importance influences. More questions will emerge as more researchers contribute to this important and growing area of research (see, for example, Thompson, Medvec, Seiden, and Kopelman, this volume, chapter 6).

REFERENCES

Arrow, H. (1997). Stability, bistability, and instability in small group influence patterns. *Journal of Personality and Social Psychology, 72,* 75–85.

Bales, R. F. (1950). *Interaction process analysis: A method for the study of small groups.* Reading, MA: Addison-Wesley.

Bales, R. F., & Slater, P. E. (1955). Role differentiation, In T. Parson, R. F. Bales, & E. A. Shils (Eds.), *Working papers in the theory of action.* Glencoe, IL: Free Press.

Bales, R. F., & Stodbeck, F. L. (1951). Phases in group problem solving. *Journal of Abnormal and Social Psychology, 46,* 485–495.

Barsade, S. G., & Gibson, D. E. (1998). Group emotion: A view from the top and bottom. In D. Gruenfeld, M. Mannix, & M. Neale (Eds.), *Research on managing groups and teams* (pp. 81–102). Stamford, CT: JAI Press.

Bavelas, J. B., Black, A., Lemery, C. R., & Mullett, J. (1987). Motor mimicry as primitive empathy. In N. Eisenberg & J. Strayer (Eds.), *Empathy and its development* (pp. 317–338). New York: Cambridge University Press.

Bennis, W. G., & Shepard, H. A. (1956). A theory of group development. *Human Relations, 9,* 415–437.

Bernieri, F. J. (1988). Coordinated movement and rapport in teacher-student interactions. *Journal of Nonverbal Behavior, 12,* 120–138.

Bernieri, F. J., Reznich, J. S., & Rosenthal, R. (1988). Synchrony, pseudosynchrony, and dissynchrony: Measuring the entrainment process in mother-infant dyads. *Journal of Personality and Social Psychology, 54,* 243–253.

Bion, W. R. (1961). *Experience in groups.* New York: Basic.

Blake, R. R., & Mouton, J. S. (1964). *The managerial grid.* Houston, TX: Gulf.

Burns, J. M. (1978). *Leadership.* New York: Harper.

Byrne, D. (1971). *The attraction paradigm.* New York: Academic Press.

Condon, W. S., & Ogston, W. D. (1967). A segmentation of behavior. *Journal of Psychiatric Research, 5,* 221–235.

Doherty, R. W., Orimoto, L., Hebb, J., & Hatfield, E. (1993). *Emotional contagion: Gender and occupational difference.* Unpublished manuscript, University of Hawaii, Honolulu.

Duclos, S. E., Laird, J. D., Schneider, E., Sexter, M., Stern, L., & Van Lighten, O. (1989). Emotion-specific effects of facial expressions and postures on emotional experience. *Journal of Personality and Social Psychology, 57,* 100–108.

Evans, C. R., & Dion, K. L. (1991). Group cohesion and performance: A meta-analysis. *Small Group Research, 22,* 175–186.

Festinger, L. (1950). Informal social communication. *Psychological Review, 57,* 271–282.

Fiedler, F. E. (1981). Leadership effectiveness. *American Behavioral Scientist, 24,* 619–632.

Forgas, J. P. (1990). Affective influences on individual and group judgments. *European Journal of Social Psychology, 20,* 441–453.

Forgas, J. P. (1992). Affect in social perceptions: Research evidence and an integrative model. In W. Stroebe & M. Hewstone (Eds.), *European review of social psychology* (Vol. 3, pp. 183–224). New York: Wiley.

Frijda, N. H. (1986). *The emotions.* Cambridge, UK: Cambridge University Press.

George, J. M. (1990). Personality, affect, and behavior in groups. *Journal of Applied Psychology, 75,* 107–166.

George, J. M. (1991). State or trait: Effects of positive mood on prosocial behaviors at work. *Journal of Applied Psychology, 76,* 299–307.

George, J. M. (1995). Leader positive mood and group performance: The case of customer service. *Journal of Applied Social Psychology, 25,* 778–794.

George, J. M. (1996). Group affective tone. In M. A. West (Ed.), *Handbook of work group psychology.* Chichester, UK: Wiley.

George, J. M., & Brief, A. P. (1992). Feeling good – doing good: A conceptual analysis of the mood at work-organizational spontaneity relationship. *Psychological Bulletin, 112,* 310–329.

Gersick, C. J. G. (1988). Time and transition in work teams: Toward a new model of group development. *Academy of Management Journal, 31,* 9–41.

Hackman, J. R. (1991). Group influences on individuals in organizations. In Marvin D. Dunnette & Laetta M. Hough (Eds.), *Handbook of industrial and organizational psychology* (Vol. 3, pp. 199–267). Palo Alto, CA: Consulting Psychologists Press.

Hackman, J. R., & Morris, C. G. (1975). Group tasks, group interaction process, and group performance effectiveness: A review and proposed integration. In L. Berkowitz (Ed.), *Advances in experimental social psychology* (Vol. 8, pp. 45–99). New York: Academic Press.

Hatfield, E., Cacioppo, J. T., & Rapson, R. (1992). Emotional contagion. In M. S. Clark (Ed.), *Review of personality and social psychology: Vol. 14. Emotion and social behavior* (pp. 151–177). Newbury Park, CA: Sage.

Hatfield, E., Cacioppo, J. T., & Rapson, R. (1993). Emotional contagion. *Current Directions in Psychological Science, 2,* 96–99.

Hatfield, E., Cacioppo, J. T., & Rapson, R. (1994). *Emotional contagion.* New York: Cambridge University Press.

Hersey, P., & Blanchard, K. H. (1976). Leader effectiveness and adaptability description (LEAD). In J. W. Pfeiffer & J. E. Jones (Eds.), *The 1976 annual handbook for group facilitators* (Vol. 5). La Jolla, CA: University Associates.

Hertel, G., & Fiedler, K. (1994). Affective and cognitive influences in a social dilemma game. *European Journal of Social Psychology, 24,* 131–145.

Hertel, G., Neuhof, J., Theuer, T., & Kerr, N. L. (under review). *Mood effects on cooperation in small groups: Does positive mood simply lead to more cooperation?*

Hinsz, V. B. (1991). Smile and (half) the world smiles with you, frown and you frown alone. *Personality and Social Psychology Bulletin, 17,* 586–592.

Hinsz, V. B., Tindale, R. S., & Vollrath, D. A. (1997). The emerging conceptualization of groups as information processors. *Psychological Bulletin, 121,* 43–64.

Hochschild, A. R. (1979). Emotion work, feeling *rules,* and social structure. *American Journal of Sociology, 85,* 551–575.

Hochschild, A. R. (1983). *The managed heart: Commercialization of human feelings.* Berkeley, CA: University of California Press.

Hogg, M. A. (1992). *The social psychology of group cohesiveness: From attraction to social identify.* New York: New York University Press.

Hogg, M. A. (2001). Social categorization, depersonalization and group behavior. In M. A. Hogg & S. Tindale (Eds.), *Blackwell handbook of social psychology: Group processes* (pp. 56–85). Oxford: Blackwell Publishing.

House, R. L., & Baetz, M. L. (1979). Leadership: Some empirical generalizations and new research directions. *Research in Organizational Behavior, 1,* 341–423.

Isen, A. M. (1975). *Positive affect, accessibility of cognitions, and helping.* Paper presented at the Eastern Psychological Association Convention.

Isen, A. M. (1984). Toward understanding the role of affect in cognition. In Robert S. Wyer & Thomas Srull (Eds.), *Handbook of social cognition* (pp. 179–236). Hillsdale, NJ: Erlbaum.

Jaffe, J., & Feldstein, S. (1970). *Rhythms of dialogue.* New York: Academic Press.

James, L. R., Demaree, R. G., & Wolf, G. (1984). Estimating within-group interrater reliability with and without response bias. *Journal of Applied Psychology, 69,* 85–98.

Jackson, J. (1966). A conceptual and measurement model for norms and roles. *Pacific Sociological Review, 9,* 35–47.

Katz, D., & Kahn, R. L. (1978). *The social psychology of organizations.* New York: Wiley.

Kelly, J. R. (1987). *Mood and interaction.* Unpublished dissertation, University of Illinois, Urbana-Champaign.

Kelly, J. R. (1988). Entrainment in individual and group behavior. In J. E. McGrath (Ed.), *The social psychology of time: New perspectives* (pp. 89–110). Newbury Park, CA: Sage.

Kunda, G. (1992). *Engineering culture: Control and commitment in a high-tech corporation.* Philadelphia, PA: Temple University Press.

Larsen, R. J., Kasimatis, M., & Frey, K. (1990). *Facilitating the furrowed brow: An unobtrusive test of the facial feedback hypothesis applied to negative affect.* Unpublished manuscript, University of Michigan, Ann Arbor.

Le Bon, G. (1896). *The crowd: A study of the popular mind.* London: Ernest Benn.

Levine, J. M., & Moreland, R. L. (1990). Progress in small group research. *Annual Review of Psychology, 41,* 585–634.

Lott, A., & Lott, B. (1965). Group cohesiveness as interpersonal attraction: A review of relationships with antecedent and consequent variables. *Psychological Bulletin, 64,* 259–309.

Mann, R. D. (1959). A review of the relationship between personality and performance in small groups. *Psychological Bulletin, 56,* 241–270.

McDougall, W. (1923). *Outline of psychology.* New York: Scribner.

McGrath, J. E. (1984). *Groups: Performance and interaction.* Englewood Cliffs, NJ: Prentice-Hall.

McGrath, J. E. (1991). Time, interaction, and performance (TIP): A theory of groups. *Small Group Research, 22,* 147–174.

McGrath, J. E., & Kelly, J. R. (1986). *Time and human interaction: Toward a social psychology of time.* New York: Guilford.

McIntosh, D. N., Druckman, D., & Zajonc, R. B. (1994). Socially induced affect. In D. Druckman & R. A. Bjork (Eds.), *Learning, remembering, believing: Enhancing human performance* (pp. 251–276). Washington, DC: National Academy Press.

Mudrack, P. E. (1989). Group cohesiveness and productivity: A closer look. *Human Relations, 9,* 771–785.

Mullen, B., & Copper, C. (1994). The relation between group cohesiveness and performance: An integration. *Psychological Bulletin, 115,* 210–227.

Nowlis, V. (1966). Research with the mood adjective checklist. In S. S. Tomkin & C. E. Izard (Eds.), *Affect, cognition, and personality* (pp. 352–389). New York: Springer.

Parsons, T. C., & Bales, R. F. (1955). *The family, socialization, and interaction process.* Glencoe, IL: Free Press.

Plutchik, R. (1980). *Emotion: A psychoevolutionary synthesis.* New York: Harper & Row.

Poole, M. S. (1983). Decision development in small groups: III. A multiple sequence model of group decision development. *Communication Monographs, 50,* 321–341.

Ridgeway, C., & Johnson, C. (1990). What is the relationship between socio-emotional behavior and status in task groups? *American Journal of Sociology, 95,* 1189–1212.

Schneider, B. (1987). The people make the place. *Personnel Psychology, 40,* 437–453.

Schutz, W. C. (1966). *The interpersonal underworld.* Palo Alto, CA: Science and Behavior Books.

Schwarz, N., & Clore, G. L. (1988). How do I feel about it? The informative function of affective states. In K. Fiedler & J. P. Forgas (Eds.), *Affect, cognition, and social behavior* (pp. 42–62). Göttingen, Germany: Hogrefe.

Siegman, A. W., & Reynolds, M. (1982). Interviewer-interviewee nonverbal communications: An interactional approach. In M. Davis (Ed.), *Interaction rhythms: Periodicity in communicative behavior* (pp. 249–277). New York: Human Sciences Press.

Sinclair, R. C., & Mark, M. M. (1992). The influence of mood state on judgment and action. In L. L. Martin & A. Tesser (Eds.), *The construction of social judgments* (pp. 165–193). Hillsdale, NJ: Erlbaum.

Staw, B. M., Sandelands, L. E., & Dutton, J. E. (1981). Threat-rigidity effects in organizational behavior: A multilevel analysis. *Administrative Science Quarterly, 26,* 501–524.

Stokes, J. P. (1983). Components of group cohesion: Intermember attraction, instrumental value, and risk taking. *Small Group Behavior, 14,* 163–173.

Strack, F., Martin, L. L., & Stepper, S. (1988). Inhibiting and facilitating conditions of facial expressions: A non-obtrusive test of the facial feedback hypothesis. *Journal of Personality and Social Psychology, 54,* 768–776.

Sullins, E. S. (1989). Perceptual salience as a function of nonverbal expressiveness. *Personality and Social Psychology Bulletin, 15,* 584–595.

Sullins, E. S. (1991). Emotional contagion revisited: Effects of social comparison and expressive style on mood convergence. *Personality and Social Psychology Bulletin, 17,* 166–174.

Thibaut, J. W., & Kelley, H. H. (1959). *The social psychology of groups.* New York: Wiley.

Tickle-Degnen, L., & Rosenthal, R. (1987). Group rapport and nonverbal behavior. *Review of Personality and Social Psychology, 9,* 113–136.

Tuckman, B. W. (1965). Developmental sequence in small groups. *Psychological Bulletin, 63,* 384–399.

Tuckman, B. W., & Jensen, M. A. C. (1977). Stages in small group development revisited. *Group and Organizational Studies, 2,* 419–427.

Tversky, A., & Kahneman, D. (1973). Availability: A heuristic for judging frequency and probability. *Cognitive Psychology, 5,* 207–232.

Van Maanen, J., & Kunda, G. (1989). Real feelings: Emotional expression and organizational culture. *Research in Organizational Behavior, 11,* 43–103.

Wallbott, H. G., & Scherer, K. R. (1986). The antecedents of emotional experiences. In Klaus R. Scherer, Harold G. Wallbott, & Angela B. Summerfield (Eds.), *Experiencing emotion: A crosscultural study* (pp. 69–97). Cambridge, UK: Cambridge University Press.

Warner, R. (1988). Rhythm in social interaction. In J. E. McGrath (Ed.), *The social psychology of time: New perspectives* (pp. 64–88). Newbury Park, CA: Sage.

Watson, D., & Clark, L. A. (1984). Negative affectivity: The disposition to experience aversive emotional states. *Psychological Bulletin, 96,* 465–490.

Wheelan, S. A. (1990). *Facilitating training groups.* New York: Praeger.

Wheelan, S. A. (1994). *Group processes: A developmental perspective.* Needham Heights, MA: Allyn & Bacon.

Williams, W. M., & Sternberg, R. (1988). Group intelligence: Why some groups are better than others. *Intelligence, 12,* 351–377.

Woodman, R. W., Sawyer, J. E., & Griffin, R. W. (1993). Toward a theory of organizational creativity. *Academy of Management Review, 18,* 293–321.

Worth, L. T., & Mackie, D. M. (1987). Cognitive mediation of positive affect in persuasion. *Social Cognition, 5,* 76–94.

CHAPTER SIX

Affect as a Cause of Intergroup Bias

David Wilder and Andrew F. Simon

In this chapter we will consider the role of affect in intergroup bias. Does a person's affective state influence the likelihood of engaging in bias against outgroups? Venerable common sense suggests a relationship. Whether at a rally before a football game or a political demonstration, agitation and emotional fervor appear to exacerbate hatred of rivals and enemies. Certainly the social psychological literature on the antecedents of aggression supports this premise. Research has consistently demonstrated that aversive stimuli generate anger which, in turn, frequently accentuates social aggression (e.g., Berkowitz, 1990, 1993). When our feelings are unpleasant, should we not be more distrustful of and hostile toward others? When our feelings are pleasant, should we not be more beneficent in our thoughts and behaviors?

Indeed, the proposition that affect affects intergroup bias surely seems redundant. Prejudice is an attitude toward members of a social group or category and therefore, as an attitude, has an affective component. More broadly, intergroup bias has traditionally been viewed as having three components: prejudice, stereotypes, and discrimination. Although conceptually distinct, these components of bias are related. In a recent literature review, Dovidio, Brigham, Johnson, and Gaertner (1996) reported a significant correlation of .32 between prejudice and discrimination among Whites. The classic treatise on prejudice by Gordon Allport (*The Nature of Prejudice*, 1954) is chock full of examples in which affect is both a cause and an effect of bias between groups.

Several theories of prejudice and intergroup bias have considered affect to be either a direct antecedent or a contributing factor to intergroup bias. In the theory of the authoritarian personality, Adorno and colleagues (Adorno, Frenkel-Brunswick, Levinson, & Sanford, 1950) argued that prejudice is the result of conflict and anxiety generated by children's relationships with their parents. Reflecting the influence of behaviorism and psychoanalytic theory, Dollard and associates (Dollard, Doob, Miller, Mowrer, & Sears, 1939) proposed that intergroup bias is the product of displaced hostility triggered by frustration. As a vast literature of aggression research would later demonstrate, frustration generates anger that, in turn, fosters harmful behaviors including aggression and discrimination (Berkowitz, 1990, 1993). The realistic conflict theory of prejudice (e.g., Levine & Campbell,

1972; Sherif, 1966) offered a similar argument: Conflict between groups over limited re-sources or incompatible goals gives rise to enmity between the groups which, in turn, is manifested in biased attitudes and behaviors. Social identity theorists (Tajfel, 1982; Turner, 1987) have hypothesized that one function of intergroup bias is to maintain and even enhance the self-esteem of group members. Consequently, threats to one's self-esteem should generate negative affect and foster bias against outgroups as a means of maintaining a favorable sense of self (Hunter, Platow, & Howard, 1996; Hunter, Platow, Bell, & Kypri, 1997; Lemyre & Smith, 1985; Messick & Mackie, 1989; Meindl & Lerner, 1984; Oakes & Turner, 1980).

Just as negative affect appears to foster bias, there is also evidence that persons respond to bias with intense negative reactions (Allport, 1954; Brewer, 1981; Campbell, 1975; Kramer & Messick, 1998; Stephan & Stephan, 1985; Trivers, 1971). Quite often this negative reaction takes the form of anger accompanied by a desire for retribution and revenge against the offending outgroup (Bies, 1987; Bies, Tripp, & Kramer, 1996). Although most likely to yield negative affect, victims of bias can at times take solace in making downward social comparisons to others who are even worse off than themselves (e.g., Wills, 1981).

Certainly those who perpetrate bias may derive both material and psychological benefit from their actions. Such benefit can include enhanced self-esteem (e.g., Hunter et al., 1996, 1997; Messick & Mackie, 1989). Nevertheless, engaging in bias does not inevitably yield positive affect. Inflicting bias can be a source of disquiet if retaliation is likely. In addition, bias may generate guilt if it violates personal standards or internalized norms of equity. Of course, rationalization and justification of bias may be attempted to assuage any discomfort. Furthermore, one need not engage in bias to reap its rewards nor suffer from bias to feel its pains. These effects can be experienced vicariously through shared membership in groups or empathy toward groups in which others mete out or receive bias.

Domain and Definitions

In this chapter we will review the theory and research that have examined how affective states influence the display of intergroup bias. Before plunging into this pool of research, we need to define "affect" and "bias." Affect refers to either a mood state or an emotion. An emotion, in turn, is a specific feeling that has an identifiable source and target (Isen, 1984, 1987). Emotions (e.g., anger, disgust, joy) often impel a person to act and are, therefore, considered "hot." A mood generally refers to a more diffuse feeling (e.g., unpleasantness) that is often less intense and less focused than an emotion. Distinctions between emotions and moods are not consistently made in this literature. Consequently, mood and emotion will be lumped together under the broader term, "affect." Thus, affect includes emotions such as fear and anger that are frequently provoked by specific threats as well as more diffuse moods such as happiness and sadness (Forgas, 1995).

Bias encompasses discrimination, prejudice, or stereotypes. Discrimination is differential treatment of groups because of their group labels; in particular, favoritism of one's own group (ingroup) relative to another group (outgroup) in the absence of a legitimate basis for that favoritism. Prejudice is dislike of an outgroup or greater liking of an ingroup relative to an outgroup. Stereotypes refer to beliefs about attributes or characteristics generally held by members of a group; especially beliefs that are unflattering or unfavorable.

Simply put, will the presence of affect increase or decrease bias between groups? Although it is a simple question, research does not answer with a simple yes or no. Part of this may be due to differences in procedures across studies and especially to differences in the manipulation of affective states. In the typical experiment, affect is induced and then subjects read about or interact with a member (or members) of an outgroup. Finally, subjects evaluate those outgroup members or the outgroup as a whole. For purpose of experimental control, the affect manipulation is usually independent of the outgroup and is induced in a number of ways such as giving subjects a reward (e.g., Dovidio, Gaertner, Isen, & Lawrence, 1995), threatening subjects with embarrassment or pain (e.g., Wilder & Shapiro, 1989a), asking subjects to recall a pleasant or unpleasant past event (e.g., Forgas, 1989), or having subjects read or view unpleasant information (e.g., Mackie, Queller, & Stroessner, 1994). Thus, manipulation of affect is usually independent of the outgroup (incidental affect) rather than caused by the outgroup (integral affect; Bodenhausen, 1993). Use of incidental affect avoids the confounding present in natural groups that have a specific affect associated with them.

The Impact of Affect on Bias: Explanations and Literature Review

Five reasonable hypotheses have been proposed by researchers to account for the relationships they have observed between affect and intergroup bias. These explanations are not mutually exclusive or necessarily independent of one another. Three of these (affect consistency, affect as information, affect infusion) are related in that they posit some degree of consistency between affective valence and intergroup judgments. The other two (mood and general knowledge, distraction) do not presume consistency between affect and judgments. Rather, the mood and general knowledge hypothesis predicts an asymmetry such that positive affect promotes superficial processing and the use of stereotypes whereas negative affect encourages more careful consideration of information. Finally, the distraction hypothesis argues that strong affect, regardless of valence, distracts the perceiver from careful attention to the outgroup and, consequently, leads to increased reliance on existing stereotypes and prejudice.

Affect consistency

Affect primes consistent cognitions and, therefore, disposes consistent behaviors. Positive affect should trigger positive cognitions and actions, and negative affect should foster negative thoughts and behaviors. This hypothesis fits with spreading-activation models of cognitive organization (e.g., Bower, 1981), cognitive consistency theories (e.g., Abelson et al., 1968), and learning theory based on temporal association (e.g., Byrne & Clore, 1970; Clore & Byrne, 1974; Staats & Staats, 1958; see also Zillman, 1983, for a conceptually similar argument that links arousal to aggression via excitation transfer). Extrapolating from these various, but convergent, approaches yields the simple prediction that the induction of positive affect should lessen negative affect, beliefs, and behavior directed toward an outgroup. If we are feeling good, then we should be less likely to respond unkindly to those around us. Conversely, negative affect should activate unpleasant thoughts and, therefore, encourage bias between groups.

In an experiment showing support for the affect consistency hypothesis, Forgas and Moylan (1991) showed subjects films that provoked either a positive, negative, or neutral mood. As part of an unrelated experiment, subjects viewed drawings of heterosexual dyads in which both persons were members of the same race or one person was Asian and one was Caucasian. Overall, subjects in a pleasant mood rated the stimulus persons more positively than subjects in an unpleasant mood did. In addition, there was a significant interaction between mood and the racial pairing: Subjects in a good mood rated the same-race and mixed-race pairs similarly; however, subjects in an unpleasant mood rated the mixed-race pairs as less competent and likable than the matched-race pairs. According to Forgas and Moylan, the mixed-race pairs presented a more complex, unusual stimulus for subjects and, therefore, demanded greater processing when evaluations were made. Consequently, a subject's mood was likely to influence judgments in a manner consistent with the literature on affect-cognition consistency (e.g., Bower, 1981; Isen, 1984). A negative mood made salient more negative conditions than a positive mood did.

Dovidio et al. (1995) also reported findings showing consistency between affect and judgments. When subjects were made happy, they responded more positively to members of an outgroup. Consistent with their theory of the benefits of a superordinate categorization, they found that subjects' perception of being in a common group with the target outgroup members mediated the relationship between affect and evaluation. Positive affect was significantly related to feelings of a common ingroup identity with members of the outgroup and that, in turn, was significantly predictive of a positive response to the outgroup.

Affect as information

Awareness of affect should instigate an attempt to explain it (Schachter & Singer, 1962). If the source of the affect is not apparent, the affect will be used as information to interpret the situation (Schwarz, 1990; Schwarz & Bless, 1991; Schwarz & Clore, 1988). The affect as information hypothesis can be viewed as a restricted relative of the affect consistency premise. The latter stipulates a generalization of affect to stimuli present when the affect is present. The former maintains that spreading occurs only when the affect has not been explained away; in other words, when the affect has not been compartmentalized and separated from ongoing thought. Therefore, if there is unexplained affect, predictions of the affect as information hypothesis should be similar to the affect consistency hypothesis. In an intergroup setting unexplained positive affect may be attributed to the outgroup and reduce bias whereas unexplained negative affect should exacerbate bias.

Affect infusion

Recently Forgas (1995) proposed the affect infusion model (AIM) to explain the influence of affect on social judgments. Forgas argued that the processing strategies a person adopts determine the extent to which affect infuses or influences judgments. He identified four judgmental strategies that perceivers use: direct access, motivated, heuristic, and substantive processing. Direct access (direct retrieval of stored information) and motivated processing (directed processing in response to motivational pressures; e.g., motivation to be accurate) result in little affect infusion. These strategies involve relatively narrow and closed search processes which, in turn, allow little opportunity for affect to influence cognition.

On the other hand, heuristic and substantive strategies are more constructive and take longer to complete. As a result, heuristic and substantive strategies afford more opportunity for affective states to influence information processing. Heuristic processing occurs when perceivers lack prior information and a strong motivational goal yet desire to minimize their effort. They, therefore, rely on shortcuts or heuristics (e.g., Brewer, 1988; Paulhus & Lim, 1994). Using heuristics opens judgments to the infusion of prevailing affect. Heuristic processing according to Forgas appears to be comparable to what others refer to as category-based processing (Brewer, 1988; Fiske & Neuberg, 1990) or peripheral processing (Petty & Cacioppo, 1986a, 1986b). Finally, substantive processing involves the selection and integration of novel information. This is the most complex type of judgment and requires the most cognitive effort. The process of learning and integrating new information opens perceivers to the influence of their current affective state. Substantive processing is similar, if not identical, to what others refer to as individual-based processing in which careful consideration is given to individuating or personal information about the targets (Brewer, 1988; Fiske & Neuberg, 1990). It is also reminiscent of the concept of central processing in the attitude change literature (Petty & Cacioppo, 1986a, 1986b).

Which strategy a perceiver adopts is determined by task requirements. In general, perceivers are thought to be cognitive misers and will adopt the processing strategy that requires the least effort yet is sufficient to be responsive to task and social demands. If affect does influence or infuse judgments, then it does so in a manner consistent with the mood state. Like the affect consistency hypothesis, the AIM model predicts greater intergroup bias when perceivers are experiencing negative affect. However, the AIM model forecasts mood effects only when perceivers use heuristic or substantive processing strategies.

In support of the affect infusion hypothesis, Forgas (1989, 1995) reported that atypical targets elicited longer and more elaborate processing by subjects. Longer processing resulted in greater mood infusion; that is, the effects of the subjects' mood state had more impact on judgments of targets when processing time increased. As a result, subjects in a positive mood made more favorable judgments of atypical targets. But those subjects who experienced a negative mood made more unfavorable judgments of atypical targets. The effect of mood state on outgroup judgments was mediated by the amount of time processing information about the outgroup targets which, in turn, was determined by the typicalness of the target. Thus, based on Forgas' findings, one would expect that judgments of atypical or unusual outgroup members will be more influenced by a perceiver's mood state than judgments of more representative outgroup members. Moreover, the direction of influence will be consistent with the valence of the mood state.

Mood and general knowledge

Mood may affect judgments by influencing a person's motivation to do detailed processing. Specifically, a positive mood may signal that the present situation is safe and, therefore, vigilance is unnecessary (Bless, 1994, cited in Bless, Schwarz, & Kemmelmeier, in press; Bless & Fiedler, 1995; Schwarz, 1990; Schwarz & Bless, 1991). On the other hand, a negative mood signals an aversive, and perhaps threatening, environment in which vigilance is important. Consequently, greater attention should be paid to the external environment under conditions of unpleasant than pleasant mood. This, in turn, should encourage more substantive examination of stimuli by persons in a negative mood state relative to those who are happy. The bottom line is that the use of stereotypes should be greater among happy than among sad or angry persons.

Evidence from the persuasion literature is consistent with this train of thought. Sad persons are more influenced by strong than by weak arguments which suggests that sadness fosters more substantive or central processing. On the other hand, happy persons are equally influenced by strong and weak arguments, indicative of heuristic or peripheral processing (Bless, Mackie, & Schwarz, 1992; Clore, Schwarz, & Conway, 1994; Fiedler, 1991; Mackie & Worth, 1989; Schwarz, Bless, & Bohner, 1991; Sinclair, Mark, and Clore, 1994).

Turning to research on affect and bias, Mackie and her colleagues have conducted a program of research examining the role of positive mood on bias (Mackie, Queller, Stroessner, & Hamilton, 1996; Stroessner & Mackie, 1993). Overall, they have found that positive affect is associated with greater stereotyping. Their findings are most easily explained by the mood as general knowledge and distraction hypotheses (to follow).

In one of their earlier investigations (Mackie, Hamilton, Schroth, Carlisle, Gersho, Meneses, Nedler, & Reichel, 1989), they had subjects read a series of trait statements about target persons following a mood induction. As the first of two experiments, subjects watched a videotape designed to create a happy, sad, or neutral mood. Then they read statements containing two attributes (either positive or negative) about fictitious persons who were either described as construction workers, lawyers, or policemen. Subjects estimated the frequency with which each trait had described the members of each job category. Results revealed an illusory correlation effect (Hamilton & Rose, 1980) in which subjects overestimated the association between stereotypic traits and occupations. Of interest was that the illusory correlation was strongest for happy subjects.

Stroessner and Mackie (1992) induced either a positive or a neutral mood using the manipulation cited in the last paragraph. Then all subjects read descriptions of members of an unnamed group. Descriptions gave trait information relevant to intelligence, sociability, stupidity, and friendliness. The variability of the information was manipulated so that subjects had information indicating either high or low variability of these traits among the unnamed target group. Subjects in the neutral mood condition accurately reported greater variability in the group when they had seen more variable information. However, subjects experiencing a positive mood reported relatively low variability (or greater homogeneity) even when they had seen highly variable information.

Mackie, Queller, and Stroessner (1994) examined the impact of a pleasant mood on perceptions of outgroup homogeneity by varying the dispersion of information inconsistent with stereotypes of a group. For some subjects stereotype inconsistent behavior was concentrated in a few group members; for other subjects the stereotype inconsistent information was dispersed across many group members. In the neutral mood condition, subjects accurately estimated less consistency and greater atypicality among group members when counterstereotypic information was dispersed. However, when subjects had experienced a positive mood, they reported that the information they had seen was typical and consistent with stereotypes in both the dispersed and concentrated conditions. Hence, a positive mood appeared to enhance perceptions of outgroup homogeneity which might well contribute to the development of stereotypes.

Using a similar procedure in which subjects were exposed to both stereotypic and nonstereotypic information about an outgroup, Stroessner and Mackie (1992) asked subjects to rate the extent to which two stereotypic and two nonstereotypic traits were represented in the group. Subjects in the neutral condition rated the group equally across the traits (which, as the authors argued, most likely reflected the mix of information given them). Happy subjects, however, rated the stereotypic traits as more characteristic of the group and the nonstereotypic traits as less characteristic of the group.

Bodenhausen, Kramer, & Susser (1994) also examined the relationship between positive mood and judgments of an outgroup. Consistent with research reported by Mackie and her colleagues, they found that positive mood led to greater stereotypic judgments of an outgroup target. In a series of experiments they found no evidence that this relationship was due to cognitive deficits such as distraction. (To do so, they used mood manipulations that were unlikely to diminish cognitive capacity such as smells and having subjects contort their faces to display the desired affect.) Apparently, subjects did not stereotype more because they were distracted by their pleasant mood and paid less attention to information about the outgroup target. However, this effect for happy mood was eliminated when subjects were made accountable for their judgments. The accountability manipulation presumably caused subjects to focus more carefully on the individuating information presented to them, so their judgments of the targets were less affected by group stereotypes.

In a series of experiments, Bless, Schwarz, and Kemmelmeier (in press) varied both the mood of subjects (happy, neutral, sad) and the consistency of a target person vis-à-vis subjects' expectations about the target person's group. Target characteristics were either positive or negative, and stereotypes of the target group were either positive or negative. When subjects were feeling sad, evaluations of the target person were influenced only by the valence of the individuating information. Sad subjects rated the target with positive characteristics more favorably than the target with negative characteristics. Stereotypes based on the target's group membership had no influence on judgments. On the other hand, subjects experiencing a happy mood rated the target most favorably when the target had positive characteristics and the target's group was also thought to be positive. Thus, subjects made more stereotypic judgments of the target outgroup member when his behavior matched the expectations of the outgroup. This finding is consistent with the general pattern that happy subjects stereotype more than sad subjects. However, when the target's characteristics were negative, happy subjects showed a contrast effect and rated the target most unfavorably when the target's group was positive.

Overall, these studies by Mackie, Bodenhausen, Bless and their co-authors have found that positive affect usually causes superficial processing and greater stereotyping. Among the five hypotheses presented at the outset of this section, their findings are most consistent with the mood as general knowledge hypothesis and the distraction hypothesis (discussed next) and less supportive of the consistency-based explanations (affect consistency, affect as information, affect infusion).

Distraction

Affect may sap attention from other ongoing activities. Attending to and coping with affect can distract a person from other stimuli and, consequently, may disrupt processing of other activities (Wilder & Simon, 1996). In an intergroup situation affect may distract a perceiver from the behavior of the outgroup. This possibility is based on the premise that attention is a zero-sum game. The more affect saps attention, the less there is available to deal with other activities. As a result, persons rely on well-learned habits (e.g., stereotypes) in lieu of careful attention to their immediate environment.

A similar argument has been made in other literatures. Research on helping has shown that sad moods sometimes increase and sometimes decrease helping. One determinant appears to be the focus of the sad person's attention. When attention is focused inwardly, helping decreases, in part, because need for aid may be less noticed (e.g., Pyszczynski & Greenberg, 1987). In addition, Fiske and Morlin (1996) have argued that anxiety due to powerlessness can lead to a reduction of processing capacity. One way in which this may occur is that the anxiety allows intrusive thoughts that interfere with attention to the task at hand.

Applied to intergroup relations, the distraction hypothesis predicts that strong affect should enhance reliance on existing prejudice and stereotypes when evaluating members of an outgroup. Strong affect should increase perceptions of outgroup homogeneity and, consequently, should lessen the impact of atypical behavior in the outgroup. The distraction hypothesis seems to be most applicable to situations involving relatively "hot" affect such as anger or anxiety at the prospect of an imminent threat. Anxiety, for example, has been associated with a narrowing of one's focus of attention (Easterbrook, 1959; Kahneman, 1973). Distraction appears less relevant to the milder mood inductions used in the many happy–sad experiments (Bodenhausen, Kramer, & Susser, 1994). Nevertheless, a distraction explanation may partially account for the differential effects of happy versus sad moods predicted by the mood and general information hypothesis. Bless, Schwarz, and Kemmelmeier (in press) point to evidence that more positive than negative information is stored in memory and that positive information is better connected than negative. Consequently, if a positive mood state activates similarly valenced cognitions, the potential for interference and distraction is greater for persons in a positive mood state. Consistent with a distraction prediction, being in a pleasant mood should decrease processing capacity and increase reliance on heuristics, such as stereotypes, when making judgments of others (Macrae, Milne, & Bodenhausen, 1994).

In a set of studies relevant to the distraction hypothesis, Bodenhausen and his colleagues (Bodenhausen & Kramer, 1990; Bodenhausen, Sheppard, & Kramer, 1994) looked at the relationship between negative moods and stereotyping. They reported that happiness and anger increased reliance on stereotypes but that sadness had no effect as compared to a neutral control. Both happy and angry subjects appeared to rely more on heuristic cues when making judgments and less on individuating or particular information. From the standpoint of the distraction hypothesis, anger and happiness are likely to be "hotter" emotions than sadness and, therefore, more likely to distract subjects from careful attention to the task, thereby increasing the likelihood of their making stereotypic judgments.

Baron, Burgess, Kao, and Logan (1990) examined the impact of anxiety on stereotyping in a dental setting. In the first of two experiments subjects completed a mood measure assessing their anxiety while waiting for a dentist appointment. Then they read a series of sentences involving members of occupational groups (e.g., "Sue, a librarian, is wise and gentle"). The statements systematically varied how stereotypic were the actors' behaviors. Anxious subjects significantly overestimated the correlation between stereotypic traits and members of the corresponding occupation.

In Baron et al.'s (1990) second study, subjects were provided with information about dental procedures that was designed to generate either high or low fear. Then they were exposed to a weak persuasive message that was presented with superficial cues suggesting a strong message (e.g., applauding audience). Baron et al. reasoned that subjects who examined the message carefully would rate it poorly whereas those who superficially examined the message would judge it to be more convincing. The latter subjects would be more affected by the peripheral cues and presentation style of the speaker. As expected, subjects in the high fear condition rated the message as more persuasive than subjects in the low fear condition. These findings suggest that high fear led to superficial processing of the message.

A set of experiments by Wilder and Shapiro (1989a, 1989b, 1991; Wilder, 1993a, 1993b) investigated the impact of anxiety on judgments of an outgroup member who behaved contrary to expectations about his group. Following Stephan and Stephan (1985), Wilder and Shapiro reasoned that intergroup contact may not improve relations between groups when anxiety is generated in anticipation of the contact. Such anxiety (and any attempts to cope with it) may poison the interaction, not only because the negative affect is associated with the outgroup, but also because it interferes with information processing in the contact setting. To the extent that anxiety distracts individuals, they should be more likely to interpret the contact experiences in terms of their expectations or stereotypes of the outgroup. In a series of experiments, subjects were made anxious at the prospect of either making an embarrassing speech, posing for some embarrassing pictures, or receiving a set of electric shocks. Then they viewed a tape of a group interaction in which one of the four group members behaved quite differently from the majority (e.g., he behaved incompetently while the other members behaved competently). Subjects who were anxious underestimated the degree to which the deviant differed from the majority. Thus, anxious subjects were more likely than nonanxious subjects to judge the deviant to be acting according to expectations about the group, based on the majority's behavior. (Note that the same findings were obtained whether the group's behavior was positive and the deviant's negative or vice versa.) Moreover, self-reported anxiety was significantly correlated with judgments that assimilated the deviant's behavior in the direction of the majority.

In one of these experiments, following the mood induction, subjects viewed a set of humorous cartoons designed to reduce anxiety. These subjects did not make more stereotypic judgments of the deviant outgroup member. This finding, coupled with the strong, positive correlations between self-reported anxiety and stereotypic judgments in these studies, suggests that anxiety was a causal factor in subjects' stereotypic evaluations of the outgroup member.

Overall, findings from research conducted by Baron, Wilder, and their associates have been largely consistent with the distraction hypothesis. When subjects were anxious, they were more likely to overlook counterstereotypic information and relied on stereotypes when making judgments of outgroup members.

In sum, each of the five hypotheses that various researchers have posed to explain affect–bias effects has generated some support. Much of the research looking at affect and bias has compared pleasant (happy) versus unpleasant (sad, angry) moods. In this literature the general finding has been that pleasant mood, anger, and anxiety encourage greater reliance on pre-existing stereotypes and attitudes toward the outgroup. In general, sad mood appears to have no impact beyond that of a no-mood manipulation. However, manipulations that increase perceivers' processing of target information result in stronger mood congruent effects on judgments. How might we account for this pattern of findings?

A Two-step Model Linking Affect and Intergroup Bias

We have briefly reviewed five explanations of when and why affect may influence judgments of outgroups. Clearly, several of these hypotheses draw from each other and several make similar predictions. Collectively, the five hypotheses address two distinct issues: allocation of attention and infusion of affect. The distraction and mood and general knowledge hypotheses focus on how affect may influence perceivers' allocation of attention. The affect consistency, affect as information, and affect infusion hypotheses deal with the extent of influence affect has on judgments once attention has been directed. As a gambit for research, we suggest the following synthesis: Affect influences intergroup judgments by both influencing the direction of attention and the valence of subsequent cognitions about the outgroup.

1. *Allocation of attention.* Two variables determine how affect shapes what persons attend to and use as grist for judgments of outgroups: valence of affect and strength of affect.

(a) Valence of affect. Negative affect commands greater vigilance than does positive affect. As discussed by Bless et al. (in press), this may be due to the greater threat inherent in negative affect (especially anxiety and fear). It may also reflect greater informational value of negative events (e.g., Jones & Davis, 1965). In a broader sense, it may reflect the function of conscious thought as a problem-solving mechanism for humans. We tune to negative affect because that is precisely what our active thought processes are designed to address. Pleasant affect, while sought out, lulls us to bliss and dulls our attentiveness.

In addition, Isen and her colleagues (Isen & Daubman, 1984; Isen, Niedenthal, & Cantor, 1992) have shown that positive affect broadens cognitive categories so that nontypical exemplars are more readily included. Applied to the mood and bias literature, positive affect may encourage perceivers to see the similarities in their environment and, therefore, underestimate the differences between target persons and the group to which they belong. Simply put, happy perceivers will overlook (or underweight) individuating information in favor of their expectations about the group category to which the target belongs.

(b) Strength of affect. Strong, "hot" emotion grabs more attention than cooler moods. Although strength of affect has not been manipulated systematically in this research area, comparisons across studies support this argument. Studies involving anxiety and arousal (Baron et al., 1990; Wilder & Shapiro, 1989a, 1989b) have provided evidence that strong affect can distract subjects from careful attention to the behavior of outgroup members and increase reliance on stereotypic and biased beliefs. Outgroup members were judged to be more homogeneous and their behavior more consistent with stereotypes when subjects were under high arousal as a result of an anxiety manipulation. Moreover, distraction produced by anxiety was significantly related to bias. The more anxious and distracted subjects reported themselves to be, the more biased they were in their judgments of outgroup members.

Note that the Wilder and Shapiro experiments differed from others in the mood–bias literature in that affect was generated by the expectation of a forthcoming unpleasant or fearful interaction. Thus, when subjects attended to the stimulus persons they had no opportunity to compartmentalize or dissociate their anxiety from the task at hand because resolution of the anxiety was yet to come. On the other hand, in the typical studies in the Bodenhausen, Mackie, and Forgas research programs, mood induction was presented to subjects as part of a separate experiment that preceded exposure to outgroup members. It seems to us that any distraction that may have been created by subjects having to focus on their emotions and cope with them would be minimized under this "two experiment" paradigm. Consequently, we suspect that the emotions experienced in the Wilder and Shapiro procedures were more intense and likely to produce coping responses that distracted subjects from careful attention to the target outgroup.

2. *Infusion of affect.* The affect consistency, affect as information, and affect infusion hypotheses posit that more mood congruent cognitions should be made salient with more in-depth cognitive processing. Literature on affect and bias has identified at least three variables that may influence processing strategies and, therefore,, degree of affect infusion: motivational demands, temporal demands, and target demands.

(a) Motivational demands. To the extent that perceivers are motivated to be accurate in their judgments, they will give greater weight to individuating information and less to general knowledge schemas such as stereotypes (Fiske & Neuberg, 1990; Kruglanski, 1989). In several studies, when happy persons were motivated to process stimulus information more carefully, they did not rely on stereotypes more than did neutral or sad perceivers (Bless et al., 1990; Bodenhausen et al., 1994). For instance, Queller, Mackie, and Stroessner (1994, cited in Mackie, Queller, Stroessner, & Hamilton, 1996) manipulated subjects' mood states (neutral or happy) and had subjects read descriptions of members of a group of "Big Brothers." Half of their subjects were asked to form a simple impression of the group. These subjects showed the typical mood effect: happy subjects perceived the Big Brothers as more homogeneous than did neutral subjects. The other subjects were asked to sort the descriptions into piles based on similarity and then form an impression of the group. Subjects who had attended more closely to the information by sorting the cards on the basis of similarity did not display the happy–neutral mood difference. Using a different manipulation, Bodenhausen, Kramer, and Susser (1994, experiment 4) also varied how accountable subjects were for their judgments. Increasing accountability resulted in happy subjects processing information more carefully and making less stereotypic judgments.

The motivational demands perceivers carry into a situation clearly affect where they will allocate their attention and what cognitive strategies they will adopt. Thus, motivation to be accurate is likely to lead to more meticulous consideration of specific individuating information about targets than is motivation for a quick judgment. The former should lead to greater affect infusion because of the longer time spent processing information in making the judgment (Forgas, 1995). A snap judgment, by contrast, is likely to be based more strongly on pre-existing bias. As Forgas (1995) has argued in his AIM model, processing strategies influence the amount of time spent making judgments and, therefore, the opportunity of affect to infuse on judgments by arousing affect-consistent cognitions. This leads us to our second variable: temporal demands.

(b) Temporal demands. The more time spent processing information, the greater is the opportunity for affect to infuse the judgment process (Forgas, 1995). On the other hand, under severe time constraint, judgments tend to be more heuristic and homogeneous. For example, Stroessner and Mackie (1992) varied how much time subjects had to look at descriptions of members of another group. When they had only three seconds between stimuli, they found that happy subjects perceived greater homogeneity in the outgroup than did neutral subjects. However, this difference was significantly reduced when time between stimulus presentations was increased to seven seconds. Their findings indicate that the relationship between mood and stereotyping may be affected by the time available for processing information. With less time to process stimuli, happy subjects were less attentive to variability and, by implication, more reliant on their expectation of similarity within the outgroup.

(c) Target demands. Judgments of an outgroup or of specific members are made in a social context. Context is provided by the presence of others (e.g., bystanders, other outgroup members), or, at minimum, by the expectations associated with the outgroup. In either case, evidence indicates that outgroup members who appear to he atypical or who engage in unexpected behavior elicit close inspection. As a result, their individuating characteristics and behavior exercise greater impact on judgments than do simple group stereotypes (Bless et al., in press; Fiske & Neuberg, 1980).

In sum, to the extent perceivers are motivated to process information carefully and have sufficient time to do so, to the extent affect is not so strong as to distract them from attending to the actions of the target, and to the extent the target is atypical in word or deed, perceivers' judgments will be based more strongly on individuating information present in the situation and less on stereotypes and prejudice about the outgroup. Moreover, closer attention to the target will promote more affect infusion such that positive mood should lead to a more positive evaluation and negative mood to a more negative evaluation of the target.

Implications for Intergroup Contact

In closing, consider some implications that can be drawn from the affect–bias literature for that venerable solution to intergroup bias: the contact hypothesis. Although not always made explicit, the contact hypothesis is grounded in the supposition that contact between groups will more likely improve relations if the contact generates positive rather than negative affect. Certainly, reviews of the contact literature have concluded that a pleasant experience, while not sufficient, contributes to successful interactions (e.g., Allport, 1954; Amir, 1969; Brewer & Miller, 1984; Hewstone & Brown, 1986; Pettigrew, 1986, 1998; Stephan, 1987; Wilder, 1984). On the other hand, cooperative contact that is unsuccessful is less likely to improve intergroup relations (Worchel, 1986). Failure in the contact setting generates negative affect which, in turn, can poison the contact experience. Negative experiences can trigger affect-consistent cognitions, including memories of past unpleasantness with the outgroup. Failure, thereby, reinforces negative stereotypes and prejudice toward the outgroup.

The prospect of contact with members of a disliked or threatening outgroup can be a source of considerable anxiety (Islam & Hewstone, 1993; Pettigrew, 1998; Stephan & Stephan, 1985). Anxiety, in turn, can undermine any beneficial impact of a contact experience by causing persons to either avoid the contact, misconstrue the experience, or behave in a defensive manner that may poison the experience (Stephan & Stephan, 1985; Wilder & Simon, 1996). In a field study in Bangladesh, Islam and Hewstone (1993) reported that contact between Hindu and Muslim students resulted in more favorable attitudes toward the respective outgroups and a reduction of reported anxiety when the contact was of high quality (e.g., intimate rather than superficial). Interestingly, they also reported that anxiety was positively associated with contact with outgroup members who were viewed as more typical of their group. Evidently, the more typical the outgroup members, the more they possessed undesirable or threatening characteristics associated with existing prejudice. This finding gives pause to the recommendation that contact with typical outgroup members is most likely to result in the generalization of that experience to attitudes about the outgroup as a whole (Hewstone & Brown, 1981; Wilder, 1984). Contact with typical outgroup members may be of little benefit if it also generates anxiety that vitiates the contact experience. Given that anxiety may interfere with successful contact experiences, what other implications might be drawn from the literature on affect and bias that bear upon the contact hypothesis?

If we apply research on affect and bias to the contact situation, we immediately stumble. Much of the reviewed research indicates that happiness, anger, and anxiety foster superficial processing and reliance on existing prejudice and stereotypes. On the other hand, other research suggests that a sad or a neutral mood is more conducive to noticing and carefully processing information in a contact situation. This pattern of findings augurs poorly for the beneficial effects of pleasant contact with an outgroup.

Although it is tempting to infer that a good mood might be detrimental to reducing bias, that nonobvious "man bites dog" conclusion would be premature for two reasons. First, Stroessner, Hamilton, and Mackie (1992) have evidence that a positive mood can prevent the formation of stereotypes based on illusory correlations. In their experiment happy or neutral subjects were exposed to a standard illusory correlation paradigm (Hamilton & Gifford, 1976). They saw information about two groups (A and B): 24 descriptions of group A – 16 desirable and 8 undesirable behaviors; 12 descriptions of group B – 8 desirable and 4 undesirable behaviors. Thus, the proportion of desirable and undesirable descriptors were the same for both groups. In the neutral mood condition subjects rated group B less favorably than group A (illusory correlation effect). Thus, the less frequent and, therefore, more distinct negative behaviors had a greater impact for evaluations of group B. On the other hand, in the happy mood condition, both groups were rated equally. Stroessner et al. argued that the happy mood resulted in less careful processing of the information. Consequently, happy subjects were less attendant to the distinctive negative information about group B and less likely to form a negative stereotype.

Second, as the research on affect infusion (e.g., Forgas, 1995; Forgas & Fiedler, 1996) has demonstrated, the influence of mood on thoughts and actions tends to be affect-consistent and more pronounced with additional processing time. The key for successful contact, then, appears to be to encourage persons in a pleasant mood to attend closely to the actions of the outgroup in the positive contact setting. Close attention to the outgroup's actions should counter the superficial processing tendency associated with a positive mood, should provide opportunity for greater affect infusion, and should generate concrete positive experiences that prolong the positive mood state.

Close attention to the outgroup can he facilitated by the factors discussed above: motivational demands, temporal demands, and task demands. Prompting interactants for accuracy, allowing sufficient time for positive mood infusion, and presenting them with contact persons who clearly disconfirm biases should provide the opportunity both for maximum mood infusion and generation of positive cognitions that are inconsistent with existing biases (Hewstone & Lord, 1998; Wilder, 1984). This recommendation fits with what is known about successful contact (e.g., Amir, 1969). Past research has concluded that contact is most successful when it involves cooperative pursuit of shared goals, equal status, intimacy, and support from others. Moreover, as Pettigrew (1998) has pointed our, positive contact is more likely to be successful if it occurs frequently and if each experience is not so brief as to preclude the formation of friendship bonds across groups.

These are all conditions that are likely to lead to careful processing of information and the opportunity for infusion of positive affect.

Conclusions

The notion that affective states can influence judgments of groups is certainly not new (e.g., Allport, 1954). What is relatively recent, however, is a body of literature that has examined the impact of different affective states on judgments of outgroups using carefully controlled experiments. This chapter has focused on that literature and five hypotheses that have been offered to explain the role of affect in intergroup judgments. We have offered a two-component synthesis of those hypotheses: The influence of affect on intergroup judgments is mediated by how the affect influences allocation of attention and opportunity for infusion.

It should be noted that most of this literature has been generated by laboratory experiments in which affect is manipulated independently of the judged outgroup; that is, incidental to the outgroup (Bodenhausen, 1993). One may question whether the same findings would be observed were the affect integral; that is, caused by or attributed to the outgroup. One set of experiments (Wilder & Shapiro, 1989a) did employ integral affect by having the manipulation of affect linked to the behavior of members of the target outgroup. The results from this study were the same as when affect was manipulated incidental to the outgroup.

Finally, it should be noted that this literature has focused on judgments of outgroups. But certainly affect also exerts influence on judgments of ingroups. (In a recent chapter in this handbook series, Kelly (in press) has looked at mood and emotion within groups.) Affective relations among ingroup members may very likely contribute to affect directed toward an outgroup. (For example, see Allport's (1954) discussion of projection.) In a complementary fashion, affect generated by an outgroup may influence judgments of the ingroup. There is evidence that the mere salience of an outgroup is sufficient to make salient a perceiver's relevant ingroup (Wilder & Shapiro, 1986). Because outgroups and corresponding ingroups are linked, it is probable that affect associated with one has implications for affect and judgments toward the other. One direction that may prove fruitful is to expand the current research beyond examining how affect influences judgments of outgroups to a broader consideration of the influence of affect on judgments of ingroup–outgroup pairings.

REFERENCES

Abelson, R. P., Aronson, E., McGuire, W. J., Newcomb, T. M., Rosenberg, M. J., & Tannenbaum, P. H. (1968). *Theories of cognitive consistency.* Chicago, IL: Rand McNally.

Adorno, T. W., Frenkel-Brunswick, E., Levinson, D., & Sanford, R. N. (1950). *The authoritarian personality.* New York: Harper.

Allport, G. W. (1954). *The nature of prejudice.* Cambridge, MA: Addison-Wesley.

Amir, Y. (1969). Contact hypothesis in ethnic relations. *Psychological Bulletin, 71,* 319–342.

Baron, R. S., Burgess, M. L., Kao, C. F., & Logan, H. (1990). *Fear and superficial social processing: Evidence of stereotyping and simplistic persuasion.* Paper presented at the annual convention of the Midwestern Psychological Association, Chicago, IL.

Berkowitz, L. (1990). On the formation and regulation of anger and aggression: A cognitive-neoassociationistic analysis. *American Psychologist, 45,* 494–503.

Berkowitz, L. (1993). *Aggression: Its causes, consequences, and control.* New York: McGraw-Hill.

Bies, R. J. (1987). The predicament of injustice: The management of moral outrage. In L. Cummings & B. M. Staw (Eds.), *Research in organizational behavior* (Vol. 9, pp. 289–319). Greenwich, CT: JAI.

Bies, R. J., Tripp, T. M., & Kramer, R. M. (1996). At the breaking point: Cognitive and social dynamics of revenge in organizations. In J. Greenberg & R. Giacalone (Eds.), *Antisocial behavior in organizations.* Thousand Oaks, CA: Sage.

Bless, H., & Fiedler, K. (1995). Affective states and the influence of activated general knowledge. *Personality and Social Psychology Bulletin, 21,* 766–778.

Bless, H., Mackie, D. M., & Schwarz, N. (1992). Mood effects on encoding and judgmental processes in persuasion. *Journal of Personality and Social Psychology, 63,* 585–595.

Bless, H., Schwarz, N., & Kemmelmeier, M. (in press). Mood and stereotyping: Affective states and the use of general knowledge structures. In W. Stroebe & M. Hewstone (Eds.), *European review of social psychology* (Vol. 7). New York: Wiley.

Bodenhausen, G. V. (1993). Emotions, arousal, and stereotypic judgments: A heuristic model of affect and stereotyping. In D. M. Mackie & D. L. Hamilton (Eds.), *Affect, cognition, and stereotyping* (pp. 13–37). San Diego, CA: Academic Press.

Bodenhausen, G. V., & Kramer, G. P. (1990). *Affective states trigger stereotypic judgments.* Paper, presented at the annual convention of the American Psychological Society, Dallas, TX.

Bodenhausen, G. V., Kramer, G. P., & Susser, K. (1994). Happiness and stereotypic thinking in social judgment. *Journal of Personality and Social Psychology, 66,* 621–632.

Bodenhausen, G. V., Sheppard, L. A., & Kramer, G. P. (1994). Negative affect and social judgment: The differential impact of anger and sadness. *European Journal of Social Psychology, 24,* 45–62.

Bower, G. H. (1981). Mood and memory. *American Psychologist, 36*, 129–148.

Brewer, M. B. (1981). Ethnocentrism and its role in interpersonal trust. In M. B. Brewer & B. E. Collins (Eds.), *Scientific inquiry and the social sciences* (pp. 345–360). San Francisco, CA: Josey-Bass.

Brewer, M. B. (1988). A dual-process model of impression formation. In T. K. Srull & R. S. Wyer (Eds.), *Advances in social cognition* (Vol. 1, pp. 1–36). Hillsdale, NJ: Erlbaum.

Brewer, M. B., & Miller, N. (1984). Beyond the contact hypothesis: Theoretical perspectives on desegregation. In N. Miller & M. B. Brewer (Eds.), *Groups in contact: The psychology of desegregation* (pp. 281–302). Orlando, FL: Academic Press.

Byrne, D., & Clore, G. L. (1970). A reinforcement model of evaluation responses. *Personality: An International Journal, 1*, 103–128.

Campbell, D. T. (1975). On the conflict between biological and social evolution and between psychology and moral tradition. *American psychologist, 30*, 1103–1126.

Clore, G. L., & Byrne, D. (1974). The reinforcement affect model of attraction. In L. Huston (Ed.), *Foundations of interpersonal attraction* (pp. 143–170). San Diego, CA: Academic Press.

Clore, G. L., Schwarz, N., & Conway, M. (1994). Cognitive causes and consequences of emotion. In R. S. Wyer & T. K. Srull (Eds.), *Handbook of social cognition* (2nd ed., pp. 323–417). Hillsdale, NJ: Erlbaum.

Dollard, J., Doob, L. W., Miller, N. E., Mowrer, O. H., & Sears, R. R. (1939). *Frustration and aggression.* New Haven, CT: Yale University Press.

Dovidio, J. F., Brigham, J., Johnson, B. T., & Gaertner, S. L. (1996). Stereotyping, prejudice, and discrimination. In N. Macrae, C. Stangor, & M. Hewstone (Eds.), *Foundations of stereotypes and stereotyping* (pp. 337–366). Hillsdale, NJ: Erlbaum.

Dovidio, J. F., Gaertner, S. L., Isen, A. M., & Lawrence, R. (1995). Group representations and intergroup bias: Positive affect, similarity, and group size. *Personality and Social Psychology Bulletin, 21*, 856–865.

Easterbrook, J. A. (1959). The effect of emotion on cue utilization and the organization of behavior. *Psychological Review, 66*, 183–201.

Fiedler, K. (1991). On the task, the measures and the mood in research on affect and social cognition. In J. P. Forgas (Ed.), *Emotion and social judgment* (pp. 83–104). Elmsford, NY: Pergamon Press.

Fiske, S. T., & Morlin, B. (1996). Stereotyping as a function of personal control motives and capacity constraints: The odd couple of power and anxiety. In R. M. Sorrentino & E. T. Higgins (Eds.), *Handbook of motivation and cognition: The interpersonal context* (Vol. 3, pp. 322–346). New York: Guilford.

Fiske, S. T., & Neuberg, L. (1990). A continuum of impression formation, from category-based to individuating processes: Influences of information and motivation on attention and interpretation. In M. Zanna (Ed.), *Advances in experimental social psychology* (Vol. 23, pp. 1–74). San Diego, CA: Academic Press.

Forgas, J. P. (1989). Mood effects on decision-making strategies. *Australian Journal of Psychology, 41*, 197–214.

Forgas, J. P. (1995). Mood and judgment: The affect infusion model (AIM). *Psychological Bulletin, 117*, 39–66.

Forgas, J. P., & Fiedler, K. (1996). Us and them: Mood effects on intergroup discrimination. *Journal of Personality and Social Psychology, 70*, 28–40.

Forgas, J. P., & Moylan, S. J. (1991). Affective influences on stereotype judgments. *Cognition and Emotion, 5*, 379–397.

Hamilton, D. L., & Gifford, R. K. (1976). Illusory correlation in interpersonal perception: A cognitive basis of stereotypic judgments. *Journal of Experimental Social Psychology, 12*, 392–407.

Hamilton, D. L., & Rose, T. L. (1980). Illusory correlation and the maintenance of stereotypic belief. *Journal of Personality and Social Psychology, 19,* 832–845.

Hewstone, M., & Brown, R. (1986). Contact is not enough: An intergroup perspective on the contact hypothesis. In M. Hewstone & R. Brown (Eds.), *Contact and conflict in intergroup encounters* (pp. 169–195). Oxford, UK: Blackwell.

Hewstone, M., & Lord, C. G. (1998). Changing intergroup cognitions and intergroup behavior: The role of typicality. In C. Sedikides, J. Schopler, & C. A. Insko (Eds.), *Intergroup cognition and intergroup behavior* (pp. 367–392). Mahwah, NJ: Erlbaum.

Hunter, J. A., Platow, M. J., Bell, L. M., & Kypri, K. (1997). Intergroup bias and self-evaluation: Domain-specific self-esteem, threats to identity and dimensional importance. *British Journal of Social Psychology, 36,* 405–426.

Hunter, J. A., Platow, M. J., & Howard, M. L. (1996). Social identity and intergroup evaluative bias: Realistic categories and domain specific self-esteem in a conflict setting. *European Journal of Social Psychology, 26,* 631–647.

Isen, A. (1984). Toward understanding the role of affect in cognition. In R. S. Wyer & T. K. Srull (Eds.), Handbook of social cognition (Vol. 20, pp. 179–236). Hillsdale, NJ: Erlbaum.

Isen, A. (1987). Positive affect, cognitive processes and social behavior. In L. Berkowitz (Ed.), *Advances in experimental social psychology* (Vol. 20, pp. 203–253). San Diego, CA: Academic Press.

Isen, A. M., & Daubman, K. A. (1984). The influence of affect on categorization. *Journal of Personality and Social Psychology, 47,* 1206–1217.

Isen, A. M., Niedenthal, P. M., & Cantor, N. (1992). An influence of positive affect on social categorization. *Motivation and Emotion, 16,* 65–78.

Islam, M. R., & Hewstone, M. (1993). Dimensions of contact as predictors of intergroup anxiety, perceived out-group variability, and out-group attitude: An integrative model. *Personality and Social Psychology Bulletin, 19,* 700–710.

Kahneman, D. (1973). *Attention and effort.* Englewood Cliff, NJ: Prentice-Hall.

Kelly, J. R. (in press). Mood and emotion in groups. In M. Hogg & S. Tindale (Eds.), *Blackwell handbook in social psychology, Vol. 3: Group Processes.* Oxford, UK: Blackwell.

Kramer, R. M., & Messick, D. M. (1998). Getting by with a little help from our enemies: Collective paranoia and its role in intergroup relations, In C. Sedikides, Schopler, & C. A. Insko (Eds.), *Intergroup cognition and intergroup behavior* (pp. 233–255). Mahwah, NJ: Erlbaum.

Jones, E. E., & Davis, K. E. (1965). A theory of correspondent inferences: From acts to dispositions. In L. Berkowitz (Ed.), *Advances in experimental social psychology* (Vol. 2). New York: Academic Press.

Kruglanski, A. W. (1989). *Lay epistemics and human knowledge: Cognitive and motivational bases.* New York: Plenum.

Lemyre, L., & Smith, P. M. (1985). Intergroup discrimination and self-esteem in the minimal group paradigm. *Journal of Personality and Social Psychology, 49,* 660–670.

LeVine, R. A., & Campbell, D. T. (1972). *Ethnocentrism: Theories of conflict, ethnic attitudes, and group behavior.* New York: Wiley.

Mackie, D. M., Hamilton, D. L., Schroth, H. A., Carlisle, C. J., Gersho, B. F., Meneses, M., Nedler, B. F., & Reichel, L. D. (1989). The effects of induced mood on expectancy-based illusory correlations. *Journal of Experimental Social Psychology, 25,* 524–544.

Mackie, D. M., Queller, S., & Stroessner, S. J. (1994). The impact of positive mood on perceptions of behavioral consistency and member typicality in social groups. Unpublished manuscipt, University of California, Santa Barbara.

Mackie, D. M., Queller, S., Stroessner, S. J., & Hamilton, D. L. (1996). Making stereotypes better or worse: Multiple roles for positive affect in group impressions. In R. M. Sorrentino & E. T. Higgins (Eds.), *Handbook of motivation and cognition* (Vol. 3, pp. 371–396). New York: Guilford Press.

Mackie, D. M., & Worth, L. T. (1989). Cognitive deficits and the mediation of positive affect in persuasion. *Journal of Personality and Social Psychology, 57*, 27–40.

Macrae, C. N., Milne, A. B., & Bodenhausen, G. V. (1994). Stereotypes as energy-saving devices: A peek inside the toolbox. *Journal of Personality and Social Psychology, 66*, 37–47.

Meindl, J. R., & Lerner, M. (1984). Exacerbation of extreme responses to an out-group. *Journal of Personality and Social Psychology, 47*, 71–84.

Messick, D. M., & Mackie, D. M. (1989). Intergroup relations. In M. R. Rosenzweig & W. Porter (Eds.), *Annual review of psychology* (Vol. 40, pp. 45–81). Palo Alto, CA: Annual Reviews.

Oakes, P. J., & Turner, J. C. (1980). Social categorization and intergroup behaviour: Does minimal intergroup discrimination make social identity more positive? *European Journal of Social Psychology, 10*, 295–301.

Paulhus, D. L., & Lim, T. K. (1994). Arousal and evaluative extremity in social judgments: A dynamic complexity model. *European Journal of Social Psychology, 24*, 89–100.

Pettigrew, T. F. (1986). The intergroup contact hypothesis reconsidered. In M. Hewstone & R. Brown (Eds.), *Contact and conflict in intergroup encounters* (pp. 169–195). Oxford, UK: Blackwell.

Pettigrew, T. F. (1998). Intergroup contact theory. *Annual review of psychology* (Vol. 49, pp. 65–85). Annual Reviews.

Petty, R. E., & Cacioppo, J. T. (1986a). The elaboration likelihood model of persuasion. In L. Berkowitz (Ed.), *Advances in experimental social psychology* (Vol. 19). New York: Academic Press.

Petty, R. E., & Cacioppo, J. T. (1986b). *Communication and persuasion: Central and peripheral routes to attitude change*. New York: Springer-Verlag.

Pyszczynski, T. A., & Greenberg, J. (1987). Depression, self-focused attention, and self-regulatory presevation. In C. R. Snyder & C. E. Ford (Eds.), *Coping with negative life events: Clinical and social psychological perspectives* (pp. 105–129). New York: Plenum Press.

Schachter, S., & Singer, J. (1962). Cognitive, social, and physiological determinants of the emotional state. *Psychological Review, 69*, 379–399.

Schwarz, N. (1990). Feelings as information: Informational and motivational functions of affective states. In R. M. Sorrentino & E. T. Higgins (Eds.), *Handbook of motivation and cognition: Foundations of social behavior* (Vol. 2, pp. 527–561). New York: Guilford.

Schwarz, N., & Bless, H. (1991). Happy and mindless, but sad and smart? The impact of affective states on analytic reasoning. In J. Forgas (Ed.), *Emotion and social judgments* (pp. 55–71). Oxford, UK: Pergamon.

Schwarz, N., Bless, H., & Bohner, G. (1991). Mood and persuasion: Affective states influence the processing of persuasive communications. In M. Zanna (Ed.), *Advances in experimental social psychology* (Vol. 24, pp. 161–197). New York: Academic Press.

Schwarz, N., & Clore, G. L. (1988). How do I feel about it? The informative function of affective states. In K. Fiedler & J. P. Forgas (Eds.), *Affect, cognition, and social behavior* (pp. 44–62). Göttingen, Germany: Hogrefe.

Sherif, M. (1966). *In common predicament: Social psychology of intergroup conflict and cooperation*. Boston, MA: Houghton-Mifflin.

Sinclair, R. C., Mark, M. M., & Clore, G. L. (1994). Mood-related persuasion depends on mis-attributions. *Social Cognition, 12*, 309–326.

Staats, A. W., & Staats, C. K. (1958). Attitudes established by classical conditioning. *Journal of Abnormal and Social Psychology, 57*, 37–40.

Stephan, W. G. (1987). The contact hypothesis in intergroup relations. In C. Hendrick (Ed.), *Review of personality and social psychology* (Vol. 9, pp. 13–40). Newbury Park, CA: Sage.

Stephan, W. G., & Stephan, C. W. (1985). Intergroup anxiety. *Journal of Social Issues, 41*, 157–175.

Stroessner, S. J., Hamilton, D. L., & Mackie, D. M. (1992). Affect and stereotyping: The effect of induced mood on distinctiveness-based illusory correlations. *Journal of Personality and Social Psychology, 62,* 564–576.

Stroessner, S. J., & Mackie, D. M. (1992). The impact of induced affect on the perception of variability in social groups. *Personality and Social Psychology Bulletin, 18,* 546–554.

Stroessner, S. J., & Mackie, D. M. (1993). Affect and perceived group variability: Implications for stereotyping and prejudice. In D. M. Mackie & D. L. Hamilton (Eds.), *Affect, cognition, and stereotyping: Interactive processes in group perception* (pp. 63–86). San Diego, CA: Academic Press.

Tajfel, H. (1982). *Social identity and intergroup behaviour.* Cambridge, UK: Cambridge University Press.

Trivers, R. L. (1971). The evolution of reciprocal altruism. *Quarterly review of Biology, 46,* 35–57.

Turner, J. C. (1987). *Rediscovering the social group: A self-categorization theory.* Oxford, UK: Basil Blackwell.

Wilder, D. A. (1984). Intergroup contact: The typical members and the exception to the rule. *Journal of Experimental Social Psychology, 20,* 177–194.

Wilder, D. A. (1993a). The role of anxiety in facilitating stereotypic judgments of outgroup behavior. In D. M. Mackie & D. L. Hamilton (Eds.), *Affect, cognition, and stereotyping: Interactive processes in group perception* (pp. 87–109). San Diego, CA: Academic Press.

Wilder, D. A. (1993b). Freezing intergroup evaluations: Anxiety fosters resistance to counter-stereotypic information. In M. A. Hogg & D. Abrams (Eds.), *Group motivation: Social psychological perspectives* (pp. 68–86). New York: Harvester/Wheatsheaf.

Wilder, D. A., & Shapiro, P. (1989a). Role of competition-induced anxiety in limiting the beneficial impact of positive behavior by an outgroup member. *Journal of . . .*

Wilder, D. A., & Shapiro, P. (1989b). Effects of anxiety on impression formation in a group context: An anxiety-assimilation hypothesis. *Journal of Experimental Social Psychology, 25,* 482–499.

Wilder, D. A., & Shapiro, P. (1991). Facilitation of outgroup stereotypes by enhanced ingroup identity. *Journal of Experimental Social Psychology, 27,* 431–452.

Wilder, D. A., & Simon, A. F. (1996). Incidental and integral affect as triggers of stereotyping. In R. M. Sorrentino & E. T. Higgins (Eds.), *Handbook of motivation and cognition: The interpersonal context* (Vol. 3, pp. 397–419). New York: Guilford Press.

Wills, T. A. (1981). Downward comparison principles in social psychology. *Psychological Bulletin, 90,* 245–271.

Worchel, S. (1986). The role of cooperation in reducing intergroup conflict. In S. Worchel & W. G. Austin (Eds.), *Psychology of intergroup relations* (2nd ed., pp. 288–304). Chicago, IL: Nelson-Hall.

Zillman, D. (1983). Transfer of excitation in emotional behavior. In J. T. Cacioppo & R. E. Petty (Eds.), *Social psychophysiology.* New York: Academic Press.

PART II

Social Motivation

Introduction

The eight readings in this Part also span the breadth of social psychology. The first two readings share a focus on the key motivational concept of goals. Dunning, whose chapter explores motives underlying social cognition, highlights three general goals – the desire for knowledge, the desire for affirmation, and the desire for coherence – that help us to understand the question of what instigates social judgment in everyday life. Oettingen and Gollwitzer consider the nature of goals in more detail, exploring the determinants and processes of how goals emerge and how they are implemented (including detailed analysis of the concepts of goal setting and goal striving).

The next two readings concern the self, specifically how the self is evaluated, or self-esteem. As the reading by Tesser makes clear, self-esteem is a concept that draws together research on both motivation and emotion, whether we conceptualize self-esteem as a trait or a state variable. Leary, in the next contribution, reminds us that the deliberate efforts we make to convey a public image of ourselves to other people are uniquely human, and that the image we seek to present does not always or necessarily match our private view of ourselves. As Leary points out, the self is not only a cognitive structure that permits self-reflection and organizes information about the self, it also has motivational features. His chapter deals specifically with the motive of self-enhancement (maintaining a positive image of oneself) and argues that a single process is involved in enhancement of both the private self and the public self.

The central importance of motivation in interpersonal relations and close relationships is illustrated by the next two readings, both of which include an analysis of empathy. Ickes and Simpson consider the general rule, that relationship partners will typically seek to make accurate, rather than inaccurate, inferences about each other's thoughts and feelings, for the good of their relationship. However, they also summarize findings that support two exceptions to this general rule of empathic accuracy, and show that partners sometimes use motivated inaccuracy to protect themselves and their relationships, and are sometimes motivated to make accurate interpersonal perceptions even when this incurs high costs, both in personal and relationship terms. Dovidio and Penner include empathy as a key factor in why people help others, often at high costs to themselves. Their analysis of motives involved in helping is not, however, restricted to empathy, and includes several other cognitive and affective inferences. More generally, this chapter answers not only the question of why people help, but also when they do so and which (types of) people, in particular, are most likely to help.

The last two readings in this Part explore motives in intragroup and intergroup settings. Darley highlights one key set of motives in social and organizational domains, those concerning social comparison. His chapter is especially concerned with the motive to show that one can perform one's task within a group well and, relatedly, the motive to gain group esteem by performing well (and avoid loss of self-esteem due to performing poorly). Finally, Mummendey and Otten explore some of the darkest consequences of motivational biases in the area of intergroup relations. Their analysis of the determinants of hostility and antagonism against outgroups shows that motivational influences are strongly implicated in extreme forms of outgroup derogation.

CHAPTER SEVEN

On the Motives Underlying Social Cognition

David Dunning

One of the most popular metaphors in social psychology over the past thirty years has been that of person as computer. Like a computer, people input information about others, process it, and then produce some judgmental output that can take the form of an evaluation, attribution, or prediction. The metaphor has proven to be a useful one, given the voluminous research it has generated about the sophisticated (albeit imperfect) "software" people use to reach judgments about themselves and their social worlds.

However, thirty years of research on social cognition has surprisingly ignored, although not completely, one important task that the mindful computer must complete: it must monitor when a judgment is called for, if at all, among all the myriad of opportunities it has for social judgment every day. This fact has been finessed for decades in social psychology, in that it has been the experimenter who acts as the instigator of social judgment, providing participants with a target to judge and a questionnaire that specifies what issues participants must address.

But who, or rather what, acts as an instigator of social judgment in everyday life? People clearly cannot mull over and analyze all the actions of all the people they meet on all personality dimensions ever identified. To do so would render the mindful computer as one sitting in an easy chair, lost in contemplation over a social world it is too preoccupied to join. The social computer requires a mechanism that tells it to run its arsenal of applications and software selectively, ignoring many circumstances that could potentially call for judgmental efforts. But that is not all. The social computer requires a mechanism that tells it when enough is enough, that sufficient information has been gathered or that enough processing has ensued. Finally, the social computer needs a mechanism that monitors the conclusions that it reaches, to make sure that these conclusions do not violate principles that it wishes to honor.

Some researchers, especially those on the more cognitive side, will wince at the way I am introducing these issues. To them, I suggest that the social computer requires a homunculus

Preparation of this chapter was financially supported by National Institute of Mental Health Grant ROI-56072.

that peers into the social world, hitting the "execute" button when it is time to analyze the behavior of self and others, monitoring the social computer's programs as they proceed through their subroutines. It is often considered bad form, and appropriately so, to refer to cognitive mechanisms as a homunculus. The term conjures images of an unpredictable and incomprehensible apparatus, one even imbued with free will, that is invoked by psychological researchers when they cannot account for the phenomena they observe.

However, I submit that the discomfort of these researchers is misplaced, for two specific reasons. First, it is inescapable that the social computer requires the mechanism that handles the tasks of instigator, terminator, and monitor of social judgment. Indeed, such functions are often referred to in cognitive psychology as *executive functions*, and although they are often difficult to account for, an adequate portrayal of social cognitive processes requires some understanding of the executive mechanisms governing social thought.

Second, and most important, several decades of research in social psychology reveal that this executive or homunculus hardly operates as an unpredictable free agent. Several principles shape when the creature will start the social judgment process and control the conclusions it reaches. In particular, in this chapter I highlight the goals or motives that preoccupy the executive as it monitors the social judgmental process. If one scans the last fifty years of social psychological research, one finds three general goals that the executive "has in mind" as it carries out its duties. First, and most obvious, the executive has a *desire for knowledge* about its environment. It must reach conclusions about itself and other people in order to navigate its social world without too much pain and folly and hopefully with much success and reward. Second, the executive possesses a *desire for affirmation* of the competence of its owner, in that it acts to bolster favorable images of self. Finally, the executive possesses a *desire for coherence*, being interested in making sure that all new information is consistent with the beliefs it already has.

In this chapter, I discuss each desire and describe what social psychological research has to say about the executive's pursuit of it. I explain how each need shapes and molds social judgment. I also talk about controversies that research on these motives has prompted. I end the chapter with observations about current research on motivation.

Desire for Knowledge

The executive is curious. By that, I mean it possesses a strong motive to acquire information about its world. Indeed, many scholars have noted that curiosity is a motive that is surprisingly strong among humans. People like to know the answers to questions even when it provides no direct benefit to them, a situation that befuddles traditional economic analysis (Loewenstein, 1994). All of us have had the experience of sitting in front of the television watching some infotainment program, vowing to turn the set off at the next commercial break, only to have a television announcer tease us with a trivia question (such as, "Which city in the United States has the highest percentage of citizens holding college degrees?") that makes us stay with the program against our best wishes.

More formal documentation of the power of curiosity comes from work on behavioral economics, which shows that people will forego money in order to see a photograph of an individual after being shown pictures of that individual's body parts, even though seeing the entire person carries no personal consequences for them (Loewenstein, 1994). That the power of curiosity is counterintuitively strong comes from work showing that people mispredict how much of an appetite they have for trivia. When given a hypothetical choice between knowing the answer to trivia questions versus some candy bars to take home with them, people intuit that they would rather have the candy bars. However, when given an actual choice, people opt for feeding their curiosity and finding out the answers (Loewenstein, Prelec, & Shatto, 1997). (Do not worry, if you keep reading, you will find the answer to the college degree question.)

Conditions promoting curiosity

As such, one straightforward and prevalent motive that preoccupies the social cognitive executive is the simple need to know. However, that curiosity must be selective or the individual would be overwhelmed with puzzles to solve and answers to find. Clearly, people are more curious about some matters (e.g. what's my next door neighbor's annual income?) than they are about others (e.g. is income inequality rising in my country?), so what distinguishes the former situation from the latter?

Prior information. Surprisingly, people are more curious about issues to the extent that they are familiar and well-informed about them. Children are more interested in finding out the answers to questions posed about familiar animals than they are about unfamiliar ones (Berlyne, 1954). College students are more curious about answers for questions they are confident they know the answer already than they are questions they do not have a clue about (Crandall, 1971). The greater people rate their knowledge in a particular domain, the more they want to know the answers to questions in those domains (Jones, 1979). To be sure, when people are so knowledgeable that they feel they already *know* with certainty the answers to the questions posed, they are not all that curious about confirming that fact (Crandall, 1971) However, below absolute certainty people tend to desire the answers to questions they believe they are knowledgeable about.

Expectancy violation. People become curious when some new piece of information fails to conform to their expectations. When such expectancy violations occur, people expend great effort to find ways to dismiss or explain away the data, or reconcile those data with their preconceptions. Work on spontaneous attributional activity demonstrates this the best. It is when people are confronted with surprising information that they think the hardest about the causes of other persons' or their own behavior.

For example, Pyszczynski & Greenberg (1981) presented participants with another person that they were about to meet in a "get acquainted" conversation. While waiting for that conversation, they saw that person either agree or refuse to help out the experimenter with another task, with that task being either trivial or time-consuming. Participants subsequently wanted to see more information about the target when the target's behavior violated their expectancies about social norms (i.e. refused to do the trivial task or agreed to do the onerous one) than when the target's behaviors conformed to them. In a similar vein, Hastie (1984) discovered that people engage in spontaneous attributional activity when presented with another person's behavior (e.g. won a chess game) that violated their expectations of that person (e.g. he is rather unintelligent). In these situations, participants were more likely to list attributions for the behavior in their thoughts than they were when the target's behavior conformed to expectations (see also Clary & Tesser, 1983, for similar data). Evidence of such spontaneous cognition work is also apparent in real world contexts. Businesses take greater pains to explain the reasons for unexpected failures or successes in their annual reports than they do expected outcomes (Bettman & Weitz, 1983).

The role of hedonic consequences

The motive toward curiosity does serve a purpose. The ability to possess knowledge and an understanding of the social world gives people predictability and control over their social worlds. Such predictability and control allows people to adapt their behavior toward ways that provide the most pleasure and avoid the most pain. As such, the primary purpose of social cognition is to guide people in their actions (for discussions, see Heider, 1958; Trope, 1986).

Nowhere was that statement made so explicitly than by traditional attribution theorists, who stated that "The attributor is not simply a seeker after knowledge. His [or her] latent goal in gaining knowledge is that of effective management of himself [or herself] and his [or her] environment" (Kelley, 1972, p. 22). As such, it stands to reason that people are more curious about others when the actions of those others carry consequences for the social perceiver. Perhaps more important, this deeper curiosity often leads to more accurate conclusions about other people. Consider the following conditions.

Outcome dependency.   People think more effortfully about other people when the outcomes they will experience depend on those other people. This fact was perhaps best demonstrated by Berscheid and colleagues in a study of dating relationships (Berscheid, Graziano, Monson, & Dermer, 1976). Berscheid and colleagues brought college student volunteers into the laboratory and coaxed them into dating for five weeks only those individuals that the researchers had specified. The volunteers then watched videotaped interviews of three study participants, all of the opposite sex. Some participants were told that one specific interview was of a person they would be dating (indeed, some participants were told that this was the *only* person they would be allowed to date, inside and outside of the study, for five weeks). Participants paid more attention to the interviews of their putative dating partners and remembered more about them. They also made more extreme and confident trait attributions about their designated dating partners than they did of the other targets, indicating that they had thought long and hard about those specific individuals who could bring joy or boredom to the next few weeks of their lives.

Beyond making people think more deeply, outcome dependency also makes people think more accurately. Monson, Keel, Stephens, & Genung (1982) showed that people made more appropriate attributions for the behavior of other people when they expected to interact with them in a Prisoner's Dilemma Game. Erber & Fiske (1984) discovered that people paid more attention to information that was inconsistent with their prior expectations about the competence of another person when their chance of winning a prize depended, in part, on that person's skill.

Indeed, Neuberg & Fiske (1987) demonstrated that outcome dependency can cause people to put aside their stereotypes and to pay more attention to specific information about the attributes and strengths of another person. They asked college students to play an interactive "creativity" game with an individual who had just been released from the hospital after his schizophrenia had gone into remission. Students who had to work with the former patient to win a prize in the game, relative to those who did not, spent more time looking over information about the patient before the game started. As a consequence, those participants tended to view the formerly mentally ill individual more positively, thus dismissing their stereotype of schizophrenic patients.

Self-improvement.   People also desire knowledge, particularly about the self, when presented with situations that call for self-improvement. Usually, this means after confronting a failure. For example, when university students fail a test of "professional skills," they exhibit more causal reasoning than when they succeed, regardless of whether that failure was expected or unexpected (Bohner, Bless, Schwarz, & Strack (1988); see Weiner (1985) for similar findings, and Bless (2001) about the role played by negative affect in information processing). In a survey asking people questions about themselves, people cite situations in which they have experienced a failure or a threat, as well as situations in which they are about to confront some future challenge (Taylor, Neter, & Wayment, 1995). No other type of situation comes close in prompting people to evaluate themselves (see Biernat and Billings, (2001), this volume, for a discussion).

Accountability.   Social reproach is an unpleasant prospect. As such, when people must justify their opinions and beliefs to others, that is, when they are *accountable*, they take more care and apply more effort toward the formation of those opinions (for a review, see Tetlock, 1992). In a wide-ranging series of studies, Tetlock showed that making people accountable for their judgments was a substantial palliative that prevented people from falling prey to many biases and errors. First, accountability made people consider many alternative interpretations of the facts they received. It also prompted them to spend more effort integrating the facts they confronted, finding causal or conceptual links between them. As a consequence, the judgments that people reached were of better quality than the judgments people reached with no accountability. In addition, when accountable, people were found to have more insight into the determinants of their judgments. They processed persuasive communications more thoughtfully, paying more attention to the quality of arguments presented. They failed to succumb to the *correspondence bias* (also known as the *fundamental attribution error*), which refers to the overweighing of personal characteristics of others and the underweighing of situational factors, when explaining the behavior of others. They made more accurate predictions about the responses of others, and more correctly gauged the likelihood that those predictions would later prove to be right.

However, three caveats must be mentioned about this impact of accountability on social thought. First, at times accountability can prompt people to give too much weight to information that is irrelevant to the judgmental task at hand, thus leading them to under-weight diagnostic information, a tendency known as the *dilution effect* (Tetlock, 1992). Second, people must not know the opinions and beliefs of the individuals they must justify their attitudes to. When they have such knowledge, they tend to bend their beliefs "lazily" in the direction of those individuals (Tetlock, 1983). Third, people must be told they are accountable *before* they begin to consider information and form their judgments. If they reach an opinion first, and then are told they are accountable for it, a very different motive with a very different outcome ensues.

Need for control

Central to any treatment of the desire for knowledge is the issue of control. People desire knowledge so that they can predict and control their worlds. Thus, it is not surprising that events that question an individual's control over his or her environment motivate the individual toward gathering information and thinking through their opinions. For example, after Swann, Stephenson, & Pittman (1981) gave participants failure feedback on an intellectual task, participants subsequently asked for more information about a person they were about to interview.

In addition, questioning people's control paradoxically makes them more competent in social cognitive tasks. In one such study, questioning participants' control made them more accurate in distinguishing information they had actually received about another person as opposed to information that could only be inferred (Pittman & D'Agostino, 1989). In another study, participants whose ability to control their fates was questioned made arguably more accurate attributions about another person's behavior, noticing whether the target had written an essay for pay or privately in his diary, inferring weaker attitudes in the former case than they did in the latter (Pittman & Pittman, 1980). This need for control may also explain another curious finding, namely, that depressives tend to think more analytically and carefully about social information, and with the consequence of falling prey to fewer biases in judgment. To the extent that depressed individuals are motivated to regain cognitive control over their lives, they would be inclined to think more carefully about the information they are given (see Bless, 2001, and Edwards & Weary, 1993).

Individual differences

Finally, there are stable individual differences in who is curious about their world and wishes to contemplate it (see also Suedfeld & Tetlock, 2001). People, for example, differ in their level of *uncertainty orientation* (Roney & Sorrentino, 1995). Uncertainty-oriented individuals are motivated toward discovery, finding out facts about their worlds and particularly about themselves. Certainty-oriented individuals are more interested in avoiding ambiguity and bolstering previously held beliefs.

People also differ in their motivation to pursue effortful, deliberative, and thoughtful analysis. High *need for cognition* individuals seek out and mull over information they receive about their social worlds, and enjoy doing so, more than their low *n cog* peers (Cacioppo &

Petty, 1982). In several different empirical demonstrations, high *n cog* participants seek out more information about other people, generate more thoughts about the information they were given, pay more attention to the quality of the arguments they are presented when considering social issues, and, perhaps most telling, remember the information they were given more accurately than low *n cog* individuals (for a review, see Cacioppo, Petty, Feinstein, & Jarvis, 1996).

The need for closure

Curiosity and discovery are good things, but sometimes people need not only to think about an issue or to get to an answer, but they need to know an answer *now*. Kruglanski and colleagues (for a review, see Kruglanski & Webster, 1996) have delineated the important role played by this *motive toward closure*, that is, needing an answer to a question, any answer, immediately. They have heightened people's desire for immediate answers, for example, by putting people under time constraints or placing them in a room with a noisy and bothersome printer. When need for closure is increased, people consider fewer possible solutions to intellectual puzzles and express more confidence in the conclusions they reach. They are more likely to base their impressions of others on the first few pieces of information they obtain and are more likely to attribute the person's behavior to dispositional rather than to situational factors. They are also more likely to base their judgments of others on relevant stereotypes.

Other researchers have identified another motivation that attends people's curiosity about the world. People harbor the motivation to seek a simple and manageable cognitive representation of their world, although people differ in the degree of this *personal need for structure* (Neuberg & Newsom, 1993). People high on the need for personal structure, relative to their peers, are more likely to "organize social and nonsocial information in less complex ways" (Neuberg & Newsom, 1993, p. 113). Consistent with this assertion, people high on the need have been found to interpret ambiguous information to be more consistent with previously held stereotypes. A woman experiencing trouble in her college classes, for example, is imbued with more traditionally female attributes (e.g. irrationality). High need individuals are also more likely to simplify their world by forming stereotypes, even clearly erroneous ones, of novel groups (Schaller, Boyd, Yohannes, & O'Brien, 1995). (The answer to the college degree question is Los Alamos, New Mexico.)

Desire to Affirm

If there is any theme that emerges again and again in social psychology, it is that the executive of social cognition is a prideful one. In its observations about its owner and the owner's place in the social world, the executive is eager to affirm the belief that its owner is a competent, masterful, successful, and moral individual.

There is evidence everywhere that the executive is successful in its mission to affirm its owner. If one examines the self-esteem of the typical individual, one finds that the individual tends to hold overly positive views of self (for a provocative review, see Taylor & Brown,

1988). The typical person, on average, states that he or she is more capable and moral than his or her peers, a finding that defies the logic of statistics (Alicke, 1985; Dunning, Meyerowitz, & Holzberg, 1989). For example, in a survey of nearly one million American high school seniors, virtually all said they were above average in "getting along with others," with nearly 60 percent stating that they were in the top 10 percent in this ability (College Board, 1976–1977), a collection of self-views that defy objective analysis. People also tend to believe they have more control over events than they objectively do. For example, people overestimate their control over the throw of a pair of dice, a blatantly chance event (Langer, 1975). They also overestimate their ability to predict future events (Vallone, Griffin, Lin, & Ross, 1990), and to finish tasks before they are due (Buehler, Griffin, & Ross, 1994). They are also overly optimistic relative to objective criteria in their ability to bring about positive life events (such as a happy marriage and a well-paying job) while avoiding negative ones (divorce and crime victimization) (Weinstein, 1980).

The theme that people guide their judgments toward self-affirmation has emerged in so many ways in so many contexts that it has arguably reached the status of being a truism that produces both nods and yawns from those who hear it. However, it is just not that simple. Two complications have dogged this truism since social psychologists started to study it in earnest in the 1940s. First, it is often devilishly hard to show that any bias in social cognition, no matter how congenial it is to the social perceiver, is indisputably prompted by the motive to bolster self-worth. Second, the motive to self-affirm fails to show up in contexts where it should be playing a starring role. Let us consider each complication in turn.

Documenting self-affirmation biases

The cycle of research involving self-affirmation processes often involves three phases. In the first phase, researchers present evidence that the motive to affirm positive images of self leads to a judgmental bias. In the second phase, other researchers show how nonmotivational processes could produce the same bias. In the third phase, researchers struggle to construct clever experiments to decide which account is correct. Or they just give up. In social psychology, there are two instances in which supposed self-affirmational biases were documented, only to have the affirmational origin of those biases called into question.

The new look in perception.   In the late 1940s, many experimental psychologists asserted that perceptions and representations of the social world were fundamentally shaped by needs, wants, and desires, in a movement that became known as the "New Look" (Erdelyi, 1974). For example, poor children guessed that coins were larger than did rich children, presumably because the need for money especially felt by poor children led them literally to see those coins as bigger (Bruner & Goodman, 1947). People had a more difficult time recognizing threatening words (e.g. *homicide*) when they were flashed on a T-scope than they did more common words (e.g. *flower*), indicating a filter that inhibited the recognition of ominous stimuli, a phenomenon known as *perceptual defense* (Bruner & Klein, 1960).

However, the basic findings of the New Look approach fell under both logical and empirical critiques, with the latter being most devastating. For example, the finding that people failed to recognize threatening words as efficiently as they did nondescript ones was finally attributed to the fact that threatening words were less frequent, and thus less familiar, than were their nonthreatening counterparts (Broadbent, 1967). The New Look never recovered from these critiques, and research in this tradition evaporated as the 1950s turned into the 1960s.

Self-serving attributions.   In the 1970s, a similar cycle emerged for people's attributions for their successes and failures. The basic finding was that people attributed their successes to their own abilities, whereas they attributed their failures to mercurial external forces such as task difficulty or luck (for a review, see Zuckerman, 1979), an apparent motivational phenomenon. However, a number of scholars noted that this so-called self-serving attributional pattern was also logically warranted. In particular, given that people often have good reason to expect that they will succeed, it is only natural for them to attribute their successes to their own capacities and their failures to some exceptional or interfering circumstance in the environment, or to just bad luck (Miller & Ross, 1975).

Failures of the motive to appear

At times, the executive seems surprisingly disinterested in maintaining self-esteem. Nowhere is this surprising disinterest more apparent than in the gathering of social information. According to the tenets of a self-affirmation motive, people should selectively expose themselves to information that is congenial to treasured beliefs rather than information that is contradictory.

However, early research on selective exposure failed to find any consistent results that would support the notion of a defensive executive. When people were given a chance to look over information that supported or threatened their recent purchase of a car, supported or denigrated the political candidate of their party, or suggested that cigarette smoking caused or did not cause cancer, some studies showed a preference for congenial information, some no preference, and others a preference for threatening information (Freedman & Sears, 1965).

Another research program, coming several years after these studies, also showed a surprising absence of self-affirmational motives in situations where people evaluated their own abilities. For example, Trope (1980) examined when people wanted feedback about themselves. He found that people preferred to receive feedback about themselves equally in situations in which they could succeed or fail, and equally in situations in which success or failure carried decisive information about themselves. In short, people were just as willing to receive potentially self-damning information as they were self-glorifying data.

The knowledge versus the affirmation motive

It is worth pausing to reflect on these failures to find a selective exposure effect, for the counterintuitive nature of these findings does force one to consider when the need to know will drive people's cognition and when the need to self-affirm will. If one takes a long, hard look at how self-affirmational motives bias human judgment, one begins to see the situational factors that promote the need to know over the need to affirm, and vice versa.

Explicitness of informational choices.   If one scrutinizes the methods of the studies reviewed above, one finds that they have one telling common element. These studies present participants with an explicit and rather transparent choice between receiving congenial versus uncongenial information (Freedman & Sears, 1965), or between diagnostic versus nondiagnostic tests (e.g. Trope, 1980). In short, the uncongenial option was an explicit option that the participant had to consider.

A different picture of selective exposure arises when the choice between congenial and uncongenial options is not so explicit. For example, Pyszczynski, Greenberg, & LaPrelle (1985) led participants to succeed or fail on a test of social sensitivity. They were then given the option of seeing how other participants had performed. After failure, participants asked to see the responses of a greater number of other participants when they were led to believe that those others had performed badly as opposed to well, a selective exposure effect that seems designed to affirm the self. Note, however, participants were not given an explicit choice between seeing bolstering or threatening information. Given the between-subject nature of this design, participants never had to choose explicitly between looking at people who had outperformed versus underperformed them.

Similar effects arise when people search their memories for information consistent with flattering conclusions. Sanitioso, Kunda, & Fong (1990) led participants to believe that either extraversion or introversion was related to success in life pursuits. Not surprisingly, participants in the former condition later described themselves as more extraverted than did their counterparts in the latter. In examining how people could revise their self-images in such flattering ways, Sanitioso, et al. found evidence for a selective exposure effect in memory search. Participants in the extraversion condition selectively searched their memories for data that they had acted in extraverted ways in the past; participants in the introversion condition selectively searched for memories of introverted behavior. Again, participants had not been presented with a transparent choice between favorable and unfavorable information. With that choice obscured, people roamed free in their search through memory for information flattering to their self-images.

Finally, people reveal self-affirmation impulses via their tendency to *self-handicap* under threat. Faced with the explicit acquisition of self-relevant information that they are not sure will reflect well on them, people will sabotage their own performance if that sabotage gives them an adequate excuse for inadequate performance (Berglas & Jones, 1978). For example, college students not sure that they will succeed at an intellectual task volunteer to drink alcohol before confronting the task (Tucker, Vuchinich, & Sobell, 1981). Again, in this situation, there is no explicit choice between self-affirming and non-affirming options, and given this cover participants choose to act in self-affirming or protecting ways.

Timing of the information search.   Another circumstance that could determine whether people seek out unbiased versus congenial information depends on whether a conclusion or a decision has been made. For example, I recently traveled to an antique fair where I found a dining room table I was rather ambivalent about buying. Faced with my ambivalence,

I pulled my traveling companion aside and began peppering her with questions. After a long while, exasperated, she asked me what I wanted her to tell me. I said that I only wanted her honest opinions, regardless of the decision I made (which was true). Finally, after a tortuous back and forth, I decided to buy the table. As we walked back to the antique dealer, I turned to her again and told her from now on I only wanted to hear (which was true) why I had made the right decision.

This example, as well as rigorous empirical research, suggests that the motive that dominates thought before a decision is reached can be quite different from the motive that governs thought afterward. According to Gollwitzer and colleagues (e.g. Gollwitzer & Kinney, 1989; Oettingen & Gollwitzer, 2001), pre-decision thought is governed by a *deliberative* mind-set in which the individual dispassionately seeks out impartial and accurate information. However, after a decision has been made, people enter an *implementational* mind-set where they are focused on how to attain the goal they wish to attain. Once that Rubicon of decision has been crossed, people favor information that flatters their decisions over information that threatens them. Consistent with this analysis, people choosing between two pieces of experimental machinery do not overestimate their ability to make the machinery function. However, once people have chosen a machine and have started to try to make it function, they hold inflated views of their ability to make it work. Buttressing this general analysis, making people accountable for their decisions *after* they have reached them makes them seek out information selectively in order to bolster their decisions (Tetlock, 1992).

This distinction between pre- and post-decision phases serves as a specific example of a more general distinction that separates circumstances that prompt the need for accuracy over the need for affirmation. People seek out unbiased and accurate information when they have some control over their state of affairs. When they do not have control, they move instead toward the psychic analgesic of self-affirmation. Supporting this notion, Dunning (1995) examined when people desired accurate information about their abilities, no matter how pleasant or unpleasant that information was, versus when people would want only the pleasant information. He found that when people thought they could control the development of the ability, they desired information no matter how unpleasant it might be. When they thought they could not control the development of the trait, they tended to censor unpleasant news and gravitate toward congenial data. In a similar vein, Frey (1986) provided evidence that people seek out unfriendly information if they felt they could control its implications, that is, they had ample ammunition to refute it if need be.

Biases in interpretation

In some respects, the failures to find a universal tendency toward selective exposure should not come as a surprise, for it is not in the exposure to information that the self-affirming executive reveals its genius. Rather, its expertise lies in its interpretation once that information is received. The social cognitive executive has a vast array of strategies and techniques to evaluate, organize, and make sense of the information it receives, both pleasant and unpleasant. Because of this, unpleasant information is often neutralized once the executive has a chance to mull it over. To be sure, the executive is often constrained in the conclusions that it can reach, for its conclusions must remain plausible and justifiable (see Kunda, 1990, for a discussion of the important role played by "reality constraints"), but within those bounds the executive is likely to make judgments of the self and the social world that are quite pleasant and bolstering.

For example, unpleasant information is sometimes given *more*, not less, attention and scrutiny, with an eye toward dismissing its implications. Ditto & Lopez (1992), for example, asked people to take a test for an enzyme deficiency. Relative to a group who received favorable news, those who received an unfavorable result spent more time scrutinizing that result. They took longer to decide that the test had been completed and were more likely to repeat it.

Often, this greater scrutiny "pays off," in that it allows the executive to unloose its interpretive machinery toward discounting the information (for reviews, see Baumeister & Newman, 1994; Kunda, 1990). First, the scrutiny given to unfriendly information allows people to find flaws in that information. For example, people find methodological problems in scientific studies that question their personal views on the death penalty (Lord, Ross, & Lepper, 1979). Second, increased scrutiny can allow people to develop alternative explanations, often reasonable, for unpleasant outcomes that spare self-esteem (Ditto & Lopez, 1992). For example, people receiving a bad medical diagnosis are more likely to pay (appropriate) attention to the probability that some alternative source caused the result, or to remember irregularities in their recent behavior that could have thrown the test off (Ditto, Scepansky, Munro, Apanovitch, & Lockhart, 1998).

The interpretative expertise of the self-affirming executive is revealed by many other techniques. For example, when assessing the ability of self or others, people use biased and self-flattering definitions of those traits. When defining such traits as "talent," people tend to emphasize the attributes they possess and de-emphasize the attributes they do not (Dunning & Cohen, 1992; Dunning, Meyerowitz, & Holzberg, 1989). Thus, the behavioral criteria that people use to judge self and others are tacitly stacked in favor of the self.

As well, the affirmational executive is facile at denigrating the importance of the self's failures. When people do poorly on a task, their subsequent reaction is often one of deriding the importance of the skill involved (Tesser & Paulhus, 1983). Indeed, when people rate both their skill level in a domain and their importance they attach to it, one sees strong positive correlations (Pelham, 1991). Finally, when a person is induced to act in a way that violates his or her personal attitudes, the individual often comes to hold the attitude as trivial "in the grand scheme of things" (Simon, Greenberg, & Brehm, 1995).

The executive also minimizes the implications of its owner's shortcomings by perceiving those shortcomings to be common among others (Mullen & Goethals, 1990). For example, people who hold hidden fears (e.g. of public speaking, of spiders) tend to overestimate the percentage of the population who also holds those fears. In doing so, they reduce the distinctiveness of these failings (Suls & Wan, 1987). In contrast, people do not tend to perceive their strengths and proficiencies as common. If anything, they tend to *underestimate* their prevalence of those skills in the relevant population (Mullen & Goethals, 1990).

Finally, if all else fails, the executive is adept at finding other individuals who are worse than its owner. People often engage in downward social comparison, finding an individual whose level of skill or desirability of circumstance is inferior to the self, with this comparison activity becoming more fervent after threats to self-esteem (Biernat & Billings, 2001; Wills, 1981).

Implicit self-affirmation

Recent research suggests that the affirmational executive is not only adept but zealous in its guardianship of self-esteem. The evidence that people discount their own failings and extol their own virtues is not a surprise. However, what may be a surprise is that people not only make claims about themselves that directly bolster self-esteem, but also provide judgments of others that implicitly and indirectly enhance their own self-images. That is, even when it is another person who is to be judged and not the self, people make judgments that reflect favorably on the self.

For example, Dunning & Cohen (1992) examined the judgments made of others by "low" and "high" performers in a domain (e.g. athletics). Low performers judged virtually everybody, regardless of performance level, as pretty capable – thus allowing themselves by implication to see themselves as capable. In contrast, high performers denigrated the achievements of anyone whose performance was inferior to their own. In doing so, they could claim to be uniquely capable among their peers. Tellingly, these types of self-aggrandizing judgments were exacerbated by threats to self-esteem (Beauregard & Dunning, 1998; for similar data, see Dunning, Leuenberger, & Sherman, 1995).

Other researchers have shown that the need to bolster the self prompts people to revise their impressions of others in self-aggrandizing ways. When esteem is threatened, people are more likely to apply derogatory stereotypes in their judgments of other people (Fein & Spencer, 1997), and to denigrate the achievements of their peers in order to accentuate the superiority of their own achievements (Brown & Gallagher, 1992). When their personal mastery is questioned by asking them to think about their own death, they derogate people from other social groups or those who espouse opinions that differ from their own (Solomon, Greenberg, & Pyszczynski, 1991). People are also motivated to extol the skills of those who outperform them. By doing so, they give themselves more perceptual wiggle room to extol their own meager achievements (Alicke, LoSchiavo, Zerbst, & Zhang, 1997).

The most developed and researched model of this implicit self-affirmation is Tesser's (1988) *self-evaluation maintenance* (SEM) model. In the model, Tesser proposes two strategies that people pursue to bolster their self-esteem. First, people engage in *comparison* processes, in which they compare their abilities with those of their peers, particularly close peers. This comparison occurs for abilities that people consider important and ones in which they believe they outperform others. Second, people engage in *reflection* processes, in which they bask in the reflected glory of the proficiencies and achievements of close others. That basking, however, can occur only in domains that people consider unimportant for themselves, so that they are not threatened by the fact that close others outperform them.

In a number of ingenious studies, Tesser and colleagues have shown that the interplay of comparison and reflection processes has a number of implications for social life. People consider an ability as important to the extent that they believe they outperform people they are close to. People denigrate the performances of their peers in domains they consider self-defining, but not in domains they do not consider self-defining. People's choices of their friends are based, in part, on whether those others are inferior on self-defining abilities (better for the comparison process) yet superior in nonself-defining domains (better for the reflection process). People will even sabotage the performances of their friends in self-defining domains more than they will of strangers in order to maintain favorable comparisons (for a review, see Tesser, 1988; 2001).

Desire for Coherence

As much as nature abhors a vacuum, the executive despises incoherence in its beliefs about the world. As such, the executive is motivated to reduce the contradictions that it confronts in its social environment. As discussed above, inconsistencies between what people learn about their worlds and what they already believed is a prime instigator of curiosity. But in 1957, Leon Festinger raised the stakes. In his theory of cognitive dissonance, Festinger proposed that inconsistencies among beliefs, especially if one or both of those beliefs is important or relevant, cause negative psychological tension that must be relieved by any means necessary. There are many ways to resolve the inconsistency and thus reduce the tension. First, people can "add" cognitions that explain away the inconsistency. They can change one of the beliefs to be more compatible with the other belief. They can also trivialize the importance of either or both beliefs.

Researchers throughout the years have developed three distinct paradigms to study whether and how people resolved contradictory beliefs. In the *forced compliance* paradigm, people are asked to perform an action that goes against their beliefs and principles. In the classic first demonstration of dissonance principles, participants who were asked to lie about a dreadful experiment they had just completed, by saying that it was exciting and informative, later viewed the experiment as more enjoyable when they had little justification to lie (i.e. they were paid only $1) than when they had ample justification (i.e. they were paid $20) (Festinger & Carlsmith, 1959). In the *effort justification* paradigm, participants come to hold an object as more valuable to the extent that they had to work hard to get it, placing them in a position in which they had to justify all the effort expended. Finally, in the *free choice* paradigm, participants are given a choice between two items of similar desirability. After choosing one, participants tend to denigrate the value of the rejected item to resolve the dissonance caused by the choice (for reviews of these techniques, see Abelson, Aronson, McGuire, Newcomb, Rosenberg, & Tannenbaum, 1968; Aronson, 1969).

However, although dissonance theory has inspired the successful completion of thousands of empirical studies, it still is hardly a noncontroversial series of proposals. Almost from its inception, researchers enveloped the theory under a cloud of questions and concerns.

Controversy 1: does dissonance exist?

For example, Festinger's motivational theory generated alternative accounts based solely on cognitive or informational principles, much like had happened with research on the New Look and self-serving attributions. Bem (1972), for example, questioned whether dissonance as a "hot" and negative affective state existed at all. Instead, in his *self-perception* theory, he proposed that people add or alter cognitions in the face of inconsistency simply as a result of a dispassionate review of their actions and opinions. For example, why would people change their opinion of a dreadful experiment based on the fact that they had lied to another person about it for $1? That opinion change need not be to alleviate negative psychological tension, for just look at the facts: the participant had said the experiment was exciting, did it for only $1, and thus the study could not have been that noxious after all, QED. Hence, the so-called dissonance effect could be the logical outcome of dispassionate review of the events surrounding the "lie."

Perhaps the biggest dissonance reaction of them all was the upset and outrage expressed by dissonance researchers at Bem's (1966) reanalysis. The controversy between dissonance and self-perception perspectives prompted innumerable studies to resolve the contradiction between what dissonance researchers believed and what Bem proposed.

Over the years, those studies have produced two types of resolutions between Festinger's motivational proposal and Bem's purely cognitive alternative. First, researchers have taken great care to show that contradictions between beliefs, as produced in classic dissonance research paradigms, do indeed produce physiological arousal (Elkin & Leippe, 1986) and self-reports of negative affect (Elliot & Devine, 1994). Other evidence suggests this heightened emotion plays the role it has been proposed to play in dissonance processes. Giving people a way to explain away their arousal prompts them to be less interested in resolving inconsistencies (Zanna & Cooper, 1974). Preventing people from feeling dissonance, by letting them drink a few alcoholic beverages, also makes people disinclined to resolve dissonance (Steele, Southwick, & Critchlow, 1981). Most telling, allowing people to resolve dissonance by changing their attitudes reduces the arousal (Elkin & Leippe, 1986) and negative affect (Elliot & Devine, 1994) that they feel.

Second, researchers have taken pains to delineate conditions in which dissonance processes may govern people's reactions to contradictory events and those in which self-perception processes may prevail. Fazio, Zanna, & Cooper (1977) looked at the degree of discrepancy between the participant's attitude and the position they were asked to publicly espouse. Fazio, et al. proposed that when the discrepancy was great, so great that the position that participants were asked to support was not something they could agree with, participants should feel dissonance. However, when the discrepancy was trivial, that is, the participant did not necessarily disagree with the position they were asked to take, they should feel no dissonance, although they may change their attitudes due to self-perception processes. The experimental data agreed with this analysis. When participants wrote essays supporting a position greatly discrepant from their own, they changed their attitudes toward that position only when they did not have a chance to explain away the negative affect they were feeling. However, when the discrepancy was not so great, all participants changed their attitudes toward the position, regardless of what they were told about the "affect" they should be feeling, indicating that participants were feeling no dissonance when dealing with positions not that discrepant from their own.

Controversy 2: what causes dissonance?

The second controversy surrounding dissonance involves which specific inconsistencies, if any at all, cause the dissonant state. As Festinger (1957) originally noted, not all inconsistencies would provoke dissonance. The inconsistencies had to involve "important" cognitions and behaviors. But what made a cognition or behavior important?

There have been three major proposals to the question of which inconsistencies count. Cooper & Fazio (1984) suggested that it was not inconsistency *per se* that prompted dissonance. Instead, to provoke dissonance, a researcher had to induce participants to perform a behavior that (a) had been freely chosen and that (b) had adverse consequences that were (c) clearly foreseeable. Only then would people feel adverse emotions that they would quell via dissonance reduction. In support of this view, Sher & Cooper (1989) conducted a study showing that no inconsistent behavior need take place to arouse dissonance, but just a behavior that fulfilled the three conditions described above. They asked participants to give a speech that either favored or opposed the participant's own opinions, and independent of this varied whether the speech would result in negative consequences. Sher and Cooper found attitude change in line with the speech only in those situations in which negative outcomes would occur, regardless of whether the speech contradicted the participant's original views.

Aronson (1969) developed a completely different analysis of which inconsistencies and conditions led to dissonance. In his view, inconsistency again *per se* did not lead to dissonance but rather inconsistencies about the self. That is, people tended to possess views of themselves that they wished to maintain and bolster. When their behavior contradicted those beliefs, then they would experience dissonance and work to resolve it. Perhaps his clearest demonstration of this analysis was a series of studies conducted in the 1990s on *hypocrisy*, in which Aronson and colleagues showed that making discrepancies about the self salient led to changes in behavior.

In one such study, participants were asked to make a videotaped speech in which they attempted to persuade high school students to practice safe sex. Before beginning the speech, some participants completed a questionnaire about their own adherence to safe sex principles, which, of course, for virtually all participants turned out to be imperfect. According to Aronson and colleagues, having participants review their past failings should prompt them to see the hypocrisy between what they practiced and what they were about to preach. As such, participants in this condition should feel dissonance, and thus be motivated to reduce it. And they did, purchasing more condoms at the end of the experiment than did participants who merely gave the speech (Stone, Aronson, Crain, Winslow, & Fried, 1994). Key to this demonstration, and contradicting the proposals of Cooper & Fazio (1984), dissonance effects were obtained in situations involving no foreseeable aversive consequences (for, after all, the students' speeches could only steer their audiences toward taking more safe sex precautions).

Close to Aronson's analysis of dissonance arousal was the approach taken by Steele (1988), who also emphasized the importance of beliefs about the self in dissonance arousal. According to Steele, it was not necessarily contradictions with self-beliefs that provoked dissonance but contradictions with the specific belief that the self was a moral and effective individual. Cast a person's morality or mastery into doubt, and dissonance would kick in. Supporting this *self-affirmational* view, Steele provided many demonstrations that reminding people that they were effective and ethical individuals tended to stop dissonance processes in their tracks.

For example, in one such study, participants were asked to write essays opposing state funding for facilities for the handicapped. Participants showed dissonance effects, changing their own attitudes to be in line with the essay, unless they had been given a chance to volunteer to help a blind person. In this last situation, participants could affirm the notion that they were charitable individuals, thus making the essay less threatening (Steele & Liu, 1983).

The logical conclusion of consistency motives

At its logical conclusion, the motive toward epistemic coherence would lead people to seek out and remember only the information that confirms previously held beliefs. In the realm of beliefs about the self, that motive has been well-documented. In work on *self-verification* motives, Swann (1997) and colleagues have shown that people prefer to gather information that reaffirms views already held about the self. Of key import, people seek out this confirmatory information even when it supports negative self-beliefs.

For example, people with negative self-views pay more attention to information if they believe that information will portray them in an unfavorable light than they do information that promises to be favorable. They are also willing to pay money to receive such negative information. People also surround themselves with other individuals who verify views, even negative ones, about the self. For example, they feel more intimate with their marriage partners when those partners hold the same impression that people hold about themselves, even if those impressions are unfavorable ones. In short, people actively arrange their social environments to confirm views held of the self (for reviews, see Swann, 1990, 1997). Finally, people with low self-views distort their memory for feedback about their abilities in a self-denigrating direction, in contrast to high self-view individuals who distort in a positive direction (Story, 1998).

But why do people self-verify? At first blush, one might think that people with negative self-views simply are not as upset by negative information as are people with high self-views, and thus do not fear it. However, when people with low self-views are given negative information, they are just as unhappy and upset as are their high self-view peers (Swann, 1990). So why do low self-view individuals choose information that is emotionally punishing?

Two desires appear to underlie the motive toward self-verification. Swann, Stein-Serroussi, & Geisler (1992) asked people why they chose self-verifying information. In pouring over people's explanations, they found, first, that people desired to maintain the overarching belief that they knew themselves. By maintaining that belief, people also maintained some notion that the world was a coherent and predictable place. In people's explanations for the information they sought, these concerns over *epistemic* matters were the most frequent reason that people cited. But beyond epistemic concerns, people also expressed *pragmatic* concerns. When choosing people to interact with, participants opted for the person who was the likeliest to lead to a smooth and productive social interaction. That person was likeliest to be the individual who had an accurate impression of the information gatherer.

Current Thinking and Future Directions

Thus, scanning the social psychological literature over the decades, one sees ample empirical support for the three motives to seek out information, to make sure it is favorable, and to insure that it is consistent with prior beliefs. However, there is still much work to be done ascertaining how these motives influence human thought and action. Consider the following questions, all of which are currently receiving or deserve scientific attention.

Relation of the three motives to each other

The first question is how the motives toward knowledge, affirmation, and coherence interact with one another. Recent theorists have put forth only the simplest of conclusions about the interrelations of these motives, signaling the start of work that still has several years to go.

For example, some theorists have tackled the question of, if push ever came to shove, which motive would rank supreme over the others? Sedikides (1993) conducted a study on "self-reflection," that is, what information would people seek to find out about themselves when wrapped up in a moment of contemplation about the self. In asking people to design the questions they would ask about themselves, he found that self-enhancement ranked supreme. His participants tended to ask questions about their strong points, ones to which they already knew the answer. Other theorists have reached similar conclusions about the supremacy of the motive to affirm one's self (Baumeister, 1998; Heider, 1958).

However, there are two reasons to be cautious about making any claim about the supremacy of any motive over the others. First, which motive is supreme in any given situation likely depends on the specific circumstances surrounding that situation. Sedikides (1993), for example, found that the motive toward affirmation reigned supreme, but note that his self-reflection situation carried no concrete consequences for participants. What if college seniors had been asked about their chances to pass the course exam taking place next week? That situation carries immediate consequences for the question-asker and a very different set of motivations might have been invoked. After all, recall that people become more motivated to acquire accurate information when they are faced with decisions that carry obvious, real, and immediate consequences for them.

Second, the question of which motive is supreme presupposes that the motives are distinct. Any researcher who squints into the fact of any of these motives soon sees that they tend to morph into each other in the experiments reviewed above. For example, noticing an inconsistency in the environment may make one curious (the need to know), but if the inconsistency is relevant enough it can cause dissonance (the need for coherence). Question a person's mastery over the world (that is, make them need to affirm themselves), and sometimes the result is more attributional activity and more accurate judgment (the need to know). Make a person confront an important inconsistency and they will strive to resolve it, unless you first buttress his or her positive self-views through an exercise in self-affirmation (Steele, 1988) or by reminding them of a way in which they compare favorably with people they know (Tesser & Cornell, 1991).

In short, the three motives tend to blend in together, so much so that it is difficult to know if they are distinct. At their heart, each motive involves the same issue: the person's sense of mastery over the world. By gathering knowledge, a person renders the world comprehensible, predictable, and controllable. By pursuing the motive for self-affirmation, a person establishes that he or she is competent enough to master happy fates and avoid fearful ones. By fulfilling the motive for coherence, one gains the mastery conferred by possessing a predictable world. Scratch beneath the surface, and each motive addresses the same basic issue, and thus it is difficult to know if they are distinct or rather different manifestations of the same underlying motive (see Aronson, 1992; Tesser & Cornell, 1991, for similar conclusions).

Individual differences

A curious feature of motivational approaches to social cognitive phenomena is that they make theorists think in terms of individual differences more than they do when those theorists adopt cognitive perspectives. Consider all the individual difference variables that have been evoked in analyses of epistemic motives, such as need for cognition, need for personal structure, and uncertainty orientation. Other theorists have explored the need to self-affirm through studies of self-esteem (Blaine & Crocker, 1993) and narcissism (John & Robins, 1994). Even cognitive dissonance has been approached via an individual difference perspective, for it has been found that people high in the *preference for consistency* display dissonance effects more strongly than do their peers who are low in this need (Cialdini, Trost, & Newsom, 1995). If one looks over the history of purely cognitive approaches to social judgment, one would be hard pressed to find such a proliferation of individual difference variables.

Thus, it would not be a surprise if a re-emergence of motivational approaches in social cognition prompted more interest in individual difference work. However, three notes are worth making about such individual difference work. First, it is an interesting research question in itself why it is so much easier to think of individual differences in terms of motivational differences as opposed to cognitive ones. (Could that say something important about how people make attributions about others in their everyday world?) Second, researchers should make sure to verify that the individual differences they observe are actually due to needs and motives as opposed to some other factor. Take, for example, the need for cognition. People do differ in the tendency to engage in effortful thought (Cacioppo, Petty, Feinstein, & Jarvis, 1996), but is that due to a motive? It could simply be a predisposition toward caution and analysis, or a product of familial training, or an indication of intellectual ability, for people will tend to think hard if they are often successful at it.

The third note to be made is more telling for theoretical work on human motives. The interesting story about motives may not be how they drive human judgment in general, but how they drive the thoughts and actions of important classes of people. Take the late lamented New Look in perception. While the New Look lies largely dormant in social psychology, this perspective has arisen independently, and forcefully, in the field of psychopathology. Evidence abounds that certain clinical populations show great evidence of perceptual defense that holds many similarities to the proposals promoted by New Look theorists.

For example, Amir, Foa, & Coles (1998) found evidence that people with generalized social phobias are vigilant toward but ultimately repress any material that evokes their phobia. Amir, et al. showed social phobics and nonphobics a number of sentences that ended with words that had double meanings, one of which was socially threatening (e.g. *She wrote down the mean.*). Participants were asked if a following target word was consistent with the material in the sentence (e.g. *unfriendly*). The target word was not consistent with the sentence – but it was consistent with a socially threatening interpretation of the last word in that sentence. When the target word closely followed the stimulus sentence, social phobics relative to their nonphobic peers took longer to state that the target word was inconsistent, indicating that they had activated the socially threatening meaning of the target word. However, when the target word followed the sentence after a pause of nearly a second, social phobics were faster at denying the consistency of the target word, indicating that they had begun to inhibit the socially threatening meaning of that word.

Culture

Perhaps the most intriguing set of individual differences in social cognitive processes are those that covary with geographic borders. At first blush, it would seem to be a human universal, one hardly worth mentioning, that people are motivated to find things out, to affirm their own worth, and to see a coherent world. However, these obvious motives may not survive a transfer off the shores of North America and Europe. An emerging body of work suggests that the denizens of many cultures fail to be influenced as much, if at all, by the motivational forces (see Oyserman, 2001, for a review of research on culture).

For example, take the motive to affirm the self. In some extant studies, people of Eastern cultures, such as China and Japan, fail to show any evidence of this motive. For example, Japanese respondents fail to show any self-serving biases in their impressions of themselves, quite unlike the usual positive biases demonstrated by North American respondents. In an illustrative study, Canadian and Japanese respondents were asked to rate their ability relative to their peers. Canadian respondents tended, on average, to say that they were above average in their abilities, replicating a typical but logically impossible set of self-views. Japanese participants showed no such "above average" bias, even in situations that should be the most threatening to self-image (Heine & Lehman, 1995). These findings suggest that Japanese individuals are not interested in enhancing the self *per se*, but rather focused on criticizing the self to find ways to improve themselves. In particular, they engage in self-analysis in order to find ways that they can fit themselves into collective interpersonal relations that are harmonious (Markus & Kitayama, 1991).

As well, the desire for coherence in the social world may be an obsession found more in the West than in the East, judging from recent experiments on dissonance effects. Heine & Lehman (1997) asked Canadian and Japanese participants to choose between equally valued compact discs. Whereas Canadian participants showed the usual dissonance effect, disparaging the nonchosen compact disc relative to the chosen one, Japanese participants showed no such pattern. Interestingly, receiving positive feedback (a self-affirmation exercise) prevented Canadian participants from displaying the usual dissonance effect and receiving negative feedback exacerbated it. Feedback had no effect on Japanese participants, showing once again a lack of concern for self-affirmation.

Further data on the need for coherence reveals more subtle, and perhaps deeper, differences between Eastern and Western cultures. In a study of preferences for consistency among American and Chinese respondents, Peng (1997) found that Westerners tended to prefer propositions, as embedded in proverbs, that were logically coherent (*as the twig is bent, so grows the tree*), whereas Chinese respondents found relatively more favor in propositions that contained logical contradictions (*too humble is half proud*).

Mechanisms of motivation

Future research could also focus on what "level" motivation influences social judgment. In particular, over the past twenty years in social psychology, a distinction has emerged between processes that occur on the *explicit* level, with conscious control and effort, and those that occur on the *implicit* level, without any awareness, control, or monitoring (Banaji et al., 2001; Greenwald & Banaji, 1995). It would be useful to see the extent to which affirmational and coherence motives occur at either level. Such an investigation would be useful in answering the important question of whether the biases that these motives produce are correctable. To the extent that their influence is implicit, with their influence occurring outside of consciousness and control, correcting for motivational biases would be difficult, if not impossible. Thus, the distinction between implicit and explicit processing becomes more important as one stirs motivation into the mix of social cognition.

Parallel constraint satisfaction systems

Upon examining the style of research typically adopted to examine motivation in human judgment, one might be tempted to surmise that social psychology, if it is ever to take motivation seriously, will have to abandon its rigorous and computer based information processing methods and learn (or perhaps to relearn) how to conduct high impact psychodramas that provoke the psychic needs of participants. One would have to re-invent, for example, the style of the old dissonance experiments, which presented participants with vivid conflicts not easily resolved.

Although a return to high impact methodology might be called for, an emphasis on motivation should not cause psychological researchers to run from their personal computers. In fact, motivational perspectives on social cognition may call for an increased emphasis on computer based research tools. Consider parallel constraint satisfaction models, in which researchers set up computer simulations where they give an organism in the computer some *a priori* beliefs, and then revise some of those beliefs to see how the system alters the other beliefs it has been given. The key in such systems is that all changes must bring all beliefs in harmony, or at least in some steady state, with one another (Smith & Qweller, 2001; Smith, 1998).

One can easily see how parallel constraint satisfaction models could be useful for expressing and exploring how motivations influence social judgment. Suppose we built a system that mimicked the human desire to think well of itself, a belief that could not be changed unless under tremendous fire. We could then feed the system with social information to see how interpretations of that information and other beliefs about the "self" were changed or shaped when constrained by the overarching belief that the self is good. In fact, such a system has already been built to model processes associated with cognitive dissonance, and has done a splendid job of accounting for classic dissonance findings (Shultz & Lepper, 1996).

Concluding Remarks

At the outset of this chapter, I raised the issue of executive functions in social judgment, raising questions about what factors instigate, monitor, shape, control, and terminate the processes of social judgment. In short, I asked how we could characterize the homunculus that carries out these functions. Several systematic principles turned out to shape the efforts of that creature. Work on curiosity and the desire for knowledge shows that the creature desires information the most under circumscribed situations. Work on the desire for affirmation and coherence shows the constraints that the creature is under as it works its way toward its conclusions about the social world. For the most part, those conclusions must affirm the self-esteem of its owner and be coherent with important beliefs already possessed.

As such, the time may be ripe for turning research attention more directly on the executive functions governing social judgment. However, to do so, researchers may have to adopt research strategies that may have to differ from the usual ones used in social psychology. In particular, to determine when people spontaneously decide to judge others, and on what dimensions, researchers will have to forego handing their participants questionnaires containing predefined questions. Instead, researchers will have to present participants with opportunities to make judgments that they may choose to pass on. As well, to determine the importance and prevalence of constraints, such as affirmation and coherence, on participants' judgments, researchers will have to lie back and let participants decide when they will make judgments and invoke those constraints themselves.

These types of research paradigms will call for some cleverness, but the results of pursuing them will be useful. Like the executive, scientists are curious and like to form coherent theories of the world (and have been shown not to mind the occasional self-affirmation). Thus, to satiate these needs, scientists will have to alter the methods they use to address more completely how social judgment is motivated.

REFERENCES

Abelson, R. P., Aronson, E., McGuire, W. J., Newcomb, T. M., Rosenberg, M. J., & Tannenbaum, T. M. (1968). *Theories of cognitive consistency: A sourcebook*. Skokie, IL: Rand McNally.

Alicke, M. D. (1985). Global self-evaluation as determined by the desirability and controllability of trait adjectives. *Journal of Personality and Social Psychology, 59*, 1621–1630.

Alicke, M. D., LoSchiavo, F. M., Zerbst, J., & Zhang, S. (1997). The person who outperforms me is a genius: Maintaining perceived competence in upward social comparison. *Journal of Personality and Social Psychology, 72,* 781–789.

Amir, N., Foa, E. B., & Coles, M. E. (1998). Automatic activation and strategic avoidance of threat-relevant information in social phobia. *Journal of Abnormal Psychology, 107,* 285–290.

Aronson, E. (1969). The theory of cognitive dissonance: A current perspective. In L. Berkowitz (Ed.), *Advances in experimental social psychology* Vol. 4 (pp. 1–34). New York: Academic Press.

Aronson, E. (1992). The return of the repressed: Dissonance theory makes a comeback. *Psychological Inquiry, 3,* 303–311.

Banaji, M. R., Lemm, K. M., & Carpenter, S. J. (2001). The social unconscious. In A. Tesser & N. Schwarz (Eds.), *Blackwell handbook of social psychology: Intraindividual processes* (pp. 134–158). Oxford: Blackwell Publishing.

Baumeister, R. F. (1998). The self. In D. T. Gilbert, S. T. Fiske, & G. Lindzey (Eds.), *Handbook of social psychology* Vol. 1. 4th. edn. (pp. 680–740). New York: McGraw-Hill.

Baumeister, R. F., & Newman, L. S. (1994). Self-regulation of cognitive inference and decision processes. *Personality and Social Psychology Bulletin, 20,* 3–19.

Beauregard, K. S., & Dunning, D. (1998). Turning up the contrast: Self-enhancement motives prompt egocentric contrast effects in social judgments. *Journal of Personality and Social Psychology, 74,* 606–621.

Bem, D. J. (1966). Self-perception: An alternative interpretation of cognitive dissonance phenomena. *Psychological Review, 74,* 183–200.

Bem, D. J. (1972). Self-perception theory. In L. Berkowitz (Ed.), *Advances in experimental social psychology* Vol. 6 (pp. 1–63). New York: Academic Press.

Berglas, S., & Jones, E. E. (1978). Drug choice as a self-handicapping strategy in response to noncontingent success. *Journal of Personality and Social Psychology, 36,* 405–417.

Berlyne, D. E. (1954). An experimental study of human curiosity. *British Journal of Psychology, 45,* 256–265.

Berscheid, E., Graziano, W., Monson, T., & Dermer, M. (1976). Outcome dependency: Attention, attribution, and attraction. *Journal of Personality and Social Psychology, 34,* 978–989.

Bettmann, J. R., & Weitz, B. A. (1983). Attributions in the boardroom: Causal reasoning in corporate annual reports. *Administrative Science Quarterly, 28,* 165–183.

Biernat, M., & Billings, L. S. (2001). Standards, expectancies, social comparison. In A. Tesser & N. Schwarz (Eds.), *Blackwell handbook of social psychology: Intraindividual processes* (pp. 257–283). Oxford: Blackwell Publishing.

Blaine, B., & Crocker, J. (1993). Self-esteem and self-serving biases in reactions to positive and negative events: An integrative review. In R. F. Baumeister (Ed.), *Self-esteem: The puzzle of low self-regard* (pp. 55–85). New York: Plenum Press.

Bless, H. (2001). The consequences of mood on the processing of social information. In A. Tesser & N. Schwarz (Eds.), *Blackwell handbook of social psychology: Intraindividual processes* (pp. 391–412). Oxford: Blackwell Publishing.

Bohner, G., Bless, H., Schwarz, N., & Strack, F. (1988). What triggers causal attributions? The impact of valence and subjective probability. *European Journal of Social Psychology, 18,* 335–345.

Broadbent, D. E. (1967). Word-frequency effect and response bias. *Psychological Review, 74,* 1–15.

Brown, J. D., & Gallagher, F. M. (1992). Coming to terms with failure: Private self-enhancement and public self-effacement. *Journal of Experimental Social Psychology, 28,* 3–22.

Bruner, J. S. (1957). On perceptual readiness. *Psychological Review, 64,* 123–152.

Bruner, J. S., & Goodman, C. C. (1947). Value and need as organizing factors in perception. *Journal of Abnormal and Social Psychology, 42,* 33–44.

Bruner, J. S., & Klein, G. S. (1960). The functions of perceiving: New Look retrospective. In S. Wapner & B. Kaplan (Eds.), *Perspectives on psychological theory: Essays in honor of Heinz Werner* (pp. 61–77). New York: International Universities Press.

Buehler, R., Griffin, D., & Ross, M. (1994). Exploring the "planning fallacy": Why people underestimate their task completion times. *Journal of Personality and Social Psychology, 67*, 366–381.

Cacioppo, J. T., & Petty, R. E. (1982). The need for cognition. *Journal of Personality and Social Psychology, 42*, 116–121.

Cacioppo, J. T., Petty, R. E., Feinstein, J. A., & Jarvis, W. B. G. (1996). Dispositional differences in cognitive motivation: The life and times of individuals varying in need for cognition. *Psychological Bulletin, 119*, 197–253.

Cialdini, R. B., Trost, M. R., & Newsom, J. T. (1995). Preference for consistency: The development of a valid measure and the discovery of surprising behavioral implications. *Journal of Personality and Social Psychology, 69*, 318–328.

Clary, E. G., & Tesser, A. (1983). Reactions to unexpected events: The naive scientist and interpretative activity. *Personality and Social Psychology Bulletin, 9*, 609–620.

College Board (1976–1977). *Student descriptive questionnaire.* Princeton, NJ: Educational Testing Service.

Cooper, J., & Fazio, R. H. (1984). A new look at dissonance theory. In L. Berkowitz (Ed.), *Advances in experimental social psychology* Vol. 17 (pp. 229–268). New York: Academic Press.

Crandall, J. E. (1971). Relation of epistemic curiosity to subjective uncertainty. *Journal of Experimental Psychology, 88*, 273–276.

Ditto, P. H., & Lopez, D. L. (1992). Motivated skepticism: Use of differential decision criteria for preferred and nonpreferred conclusions. *Journal of Personality and Social Psychology, 63*, 568–584.

Ditto, P. H., Scepansky, J. A., Munro, G. D., Apanovitch, A. M., & Lockhart, L. K. (1998). Motivated sensitivity to preference-inconsistent information. *Journal of Personality and Social Psychology, 75*, 53–69.

Dunning, D. (1995). Trait importance and modifiability as factors influencing self-assessment and self-enhancement motives. *Personality and Social Psychology Bulletin, 21*, 1297–1306.

Dunning, D., & Cohen, G. L. (1992). Egocentric definitions of traits and abilities in social judgment. *Journal of Personality and Social Psychology, 63*, 341–355.

Dunning, D., Leuenberger, A., & Sherman, D. A. (1995). A new look at motivated inference: Are self-serving theories of success a product of motivational forces? *Journal of Personality and Social Psychology, 69*, 58–68.

Dunning, D., Meyerowitz, J. A., & Holzberg, A. D. (1989). Ambiguity and self-evaluation: The role of idiosyncratic trait definitions in self-serving assessments of ability. *Journal of Personality and Social Psychology, 57*, 1082–1090.

Edwards, J. A., & Weary, G. (1993). Depression and the impression-formation continuum: Piecemeal processing despite the availability of category information. *Journal of Personality and Social Psychology, 64*, 636–645.

Elkin, R., & Leippe, M. (1986). Physiological arousal, dissonance, and attitude change: Evidence for a dissonance–arousal link and a "don't remind me" effect. *Journal of Personality and Social Psychology, 51*, 55–65.

Elliot, A. J., & Devine, P. G. (1994). On the motivational nature of cognitive dissonance: Dissonance as psychological discomfort. *Journal of Personality and Social Psychology, 67*, 382–394.

Erber, R., & Fiske, S. T. (1984). Outcome dependency and attention to inconsistent information. *Journal of Personality and Social Psychology, 47*, 709–726.

Erdelyi, M. H. (1974). A new look at the New Look: Perceptual defense and vigilance. *Psychological Review, 81*, 1–25.

Fazio, R. H., Zanna, M. P., & Cooper, J. (1977). Dissonance and self-perception: An integrative view of each theory's proper domain of application. *Journal of Experimental Social Psychology, 47*, 709–726.

Fein, S., & Spencer, S. J. (1997). Prejudice as self-image maintenance: Affirming the self through derogating others. *Journal of Personality and Social Psychology, 73*, 31–44.

Festinger, L. (1957). *A theory of cognitive dissonance.* Evanston, IL: Row, Peterson.

Freedman, J. L., & Sears, D. O. (1965). Selective exposure. In L. Berkowitz (Ed.), *Advances in experimental social psychology* Vol. 2 (pp. 58–98). San Diego, CA: Academic Press.

Frey, D. (1986). Recent research on selective exposure to information. In L. Berkowitz (Ed.), *Advances in experimental social psychology* Vol. 19 (pp. 41–80). New York: Academic Press.

Gollwitzer, P. M., & Kinney, R. F. (1989). Effects of deliberative and implemental mind-sets on illusion of control. *Journal of Personality and Social Psychology, 56*, 531–542.

Greenwald, A. G. (1980). The totalitarian ego: Fabrication and revision of personal history. *American Psychologist, 35*, 608–618.

Greenwald, A. G., & Banaji, M. R. (1995). Implicit social cognition: Attitudes, self-esteem, and stereotypes. *Psychological Review, 102*, 4–27.

Hastie, R. (1984). Causes and effects of causal attribution. *Journal of Personality and Social Psychology, 46*, 44–56.

Heider, F. (1958). *The psychology of interpersonal relations.* New York: Wiley.

Heine, S. J., & Lehman, D. R. (1995). Cultural variation in unrealistic optimism: Does the West feel more invulnerable than the East? *Journal of Personality and Social Psychology, 68*, 595–607.

Heine, S. J., & Lehman, D. R. (1997). Culture, dissonance, and self-affirmation. *Personality and Social Psychology Bulletin, 23*, 389–400.

John, O. P., & Robins, R. W. (1994). Accuracy and bias in self-perception: Individual differences in self-enhancement and the role of narcissism. *Journal of Personality and Social Psychology, 66*, 206–219.

Jones, S. (1979). Curiosity and knowledge. *Psychological Reports, 45*, 639–642.

Kelley, H. H. (1972). Attribution in social interaction. In E. E. Jones, D. E. Kanouse, H. H. Kelley, R. S. Nisbett, S. Valins, & B. Weiner (Eds.), *Attribution: Perceiving the causes of behavior* (pp. 1–26). Morristown, NJ: General Learning Press.

Kruglanski, A. W., & Webster, D. M. (1996). Motivated closing of the mind: "Seizing" and "freezing." *Psychological Review, 103*, 263–283.

Kunda, Z. (1987). Motivated inference: Self-serving generation and evaluation of causal theories. *Journal of Personality and Social Psychology, 53*, 37–54.

Kunda, Z. (1990). The case for motivated reasoning. *Psychological Bulletin, 108*, 480–498.

Langer, E. J. (1975). The illusion of control. *Journal of Personality and Social Psychology, 32*, 311–328.

Lau, R. R., & Russell, D. (1980). Attributions in the sports pages: A field test of some current hypotheses in attribution research. *Journal of Personality and Social Psychology, 39*, 29–38.

Loewenstein, G. (1994). The psychology of curiosity: A review and reinterpretation. *Psychological Bulletin, 116*, 73–98.

Loewenstein, G., Prelec, D., & Shatto, C. (1997). Hot/cold intrapersonal empathy gaps and the prediction of curiosity. Unpublished manuscript, Carnegie Mellon University.

Lord, C. G., Ross, L., & Lepper, M. (1979). Biased assimilation and attitude polarization: The effects of prior theories on subsequently considered evidence. *Journal of Personality and Social Psychology, 37*, 2098–2109.

Markus, H., & Kitayama, S. (1991). Culture and the self: Implications for cognition, emotion, and motivation. *Psychological Review, 98*, 224–253.

Miller, D. T., & Ross, M. (1975). Self-serving biases in the attribution of causality: Fact or fiction? *Psychological Bulletin, 82,* 213–225.

Monson, T. C., Keel, R., Stephens, D., & Genung, V. (1982). Trait attributions: Relative validity, covariation with behavior, and prospect of future interaction. *Journal of Personality and Social Psychology, 42,* 1014–1026.

Mullen, B., & Goethals, G. R. (1990). Social projection, actual consensus and valence. *British Journal of Social Psychology, 29,* 279–282.

Neuberg, S. L., & Fiske, S. T. (1987). Motivational influences on impression formation: Outcome dependency, accuracy-driven attention, and individuating processes. *Journal of Personality and Social Psychology, 53,* 431–444.

Neuberg, S. L., & Newsom, J. T. (1993). Personal need for structure: Individual differences in the desire for simple structure. *Journal of Personality and Social Psychology, 65,* 113–131.

Oettingen, G. & Gollwitzer, P. M. (2001). Goal setting and goal striving. In A. Tesser & N. Schwarz (Eds.), *Blackwell handbook of social psychology: Intraindividual processes* (pp. 329–347). Oxford: Blackwell Publishing.

Oyserman, D. (2001). Self-concept and identity. In A. Tesser & N. Schwarz (Eds.), *Blackwell handbook of social psychology: Intraindividual processes* (pp. 499–517). Oxford: Blackwell Publishing.

Peng, K. (1997). Naive dialecticism and its effects on reasoning and judgment about contradiction. Unpublished doctoral dissertation, University of Michigan, Ann Arbor.

Pittman, T. S. (1998). Motivation. In D. T. Gilbert, S. T. Fiske, & G. Lindzey (Eds.), *Handbook of social psychology* Vol. 1. 4th. edn. (pp. 459–490). New York: McGraw-Hill.

Pittman, T. S., & D'Agostino, P. R. (1989). Motivation and cognition: Control deprivation and the nature of subsequent information processing. *Journal of Experimental Social Psychology, 25,* 465–480.

Pittman, T. S., & Pittman, N. L. (1980). Deprivation of control and the attribution process. *Journal of Personality and Social Psychology, 39,* 377–389.

Pyszczynski, T. A., & Greenberg, J. (1981). Role of disconfirmed expectancies in the instigation of attributional processing. *Journal of Personality and Social Psychology, 40,* 31–38.

Pyszczynski, T. A., Greenberg, J., & LaPrelle, J. (1985). Maintaining consistency between self-serving beliefs and available data: A bias in information processing. *Personality and Social Psychology Bulletin, 11,* 179–190.

Roney, C. J. R., & Sorrentino, R. M. (1995). Self-evaluation motives and uncertainty orientation: Asking the "who" question. *Personality and Social Psychology Bulletin, 21,* 1319–1329.

Sanitioso, R., Kunda, Z., & Fong, G. (1990). Motivated recruitment of autobiographical memory. *Journal of Personality and Social Psychology, 59,* 229–241.

Schaller, M., Boyd, C., Yohannes, J., & O'Brien, M. (1995). The prejudiced personality revisited: Personal need for structure and formation of erroneous group stereotypes. *Journal of Personality and Social Psychology, 68,* 544–555.

Sedikides, C. (1993). Assessment, enhancement, and verification determinants of the self-evaluation process. *Journal of Personality and Social Psychology, 65,* 317–338.

Sher, S. J., & Cooper, J. (1989). Motivational basis of dissonance: The singular role of behavioral consequences. *Journal of Personality and Social Psychology, 56,* 899–906.

Shultz, T. R., & Lepper, M. R. (1996). Cognitive dissonance as constraint satisfaction. *Psychological Review, 103,* 219–240.

Simon, L., Greenberg, J., & Brehm, J. (1995). Trivialization: The forgotten mode of dissonance reduction. *Journal of Personality and Social Psychology, 68,* 247–260.

Smith, E. R. (1998). Mental representations and memory. In D. T. Gilbert, S. T. Fiske, & G. Lindzey (Eds.), *Handbook of social psychology* Vol. 1. 4th. edn. (pp. 391–445). New York: McGraw-Hill.

Smith, E. R. & Queller, S. (2001). Mental representations. In A. Tesser & N. Schwarz (Eds.), *Blackwell handbook of social psychology: Intraindividual processes* (pp. 111–133). Oxford: Blackwell Publishing.

Solomon, S., Greenberg, J., & Pyszczynski, T. (1991). A terror management theory of social behavior: The psychological function of self-esteem and cultural worldview. In M. P. Zanna (Ed.), *Advances in experimental social psychology* Vol. 24 (pp. 91–159). San Diego, CA: Academic Press.

Steele, C. M. (1988). The psychology of self-affirmation: Sustaining the integrity of the self. In L. Berkowitz (Ed.), *Advances in experimental social psychology* Vol. 21 (pp. 261–302). San Diego, CA: Academic Press.

Steele, C. M., & Liu, T. J. (1983). Dissonance processes as self-affirmation. *Journal of Personality and Social Psychology, 45,* 5–19.

Steele, C. M., Southwick, L., & Critchlow, B. (1981). Dissonance and alcohol: Drinking your troubles away. *Journal of Personality and Social Psychology, 41,* 831–846.

Stone, J., Aronson, E., Crain, A. L., Winslow, M. P., & Fried, C. B. (1994). Inducing hypocrisy as a means for encouraging young adults to use condoms. *Personality and Social Psychology Bulletin, 20,* 116–128.

Story, A. L. (1998). Self-esteem and memory for favorable and unfavorable personality feedback. *Personality and Social Psychology Bulletin, 24,* 51–64.

Suedfeld, P., & Tetlock, P. E. (2001). Individual differences in information processing. In A. Tesser & N. Schwarz (Eds.), *Blackwell handbook of social psychology: Intraindividual processes* (pp. 284–304). Oxford: Blackwell Publishing.

Suls, J., & Wan, C. K. (1987). In search of the false uniqueness phenomenon: Fear and estimates of social consensus. *Journal of Personality and Social Psychology, 52,* 211–217.

Swann, W. B., Jr. (1990). To be adored or to be known: The interplay of self-enhancement and self-verification. In R. M. Sorrentino & E. T. Higgins (Eds.), *Foundations of social behavior*, vol. 2 (pp. 408–448). New York: Guilford Press.

Swann, W. B., Jr. (1997). The trouble with change: Self-verification and allegiance to the self. *Psychological Science, 8,* 177–180.

Swann, W. B., Jr., Stein-Serroussi, A., & Geisler, R. B. (1992). Why people self-verify. *Journal of Personality and Social Psychology, 62,* 392–401.

Swann, W. B., Jr., Stephenson, B., & Pittman, T. S. (1981). Curiosity and control: On the determinants of the search for social knowledge. *Journal of Personality and Social Psychology, 40,* 635–642.

Taylor, S. E., & Brown, J. D. (1988). Illusions and well-being: A social psychological perspective on mental health. *Psychological Bulletin, 116,* 193–210.

Taylor, S. E., Neter, E., & Wayment, H. A. (1995). Self-evaluation processes. *Personality and Social Psychology Bulletin, 21,* 1278–1287.

Tesser, A. (1988). Toward a self-evaluation maintenance model of social behavior. In L. Berkowitz (Ed.), *Advances in experimental social psychology* Vol. 21 (pp. 181–227). New York: Academic Press.

Tesser, A. (2001). Self-esteem. In A. Tesser & N. Schwarz (Eds.), *Blackwell handbook of social psychology: Intraindividual processes* (pp. 479–498). Oxford: Blackwell Publishing.

Tesser, A., & Cornell, D. P. (1991). On the confluence of self processes. *Journal of Experimental Social Psychology, 27,* 501–526.

Tesser, A., & Paulhus, D. (1983). The definition of self: Private and public self-evaluation management strategies. *Journal of Personality and Social Psychology, 44,* 672–682.

Tetlock, P. E. (1983). Accountability and complexity of thought. *Journal of Personality and Social Psychology, 45,* 74–83.

Tetlock, P. E. (1992). The impact of accountability on judgment and choice: Toward a social contingency model. In M. Zanna (Ed.), *Advances in experimental social psychology* Vol. 25 (pp. 331–376). San Diego, CA: Academic Press.

Trope, Y. (1980). Self-assessment, self-enhancement, and task performance. *Journal of Experimental Social Psychology, 16*, 116–129.

Trope, Y. (1986). Self-enhancement and self-assessment in achievement behavior. In R. M. Sorrentino, & E. T. Higgins (Eds.), *Handbook of motivation and cognition: Foundations of social behavior* (pp. 350–378). New York: Guilford Press.

Tucker, J. A., Vuchinich, R. E., & Sobell, M. B. (1981). Alcohol consumption as a self-handicapping strategy. *Journal of Abnormal Psychology, 20*, 220–230.

Vallone, R. P., Griffin, D. W., Lin, S., & Ross, L. (1990). Overconfident prediction of future actions and outcomes by self and others. *Journal of Personality and Social Psychology, 58*, 582–592.

Weiner, B. (1985). "Spontaneous" causal thinking. *Psychological Bulletin, 97*, 74–84.

Weinstein, N. D. (1980). Unrealistic optimism about future life events. *Journal of Personality and Social Psychology, 39*, 806–820.

Wills, T. A. (1981). Downward comparison principles in social psychology. *Psychological Bulletin, 90*, 245–271.

Zanna, M. P., & Cooper, J. (1974). Dissonance and the pill: An attribution approach to studying the arousal properties of dissonance. *Journal of Personality and Social Psychology, 29*, 703–709.

Zuckerman, M. L. (1979). Attribution of success and failure, or: The motivational bias is alive and well. *Journal of Personality, 47*, 245–287.

CHAPTER EIGHT

Goal Setting and Goal Striving

Gabriele Oettingen and Peter M. Gollwitzer

In this chapter we focus on the determinants and processes of goal emergence and goal implementation. We first address personal and situational variables leading to the formation of behavioral goals and what kind of psychological processes help or hinder goal setting. In the second part of the chapter, we discuss how set goals of different qualities predict goal attainment and which self-regulatory strategies help successful goal striving. Goal effects on cognition are discussed as possible mediators of the goal–behavior link.

The History of the Goal Concept

Behaviorists recognize goal-directed behavior by its features. Goal-directed behavior is *persistent*. A hungry rat persists in searching a maze until the pellets are reached (Tolman, 1925). Goal-directed behavior is *appropriate*. When one path is blocked, another path to the same goal is taken, or if the goal moves, the organism readily follows it. Finally, goal-directed organisms start *searching* when exposed to stimuli associated with the goal.

A behaviorist's statement that a certain piece of food is a goal for the hungry organism means (1) that the food qualifies as an incentive for the organism, and (2) that the researcher has chosen to describe the behavior of the organism relative to the food stimulus rather than relative to any other object or event. Skinner (1953) referred to goal-directedness as a shorthand description of behavior resulting from some kind of operant conditioning. Thus in the behaviorist tradition, the reference point for goal-directed behavior is not the intention or the goal set by the organism itself.

In contrast, the reference point of modern goal theories is the internal subjective goal. Goal-directed behavior refers to goals held by the individual (e.g. a person's goal to stop smoking serves as the reference point for his or her efforts to achieve this goal). Research questions focus on how and in what form goals are set and how goal setting affects behavior. The behaviorist distinctions between needs (motives), incentives, and goal-directed behavior are, however, still present in modern goal theories which consider needs (e.g. the need for approval) as forces that narrow down classes of incentives (e.g. being popular or accomplished), and see behavioral goals in the service of these incentives. For example, Geen (1995) defined an incentive as a desired outcome that subsumes several lower order goals. Incentives (e.g. being popular or accomplished) are considered to be a product of a person's need (i.e. the need for social approval) and the perceived situational opportunities (i.e. the person's friends or scientific community, respectively). Intentions to attain popularity or to accomplish outstanding scientific achievements are understood as higher order goals served by many lower order behavioral goals (e.g. intending to use the weekend to visit friends or to write an outstanding scientific article, respectively).

The modern perspective of analyzing goal-directed behaviors in relation to subjective goals has its own precursors: William James and William McDougall in America, and Narziß Ach and Kurt Lewin in Europe. In his *Principles of Psychology* (1890/1950) James held that behavior can be regulated by resolutions (i.e. intentions, subjective goals), even though this may be difficult at times. However, if certain preliminaries are fulfilled, behavior specified in resolutions comes true. McDougall (1908/1931) postulated that goals guide behavior through cognitive activity that pertains to the analysis of the present situation and the intended goal. Progress towards, and the attainment of, the goal are seen as pleasurable and thwarting and failing as painful.

In Europe, the scientific debate on goal striving was dominated by controversy between Ach and Lewin. Ach (1935) assumed that mental links between an anticipated situation and an intended behavior create what he called a determination, which urges the person to initiate the intended action when the specified situation is encountered. The strength of a determination should depend on how concretely the anticipated situation is specified and on the intensity of the intention. Determination was seen as directly eliciting the behavior without conscious intent. Lewin (1926) critically referred to Ach's ideas as a "linkage theory of intention" and proposed a need theory of intention. Goals (intentions), like needs, are assumed to assign a valence (*Aufforderungscharakter*) to objects and events in one's surroundings. Similar to basic needs (e.g. hunger) which can be satisfied by a variety of behaviors (e.g. eating fruit, vegetables, or bread), the quasi-needs associated with intentions (e.g. to be popular) may be satisfied by various behaviors (e.g. inviting one's friends for a party, buying birthday gifts). The tension associated with the quasi-need determines the intensity of goal striving. This tension depends on the strength of relevant real needs (i.e. superordinate drives or general life goals) and how strongly these are related to the quasi-need. Lewin's tension-state metaphor accounts for the flexibility of goal striving.

Many of the ideas on goal-directed behaviors as presented by James, McDougall, Ach, Lewin, and the behaviorists, have been absorbed into modern goal theories, whereby goal implementation has received much more theoretical and empirical attention than goal setting. Karoly (1993, p. 27) states that "the study of goals as dependent variables remains infrequent" and Carver & Scheier (1999) conclude that "the question of where goals come from and how they are synthesized is one that has not been well explored." We will start, then, with the question of what factors determine goal selection and which psychological processes promote goal setting.

Goal Setting

Determinants of goal setting

Assigned goals. Goals are often *assigned* by others (e.g. employers, teachers, parents). It matters who assigns goals to whom, and how the persuasive message is framed. Relevant variables may include attributes of the source, the recipient, and the message (McGuire, 1969). Locke & Latham (1990) report that source variables, such as legitimacy and trustworthiness, play an important role in the transformation of an assigned goal into a personal goal. For recipients of such assignments, perception of the goal as desirable and feasible, personal redefinition of the goal, and integration with other existing goals are important (Cantor & Fleeson, 1994). Finally, relevant message variables may be the discrepancy between the suggested goal and the recipient's respective current goal (e.g. when a very low calorie diet is suggested to a person with a moderate dieting goal), and whether fear appeals are used (e.g. information on the dramatic medical consequences of health-damaging behavior is provided). Effective sellers of goals must also consider the processing ability and motivation of the recipient as a moderator of the effects of source, recipient, and message variables on accepting assigned goals as personal goals (Petty & Cacioppo, 1986; Chaiken, 1987).

Self-set goals. Goals do not need to be assigned, as people also set goals on their own. Self-set goals, however, are often influenced by others, for example, when goals are conjointly set (e.g. in participative decision making and employee involvement; Wilpert, 1994), or when goals are adopted from highly respected models (e.g. adopting standards for self-reward; Mischel & Liebert, 1966). Cantor & Fleeson (1994) point out that social context cues, such as normative expectations of the social community, also influence goal selection.

The personal attributes that most strongly determine goal choice are perceived desirability and feasibility. People prefer to choose goals that are desirable and feasible (Ajzen, 1985; Heckhausen, 1991; Gollwitzer, 1990; Locke & Latham, 1990). Desirability is determined by the estimated attractiveness of likely short-term and long-term consequences of goal attainment. Such consequences may pertain to anticipated self-evaluations, evaluations by significant others, progress toward some higher order goal, external rewards of having attained the goal, and the joy/pain associated with moving towards the goal (Heckhausen, 1977). Feasibility depends upon people's judgments of their capabilities to perform relevant goal-directed behaviors (i.e. self-efficacy expectations; Bandura, 1997), their belief that these goal-directed behaviors will lead to the desired outcome (i.e. outcome expectations; Bandura, 1997), or the judged likelihood of attaining the desired outcome (i.e. generalized expectations; Oettingen, 1996) or desired events in general (general optimism; Scheier & Carver, 1985). The information source for efficacy expectations, outcome expectations, generalized expectations, and optimism is past experiences: one's own past performances, the observed performances of others, received relevant persuasive messages, and one's previous physiological responses to challenge (Bandura, 1997). Proper assessment of the feasibility and desirability of a potential goal also requires seeing the goal in relation to other potential goals. A goal associated with many attractive consequences may suddenly appear less desirable in light of a superordinate goal, or it might seem more feasible in connection with other, compatible goals (Cantor & Fleeson, 1994; Gollwitzer, 1990).

Estimated desirability and feasibility determine the choice of a goal's difficulty level. Festinger (1942), in his theory of resultant valence, argued that people choose goal difficulty levels where the resultant expected valence is the highest – this being a multiplicative function of the probability of success or failure and the valence of success or failure. Atkinson's (1957) risk taking model modified and extended Festinger's reasoning to make separate predictions for individuals with hope for success versus fear of failure. The latter prefer low and high difficulty levels, whereas the former choose goals of medium difficulty.

Set goals may also differ in other structural features (e.g. abstract vs. concrete) and in content (e.g. materialistic vs. social integrative). People generally prefer to set themselves abstract goals, and adopt concrete goals only when they run into problems attaining an abstract goal. According to act identification theory (Vallacher & Wegner, 1987), people conceive of their actions in rather abstract terms (e.g. cleaning the apartment) and only drop down to lower, concrete levels (e.g. vacuuming the carpet) when difficulties in carrying out the activity as construed at the higher level arise. Some people typically think of their actions in low-level terms, whereas others prefer high-level identifications (Vallacher & Wegner, 1989). This general preference for either an abstract or a concrete level of identifying actions should be reflected in the choice of abstract versus concrete goals.

Goals can be framed with a positive or negative outcome focus (i.e. goals that focus on establishing and keeping positive outcomes as compared to avoiding and ameliorating negative outcomes). Higgins (1997) argues that people construe their self either as an ideal self that they intrinsically desire to be, or as an ought self that they feel compelled to be. The former orientation focuses on promotion, whereas the latter focuses on prevention. Part of the promotion orientation is a predilection for setting goals with a positive outcome focus, whereas part of the prevention orientation is a predilection for setting goals with a negative outcome focus.

Goals can also be framed as performance versus learning goals (Dweck, 1996), also referred to as performance versus mastery goals (Ames & Archer, 1988), or ego involvement versus task involvement goals (Nicholls, 1979). Goals in the achievement domain, for example, can either focus on finding out how capable one is (performance goals) or on learning how to carry out the task (learning goals). Dweck (1996) reports that implicit theories on the nature of ability determine the preference for performance versus learning goals. If people believe that ability is fixed and cannot be easily changed (i.e. hold an entity theory of ability), they prefer performance goals. However, if people believe that ability can be improved by learning (i.e. hold an incremental theory of ability), they prefer learning goals. Similar implicit theories concerning the malleability of moral character affect the selection of punitive versus educational correctional goals.

The content of set goals is influenced by needs, wishes, and higher order goals. Ryan, Sheldon, Kasser, & Deci (1996) argue, for example, that the content of people's goals reflect their needs. Autonomy, competence, and social integration needs are expected to promote goal setting focused on self-realization rather than materialistic gains. Markus & Nurius (1986; Oyserman, 2001) argue that people conceive of themselves not only in terms of what they are (i.e. the self-concept), but also what they wish to become in the future (i.e. the possible self). These possible selves should give people ideas on what kind of personal goals they may strive for.

Once higher order goals are formed (e.g. to become a physician), they determine the contents of lower order goals. The contents of such "Be" goals determine the contents of respective "Do" goals which in turn determine the contents of respective "motor-control" goals (Carver & Scheier, 1998, p. 72; Carver, 2001). "Be" goals have been described by using terms such as current concerns (Klinger, 1977), self-defining goals (Wicklund & Gollwitzer, 1982), personal projects (Little, 1983), personal strivings (Emmons, 1996), and (individualized) life tasks (Cantor & Fleeson, 1994). Whereas choosing higher order "Be" goals should be determined by their perceived desirability and feasibility (Klinger, 1977), choosing the respective lower order "Do" goals also depends on the commitment to the respective "Be" goals (Gollwitzer, 1987).

Processes of goal setting

Reflective processes.   So far we have discussed which variables determine the choice of goals with certain structural and thematic features. We now consider the question of what triggers goal setting. Bandura (1997) suggests that having successfully achieved a set goal stimulates the setting of ever more challenging goals, due to a person's heightened sense of efficacy which is based on having successfully attained the prior goal. Others have pointed out that the core processes of goal setting involve committing oneself to achieving a certain incentive (Klinger, 1977). Heckhausen & Kuhl (1985) argued that the lowest degree of commitment to an incentive is a mere wish to attain it. A wish that is tested for feasibility becomes a want which carries a higher degree of commitment. To develop a full goal commitment (i.e. to form the intention or goal to achieve the incentive), a further relevance check must be carried out relating to necessary means, opportunities, time, relative importance, and urgency.

In their Rubicon model of action phases Heckhausen & Gollwitzer (1987; Heckhausen, 1991; Gollwitzer, 1990) assume that people entertain more wishes than they have time or opportunities to realize. Therefore they must select between wishes in order to accomplish at least some of them. The criteria for selection are feasibility and desirability. Wishes with high feasibility and desirability have the best chance to become goals. The transformation of wishes into goals is a resolution, resulting in a feeling of determination to act. Through this resolution the desired end state specified by the wish becomes an end state that the individual feels committed to achieve. To catch the flavor of this transition from wishing to willing, the metaphor of crossing the Rubicon is used.

What are the preliminaries of crossing the Rubicon? The model of action phases (Gollwitzer, 1990; Heckhausen, 1991) states that the realization of a wish demands the completion of four successive tasks: deliberating between wishes to select appropriate ones (predecision phase), planning the implementation of chosen wishes (i.e. goals or intentions) to help get started with goal-directed behaviors (preaction phase), monitoring goal-directed behaviors to bring them to a successful ending (action phase), and evaluating what has been achieved as compared to what was desired to terminate goal pursuit or to restart it (evaluation phase). People decide to "cross the Rubicon" (i.e. move from the predecision phase to the preaction phase) when they sense that the feasibility and desirability of a wish is not only acceptably high, but has been exhaustively deliberated and correctly assessed. Gollwitzer, Heckhausen, & Ratajczak (1989) observed that undecided people more readily formed goals when they had been asked to judge the likelihood of wish fulfillment and to list likely positive and negative, short-term and long-term consequences. In addition, when undecided people were lured into planning the implementation of the wish by simply connecting anticipated opportunities with intended goal-directed behaviors, they also showed a greater readiness to cross the Rubicon. Apparently, when undecided people feel that the task of assessing the feasibility and desirability of a given wish is completed, they show a greater readiness to move on and set themselves the respective goal.

A recent theory on fantasy realization (Oettingen, 1996) analyzes goal setting by delineating different routes to goal formation. The theory distinguishes between two forms of thinking about the future, expectations and free fantasies. Expectations are judgments of the likelihood that a certain future behavior or outcome will occur. Free fantasies about the future, to the contrary, are thoughts and images of future behaviors or outcomes in the mind's eye, independent of the likelihoods that these events will actually occur. For example, despite perceiving low chances of successfully resolving a conflict with a partner, people can indulge in positive fantasies of harmony.

Fantasy realization theory specifies three routes to goal setting which result from how people deal with their fantasies about the future. One route is expectancy based, while the other two are independent of expectations. The expectancy based route rests on mentally contrasting positive fantasies about the future with negative aspects of impeding reality. This mental contrast ties free fantasies about the future to the here and now. Consequently, the desired future appears as something that must be achieved and the impeding reality as something that must be changed. The resulting necessity to act raises the question: can reality be altered to match fantasy? The answer is given by the subjective expectation of successfully attaining fantasy in reality. Accordingly, mental contrasting of positive fantasies about the future with negative aspects of the impeding reality causes expectations of success to become activated and used. If expectations of success are high, a person will commit herself to fantasy attainment; if expectations of success are low, a person will refrain.

The second route to goal setting stems from merely indulging in positive fantasies about the desired future, thereby disregarding impeding reality. This indulgence seduces one to consummate and consume the desired future envisioned in the mind's eye. Accordingly, no necessity to act is experienced and relevant expectations of success are not activated and used. Commitment to act towards fantasy fulfillment reflects solely the pull of the desired events imagined in one's fantasies. It is moderate and *in*dependent of a person's perceived chances of success (i.e. expectations). As a consequence, the level of goal commitment is either too high (when expectations are low) or too low (when expectations are high).

The third route is based on merely dwelling on the negative aspects of impeding reality, thereby disregarding positive fantasies about the future. Again, no necessity to act is experienced, this time because nothing points to a direction in which to act. Expectations of success are not activated and used. Commitment to act merely reflects the push of the negative aspects of impeding reality. Similar to indulgence in positive fantasies about the future, dwelling on the negative reality leads to a moderate, expectancy *in*dependent level of commitment, which is either too high (when expectations are low) or too low (when expectations are high).

Fantasy realization theory is supported by various experimental studies. In one study (Oettingen, in press-a, Study 1) participants were confronted with an interpersonal opportunity: getting to know an attractive person. Female participants first judged the probability of successfully getting to know an attractive male doctoral student, whose picture they saw. Participants then generated positive aspects of getting to know the attractive man (e.g. love, friendship) and negative aspects of impeding reality (e.g. being shy, his potential disinterest). They were then divided into three groups for elaboration of these aspects. In the fantasy–reality contrast group, participants mentally elaborated both positive aspects of getting to know the man and negative aspects of reality standing in the way; this was done in alternating order beginning with a positive aspect. In the positive fantasy group, participants mentally elaborated only positive aspects of getting to know the man; and in the negative reality group, participants mentally elaborated only negative aspects of impeding reality.

In the fantasy–reality contrast group, goal commitment (assessed as eagerness to get to know the person and anticipated frustration in case of failure) was strictly dependent on participants' expectations, while in the positive fantasy and the negative reality groups, expectations had no effects on goal commitment. Whether expectations were low or high, goal commitment was at a medium level. Apparently, mental contrasting makes people set themselves binding goals when expectations of success are high, and it makes people refrain from goal setting when expectations of success are low. Indulging in positive fantasies and ruminating about impeding reality, to the contrary, cause goal commitment to be weakly pulled by the positive future or pushed by the negative reality, respectively.

A further experiment (Oettingen, in press-a, Study 2) with childless female doctoral students dealt with the emergence of the goal to combine work and family life. Again, mental contrasting of positive fantasies about the future with negative aspects of impeding reality made expectations determine goal commitment (assessed as anticipated frustration in case of failure, intended effort expenditure, and planning goal implementation via process simulations; Taylor, Pham, Rivkin, & Armor, 1998). Goal commitment was mild and unaffected by expectations in participants who had indulged in positive fantasies or who had dwelled on the negative reality. In both experiments only contrasting participants behaved rationally in the sense that their expectations of success determined their level of commitment. Fantasizing and ruminating participants behaved irrationally. Their level of commitment was either too high (when expectations of success were low) or too low (when expectations of success were high). A series of further experiments (Oettingen, in press-b) using various fantasy themes related to personality development (e.g. academic achievement, conflict resolution, emotional and financial independence, occupational success) and different experimental paradigms to induce the three modes of self-regulatory thought (i.e. mental contrasting, indulging in positive fantasies about the future, dwelling on impeding reality) replicated this pattern of results. Taken together, the experimental findings suggest that whether people arrive at goal commitment in a rational (expectancy based) or irrational (expectancy *in*dependent) manner depends on how they mentally deal with a desired future.

Reflexive processes. So far we have discussed goal setting as a reflective process. People think about potential goals in different ways, and based on these reflections they either choose a goal or refrain from doing so. However, goals may become activated outside of awareness

(Bargh, 1990). Bargh's automotive theory suggests that strong mental links develop between the cognitive representation of situations and the goals the individual chronically pursues within them. As a consequence of repeated and consistent pairing, these goals are activated automatically when the person enters the critical situation. The automatically activated goal then guides behavior within the situation without choice or intention. Reflective choice, originally crucial, is now by-passed.

Bargh, Gollwitzer, Lee Chai, and Barndollar (1999) tested the assumption of direct goal activation in several experiments by assessing whether directly activated goals lead to the same behavioral consequences as reflectively set goals. Indeed, nonconscious priming of an achievement goal caused participants to perform better on an intellectual task than a non-primed control group. Moreover, nonconsciously primed achievement goals led to increased persistence and a higher frequency of task resumption. By applying a dissociation paradigm it could be ruled out that these effects were based on the mere priming of the semantic concept of achievement.

The processes described by Bargh and colleagues are based on reflective goal setting at an earlier point in time. Automatization relates only to the activation of a set goal in a given situation. It seems possible, however, that goal-directed behavior can occur in the absence of previously or ad hoc set goals. As noted in the introduction, behaviorist research has shown that conscious goal setting or the nonconscious activation of the representation of a goal are not needed to produce behavior that carries features of goal-directedness. Such behavior can also be produced by applying principles of operant conditioning.

The idea that goal-directed behavior can be reflexively elicited is supported by recent work in the area of motor control that adheres to dynamic systems theorizing (Kelso, 1995). This work suggests that complex goal-directed behaviors can emerge without mental representations of goals. Moreover, robotics research (Brooks, 1991; Maes, 1994) finds that robots can be programmed to perform rather complex, goal-directed like behaviors without having to install goal concepts. Connectionist theorizing is also wary of the goal concept. Some connectionist theories completely abolish the goal concept, while others try to replace the reflective processes of goal choice by suggesting parallel constraint satisfaction models (Read, Vanman, & Miller, 1997).

Finally, Carver & Scheier (1999) point out that there might be two kinds of goal related automaticity. The first is described by Bargh (1990) in his automotive model and relates to automatization through repeated and consistent pairing of a goal with a situational context. The second relates to primitive built-in behavioral tendencies that are present also in nonhuman species. Carver and Scheier describe this type of automaticity as an intuitive, crudely differentiated "quick and dirty" way of responding to reality that provides a default response. One does not wait to form an intention, but acts immediately. This mode of responding reminds of what McClelland and his colleagues (McClelland, Koestner, & Weinberger, 1989) describe as behavior based on implicit motives. Implicit motives are believed to be biologically based, directly guiding behavior through natural incentives.

We have pointed to these reflexive origins of goal-directed behavior to make the reader aware that (as behaviorists have long asserted) behaviors carrying features of goal-directedness do not necessarily require subjective goal setting based on reflective thought or the activation of a mental representation of an existing goal. Although some theorists may question the existence and relevance of reflective goal setting or the mental representation of goals, a more challenging research question for the future is how the two (reflective and reflexive) systems interact.

Determinants of goal striving

Goal contents vary in structural features. They may be challenging or modest, specific or vague, abstract or concrete, proximal or distal, framed with a negative or positive outcome focus, and so forth. As well, goals differ thematically. All of these differences affect the success of goal striving.

Locke & Latham (1990) demonstrated that challenging goals spelled out in specific terms are superior to modest specific goals, as well as to challenging but vague (i.e. "do your best") goals in facilitating goal attainment. This effect has a number of prerequisites: frequent performance feedback, a strong goal commitment, the goal should not be too complex, and limitations in talent or situational constraints should not make goal attainment impossible. What does not seem to matter is whether goal setting is determined from outside (assigned goals), freely chosen by individuals (self-set goals), or chosen in interaction with others (participative goals). As potential mediators of the goal specificity effect Locke & Latham (1990) point to heightened persistence, focusing attention on the execution of goal-directed behaviors, a greater readiness to plan the goal pursuit, and to feedback and self-monitoring advantages.

Further structural differences between goals include time frame, outcome focus, and learning versus performance orientation. Bandura & Schunk (1981) divide the time frame of goal attainment into proximal and distal goals. Proximal goals relate to what the individual does in the present or near future, while distal goals point far into the future. Children who were weak and uninterested in mathematics pursued a program of self-directed learning (a total of 42 pages of instruction) under conditions involving either a distal goal only (42 pages in 7 sessions), or the distal goal plus proximal subgoals (6 pages per session for 7 sessions). Additional proximal goals improved the children's arithmetic scores by providing more performance feedback, thus making it easier to monitor progress in goal pursuit. However, this feedback advantage may turn into a detriment when inhibitional goals (e.g. dieting goals) are concerned, as people more readily discover failures which may cause them to give up prematurely. Indeed, Cochran & Tesser (1996) observed that the goal proximity effect is reversed for goals framed in terms of preventing failures.

Higgins (1997) reports that goals framed with a positive outcome focus lead to task performance that is strongest when both expectations of success and the incentive value of success are high; when people hold goals with a negative outcome focus this effect is less pronounced. In other words, when highly desirable and feasible wishes are transferred into goals it seems wise to frame these with a positive outcome focus. Goals with a positive outcome focus construe achievement as accomplishment, whereas goals with a negative outcome focus construe achievement as providing security.

Finally, learning goals and performance goals have different effects on performance (Dweck, 1996). Learning goals lead to better achievements than performance goals because the former allow for a more effective coping with failure than the latter. For people with performance goals, failure signals a lack of ability and thus cause reactions of giving up. People with learning goals, on the other hand, view set-backs as cues to focus on new strategies. Accordingly, their behavior is oriented toward mastering the causes of the set-back, ultimately furthering goal attainment. Elliot & Church (1997) have recently found that performance goals are less detrimental when they are framed as approach goals (e.g. I want to get good grades) rather than avoidance goals (e.g. I do not want to get bad grades).

With respect to the thematic contents of goals, Ryan, Sheldon, Kasser, & Deci (1996) suggest that goals of autonomy, competence, and social integration lead to greater creativity, higher cognitive flexibility, greater depth of information processing, and more effective coping with failure. These effects are mediated by an intrinsic self-regulation, as the needs of autonomy, competence, and social integration are assumed to further intrinsic goal striving. This positive kind of goal striving is contrasted with being unreflectively controlled from outside (e.g. goal assignments from authorities) or from inside (e.g. goal setting based on feelings of obligation). Ryan, et al. (1996) also discuss side effects of goal-directed actions. Goals based on autonomy, competence, and social integration needs are associated with higher well-being and life satisfaction. Kasser & Ryan (1993) observed that people with goals such as making money, becoming famous, and acquiring high status, experience a worse subjective well-being as compared to those with goals such as cultivating friendship or becoming active in communal services. This is particularly true for individuals who feel highly efficacious, implying that people who successfully implement materialistic goals are particularly at risk for low well-being.

Well-being has been analyzed in other goal content approaches as well. Emmons (1996) reports that a strong predictor of a person's well-being is the proportion of intimacy goals to the total number of goals. The proportion of achievement and power goals, however, tends to be negatively related to well-being. Moreover, highly abstract goals (e.g. getting to know people) tends to be associated with psychological distress (particularly anxiety and depression), whereas low level strivings (e.g. speak friendly to strangers) are linked to greater levels of psychological well-being, but also to more physical illness. Finally, having a high proportion of avoidance strivings (e.g. avoid being lonely, avoid being upset) is associated with suppressed positive mood, reduced life satisfaction, heightened anxiety, and weaker physical health.

Recently, Brunstein, Schultheiss, & Maier (in press) pointed out that structural features also matter in predicting well-being on the basis of goal pursuit. For instance, high commitment to a personal goal furthers life satisfaction only when the person perceives the personal goal as feasible; when feasibility is low, goal commitment reduces life satisfaction. Moreover, the positive effects of intimacy goals strongly depend on social support from significant others. The effects of goals on emotional well-being are also influenced by how well people's goals match their needs or implicit motives (McClelland, 1985). People with strong achievement and power needs, and goals of the same theme – as well as people with strong affiliation and intimacy needs, and goals of the same theme – report higher emotional well-being than those whose needs and goals do not match.

Processes of goal striving

Experience tells us that it is often a long way from goal setting to goal attainment. Having set a goal is just a first step, usually followed by a host of implementational problems that must be successfully solved. In the section above, predictions about successful goal attainment were made on the basis of structural and thematic properties of the set goals. A process-related approach focuses on how the problems of goal pursuit are solved by the individual. To effectively solve these problems, which pertain to initiating goal-directed actions and bringing them to a successful ending, the person needs to seize opportunities to act, ward off distractions, flexibly step up efforts in the face of difficulties, by-pass barriers, compensate for failures and shortcomings, and negotiate conflicts between goals. Various theories address how the individual effectively solves these problems of goal implementation.

Implemental mindset. The model of action phases (Heckhausen & Gollwitzer, 1987; Gollwitzer, 1990; Heckhausen, 1991) sees successful goal pursuit as solving a series of successive tasks: deliberating wishes (potential goals) and choosing between them, planning goal-directed actions and getting started, bringing goal pursuit to a successful end, and evaluating its outcome. The task notion implies that people can promote goal pursuit by developing the respective mindsets which facilitate task completion (Gollwitzer, 1990). Studies conducted on the mindsets associated with either deliberating between wishes (i.e. deliberative mindset) or with planning goal-directed actions (i.e. implemental mindset) support this idea.

When participants are asked to plan the implementation of a set goal, an implemental mindset with the following attributes originates (Gollwitzer & Bayer, 1999): participants become closed-minded in that they are no longer distracted by irrelevant information, while processing information related to goal implementation very effectively (e.g. information on the sequencing of actions). Moreover, desirability-related information is processed in a partial manner favoring pros over cons, and feasibility-related information is analyzed in a manner that favors illusory optimism. This optimism extends to an illusion of control over uncontrollable outcomes, and even holds for depressed individuals. Self-perception of important personal attributes (e.g. cheerfulness, smartness, social sensitivity) is strengthened, while perceived vulnerability to both controllable and uncontrollable risks is lowered (e.g. developing an addiction to prescription drugs or losing a partner to an early death, respectively). The implemental mindset favors goal attainment by helping the individual to effectively cope with classic problems of goal striving, such as becoming distracted, doubting the attractiveness of the pursued goal, or being pessimistic about its feasibility.

Planning. Set goals commit an individual to attaining the specified desired future, but they do not commit the individual to when, where, and how she intends to act. Such additional commitments can be added by planning goal pursuit via implementation intentions with the format of "if I encounter situation x, then I will perform the goal-directed behavior y!" Gollwitzer (1993) argued that implementation intentions are a powerful self-regulatory strategy for overcoming problems of getting started with goal-directed actions (e.g. when people are tired, absorbed with some other activity, or lost in thoughts, and thus miss good opportunities to act). In support of this hypothesis, it was observed in numerous studies (for a summary, see Gollwitzer, 1999) that difficult to reach goals benefit greatly from being furnished with implementation intentions. This effect extends to projects such as resolving important interpersonal conflicts, performing a medical self-examination, regular intake of a vitamin supplement, eating healthy foods, and doing vigorous exercise. It also holds true for people who have problems turning goals into action, such as opiate addicts under withdrawal or schizophrenic patients.

Because implementation intentions spell out links between situational cues and goal-directed behavior, it is assumed (Gollwitzer, 1993) that by forming such intentions people delegate the control of behavior to the environment, thus facilitating the initiation of goal-directed actions. The mental representations of the specified situational cues become highly activated, making these cues more accessible. Various experiments (for a summary, see Gollwitzer, 1999) demonstrate that situational cues specified in implementation intentions are more easily detected and remembered, as well as more readily attended to than comparable non-intended situations. Moreover, implementation intentions create strong associative links between mental representations of situations and actions which otherwise are achieved only through consistent and repeated pairing. As a consequence, action initiation becomes automatized. Various experiments demonstrate that the goal-directed behavior specified in implementation intentions is initiated swiftly and effortlessly in the presence of the critical situation. Moreover, the subliminal presentation of the critical situation suffices to activate cognitive concepts and knowledge relevant to the efficient initiation of the intended behavior. Finally, patients with a frontal lobe injury, who have severe deficits in the conscious and effortful control of behavior, while remaining unaffected in performing automatized behaviors, benefit greatly from forming implementation intentions.

Implementation intentions ameliorate not only problems of the initiation of goal-directed behavior, but also other problems of goal striving (Gollwitzer & Schaal, 1998). In a series of studies, implementation intentions created resistance to tempting distractions while solving tedious arithmetic problems. Moreover, set goals to escape unwanted habitual responses (i.e. stereotypical beliefs and prejudicial feelings) are more successfully attained when furnished with implementation intentions. Finally, implementation intentions can protect people from the unwanted influences of goals directly activated by situational cues (Bargh, 1990). People need only prepare themselves by setting antagonistic behavioral goals and furnish them with implementation intentions (Gollwitzer, 1999).

In summary, implementation intentions create a type of behavioral automaticity that does not originate from laborious and effortful practice. Rather, people strategically delegate their control over goal-directed behavior to anticipated, critical situational cues. This easily accessible self-regulatory strategy of forming implementation intentions can be used to increase tenacity in initiating goal-directed action. At the same time it helps to increase flexibility in escaping unwanted habits of thinking, feeling, and behaving.

There are other effective types of planning besides forming implementation intentions. Planning can be approached in a more reflective way as in mental simulations exploring possible ways to achieving a goal. Taylor, Pham, Rivkin, & Armor, (1998) call such mental simulations process simulations. If applied repeatedly, they further goal attainment, such as achieving good grades in academic exams. Apparently, repeated mental simulations of how to achieve a goal also result in firm plans.

Action versus state orientation.   Competing goal pursuits are paid particular attention in Kuhl's action control theory (for a summary, see Kuhl & Beckmann, 1994). For an ordered action sequence to occur, a current guiding goal must be shielded from competing goal intentions (e.g. the goal of making a phone call from the competing intention to tidy one's desk). Kuhl calls this shielding mechanism action control and differentiates a number of control strategies, such as attention control, emotion control, and environment control. Through environment control, for example, the individual prevents the derailing of an ongoing goal pursuit by removing competing temptations from the situation.

Whether and how effectively these strategies are used depends on the current control mode of the individual. An action-oriented person concentrates on planning and initiating of goal-directed action, responds flexibly to situational demands, and uses control strategies effectively. A state-oriented person, in contrast, cannot disengage from incomplete goals and is caught up in uncontrollable perseveration of thoughts related to aversive experiences or in dysfunctional thoughts about future successes. Action and state orientation may be induced by situational variables (e.g. a surprising event, persistent failure), but is founded in personal disposition.

Recent experimental research on state orientation has discovered a further volitional handicap. State-oriented individuals readily misperceive assigned goals as self-generated. These findings have stimulated a new theoretical perspective (Kuhl, in press) which sees the volitional control of action as a result of the cooperation of various mental sub-systems (i.e. intention memory, extension memory, intuitive behavior control, and object recognition). Action versus state orientation is understood as a parameter that modulates the cooperation between these systems thus leading to different kinds of volitional control of action with different outcomes.

Resumption of disrupted goal pursuit.   Higher order goals (e.g. to become popular) offer multiple routes to approach them. If one pathway is blocked, an individual can approach the goal another way. Self-completion theory (Wicklund & Gollwitzer, 1982) addresses this issue of compensation by analyzing self-defining goals. Such goals specify as the desired end state an identity, such as scientist, mother, or a political liberal. As many different things indicate the possession of such identities, the striving for an identity is a process of collecting these indicators (or self-defining symbols). These indicators extend from relevant material symbols (e.g. for a scientist, books and awards) to relevant self-descriptions (e.g. using titles) and performances (e.g. accomplishing important research). Whenever shortcomings in one type of symbol are encountered, an individual will experience self-definitional incomplete-ness, which leads to compensatory self-symbolizing efforts. These may take the form of pointing to the possession of alternative symbols or acquiring new symbols.

This compensation principle has been supported with various self-defining goals and different types of symbols (for a summary, see Gollwitzer & Kirchhof, 1998). Easily access-ible symbols (e.g. self-descriptions) are powerful substitutes for symbols that are harder to come by (e.g. relevant performances). Newcomers to a field of interest (e.g. science) can thus symbolize the related identity without full command of the relevant performances. Further, elderly people do not have to leave the field when age related deficits hamper performance. Research on self-completion has discovered that effective self-symbolizing requires a social reality. Compensatory efforts are particularly effective when other people notice them. This, however, has costs. Compensating individuals see others only in terms of their capability to notice compensatory efforts and thus lack social sensitivity. Also, when people make public their intention to acquire a certain self-definitional indicator (e.g. studying hard), actual effort will be reduced, as the proclamation alone produces self-definitional completeness (Gollwitzer, Bayer, Scherer, & Seifert, in press).

Finally, self-completion theory may sound similar to Steele's (1988) self-affirmation theory, but self-completion is a goal theory, not a self-esteem theory (for a different view, see Tesser, Martin, & Cornell, 1996). According to Steele, anything that makes you feel good will reaffirm a weakened self-esteem. Self-completion theory, however, postulates that self-definitional incompleteness can only be substituted for by acquiring an alternative but related symbol. Recent research demonstrates that merely reaffirming self-esteem cannot produce self-definitional completeness (Gollwitzer, et al., in press).

Mobilization of effort.   People may promote goal achievement by compensating for failures but they also try to avoid committing errors in the first place. Warding off failure becomes a pressing issue whenever difficulties mount. Brehm & Wright's (Brehm & Self, 1989; Wright, 1996) energization theory of motivation assumes that the readiness to exert effort is directly determined by the perceived difficulty of a task. As perceived difficulty increases, so does effort expenditure, unless the task is recognized to be unsolvable. There is, however, a second limit to the increase of effort in response to heightened task difficulty: potential motivation. Potential motivation is fed by need related variables (i.e. strength of the related need or higher order goal, the incentive value of the task, and the instrumentality of task completion for satisfaction or attainment). If potential motivation is low, people do not find it worthwhile to expend more effort when an easy task becomes more difficult. The upper limit of effort expenditure is low and quickly reached. If potential motivation is high, however, an increase in difficulty is matched by investment of effort up to high levels of difficulty. The upper limit of effort expenditure is high and is reached only after much effort expenditure has occurred.

Empirical tests of the theory have varied potential motivation either by offering high or low rewards for task completion or making a high reward more or less likely. Effort mobilization is usually assessed by cardiovascular responses (i.e. heart rate and systolic blood pressure). In general, low potential motivation curbs the linear relationship between task difficulty and effort. Recent research uses energization theory to understand the differences between men and women in effort on sex-typed tasks, and to explore the effects of private versus public performance conditions on effort (Wright, Tunstall, Williams, Goodwin, & Harmon-Jones, 1995; Wright, Murray, Storey, & Williams, 1997).

Discrepancy reduction.   The goal striving theories discussed so far implicitly or explicitly view goals as something attractive that the individual wants to attain. Goals are not simply "cold" mental representations that specify standards or reference points, but are cognitively explicated and elaborated incentives. Such motivational goal theories are rivaled by a more cognitive view that sees goals as specifying performance standards. According to Bandura (1997), goals have no motivational consequences per se. They only specify the conditions that allow a positive or negative self-evaluation. If the set goal is attained, positive self-evaluation prevails, whereas staying below one's goal leads to negative self-evaluation. The individual is pushed by the negative self-evaluation associated with the discrepancy, and pulled by the anticipated positive self-evaluation linked to closing the gap between the status quo and the goal. Accordingly, goals stimulate effortful action only when people notice a discrepancy between the status quo and the set goal. Bandura proposes frequent feedback as a powerful measure to stimulate goal pursuit. However, people will try to reduce a discrepancy only when they feel self-efficacious with respect to goal-directed actions.

Carver & Scheier (1998) propose a different discrepancy reduction theory of goal pursuit. Based on cybernetic control theory, the central concept of their analysis is the negative feedback loop. Carver and Scheier highlight goal pursuits' hierarchical structure and assume a cascading loop structure. Goal-directed behavior is regulated at the middle level ("Do-goals") with actions at higher levels ("Be-goals") suspended until the individual becomes self-aware. Discovery of discrepancies on the "Be-level" or the "Do-level" triggers lower level goals or behaviors aimed at discrepancy reduction, respectively. An individual tries to close discrepancies only when outcome expectations are high. However, a positive affective response as a consequence of goal attainment is not assumed, nor is the detection of a discrepancy associated with negative affect. Rather, the source of positive or negative feelings in goal pursuit is the speed of discrepancy reduction. The intensity of these feelings is regulated again in a negative feedback loop. If the speed meets a set criterion, positive feelings result, whereas negative feelings are experienced with speeds that stay below this criterion.

The discrepancy notions discussed above construe goals as "cold" mental representations of performance standards with no links to needs or incentives. This conceptualization of goals makes it difficult to explain why motivation (see Brehm and Wright's notion of potential motivation) moderates the relation between task difficulty and effort. Moreover, according to discrepancy theory an increase in task difficulty should reduce efforts at task completion, because an experienced increase in task difficulty should lead to reduced self-efficacy and less positive outcome expectations. As Brehm and Wright have repeatedly demonstrated, however, high potential motivation makes it worthwhile for people to mobilize additional effort whenever heightened task difficulty threatens task completion. Finally, Carver and Scheier's construal of the regulation of the speed of discrepancy reduction assumes that positive discrepancies (i.e. moving towards the goal too fast) are reduced as readily as negative discrepancies (i.e. moving towards the goal too slowly). However, from the perspective that goals represent a desired outcome, a person should be less motivated to reduce positive discrepancies than negative discrepancies (Gollwitzer & Rohloff, 1999).

Prospects of Future Research on Goals

Although research on the determinants and processes of goal setting and goal striving has won momentum in recent years, there are goal related phenomena that have not yet received much theoretical and empirical attention. One is the issue of goal conflict. For instance, future research will have to discover how conflicting goals emerge. Answers may come from an analysis of when and how fantasies about a desired future originate. Such visions should be a product of a person's cultural context and the needs, values, attitudes, and interests the person has developed within it. Moreover, whether a person is willing to transfer these fantasies into binding goals should depend on whether the person is ready to contrast her fantasies with reality; again, this mode of self-regulatory thought about the future may have cultural underpinnings (Oettingen, 1997).

Once set goals are in conflict, these conflicts have to be resolved. Emmons (1996) points to the possibility of creative integrations, where new goals are formed which serve both of the conflicting goals (e.g. agentic and communal strivings are reconciled by taking on communal responsibilities). Moreover, Cantor & Fleeson (1994) argue that to meet higher order life tasks (e.g. graduating from college) people can strategically link behavioral goals that apparently conflict (e.g. the conflict between studying and being with other people is reconciled by studying in a group). But more often than not, conflicts can only be resolved by giving up one goal. This raises the question of when and how people most effectively disengage from goals. Although Klinger (1977) has offered a stage theory of disengagement from incentives, systematic research on disengagement from set goals is still missing. Simply ruminating about the impediments of attaining the goal should not suffice (Martin & Tesser, 1996; Oettingen, 1996). Rather, people's low expectations of success need to be activated and used to foster active disengagement, and this becomes more likely when the desired future is mentally contrasted with negative aspects of impeding reality.

REFERENCES

Ach, N. (1935). Analyse des Willens. In E. Abderhalden (Ed.), *Handbuch der biologischen Arbeitsmethoden* Vol. 6. Berlin: Urban & Schwarzenberg.

Ajzen, I. (1985). From intentions to actions: A theory of planned behavior. In J. Kuhl & J. Beckmann (Eds.), *Action control: From cognition to behavior* (pp. 11–39). Heidelberg: Springer-Verlag.

Ames, C., & Archer, J. (1988). Achievement goals in the classroom: Students' learning strategies and motivation processes. *Journal of Educational Psychology, 80*, 260–267.

Atkinson, J. W. (1957). Motivational determinants of risk-taking behavior. *Psychological Review, 64*, 359–372.

Bandura, A. (1997). *Self-efficacy: The exercise of control.* New York: Freeman.

Bandura, A., & Schunk, D. H. (1981). Cultivating competence, self-efficacy and intrinsic interest through proximal self-motivation. *Journal of Personality and Social Psychology, 41*, 586–598.

Bargh, J. A. (1990). Auto-motives: Pre-conscious determinants of social interaction. In E. T. Higgins, & R. M. Sorrentino (Eds.), *Handbook of motivation and cognition* Vol. 2 (pp. 93–130). New York: Guilford Press.

Bargh, J. A., Gollwitzer, P. M., Lee Chai, A., & Barndollar, K. (1999). Bypassing the will: Nonconscious self-regulation through automatic goal pursuit. Manuscript submitted for publication.

Brehm, J. W., & Self, E. A. (1989). The intensity of motivation. *Annual Review of Psychology, 45*, 560–570.

Brooks, R. A. (1991). New approaches to robotics. *Science, 253*, 1227–1232.

Brunstein, J. C., Schultheiss, O. C., & Maier, G. W. (in press). The pursuit of personal goals: A motivational approach to well-being and life adjustment. In J. Brandtstädter, & R. M. Lerner (Eds.), *Action and self-development: Theory and research through the life span.* Thousand Oaks, CA: Sage.

Cantor, N., & Fleeson, W. (1994). Social intelligence and intelligent goal pursuit: A cognitive slice of motivation. In W. Spaulding (Ed.), *Nebraska symposium on motivation* Vol. 41 (pp. 125–180). Lincoln: University of Nebraska Press.

Carver, C. (2001). Self regulation. In A. Tesser & N. Schwarz (Eds.), *Blackwell handbook of social psychology: Intraindividual processes* (pp. 307–328). Oxford: Blackwell Publishing.

Carver, C. S., & Scheier, M. F. (1998). *On the self-regulation of behavior.* New York: Cambridge University Press.

Carver, C. S., & Scheier, M. F. (1999). Themes and issues in the self-regulation of behavior. In R. S. Wyer (Ed.), *Advances in social cognition.* Mahwah, NJ: Erlbaum.

Chaiken, S. (1987). The heuristic model of persuasion. In M. P. Zanna, J. M. Olson, & C. P. Herman (Eds.), *Social influence: The Ontario symposium* Vol. 5 (pp. 3–39). Hillsdale, NJ: Erlbaum.

Cochran, W., & Tesser, A. (1996). The "what the hell" effect: Some effects of goal proximity and goal framing on performance. In L. L. Martin, & A. Tesser (Eds.), *Striving and feeling* (pp. 99–120). Mahwah, NJ: Erlbaum.

Dweck, C. S. (1996). Implicit theories as organizers of goals and behavior. In P. M. Gollwitzer, & J. A. Bargh (Eds.), *The psychology of action: Linking cognition and motivation to behavior* (pp. 69–90). New York: Guilford Press.

Emmons, R. A. (1996). Striving and feeling: Personal goals and subjective well-being. In P. M. Gollwitzer, & J. A. Bargh (Eds.), *The psychology of action: Linking cognition and motivation to behavior* (pp. 313–337). New York: Guilford Press.

Festinger, L. (1942). A theoretical interpretation of shifts in level of aspiration. *Psychological Review, 49,* 235–250.

Geen, R. G. (1995). *Human motivation.* Pacific Grove, CA: Brooks/Cole Publishing.

Gollwitzer, P. M. (1987). The implementation of identity intentions. In F. Halisch, & J. Kuhl (Eds.), *Motivation, intention, and action.* Berlin: Springer.

Gollwitzer, P. M. (1990). Action phases and mind-sets. In E. T. Higgins, & R. M. Sorrentino (Eds.), *Handbook of motivation and cognition* Vol. 2 (pp. 53–92). New York: Guilford Press.

Gollwitzer, P. M. (1993). Goal achievement: The role of intentions. In W. Stroebe, & M. Hewstone (Eds.), *European review of social psychology* Vol. 4 (pp. 141–185). Chichester, UK: John Wiley.

Gollwitzer, P. M. (1999). Implementation intentions: The strategic preparation of automatic goal pursuit. *American Psychologist, 54,* 493–503.

Gollwitzer, P. M., & Bayer, U. (1999). Deliberative versus implemental mindsets in the control of action. In S. Chaiken, & Y. Trope (Eds.), *Dual process theories in social psychology* (pp. 403–422). New York: Guilford Press.

Gollwitzer, P. M., & Kirchhof, O. (1998). The willful pursuit of identity. In J. Heckhausen, & C. S. Dweck (Eds.), *Motivation and self-regulation across the life-span* (pp. 389–423). New York: Cambridge University Press.

Gollwitzer, P. M., & Rohloff, U. (1999). The speed of goal pursuit. In R. S. Wyer (Ed.), *Advances in social cognition* Vol. 12 (pp. 147–159). Hillsdale, NJ: Erlbaum.

Gollwitzer, P. M., & Schaal, B. (1998). Metacognition in action: The importance of implementation intentions. *Personality and Social Psychology Review, 2,* 124–136.

Gollwitzer, P. M., Heckhausen, H., & Ratajczak, H. (1990). From weighing to willing: Approaching a change decision through pre- or postdecisional mentation. *Organizational Behavior and Human Decision Processes, 45,* 41–65.

Gollwitzer, P. M., Bayer, U., Scherer, M., & Seifert, A. E. (in press). A motivational–volitional perspective on identity development. In J. Brandtstädter, & R. M. Lerner (Eds.), *Action and self-development.* Thousand Oaks, CA: Sage.

Heckhausen, H. (1977). Achievement motivation and its constructs: A cognitive model. *Motivation and Emotion, 1,* 283–329.

Heckhausen, H. (1991). *Motivation and action.* Heidelberg: Springer-Verlag.

Heckhausen, H., & Gollwitzer, P. M. (1987). Thought contents and cognitive functioning in motivational versus volitional states of mind. *Motivation and Emotion, 11,* 101–120.

Heckhausen, H., & Kuhl, J. (1985). From wishes to action: The dead ends and short cuts on the long way to action. In M. Frese, & J. Sabini (Eds.), *Goal-directed behavior: The concept of action in psychology* (pp. 134–159). Hillsdale, NJ: Erlbaum.

Higgins, E. T. (1997). Beyond pleasure and pain. *American Psychologist, 52,* 1280–1300.

James, W. (1890/1950). *Principles of psychology.* 2 vols. New York: Dover.

Karoly, P. (1993). Mechanisms of self-regulation: A systems view. *Annual Review of Psychology, 44,* 23–52.

Kasser, T., & Ryan, R. M. (1993). A dark side of the American dream: Correlates of financial success as a central life aspiration. *Journal of Personality and Social Psychology, 65,* 410–422.

Kelso, J. A. S. (1995). *Dynamic patterns: The self-organization of brain and behavior.* Cambridge, MA: MIT Press.

Klinger, E. (1977). *Meaning and void.* Minneapolis: University of Minnesota Press.

Kuhl, J. (in press). A functional-design approach to motivation and self-regulation: The dynamics of personality systems interactions. In M. Boekaerts, P. R. Pintrich, & M. Zeidner (Eds.), *Self-regulation: Directions and challenges for future research.* New York: Academic Press.

Kuhl, J., & Beckmann, J. (1994). *Volition and personality.* Göttingen: Hogrefe.

Lewin, K. (1926). Vorsatz, Wille und Bedürfnis. *Psychologische Forschung, 7,* 330–385.

Little, B. R. (1983). Personal projects: A rationale and methods for investigation. *Environment and Behavior, 15,* 273–309.

Locke, E. A., & Latham, G. P. (1990). *A theory of goal setting and task performance.* Englewood Cliffs, NJ: Prentice-Hall.

McClelland, D. C. (1985). *Human motivation.* Glenview, Ill.: Scott, Foresman.

McClelland, D. C., Koestner, R., & Weinberger, J. (1989). How do self-attributed and implicit motives differ? *Psychological Review, 96,* 690–702.

McDougall, W. (1908/1931). *Social psychology.* London: Methuen.

McGuire, W. J. (1969). The nature of attitudes and attitude change. In G. Lindzey, & E. Aronson (Eds.), *Handbook of social psychology* Vol. 3, 2nd. edn. (pp. 136–314). Reading, MA: Addison-Wesley.

Maes, P. (1994). Modeling adaptive autonomous agents. *Artificial Life, 1,* 135–162.

Markus, H., & Nurius, P. (1986). Possible selves. *American Psychologist, 41,* 954–969.

Martin, L. L., & Tesser, A. (1996). Some ruminative thoughts. In R. S. Wyer (Ed.), *Advances in social cognition* Vol. 9 (pp. 1–47). Mahwah, NJ: Erlbaum.

Mischel, W., & Liebert, R. M. (1966). Effects of discrepancies between observed and imposed reward criteria on their acquisition and transmission. *Journal of Personality and Social Psychology, 3,* 45–53.

Nicholls, J. G. (1979). Quality and equality in intellectual development: The role of motivation in education. *American Psychologist, 34,* 1071–1084.

Oettingen, G. (1996). Positive fantasy and motivation. In P. M. Gollwitzer, & J. A. Bargh (Eds.), *The psychology of action: Linking cognition and motivation to behavior* (pp. 236–259). New York: Guilford Press.

Oettingen, G. (1997). Culture and future thought. *Culture and Psychology, 3,* 353–381.

Oettingen, G. (in press-a). Expectancy effects on behavior depend on self-regulatory thoughts. *Social Cognition.*

Oettingen, G. (in press-b). Free fantasies about the future and the emergence of developmental goals. In J. Brandtstädter, & R. M. Lerner (Eds.), *Action and self-development: Theory and research through the life span*. Thousand Oaks, CA: Sage.

Oyserman, D. (2001). Self-concept and identity. In A. Tesser & N. Schwarz (Eds.), *Blackwell handbook of social psychology: Intraindividual processes* (pp. 499–517). Oxford: Blackwell Publishing.

Petty, R. E., & Cacioppo, J. T. (1986). *Communication and persuasion: Central and peripheral routes to attitude change*. New York: Springer-Verlag.

Read, S. J., Vanman, E. J., & Miller, L. C. (1997). Connectionism, parallel constraint satisfaction processes, and Gestalt principles: (Re)introducing cognitive dynamics to social psychology. *Review of Personality and Social Psychology*, *1*, 26–53.

Ryan, R. M., Sheldon, K. M., Kasser, T., & Deci, E. L. (1996). All goals are not created equal: an organismic perspective on the nature of goals and their regulation. In P. M. Gollwitzer, & J. A. Bargh (Eds.), *The psychology of action: Linking cognition and motivation to behavior* (pp. 7–26). New York: Guilford Press.

Scheier, M. F., & Carver, C. S. (1985). Optimism, coping, and health: Assessment and implications of generalized outcome expectancies. *Health Psychology*, *4*, 219–247.

Skinner, B. F. (1953). *Science and human behavior*. New York: Macmillan.

Steele, C. M. (1988). The psychology of self-affirmation: Sustaining the integrity of the self. In L. Berkowitz (Ed.), *Advances in experimental social psychology* Vol. 21 (pp. 261–302). New York: Academic Press.

Taylor, S. E., Pham, L. B., Rivkin, I. D., & Armor, D. A. (1998). Harnessing the imagination. *American Psychologist*, *53*, 429–439.

Tesser, A., Martin, L. L., & Cornell, D. P. (1996). On the substitutability of self-protective mechanisms. In P. M. Gollwitzer, & J. A. Bargh (Eds.), *The psychology of action: Linking cognition and motivation to behavior* (pp. 48–67). New York: Guilford Press.

Tolman, E. C. (1925). Purpose and cognition: The determinants of animal learning. *Psychological Review*, *32*, 285–297.

Vallacher, R. R., & Wegner, D. M. (1987). What do people think they're doing? Action identification and human behavior. *Psychological Review*, *94*, 3–15.

Vallacher, R. R., & Wegner, D. M. (1989). Levels of personal agency: Individual variation in action identification. *Journal of Personality and Social Psychology*, *57*, 660–671.

Wicklund, R. A., & Gollwitzer, P. M. (1982). *Symbolic self-completion*. Hillsdale, NJ: Erlbaum.

Wilpert, B. (1994). Participation research in organizational psychology. In G. d'Ydewalle, P. Eelen, & P. Bertelson (Eds.), *International perspectives on psychological science* Vol. 2 (pp. 293–310). Hove, UK: Erlbaum.

Wright, R. A. (1996). Brehm's theory of motivation as a model of effort and cardiovascular response. In P. M. Gollwitzer, & J. A. Bargh (Eds.), *The psychology of action: Linking cognition and motivation to behavior* (pp. 424–453). New York: Guilford Press.

Wright, R. A., Murray, J. B., Storey, P. L., & Williams, B. J. (1997). Ability analysis of gender relevance and sex differences in cardiovascular response to behavioral challenge. *Journal of Personality and Social Psychology*, *73*, 405–417.

Wright, R. A., Tunstall, A. M., Williams, B. J., Goodwin, J. S., & Harmon-Jones, E. (1995). Social evaluation and cardiovascular response: An active coping approach. *Journal of Personality and Social Psychology*, *69*, 530–543.

CHAPTER NINE

Self-esteem

Abraham Tesser

One of the most basic responses to any object is evaluation (Tesser & Martin, 1996). Evaluative judgments reflect the extent to which we respond to things as good or bad, likable or dislikable, positive or negative, etc. Such judgments are extremely important in distinguishing objects, persons, ideas, things, or places. They account for most of the variance in mapping semantic meaning (Osgood, Suci, & Tannenbaum, 1957). This is true in the United States as well as other cultures (Osgood, 1974). Evaluation appears to be automatic: it is made faster than other kinds of judgments (Zajonc, 1980) and, often, without a conscious goal to make such judgments (Bargh, Chaiken, Govender, & Pratto, 1992; Fazio, Sanbonmatsu, Powell, & Kardes; 1986; but see Klinger, Burton, & Pitts, in press). When evaluative responses are associated with one's self they are known as self-esteem.

Arguably, the most important thing in one's life is the self. Given the importance of evaluative responding, it is no wonder then that the evaluation of self, or self-esteem, is a topic that has occupied social psychologists almost from the beginning of the discipline in its present form (e.g. James, 1890). Not only is there a long tradition of concern with this topic, but the amount of work associated with it is prodigious (Wylie, 1974, 1979). Indeed, in a recent review of the literature, Banaji & Prentice (1994) counted over 5,000 publications on this topic.

Self-esteem is a topic of non-scientific discussion and self-help books as well. Even the state of California has recognized the importance of self-esteem in everyday functioning (California Task Force, 1990). In short, the topic is an important one from a scientific and from a non-technical point of view. It is multifaceted and the literature is extensive. Thus, given the limitations of the present format, I must be selective. I touch only on aspects of this research that I find particularly important or interesting. (Reviews of additional aspects of this topic can be found in Biernat & Billings, 2001; Dunning, 2001; and Oyserman 2001).

Support for completing this chapter was generously provided by NIMH (K05 MH01233).

Self-esteem and Affect

I have defined self-esteem as an evaluative response toward the self. An evaluative response involves judgments of good–bad. Such judgments can be primarily cognitive, i.e. cool knowledge that I am either good or bad; or affective, i.e. hot positive or negative feelings about the self. Emotion seems to be a ubiquitous participant when the valuation of self is at issue, but what is its precise role?

Brown (1993) argues that self-esteem is primarily an affective response. "Brown (1994) compared self-esteem to a parent's esteem for his or her child: the affective response seems to appear strongly and immediately, without waiting for detailed cognitive appraisals" (cited in Baumeister, 1998, p. 695). Leary & Downs (1995) also argue that affect is part and parcel with self-esteem: "Precisely speaking, people do not suffer negative emotions because their self-esteem is damaged. Rather, decreased self-esteem and negative affect are co-effects of the [same] system" (ibid., p. 134).

Measures of self-esteem often correlate with affective variables. Self-esteem shows a positive association with life satisfaction (Myers & Diener, 1995), positive affect (Brockner, 1984), and a negative association with anxiety (Brockner, 1984), hopelessness (Crocker, Luhtanen, Blaine, & Broadnax, 1994), and depression (Tennen & Hertzberger, 1987). Nevertheless, Crocker & Wolfe (1998) caution us about *equating* self-esteem with affect. They remind us that correlations reveal little about the nature of an association. The correlations could indicate that self-esteem and affect are facets of the same underlying construct. However, the correlations might reflect a state of affairs in which affect causes self-esteem or in which changes in self-esteem cause changes in affect. Further, Crocker and Wolfe point out that self-esteem and affective variables like mood are conceptually distinct (Heatherton & Polivy, 1991). One's mood can change with circumstances even while one's evaluation of self remains consistent.

Affect is clearly associated with self-evaluation. However, that association could reflect affect as a source, affect as a consequence, or affect as simply a facet or outcropping of self-evaluation. We still do not understand the precise role(s) of affect in self-evaluation and self-evaluative processes. My own best guess is that affect is both a mediator (cause) and a consequence of *change* in self-esteem. Changes in self-esteem appear to be inevitably associated with affect and emotion (Tesser & Collins, 1988). Moreover, as we will see below, these affective changes may be crucial in instigating esteem-protective behaviors (Leary & Downs, 1995; Tesser, Martin, & Cornell, 1996). Thus, while self-esteem and emotion are not identical, emotion tends to play a crucial role in the phenomenological experience of self-esteem as well as the regulation of self-esteem.

Am I Good?, Am I Bad?: Self-esteem as a Trait

Sometimes self-esteem is treated as a trait. Self-esteem is seen to be an enduring, characteristic level of self-evaluation. Individuals differ with respect to their chronic level of self-esteem and these individual differences among levels are crucial to understanding behavior. Indeed, most measures of self-esteem are of the individual difference variety. One of the most popular of these measures was developed by Morris Rosenberg (1965). Respondents are asked to indicate the extent to which they agree or disagree with ten relatively straight-forward statements such as: "I feel that I am a person of worth, at least on an equal basis with others." If self-esteem is an enduring trait, it should reveal high test–retest reliabilities. A review by McFarlin & Blascovich (1981) indicates that the Rosenberg scale and other instruments like it do show considerable stability over time.

If self-esteem is an important trait it should be related to other consequential feelings and behaviors. As noted above, trait self-esteem is related to a variety of affective states such as life satisfaction and depression (negative relationship). Reviews by Wylie (1974, 1979) indicate that it is also related to desire for control, achievement motivation, self-determination, and need for approval. Balance theory (Heider, 1958) asserts that people tend to see the world in a simple, evaluatively balanced way, i.e. good things go with good things and bad things go with bad things. Until recently, a simplified summary of the theorizing regarding trait self-esteem was like a derivation from balance theory: Self-esteem, a good trait, is positively associated with other good things and negatively associated with bad things. The empirical world, however, is not that simple.

Recent work on aggression makes the point extremely well. Although there have been a number of suggestions that violent behavior is associated with low self-esteem, Baumeister, Smart, & Boden's (1996) interdisciplinary review of the evidence is not consistent with this expectation. Rather, they find that violence becomes more likely when another person or situation contradicts a person's highly favorable view of the self. An individual whose positive self-view is accurate is less likely to be confronted with inflammatory contradictory informa-tion than an individual whose positive self-view is inflated. Baumeister, Smart, & Boden (1996) suggest that murder, assault, rape, and domestic violence are often associated with threats to honor and threats to feelings of male superiority.

Some complications

Clearly, our understanding of trait self-esteem is becoming more complex and elaborated. Our hypotheses are less predictable from the simple perspective of balance theory. Even our view of trait self-esteem as an enduring characteristic is being questioned. Kernis and his associates (see Kernis & Waschull, 1995; Greenier, Kernis, & Waschull, 1995, for reviews) have found that individuals differ not only with respect to level of self-esteem but they also differ with respect to stability in the level of their self-esteem. (Stability of self-esteem is indexed by the standard deviation in an individual's level of self-esteem measured repeatedly over time.)[1] Stability of self-esteem seems to interact in important ways with level of self-esteem to predict behavior. For example, consistent with the Baumeister, Smart, & Boden (1996) thesis, persons with unstable high self-esteem are more aggressive than others (Kernis, Grannemann, & Barclay, 1989).

Why do some individuals appear to be more stable in their self-esteem than others? One answer recognizes that self-esteem may be subject to environmental events, at least to some extent. Thus, differences in stability of self-esteem may simply reflect differences in environmental variability across persons rather than fundamental individual differences. Other answers, more consistent with the spirit of self-esteem as a trait, are beginning to emerge. The notions of self-concept clarity (Campbell, 1990; Campbell, Trapnell, Heine, Katz, Lavallee, & Lehman, 1996) and contingencies of self-esteem (Crocker & Wolfe, 1998) are examples of such answers.

Self-esteem is related to self-concept. If I think of myself as kind, moral, smart, etc. I will tend to have high self-esteem. If I think of myself as unkind or not very smart, I will tend to have low self-esteem. However, what if I am uncertain about myself? Uncertainty appears to be related to low self-esteem. Campbell (1990) compared persons high and low in self-esteem and found that persons high in self-esteem show (1) greater confidence and extremity in their beliefs about the self: (2) greater stability in their self-beliefs over time; (3) greater consistency between their general self-beliefs and situation specific self-beliefs; and (4) greater internal consistency in the way they report their self-beliefs.

Campbell's work shows that the tenuousness with which we hold self-beliefs is related to self-esteem. She did not specifically correlate uncertainty with stability of global self-esteem. It seems quite plausible, however, that self-concept clarity and stability of self-esteem are related. Indeed, one of the components of self-concept clarity is belief stability.

Crocker & Wolfe (1998) more specifically address the question of self-esteem stability in their theory of "contingencies of worth." Crocker and Wolfe suggest that individuals can be rank ordered along a continuum on which one end is non-contingent self-esteem and the other end is contingent self-esteem. Persons with non-contingent self-esteem are certain about who they are. Although they may be disappointed when things do not go as they hope or delighted when things do go well, their evaluation of self does not fluctuate. That is, even persons with non-contingent self-esteem will experience affective shifts in response to self-relevant feedback, but they will not change their evaluation of self. From Carl Rogers' (1961) point of view, these people grew up in an unconditionally accepting environment and their feelings of worth do not depend on any particular success or failure. They are also reminiscent of Deci & Ryan's (1995) notion of the autonomous or self-determined self. Note, however, that Roger's and Deci and Ryan's analogs to the non-contingent self have positive self-esteem. Crocker and Wolfe suggest that there are also persons with non-contingent low self-esteem. Persons with non-contingent self-esteem should look very much like Kernis's stable self-esteem individuals.

Persons at the contingent end of this continuum have self-esteem that fluctuates. For them, self-esteem is contingent "on the belief that they have valued attributes or competencies, on approval and regard from others, being virtuous, or the exercise of power, and some people derive a sense of self worth from their collective identities" (Crocker & Wolfe, 1998, p. 19). Thus, self-esteem will fluctuate for non-contingents depending on their own behavior or feedback. Indeed, others have measured self-esteem by assessing respondents evaluation of self in a variety of areas (e.g. Hatter, 1993, Piers & Harris, 1969) and then summing across those areas. This is not satisfactory from Crocker and Wolfe's perspective because, they argue, different people have different contingencies of self-worth that they must satisfy. Fluctuations in self-esteem must be matched to fluctuations in the individual's own area of contingency.

Crocker and Wolfe identify nine contingencies of self that are frequently encountered, at least in college students. These are others' approval, appearance, God's love, friends and family, power, self-reliance, social identity, school competence and virtue. The following contingencies of self-esteem are more important for females than for males: others' approval, appearance, God's love, and competency. Black and white respondents differ on all contingencies except power and virtue. God's love is a more important contingency of self-esteem for Blacks than for Whites; the remaining contingencies (on which there are differences) are more important for Whites than for Blacks.

From a theoretical point of view, the Crocker and Wolfe perspective is quite integrative. Trait theorists in general have gone from simple expectations that a particular trait will reveal itself consistently across situations to more sophisticated views which find consistencies by taking the individual's subjective, idiosyncratic interpretation of situations into account (Mischel & Shoda, 1998). The Crocker and Wolfe formulation has that spirit. It helps us to understand why self-esteem may fluctuate (because at least for some people self-esteem is contingent) and it identifies many of the contingencies around which self-esteem fluctuates. This perspective, however, is still in its infancy and only future research will reveal its real potential.

Trait self-esteem: How shall we know it?

All of the research on trait self-esteem that I have reviewed so far depends on conscious, deliberate self-report to assess level of self-esteem. Such measures, if they are to be taken at face value, have two crucial assumptions that we know are questionable. One assumption is that persons will accurately report their self-esteem. Here one must be concerned with a variety of issues that psychometricians deal with perennially. Do different subjects use the scale with the same calibration? We treat scale scores as if all respondents use the categories in the same way but they may not. We generally give individual scores meaning by comparing them to other people on the same dimension, i.e. nomothetically, when, indeed, the subject may be formulating his or her response by looking within him or herself and comparing dimensions, idiographically. There are potential problems with response sets such as the tendency to agree (Cronbach, 1946) and, particularly in the case of self-esteem, to try to appear socially desirable (Crowne & Marlowe, 1964).

The second issue is even more fundamental than the first. Do individuals even know how positively they evaluate the self? Are there aspects of self-esteem that are consequential but not available to conscious awareness? Recent work on implicit memory (e.g. Tulving & Schacter, 1990) and automaticity in stereotypes (e.g. Devine, 1989) and attitudes (Bargh, et al., 1992; Fazio, et al., 1986) suggests that there are important, implicit, i.e. nonconscious, elements in a variety of psychological systems. The notion that there may be automatic, non-conscious elements connected with self-esteem seems plausible.

Greenwald & Banaji (1995, p. 11) define implicit self-esteem as "the introspectively unidentified (or inaccurately identified) effect of the self attitude on evaluation of self-associated and self-dissociated objects." They see evidence for implicit self-esteem in a variety of well established phenomena: the "mere ownership effect," i.e. objects become more positively evaluated by simply belonging to the self (Feys, 1991; Beggan, 1992); the "minimal group effect," i.e. regardless of how arbitrary the grouping, members of one's own group are treated more favorably than members of other groups (e.g. Tajfel & Turner, 1986); and the "initial letter effect," where individuals tend to like the letters in their own names, particularly the first letters of their names, more than other alphabet letters (Nuttin, 1985).

No "standard measure" of implicit self-esteem has yet surfaced. However, researchers are exploring a variety of possibilities. Following Fazio (e.g. Fazio, Powell, & Herr, 1983), Cline (e.g. Cline, in progress; Cline & Tesser, 1998) is measuring "implicit attitude toward the self." She primes subjects with symbols of the self (e.g. their name), and measures individual differences in the extent to which such primes speed up or slow down the evaluation of words with clear evaluative meaning, e.g. rose, Hitler. A positive evaluation of the self should speed up the identification of positive words and slow down the identification of negative words. The technique shows some promise, at least among women. Other possibilities for measuring individual differences in implicit response systems are being developed rapidly (Greenwald, McGhee, & Schwartz, 1998: see also Bassili, 2001).

Am I Doing Better or Worse? Self-esteem as a State Variable

Concern with self-esteem as an enduring individual difference variable or trait is one approach to understanding. There is also an important, growing, and vibrant literature that focuses on the situations that lead to transient changes in self-evaluation. The component of self-esteem that fluctuates relatively rapidly, changing with circumstance, is known as state self-esteem. The regulation of state self-esteem has been the subject of thousands of studies (Banaji & Prentice, 1994).

The self-motives[2]

Underlying most of the studies of state self-esteem is the assumption that persons are motivated to achieve, maintain, or enhance a self-evaluation. Self-evaluation is a potential concern whenever there is new information or feedback about the self or some aspect of the self. If our only motive was to maintain a positive self-evaluation we would avoid or distort (potentially) negative feedback and approach or magnify the importance of (potentially) positive feedback. However, feedback may prompt other motives as well. (See Biernat & Billings, 2001, and Dunning, 2001 for more detailed reviews of the motives related to self.)

Persons may be motivated to verify their current view of self. For persons with a positive evaluation of self, the motive to enhance and the motive to self-verify lead to the same prediction, i.e. approach positive information and avoid negative information. However, for persons with a negative self-view the enhancement and verification perspectives make different predictions. According to self-verification theory, persons with a negative self-view should seek out negative feedback. Swann (e.g. 1987) and his students and associates (e.g. Swann, Stein-Seroussi, & Geisler, 1992) have provided ample evidence for the existence of a self-verification motive. However, this motive is limited in the kinds of responses it prompts and the resources necessary for it to manifest itself. We can distinguish cognitive responses to feedback (I believe it, I don't believe it) from affective responses (I enjoy it; I hate it).

Self-verification seems limited to cognitive responses (Shrauger, 1975). We can distinguish automatic behavior (quick, effortless) from controlled behavior (deliberate, effortful). Self-verification seems limited to non-spontaneous occasions (Swann, Hixon, Stein-Seroussi, & Gilbert, 1990). (See Dunning, 2001 for a more complete review of self-verification.)

Feedback about the self may trigger a third motive: accuracy. According to Trope and his colleagues (Trope, 1986) it is important that all of us have an accurate view of our strengths and our weaknesses. Distortions and selective biases can take us only so far in a world with real outcomes. An accurate self-appraisal should allow us to avoid potential failures and seek out potential success. Thus, according to this framework, we should not seek out flattering feedback nor should we seek out feedback that verifies what we think of ourselves. We should seek out feedback that is most diagnostic of our skill, abilities, and other attributes. Indeed, under certain circumstances, individuals prefer diagnostic feedback to flattering feedback (e.g. Trope, 1980). Here too, however, exposure to negative information about the self is conditional. For example, individuals are willing to expose themselves to negative information when they are uncertain about themselves and the negative feedback is diagnostic (Trope, 1982). (Note that self-verification and accuracy motives seem to conflict in their predictions about self-certainty. The greater one's self-certainty, the *lower* the accuracy motivation but the greater the motive to self-verify.) Positive mood appears to be a useful personal resource for coping with stress (Aspinwall, 1998; 2001). Trope & Neter (1994) find that prior success and good mood are important precursors to exposure to diagnostic negative information.

Sedikides (1993), a psychologist who is not strongly identified with any of these positions, conducted a study to compare the "general" power of the three motives we have discussed: self-enhancement, self-verification, and accuracy. He asked people what information they would want if they were thinking about themselves. Questions that the subjects designed themselves revealed evidence for each of the motives. However, the most important motive for explaining his data was the motive to maintain self-esteem, followed by self-verification, and accuracy. My own point of view coincides with Sedikides's data. Clearly, on occasion people self-verify or seek out accurate information *regardless* of the implications for self-evaluation. However, the more general tendency is for people to defend or enhance self-evaluation. We turn now to a discussion of how we maintain a positive self-evaluation.

The arenas of self-esteem maintenance

How the self is defended or enhanced is, perhaps, the area that has attracted the most research attention. This research attempts to elaborate the squiggles in the signature of the motive to maintain a positive self-evaluation. Indeed, by now there is evidence for so many qualitatively different psychological defense mechanisms that I previously have referred to the collection as the "self-zoo" (Tesser, Martin, & Cornell, 1996).

Since comprehensive reviews of the self-esteem maintenance literature already exist (e.g. Banaji & Prentice, 1994; Baumeister, 1998; Hoyle, Kernis, Leary, & Baldwin, 1998), I will focus only on a sample of these mechanisms. Elsewhere (Tesser, Crepaz, Collins, Cornell, & Beach, 1998), I have argued that three global approaches subsume much of the self-defense research. These approaches are social comparison, inconsistency reduction, and value expression. The approaches differ in that what they suggest constitutes a potential threat or enhancement to self-esteem and what behaviors or strategies an individual may adopt to defend or enhance the self.

Social comparison theory

A number of models suggest that the outcomes of others have consequences for one's own self-esteem (see Biernat & Billings 2001 for an elegant review of this literature). The particular approach to social comparison with which I am most familiar is the Self-Evaluation Maintenance (SEM) model (e.g. Tesser, 1988), so I will use it as an illustration. This model suggests that being outperformed by another can lower self-evaluation by inviting unflattering self-comparison, or it can raise self-evaluation – a kind of basking in reflected glory (e.g. Cialdini, Borden, Thorne, Walker, Freeman, & Sloan, 1976). These effects are enhanced with a psychologically close other. Another is psychologically close to the extent that the other shares salient features with the self, is in physical proximity with the self, etc., i.e. what Heider (1958) calls "unit relatedness" or, more recently, what group perception researchers (e.g. Hamilton, Sherman, & Lickel, 1998) call "entitativity." The relevance of the performance domain determines the relative importance of these opposing processes. Suppose the performance domain is unimportant to one's self-definition (low relevance). Then, the reflection process will be dominant and one's self-evaluation will be augmented by a close other's better performance. Suppose the performance domain is important to one's self-definition (high relevance). Then, the comparison process will be dominant and one's self-evaluation will be threatened by a close other's better performance. Thus, interacting combinations of three variables, performance, closeness, and relevance, are the antecedents to self-esteem threat or enhancement.

What might one do to enhance self-esteem or to reduce threats to self-esteem? One can change the relevance of the performance domain. This changes the relative importance of the comparison and reflection process (e.g. Tesser & Campbell, 1980; Tesser & Paulhus, 1983); or, one can increase or decrease closeness to the other and thereby amplify enhancing outcomes or dampen threatening outcomes (e.g. Pleban & Tesser 1981); or, one can increase or decrease the performance gap between self and other (Tesser & Smith, 1980).

I will continue to use the SEM model as an exemplar. However, it is important to note some recent developments that are illustrating the other side of the social comparison coin. We usually think of comparison with others affecting one's view of self. Recent research has turned this on its head and shown that one's view of self can affect the view of comparison others. For example, the poorer an individual performs in some domain, say athletics, the more charitable that individual is in evaluating the athletic performance of others – if I do poorly then people who do poorly are OK; if I do well then people who do poorly are rated down (Dunning & Cohen, 1992). Alicke, LoSciavo, Zerbst, & Zhang (1997) have shown that, under some conditions, when we are outperformed by another we don't downgrade our view of self, we upgrade the other's performance. It is less threatening to be outperformed by a "genius" than a person of normal ability.

The effect of threat to self on our view of others carries over to the group/stereotype literature. In 1950, Adorno, Frenkel-Brunswik, Levinson, and Sanford suggested that prejudice is functional: it sometimes operates to cover up our own inadequacies. Fein & Spencer (e.g. 1997; Spencer, Fein, Wolfe, Fong, & Dunn, 1998) have shown this experimentally. They have found that individuals who have experienced a threat to self-esteem show greater signs of derogating outgroups than those who are not threatened.

Cognitive consistency theory

The number of variations within this approach to self-evaluation regulation are also quite large (Abelson, Aronson, McGuire, Newcomb, Rosenberg, & Tannenbaum, 1968; Dunning, 2001; Tesser & Martin, 1996). The exemplar with which we will be concerned is cognitive dissonance theory (Festinger, 1957). As originally formulated, dissonance theory was not a theory of self-esteem. Over the years, however, at least some investigators (e.g. Aronson, 1969; Greenwald & Ronis, 1978) have come to interpret dissonance in terms of threat to self-esteem.

According to dissonance theory, self-esteem is threatened by inconsistency. Holding beliefs/cognitions that are logically or psychologically inconsistent, i.e. dissonant, with one another is uncomfortable. For example, a student's cognition that she is opposed to a tuition increase is dissonant with the cognition that she freely chose to write an essay in favor of a tuition increase and such a choice will be threatening. How might the student reduce the threatening inconsistency? She can change her attitude toward a tuition increase or she can revoke her choice to write the essay, whichever is easier. If we assume that her choice was associated with a public commitment to an experimenter, for example, then changing her attitude toward the tuition increase is likely to be easier.

Social comparison mechanisms and consistency reduction mechanisms seem to have little in common. Threat from dissonance rarely has anything to do with the performance of another, i.e. social comparison. By the same token, inconsistency is generally irrelevant to an SEM threat, whereas others' performance is crucial. Attitude change is the usual mode of dissonance threat reduction; on the other hand, changes in closeness, performance, or relevance are the SEM modes.

Value expression theory

The notion that expressing one's most cherished values can affect self-esteem also has a productive history in social psychology (e.g. Smith, Bruner, & White, 1956; Katz, 1960, Rokeach, 1985). Simply expressing who we are, stating our important attitudes and values seems to have a positive effect on self-evaluation. The specific variation of value expression theory that I deal with here is self-affirmation theory (e.g. Steele, 1988).

According to Steele, self-evaluation has at its root a concern with a sense of global self-integrity. The concept of integrity is very broad. For example, Steele interprets the active ingredient of learned helplessness (e.g. Liu & Steele, 1986) and of many dissonant situations (e.g. Steele & Liu, 1983) to be a threat to self-integrity rather than a threat due to the experience of inconsistency. Self-integrity refers to holding self-conceptions and images that one is "adaptively and morally adequate, that is, as competent, good, coherent, unitary, stable, and capable of free choice, capable of controlling important outcomes, and so on" (Steele, 1988, p. 262).

If the locus of the threat to self-esteem is self-integrity then the behavior to reduce that threat is self-affirmation or a declaration of the significance of an important self-value. Since self-integrity is presumed to be general, the content of the affirmed self-value and the content of the threat to self-esteem may be totally independent. Although "self-integrity" is rather general, Steele has relied heavily on value expression to boost self-esteem. Note that the behavior of reaffirming a cherished value is qualitatively different from the SEM behaviors of changing closeness, relevance, or performance, or the dissonance behavior of attitude change.

Is self-esteem regulation one arena or many arenas?

If the antecedent circumstances and the resulting behaviors of different mechanisms are distinct, one may very well question whether there is a single self-esteem or three independent types of self-esteem. Each type identifies a qualitatively different variable to which self-evaluation is sensitive, i.e. social comparison, inconsistency, and value expression, and each has a qualitatively different behavioral strategy for regulating self-esteem.

Lewin (1935) and his students, particularly Ovsiankina (1928), have identified at least one way of addressing this question (see Tesser, Martin, & Cornell, 1996, for a discussion). Think of maintaining self-esteem as a goal. Goals have the property of equifinality (Heider, 1958), i.e. the path to the goal is irrelevant; one instrumentality is substitutable for another. If each of the self-esteem mechanisms is describing different ways of regulating a singular self-esteem, then one mechanism should be substitutable for another. A threat to self-esteem due to inconsistency may be reduced by basking in the reflected glory of a close other; a boost to the self via value expression may buffer the threat due to negative comparison, etc. On the other hand, there may be separate ego needs, e.g. a concern with ambiguity/inconsistency (e.g. Cialdini, Trost, & Newsom, 1995), or a concern with competence (e.g. White, 1959), for example. In this case, a threat due to dissonance would not be reduced by basking.

Evidence for substitutability

In a substitutability design an individual's self-esteem is altered via one mechanism and then the individual engages in a second mechanism. If the second mechanism "satisfies" the goal, the individual will not resume behavior connected with the first mechanism. Claude Steele's work on substitutability of self-evaluation mechanisms is perhaps the most elegant. Steele & Liu (1983) demonstrated that the self-affirmation mechanism could substitute for cognitive dissonance reduction. Participants were given high or low choice to write a counter-attitudinal essay (dissonance manipulation). Some participants then filled out a questionnaire concerning a very important value and others were given a questionnaire irrelevant to their values (self-affirmation manipulation). A measure of dissonance reducing attitude change was then administered. The typical dissonance finding was obtained for those participants who were given a questionnaire covering an unimportant value but not for participants that affirmed an important value. Self-affirmation appeared to eliminate the threat produced by dissonance, i.e. self-affirmation can substitute for or "turn off" dissonance reduction.

There is also evidence that self-affirmation affects the comparison and reflection processes associated with the SEM model. Tesser & Cornell (1991) allowed participants to affirm or not affirm an important aspect of the self and then gave subjects an SEM threat. Results indicated that when participants affirmed an important aspect of their self, the SEM threat pattern was completely eliminated. These results indicate that self-affirmation substitutes for SEM processes. The ability to affect other self-esteem maintaining processes is not limited to self-affirmation. Tesser & Cornell (1991, Study 2 and 3) observed that certain SEM situations could substitute for dissonance reduction. More recent work (Tesser, et al., 1998) rounds out the picture by showing that cognitive dissonance (Study 2) and SEM mechanisms (Study 1) substitute for self-affirmation and that dissonance substitutes for SEM (Study 3).

The confluence model

I have described the work above to give the reader a feel for the kind of research connected with the maintenance and regulation of self-evaluation. There are a couple of noteworthy aspects of this work. First, there is a dramatic diversity of approaches. In spite of different antecedents and consequences associated with each, under certain conditions, they substitute for one another in regulating self-esteem.[3] The metaphor I find apt is that of the confluence of a river. The streams entering the river may be separate but once they converge with the river the waters are indistinguishable. Regardless of the source of the water the river may be channeled in many different directions.

Evolution and Self-esteem

Given its importance it may be surprising to learn that empirical, experimental research on the origins of self-esteem are relatively recent. We are only beginning to address questions about the origins of self-esteem. (Our discussion of these issues draws heavily on the work of Leary & Downs, 1995, and Beach & Tesser, in press.)

A number of answers have been suggested to the question as to why there is a need for a positive view of self. Earlier I briefly discussed the relationship between self-esteem and emotion. I noted that changes in self-esteem tend to be associated with changes in affect (Tesser & Collins, 1988; Tesser, Millar, & Moore, 1988). Increased self-esteem is associated with positive affect and decreased self-esteem is associated with negative affect. Trait self-esteem tends to be related to affective traits such as depression and anxiety (Taylor & Brown, 1988). This suggests that the motive for positive self-esteem derives from preferences for positive affective states. One problem with this explanation is that it does not tell us why positive emotions tend to be associated with positive evaluations of the self.

Another suggestion is that people prefer high self-esteem because it helps them toward goal achievement. Indeed, self-esteem is associated with achievement. People high in self-confidence, e.g. self-efficacy (Bandura, 1977), tend to perform better and persist longer at various tasks. However, high self-esteem can also have negative consequences for achievement. Persons high in self-esteem may take on unrealistically difficult tasks. Indeed, persons high in self-esteem tend to persist longer even at impossible tasks (McFarlin, Baumeister, & Blascovich, 1984).

Some explanations have a decidedly evolutionary cast. Barkow's (1980) notion that self-esteem is an indicator of dominance in a group comes from evolutionary psychology. Pre-homonid groups had dominance hierarchies. Individuals higher in the dominance hierarchy had greater access to mates, food, and all the other amenities of social life. With the development of cognitive abilities, came the ability to keep track of one's place in the hierarchy and the motivational mechanism, self-esteem, for moving toward dominance. Indeed, status within an organization affects self-esteem and may even be more important than resource favorability in shaping feelings of connectedness to organizations (Kramer & Neale, 1998).

Perhaps the most thoroughly researched explanation for the origin of self-esteem is provided by terror management theory. Pyszczynski, Greenberg, & Solomon (1997) suggest that with the evolutionary emergence of self-consciousness comes the awareness of death. The notion of the finality of death produces terror. Being a part of one's culture reduces that terror because the culture lives on or because it promises an afterlife. Thus, as long as the individual remains part of a viable culture he may achieve a kind of immortality. Self-esteem may have evolved as an affective indicator of the extent to which the individual is meeting cultural standards. As such, self-esteem is a buffer against the terror of death.

There have been many successful tests of terror management theory. Since the terror of death is central, it follows that concerns with cultural standards will be particularly pronounced when death is made salient. A number of studies using a variety of measures have confirmed this prediction. For example, people induced to think about death evaluate cultural heroes more positively, and cultural transgressors more negatively than people not thinking about death (Greenberg, Pyszczynski, Solomon, Rosenblatt, Veeder, Kirkland, & Lyon, 1990). People who focus on death also show greater attraction to persons who share their religious beliefs than people not focused on death (Greenberg, Simon, Pyszczynski, Solomon, & Chatel, 1992). The body of evidence for this theory is impressive. However, the theory is not comprehensive. There appear to be changes in self-esteem even when death is not salient and even when social norms are not at stake. For example, it is difficult to see how social comparison information makes one's death more or less salient and which social norms are being violated when another outperforms the self.

From the point of view of terror management theory, self-esteem derives from upholding cultural standards. Perhaps upholding cultural standards is related to self-esteem, at least to some extent, because upholding cultural standards makes us more attractive to the persons around us. Thus, another explanation for the origin of self-esteem is that it evolved as a sociometer (Leary & Downs, 1995). In a very broad-ranging review, Baumeister & Leary (1995) have shown the importance of social belonging and described the pain of being excluded from important groups. Indeed, as *homo sapiens* were emerging in the late Pleistocene, group life was crucial to survival. Maintenance of social bonds was clearly important for mating, defense, the acquisition of food, shelter, etc. One might suppose that only those who were able to maintain relationships and not be excluded from social groups survived. Given the importance of maintaining group membership, some mechanism should have evolved to avoid social exclusion (but see Maryanski & Turner, 1992). According to Leary & Downs (1995) self-esteem is such a mechanism. It functions "as a sociometer that (1) monitors the social environment for cues indicating disapproval, rejection, or exclusion and (2) alerts the individual via negative affective reactions when such cues are detected" (Leary & Downs, 1995, p. 129).

It is impossible to test directly a specific evolutionary path, and difficult to test the "innateness" of the need to belong. However, a review of the literature (Baumeister & Leary, 1995) and several new studies are consistent with the sociometer idea. For example, Leary, Tamdor, Terdal, & Downs (1995) presented subjects with different behaviors (Study 1) and asked them to rate the extent to which others would reject them if they engaged in the behavior. Later, subjects rated the extent to which they would experience esteem-deflating emotions, e.g. shame, dejection, worthlessness, if they engaged in the behavior. They found a substantial positive correlation between these two sets of ratings. In a second study, subjects reported on personal events that had a positive or negative impact on their self-feelings. They then rated their self-feelings and the extent to which each of the situations involved social exclusion. Again, the correlation between these variables was significant. In a third and fourth study, subjects were randomly assigned to be either accepted or rejected by a group or another person. Rejected subjects showed greater negative self-feelings. These studies clearly suggest that behaviors or situations associated with exclusion are also associated with decrements in self-esteem.

The Leary and Downs hypothesis is plausible but I (Beach & Tesser, in press) believe that it does not go far enough. Leary and Downs suggest that self-esteem is rooted in concerns with being excluded by others. Certainly, however, we are not equally concerned with being excluded by all people and all groups. The SEM model (described above) captures that intuition. It suggests that the social consequences to self-esteem are amplified in the context of psychologically close others rather than distant others. Thus, self-esteem may be a more sensitive sociometer to exclusion among close than among distant others. This seems to make good sense from an evolutionary perspective. Certainly, there is an adaptive advantage to being concerned with those who are close, e.g. one's own group, than with members of other groups.

Leary and Downs (along with William James, 1890) recognize that the self-esteem of different people is sensitive to feedback in different domains. "People can follow many routes to social acceptance. Only when people have staked their connections to others on certain aspects of themselves should their self-esteem be affected by events that reflect on those aspects" (Leary & Downs, 1995, p. 137). However, Leary and Downs do not specify how certain aspects of the self become important to connections with others. The SEM model also recognizes the idea of different domains of self-esteem. The SEM construct of relevance refers to the extent to which doing well in some particular domain is important to the self.

Again, an evolutionary account of the SEM prediction is not very difficult to construct. Clearly, there is a selective advantage in avoiding conflict and feeling good about members of one's own group. The tendency for conflict within groups would be reduced if individuals specialize in what they do. For example, if A is hunting while B is mending there is less reason and opportunity for conflict than if both hunted and mended. This would be particularly true if A was better at hunting and B was better at mending.[4] Indeed, A could be attracted to B because her mending produces something valuable to the group but does not threaten his own contribution and value to the group. The SEM model describes just such an adaptation. It predicts that one is unlikely to adopt a self-definition (role) involving an area in which a close other outperforms self. The consequence of this prediction is movement toward role specialization within the group and positive affect associated with other group members' achievements (the reflection process). This adaptation is quite specific but has important and relatively general consequences.

In sum, the current intellectual zeitgeist sees self-esteem as an adaptation to social rather than individual demands. For the most part, the accounts we reviewed here suggest that self-esteem is conditioned on our acceptability to others. Leary makes this point directly; Barkow in terms of social status; and terror management theory in terms of upholding cultural standards. The SEM model augments these accounts by predicting which persons and which self-aspects are likely to have the greatest impact on self-esteem.

A Coda on Culture

Thinking about evolution inevitably brings to mind questions about culture. Perhaps the work that most strongly captured the imagination and energies of self researchers in the 1990s was Markus & Kitayama's (1991) distinction between the independent self (e.g. distinct, autonomous, unique self) and the interdependent self (e.g. relational, connected, sociocentric self). This work suggests that our emphasis on striving for independence and realization of our own, unique personal potential may be a result of immersion in Western culture. In contrast, Southern European and Asian cultures put an emphasis on conformity, a self that "fits in" with important others. Triandis (1989) worked with a more articulated view of the self: private self (own view of stares, traits, personal behavior); public self (generalized other's view of self), and collective self (specific group's view of self, e.g. family's view of self). More importantly, he studied cultural variables that are likely to be associated with an emphasis on one or the other aspects of self. For example, cultures that are more complex are associated with accentuation of public and private aspects of self. Individualistic cultures are associated with an emphasis on the private self and a de-emphasis of the collective self. Collectivism, external threat, and competition with outgroups increase the emphasis on the collective aspects of self.

Research addressing cultural influences on self is enjoying a new popularity. Moreover, the cultural view holds great promise for understanding the self. I present only a cursory view here because of space constraints and because the cultural position is thoroughly explored in Miller (2001) and Oyserman (2001).

Summary

We defined self-esteem as an evaluation of the self and suggested that changes in self-esteem are associated with affect. Self-esteem is sometimes treated as a trait. Classic research indicates that trait measures of self-esteem show good reliability and relate to a variety of other "good" attributes. More recent work suggests that self-esteem may be unstable or contingent, at least for some people, and that high levels of self-esteem sometimes may be related to "bad" attributes such as aggression. A second research tradition treats self-esteem as a state variable. Work in this tradition sometimes pits the motive to maintain a positive self-evaluation against other motives such as desires for accuracy or self-verification. There is evidence for all three of these motives, although the need to maintain a positive evaluation seems to be the most pervasive. There are many strategies for maintaining self-esteem, including the use of social comparison, cognitive consistency, and value expression. The observation that these strategies are qualitatively different from one another raises the question of whether there is one or several arenas of self-evaluation maintenance. Patterns of substitutability in these strategies suggest that self-esteem is a unitary motive. Finally, a review of conjecture regarding the evolutionary antecedents of self-esteem revealed a variety of approaches suggesting that self-esteem evolved to solve social problems.

NOTES

1 The standard deviation is sensitive to systematic changes such as increases and decreases in self-esteem as well as random fluctuations. Research attempting to distinguish and understand such patterns is needed.

2 In the interest of brevity, the discussion of state self-esteem ignores chronic individual differences in self-esteem. It should be noted that differences in trait self-esteem are dearly related to self-enhancing behaviors (e.g. Blaine & Crocker, 1993) and may be related to the other motives as well.

3 Substitutability is not always observed. For example, Stone, Weigand, Cooper, & Aronson (1997) have shown that if people have a direct means of dealing with a threat to self-esteem they prefer the direct route to substituting a different mechanism.

4 The activities chosen for illustration are sex linked. Indeed, the earliest signs of specialization and role differentiation in evolutionary history center on gender and age distinctions.

REFERENCES

Abelson, R. P., Aronson, E., McGuire, W. J., Newcomb, T. M., Rosenberg, M. J., & Tannenbaum, P. H. (Eds.) (1968). *Theories of cognitive consistency: A source book*. Chicago: Rand McNally.

Adorno, T. W., Frenkel-Brunswik, E., Levinson, D. J., & Sanford, R. N. (1950). *The authoritarian personality*. New York: Harper & Row.

Alicke, M. D., LoSchiavo, F. M., Zerbst, J., & Zhang, S. (1997). The person who outperforms me is a genius: Maintaining perceived competence in upward social comparison. *Journal of Personality and Social Psychology, 73*, 781–789.

Aronson, E. (1969). The theory of cognitive dissonance: A current perspective. In L. Berkowitz (Ed.), *Advances in experimental social psychology*, Vol. 4 (pp. 2–32). New York: Academic Press.

Aspinwall, L. G. (1998). Rethinking the role of positive affect in self regulation. *Motivation and Emotion, 22*, 1–32.

Aspinwall, L. G. (2001). Dealing with adversity: Self-regulation, coping, adaptation, and health. In A. Tesser & N. Schwarz (Eds.), *Blackwell handbook of social psychology: Intraindividual processes* (pp. 591–614). Oxford: Blackwell Publishing.

Banaji, M. R., & Prentice, D. A. (1994). The self in social contexts. *Annual Review of Psychology, 45*, 297–332.

Bandura, A. (1977). Self-efficacy: Toward a unifying theory of behavioral change. *Psychological Review, 84*, 191–215.

Bargh, J. A. (1992). Why subliminality might not matter to social psychology: Awareness of the stimulus vs awareness of its influence. In R. F. Bornstein & T. S. Pittman (Eds.) *Perception without awareness* (pp. 236–255). New York. Guilford Press.

Bargh, J. A., Chaiken, S., Govender, R., & Pratto, F. (1992). The generality of the automatic attitude activation effect. *Journal of Personality and Social Psychology, 62*, 893–912.

Barkow, J. (1980). Prestige and self-esteem: A biosocial interpretation. In D. R. Omark, F. F. Strayer, & D. G. Freedman (Eds.), *Dominance relations* (pp. 319–332). New York: Garland.

Bassili, J. N. (2001). Cognitive indices of social information processing. In A. Tesser & N. Schwarz (Eds.), *Blackwell handbook of social psychology: Intraindividual processes* (pp. 68–88). Oxford: Blackwell Publishing.

Baumeister, R. F. (1998). The self. In D. T. Gilbert, S. T. Fiske, & G. Lindzey (Eds.), *Handbook of social psychology*, 4th. edn. (pp. 680–740). New York: McGraw-Hill.

Baumeister, R. F., & Leary, M. R. (1995). The need to belong: Desire for interpersonal attachments as a fundamental human motivation. *Psychological Bulletin, 117*, 497–529.

Baumeister, R. F., Smart, L., & Boden, J. M. (1996). Relation of threatened egotism to violence and aggression: The dark side of high self-esteem. *Psychological Review, 103*, 5–33.

Beach, S. R. H., & Tesser, A. (in press). Self-evaluation maintenance and evolution: Some speculative notes. In J. Sulls & L. Wheeler (Eds.), *Handbook of Social Comparison*. Mahwah, NJ: Lawrence Erlbaum.

Beggan, J. K. (1992). On the social nature of nonsocial perception: The mere ownership effect. *Journal of Personality and Social Psychology, 62*, 229–237.

Biernat, M., & Billings, L. S. (2001). Standards, expectancies, social comparison. In A. Tesser & N. Schwarz (Eds.) *Blackwell handbook of social psychology: Intraindividual processes* (pp. 257–283). Oxford: Blackwell Publishing.

Blaine, B., & Crocker, J. (1993). Self-esteem and self-serving biases in reactions to positive and negative events. In R. Baumeister (Ed.), *Self-esteem: The puzzle of low self-regard* (pp. 55–85). New York: Plenum.

Brockner, J. (1984). Low self-esteem and behavioral plasticity: Some implications for personality and social psychology. In L. Wheeler (Ed.), *Review of personality and social psychology*, Vol. 4 (pp. 237–271).

Brown, J. D. (1993). Self-esteem and self-evaluation: Feeling is believing. In J. Suls (Ed.), *Psychological perspectives on the self*, Vol. 4 (pp. 27–58). Hillsdale, NJ: Erlbaum.

Brown, J. D. (1994). Self-esteem: It's not what you think. Paper presented at the Society for Experimental Social Psychology, Lake Tahoe, NY.

California Task Force to Promote Self-Esteem and Personal and Social Responsibility (1990). *Toward a state of self-esteem*. Sacramento, CA: California State Department of Education.

Campbell, J. D. (1990). Self-esteem and clarity of the self-concept. *Journal of Personality and Social Psychology, 99*, 538–549.

Campbell, J. D., Trapnell, P. D., Heine, S. J., Katz, I. M., Lavallee, L. F., & Lehmen, D. R. (1996). Self-concept clarity: Measurement, personality correlates, and cultural boundaries. *Journal of Personality and Social Psychology, 70*, 141–156.

Cialdini, R. B., Trost, M. R., & Newsom, J. T. (1995). Preference for consistency: The development of a valid measure and the discovery of surprising behavioral implications. *Journal of Personality and Social Psychology, 69,* 318–328.

Cialdini, R. B., Borden, R. J., Thorne, A., Walker, M. R., Freeman, S., & Sloan, L. R. (1976). Basking in reflected glory: Three (football) field studies. *Journal of Personality and Social Psychology, 34,* 366–375.

Cline, J. (in progress). Development of an unobtrusive measure of the automatically activated affect associated with adult attachment representations. Dissertation, University of Georgia, Athens, GA.

Cline, J., & Tesser, A. (1998). Toward an unobtrusive measure of affect associated with attachment representations. Poster, American Psychological Association. San Francisco: American Psychological Association.

Crocker, J., & Wolfe, C. (1998). Contingencies of worth. Unpublished manuscript. Ann Arbor: University of Michigan.

Crocker, J., Luhtanen, R. K., Blaine, B., & Broadnax, S. (1994). Collective self-esteem and psychological well-being among Black, White, and Asian college students. *Personality and Social Psychology Bulletin, 20,* 503–513.

Cronbach, L. J. (1946). Response sets and test validity. *Educational and Psychological Measurement, 6,* 475–494.

Crowne, D., & Marlowe, D. (1964). *The approval motive.* New York: Wiley.

Deci, E. L., & Ryan, R. M. (1995). Human anatomy: The basis for the true self-esteem. In M. H. Kernis (Ed.), *Efficacy, agency, and self-esteem* (pp. 31–49). New York: Plenum.

Devine, P. G. (1989). Stereotypes and prejudice: Their automatic and controlled components. *Journal of Personality and Social Psychology, 56,* 5–18.

Dunning, D. (2001). On the motives underlying social cognition. In A. Tesser and N. Schwarz (Eds.), *Blackwell handbook of social psychology: Intraindividual processes* (pp. 348–374). Oxford: Blackwell Publishing.

Dunning, D., & Cohen, G. L. (1992). Egocentric definitions of traits and abilities in social judgment. *Journal of Personality and Social Psychology, 63,* 341–355.

Fazio, R. H., Powell, M. C., & Herr, P. M. (1983). Toward a process model of the attitudebehavior relation: Accessing one's attitude upon mere observation of the attitude object. *Journal of Personality and Social Psychology, 44,* 723–735.

Fazio, R. H., Sanbonmatsu, D. M., Powell, M. C., & Kardes, F. R. (1986). On the automatic activation of attitudes. *Journal of Personality and Social Psychology, 50,* 229–238.

Fein, S., & Spencer, S. J. (1997). Prejudice as self-image maintenance: Altering the self through negative evaluation of others. *Journal of Personality and Social Psychology, 73,* 31–44.

Festinger, L. (1957). *A theory of cognitive dissonance.* Stanford: Stanford University Press.

Feys, J. (1991). Briefly induced belongingness to self and preference. *European Journal of Social Psychology, 21,* 547–552.

Greenberg, J., Simon, L., Pyszczynski, T., Solomon, S., & Chatel, D. (1992). Terror management and tolerance: Does mortality salience always intensify negative reactions to others who threaten one's world view? *Journal of Personality and Social Psychology, 63,* 212–220.

Greenberg, J., Pyszczynski, T., Solomon, S., Rosenblatt, A., Veeder, M., Kirkland, S., & Lyon, S. (1990). Evidence for terror management theory II: The effects of mortality salience on reactions to those who threaten or bolster the cultural worldview. *Journal of Personality and Social Psychology, 58,* 308–318.

Greenberg, J., Solomon, S., Pyszczynski, T., Rosenblatt, A., Burling, J., Lyon, D., Simon, L., & Pinel, E. (1992). Why do people need self-esteem? Converging evidence that self-esteem serves an anxiety buffering function. *Journal of Personality and Social Psychology, 63,* 913–922.

Greenier, K. D., Kernis, M. H., & Waschull, S. B. (1995). Not all high (or low) self-esteem people are the same: Theory and research on stability of self-esteem. In M. H. Kernis (Ed.), *Efficacy, agency and self-esteem* (pp. 51–72). New York: Plenum.

Greenwald, A. G., & Banaji, M. (1995). Implicit social cognition: Attitudes, self-esteem and stereotypes. *Psychological Review, 102,* 4–27.

Greenwald, A. G., & Ronis, D. L. (1978). Twenty years of cognitive dissonance: Case study of the evolution of a theory. *Psychological Review, 85,* 53–57.

Greenwald, A. G., McGhee, D. E., & Schwartz, J. L. K. (1998). Measuring individual differences in implicit cognition: The implicit association test. *Journal of Personality and Social Psychology, 74,* 1464–1480.

Hamilton, D. L., Sherman, S. J., & Lickel, B. (1998). Perceiving social groups: The importance of the entitativity continuum. In C. Sedikides & J. Schopler (Eds.), *Intergroup cognition and intergroup behavior* (pp. 47–74). Mahwah, NJ: Lawrence Erlbaum Associates.

Hatter, S. (1993). Causes and consequences of low self-esteem in children and adolescents. In R. G. Baumeister (Ed.), *Self-esteem: The puzzle of low self-regard* (pp. 87–116). New York: Plenum.

Heatherton, T. F., & Polivy, J. (1991). Development and validation of a scale of measuring state self-esteem. *Journal of Personality and Social Psychology, 60,* 895–910.

Heider, F. (1958). *The psychology of interpersonal relations.* New York: Wiley.

Hoyle, R., Kernis, M. H., Leary, M. R., & Baldwin, M. W. (1998). *Identity, esteem, regulation.* Boulder, CO: Westview Press.

James, W. (1890). *The principles of psychology.* Vol. 1. New York: Dover.

Johnson, M. M. S. (1986). The initial letter effect: Egoaattachment or mere exposure? Unpublished doctoral dissertation, Ohio State University.

Katz, D. (1960). The functional approach to the study of attitudes. *Public Opinion Quarterly, 24,* 163–204.

Kernis, M. H., & Waschull, S. B. (1995). The interactive roles of stability and level of self-esteem: Research and theory. In M. Zanna (Ed.), *Advances in Experimental Social Psychology, 27,* 93–141.

Kernis, M. H., Granneman, B. D., & Barclay, L. C. (1989). Stability and level of self-esteem as predictors of anger arousal and hostility. *Journal of Personality and Social Psychology, 56,* 1013–1022.

Klinger, M. R., Burton, P. C., & Pitts, G. S. (in press). Mechanisms of unconscious priming I: Response competition not spreading activation. *Journal of Experimental Psychology: Learning, Memory & Cognition.*

Kramer, R. M., & Neale, M. A. (Eds.) (1988). *Power and influence in organizations.* Thousand Oaks, CA: Sage.

Leary, M. R., & Downs, D. L. (1995). Interpersonal functions of the self-esteem motive: The self-esteem system as a sociometer. In M. Kernis (Ed.), *Efficacy, agency, and self-esteem* (pp. 123–144.) New York: Plenum.

Leary, M. R., Tamdor, E. S., Terdal, S. K., & Downs, D. L. (1995). Self-esteem as an interpersonal monitor: The sociometer hypothesis. *Journal of Personality and Social Psychology, 68,* 518–530.

Lewin, K. (1935). *A dynamic theory of personality: Selected papers.* Trans. D. E. Adams and K. E. Zener. New York: McGraw-Hill.

Liu, T. J., & Steele, C. M. (1986). Attributional analysis as self-affirmation. *Journal of Personality and Social Psychology, 51,* 531–540.

McFarlin, D. B., & Blascovich, J. (1981). Effects of self-esteem and performance on future affective preferences and cognitive expectations. *Journal of Personality and Social Psychology, 40,* 521–531.

McFarlin, D. B., Baumeister, R. F., & Blascovich, J. (1984). On knowing when to quit: Task failure, self-esteem, advice and non-productive persistence. *Journal of Personality, 52,* 138–155.

Markus, H., & Kitayama, S. (1991). Culture and the self: Implications for cognition, emotion, and motivation. *Psychological Review, 98,* 224–253.

Maryanski, A., & Turner, J. H. (1992). *The social cage: Human nature and the evolution of society.* Stanford: Stanford University Press.

Miller, J. G. (2001). The cultural grounding of social psychology theory. In A. Tesser and N. Schwarz (Eds.), *Blackwell handbook of social psychology: Intraindividual processes* (pp. 22–43). Oxford: Blackwell Publishing.

Mischel, W., & Shoda, Y. (1998). Reconciling processing dynamics and personality dispositions. *Annual Review of Psychology, 49,* 229–258.

Myers, D. G., & Diener, E. (1995). Who is happy? *Psychological Science, 6,* 10–19.

Nuttin, J. M. (1985). Narcissism beyond Gestalt and awareness: The name letter effect. *European Journal of Social Psychology, 15,* 353–361.

Osgood, C. E. (1974). Probing subjective culture: I. Cross-linguistic tool-making. *Journal of Communication, 24,* 21–35.

Osgood, C. E., Suci, G. J., & Tannenbaum, P. H. (1957). *The measurement of meaning.* Urbana: University of Illinois Press.

Oyserman, D. (2001). Self-concept and identity. In A. Tesser & N. Schwarz (Eds.), *Blackwell handbook of social psychology: Intraindivual processes* (pp. 499–517). Oxferd: Blackwell Publishing.

Ovsiankina, M. (1928). Die Wiederaufnahme unterbrochener Handlugen. *Pyschologische Forschung, 11,* 302–379.

Piers, E., & Harris, D. (1969). *Piers–Harris children's self-concept scale.* Los Angeles: Western Psychological Services.

Pleban, R., & Tesser, A. (1981). The effects of relevance and quality of another's performance on interpersonal closeness. *Social Psychology Quarterly, 44,* 278–285.

Pyszczynski, T., Greenberg, J., & Solomon, S. (1997). Why do we need what we need? A terror management perspective on the roots of human motivation. *Psychological Inquiry, 8,* 1–20.

Rogers, C. R. (1961). *On becoming a person.* Boston: Houghton Mifflin.

Rokeach, M. (1985). Inducing change and stability in belief systems and personality structures. *Journal of Social Issues, 41,* 153–171.

Rosenberg, M. (1965). *Society and the adolescent self-image.* Princeton, NJ: Princeton University Press.

Sedikides, C. (1993). Assessment, enhancement, and verification determinants of the self-evaluation process. *Journal of Personality and Social Psychology, 65,* 317–338.

Shrauger, J. S. (1975). Responses to evaluation as a function of initial self-perceptions. *Psychological Bulletin, 82,* 581–596.

Smith, M. B., Bruner, J. S., & White, R. W. (1956). *Opinions and personality.* New York. Wiley.

Spencer, S. J., Fein, S., Wolfe, C. T., Fong, C., & Dunn, M. A. (1998). Automatic activation of stereotypes: The role of self-image threat. *Personality and Social Psychology Bulletin, 24,* 1139–1152.

Steele, C. M. (1988). The psychology of self-affirmation: Sustaining the integrity of the self. In L. Berkowitz (Ed.), *Advances in experimental social psychology,* Vol. 21 (pp. 261–302). New York: Academic Press.

Steele, C. M., & Liu, T. J. (1983). Dissonance processes as self-affirmation. *Journal of Personality and Social Psychology, 45,* 5–19.

Stone, J., Wiegand, A. W., Cooper, J., & Aronson, E. (1997). When exemplification fails: Hypocrisy and the motive for self-integrity. *Journal of Personality and Social Psychology, 72,* 1, 54–65.

Swann, W. B. (1987). Identity negotiation: Where two roads meet. *Journal of Personality and Social Psychology, 53,* 1038–1051.

Swann, W. B., Stein-Seroussi, A., & Geisler, R. B. (1992). Why people self-verify. *Journal of Personality and Social Psychology, 62,* 392–401.

Swann, W. B., Hixon, J. G., Stein-Seroussi, A., & Gilbert, D. T. (1990). The fleeting gleam of praise: Cognitive processes underlying behavioral reactions to self-relevant feedback. *Journal of Personality and Social Psychology, 59,* 17–26.

Tajfel, H., & Turner, J. C. (1986). The social identity theory of intergroup behavior. In S. Worchel & W. G. Austin (Eds.), *Psychology of intergroup relations* (pp. 7–24). Chicago: Nelson-Hall.

Taylor, S. E., & Brown, J. D. (1988). Illusion and well-being: A social psychological perspective on mental health. *Psychological Bulletin, 103,* 193–355.

Tennen, H., & Herzberger, S. (1987). Depression, self-esteem, and the absence of self-protective attributional biases. *Journal of Personality and Social Psychology, 52,* 72–80.

Tesser, A. (1988). Toward a self-evaluation maintenance model of social behavior. In L. Berkowitz (Ed.), *Advances in experimental social psychology,* Vol. 21 (pp. 181–227). New York: Academic Press.

Tesser, A., & Campbell, J. (1980). Self-definition: The impact of the relative performance and similarity of others. *Social Psychology Quarterly, 43,* 341–347.

Tesser, A., & Collins, J. (1988). Emotion in social reflection and comparison situations: Intuitive, systematic, and exploratory approaches. *Journal of Personality and Social Psychology, 55,* 695–709.

Tesser, A., & Cornell, D. P. (1991). On the confluence of self-processes. *Journal of Experimental Social Psychology, 27,* 501–526.

Tesser, A., & Martin, L. (1996). The psychology of evaluation. In E. T. Higgins & A. W. Kruglanski (Eds.), *Social psychology: Handbook of basic principles* (pp. 400–432). New York: Guilford Press.

Tesser, A., & Paulhus, D. (1983). The definition of self: Private and public self-evaluation maintenance strategies. *Journal of Personality and Social Psychology, 44,* 672–682.

Tesser, A., & Smith, J. (1980). Some effects of friendship and task relevance on helping: You don't always help the one you like. *Journal of Experimental Social Psychology, 16,* 582–590.

Tesser, A., Martin, L., & Cornell, D. (1996). On the substitutability of self-protective mechanisms. In P. M. Gollwitzer & J. A. Bargh (Eds.), *The psychology of action: Linking motivation and cognition to behavior* (pp. 48–67). New York: Guilford Press.

Tesser, A., Millar, M., & Moore, J. (1988). Some affective consequences of social comparison and reflection processes: The pain and pleasure of being close. *Journal of Personality and Social Psychology, 54,* 49–61.

Tesser, A., Crepaz, N., Collins, J., Cornell, D., & Beach, S. R. H. (1998). Confluence of self-defense mechanisms: On integrating the self zoo. Manuscript under review.

Triandis, H. C. (1989). The self and social behavior in differing cultural contexts. *Psychological Review, 96,* 506–520.

Trope, Y. (1980). Self-assessment, self-enhancement and task preference. *Journal of Experimental Social Psychology, 16,* 116–129.

Trope, Y. (1982). Self-assessment and task performance. *Journal of Experimental Social Psychology, 18,* 201–215.

Trope, Y. (1986). Self-enhancement and self-assessment in achievement behavior. In R. M. Sorrentino & E. T. Higgins (Eds.), *Handbook of motivation and cognition: Foundations of social behavior,* Vol. 2 (pp. 350–378). New York: Guilford Press.

Trope, Y., & Neter, E. (1994). Reconciling competing motives in self-evaluation: The role of self-control in feedback seeking. *Journal of Personality and Social Psychology, 66,* 646–657.

Tulving, E., & Schacter, D. (1990). Priming and human memory systems. *Science, 267,* 301–306.

White, R. W. (1959). Motivation reconsidered: The concept of competence. *Psychological Review, 66,* 296–333.

Wylie, R. C. (1974). *The self-concept.* Revd. edn. Vol. 1. Lincoln: University of Nebraska Press.

Wylie, R. C. (1979). *The self-concept.* Revd. edn. Vol. 2. Lincoln: University of Nebraska Press.

Zajonc, R. B. (1980). Feeling and thinking: Preferences need no inferences. *American Psychologist, 35,* 151–175.

CHAPTER TEN

The Self We Know and the Self We Show: Self-esteem, Self-presentation, and the Maintenance of Interpersonal Relationships

Mark R. Leary

As the capacity for self-reflection evolved among the prehistoric people from whom modern human beings descended, they presumably became aware that other individuals did not always see them the way that they saw themselves. This realization was a benchmark in human social life because it involved the emergence of a private sense of self that the individual knew was not accessible to others and created the possibility that people could purposefully convey images of themselves that were inconsistent with how they knew themselves to be. Many other animals engage in displays that, in one sense, do not jibe with how they really are (fluffing hair or feathers to appear larger, for example), and chimpanzees have been observed to deceive other chimps and their human caretakers (de Waal, 1986). But other animals' efforts at self-presentation pale in comparison to those of human beings, limited by their meager ability to self-reflect (Gallup, 1977; Gallup & Suarez, 1986). Only in human beings do we see deliberate efforts to convey a public image to other people, an image that may or may not mesh with the individual's private view of him- or herself.

Following James's (1890) seminal descriptions of various public and private aspects of the self, two traditions emerged in the study of the self, one focusing primarily on the private, subjective self and the other on the social, public self. Early theorists and researchers interested in the private self explored how people develop a sense of self, the factors that determine the nature of people's self-concepts, the psychological motives that affect their self-views, and the emotional and behavioral implications of how people perceive themselves (Cooley, 1902; Lecky, 1945; Mead, 1934; Rogers, 1959; Rosenberg, 1965; Wylie, 1961).

Interest in the public or social self was spurred by developments in sociology, particularly those that emerged from the symbolic interactionist and dramaturgical perspectives. Goffman (1959), for example, championed a purely public characterization of the self, proposing that the only true self was the public one. In discussing the link between the self and self-presentation, Goffman wrote: "A correctly staged and performed scene leads the audience to impute a self to a performed character, but this imputation – this self – is a *product* of a scene that comes off and is not a *cause* of it" (p. 252, italics in original). He cautioned that the self should not be regarded as an internal, organic thing but rather as the dramatic effect of a person's public presentation. When social psychologists began to explore the dynamics of self-presentation (e.g., E. E. Jones, 1964; Jones, Gergen, & Jones, 1963), they adopted a view of the self that drew from both the psychological and sociological traditions. They assumed the existence of a private psychological self, but saw as one of its functions the management of a public identity.

Although early symbolic interactionists had discussed the interplay between the self as known to the individual and the self as seen by others (Cooley, 1902; Mead, 1934), psychological theory and research on the private vs. public aspects of the self were, for the most part, pursued separately for many years. Researchers who were interested in the inner workings of the self did not deny that private psychological processes affect people's public persona and vice versa, but they were interested primarily in the intrapsychic aspects of the self. In contrast, researchers interested in the public self did not ignore ways in which the public, social self was influenced by the private, psychological self, but they were interested primarily in the interpersonal factors that affect the kinds of public selves that people present to others, and the private self took a back seat.

Since the 1980s, however, much has been written about the relationship between the private and public aspects of the self (e.g., Baumeister, 1982a, 1986; Carver & Scheier, 1981; Greenwald, 1982; Greenwald & Breckler, 1985; Leary & Baumeister, 2000; Schlenker, 1985, 1986), but it is not my intention to review this extensive literature here. Rather, my interest in this chapter is on one particular motivational feature of the private and public selves.

Private and Public Self-enhancement

The self is not only a cognitive structure that permits self-reflection and organizes information about oneself but has motivational features as well. Three self-motives have attracted the most attention: self-consistency (the motive to maintain, if not verify, one's existing view of oneself), self-evaluation (or self-assessment; the motive to see oneself accurately), and self-enhancement (the motive to maintain a positive image of oneself) (see Hoyle, Kernis, Leary, & Baldwin, 1999; Sedikides, 1993). Of these, our interest in this chapter is in self-enhancement. Researchers in both traditions have posited the existence of a fundamental self-enhancement motive that prompts people to construe themselves in favorable, socially desirable ways. These two enhancement motives – one involving the private self and one involving the public self – have been regarded as separate, but I will make the case that they are aspects of a single process.

Private self-enhancement: the self-esteem motive

Most psychologists accept the assumption that people are motivated to maintain a positive evaluation of themselves. Greenwald (1980) provided perhaps the most vivid characterization of the self-esteem motive, which he compared to a totalitarian political regime. Just as a totalitarian government suppresses information and rewrites history to preserve a particular desired image of the government, the "totalitarian ego" distorts the facts about oneself and rewrites one's memory of personal history to maintain one's own positive evaluation. Some writers have suggested that people not only want to feel good about themselves but *need* to do so, elevating self-esteem from something people merely like to have to something that they require in order to function optimally.

The assumption that people have a motive (or need) for self-esteem has guided a great deal of research. The self-esteem motive has been used to explain a variety of behaviors, including self-serving attributions, self-affirmation, self-handicapping, rationalization, social comparison, derogation of outgroups, and defensive pessimism (for reviews, see Blaine & Crocker, 1993; Hoyle et al., 1999, chap. 7). Furthermore, deficiencies in self-esteem have been blamed for problems as diverse as depression, unwanted pregnancies, drug abuse, illiteracy, and child abuse (Branden, 1994; Mecca, Smelser, & Vasconcellos, 1989).

Public self-enhancement: self-presentation

Theorists interested in the public self have posited an analogous motive to self-esteem, suggesting that people are typically motivated to be evaluated positively by others. Given that being regarded favorably by other people is a prerequisite for many positive outcomes in life – respect, friendship, romantic relationships, job success, and so on – it is not surprising that people are generally motivated to be perceived positively and to pursue others' approval.

The primary way in which people seek social approval and its attendant benefits is through conveying particular images of themselves to others – that is, through *self-presentation* or *impression management* (Baumeister, 1982a; Leary & Kowalski, 1990; Schlenker, 1980). People are highly motivated to project positive, socially desirable impressions of themselves, and are quite versatile in how they do so. Through what they say about themselves, the attitudes they express, their explanations of their behavior, their physical appearance, the people with whom they associate, their possessions, and other means, people convey impressions that they think will lead to desired reactions from other people (Leary, 1995; Schlenker, 1980).

Although people usually want to make "good" impressions and to be evaluated favorably, in some instances they believe that their interests will be best served by projecting an undesirable impression that carries a high probability of being evaluated negatively. For example, people may want to be seen as emotionally unstable to reduce the demands that other people place on them, or as threatening and hostile in order to coerce other people to behave in certain ways (Jones & Pittman, 1982; Shepperd & Kwavnick, 1999). In such cases, people are willing to sacrifice others' positive evaluations and good will in order to obtain other goals. Although people sometimes resort to undesirable self-presentations, the predominant self-presentational motive is clearly self-enhancement (Jones & Pittman, 1982).

Integrating private and public enhancement

Thus, a self-enhancement motive has been postulated with reference to both the private self that is known only to the individual and the public self that is shown to other people. Several efforts have been made to provide overarching conceptual frameworks that encompass both the private and public selves (e.g., Baumeister & Tice, 1986; Greenwald, 1982; Greenwald & Breckler, 1985; Scheier & Carver, 1983; Schlenker, 1985, 1986), but none of them explicitly addresses the common self-enhancement process that is the focus of this chapter.[1] Before examining the common link between private and public self-enhancement, it is necessary to address two fundamental issues that underlie our understanding of these processes – one involving the distinction between the private and the public self, and the other involving the function of private self-enhancement.

The private and public self.   Although many psychologists have drawn a distinction between the public and private selves, strictly speaking, there is actuality only one self, and it is private. The term "self" has been used in many ways over the years to refer to a variety of thoughts, behaviors, beliefs, abilities, motives, and other psychological processes. However, at the most fundamental level, the self is the cognitive apparatus that permits self-reflexive thought – the cognitive structures and associated processes that permit people to take themselves as an object of their own thought and to think consciously about themselves. Most other animals apparently do not possess the neural substrate that underlies this cognitive apparatus for, with the exception of certain great apes, other taxa do not appear to be capable of self-reflection (Gallup & Suarez, 1986). As a literary or theoretical device, we sometimes find it useful to talk about the private and public selves as different types of self, and I am not disputing these uses of the terms. Yet, if we think critically about what the psychological self really is, we see that it resides in the cognitive-affective apparatus of the individual and that all self-processes involve self-reflection – that is, the private self.

The term "public self" has been used to refer to three distinct entities: the image that an individual conveys to other people (including the person's reputation and roles), the individual's beliefs about his or her public image (i.e., how the individual thinks he or she is perceived by others), and the impressions that other people actually hold of the person. Whichever of these we may mean when we refer to the public self, we are referring to a very different concept than the private psychological self that permits people to think about and deliberately control these public impressions. Unless we endorse Goffman's (1959) radical dramaturgical view of the self described earlier, what we commonly call the public self is not a "self" at all, but rather behaviors from which other people and the individual him- or herself draw inferences about the person's characteristics, motives, feelings, roles, and other attributes. Depending on whether we're talking about the person's beliefs about his or her public image or about others' impressions, this so called public self resides either within the individual's own private sense of self or in others' minds, respectively. In either case, it is not a "self" in the true sense of the term. The importance of this point is not merely semantic. How we explain the relationship between the so-called private and public selves – particularly, how we account for the relationship between self-esteem and self-presentation – depends heavily on how we conceptualize these constructs.[2]

The function of self-esteem.   A second issue that is fundamental to understanding private and public self-enhancement involves the function of the self-esteem motive. The fact that people want *other individuals* to view them positively seems easy to explain: good things come to those who make good impressions. But why are people so concerned with their own *self*-evaluations? What benefits, if any, does trying to maintain one's self-esteem confer?

As noted, most researchers have implicitly assumed that people simply "need" self-esteem for its own sake, but most have not considered why this should be so. Theorists who have considered the function of self-esteem have tended to arrive at one of three general conclusions. First, some writers have argued that people seek self-esteem because high self-esteem promotes effective living by enhancing people's ability to cope with threats (e.g., Bednar, Wells, & Peterson, 1989), bolstering self-confidence (Branden, 1994), or promoting psychological well-being (Greenberg et al., 1992; Taylor & Brown, 1988). However, several facts raise questions about these explanations of self-esteem: (1) high self-esteem is not always associated with better coping than low self-esteem (Baumeister, Heatherton, & Tice, 1993; Baumeister, Smart, & Boden, 1996); (2) although self-efficacy beliefs facilitate coping, a causal role of self-esteem per se in behavior has not been established (Dawes, 1994; Leary, 1999); and (3) positive illusions about oneself are as likely to be maladaptive as adaptive (Asendorpf & Ostendorf, 1998; Colvin & Block, 1994; Colvin, Block, & Funder, 1995).

A second line of thought suggests that self-esteem is integrity of the self. For example, Deci and Ryan (1995) proposed that people possess true self-esteem when they behave in ways that are consistent with their true selves (as opposed to behaving for extrinsic reasons), a contemporary version of the humanistic perspective that ties self-esteem to authenticity (Rogers, 1959). Steele and his colleagues have offered a similar approach, suggesting that the self-system functions to maintain self-integrity – the person's perception of moral and adaptive adequacy (Steele, 1988; Steele, Spencer, & Lynch, 1993; Spencer, Josephs, & Steele, 1993). However, it remains unclear precisely what tangible benefits people derive from behaving congruently or seeing themselves as morally adequate.

A third approach suggests that people do not pursue self-esteem for its own sake but rather use subjective feelings of self-esteem as an indicator of some other desired social commodity, such as dominance (Barkow, 1980) or social acceptance (Leary & Downs, 1995). This approach is particularly useful for our purposes because it provides a direct link between self-esteem and self-presentation by conceptualizing self-esteem as a gauge of interpersonal effectiveness, thus showing why private feelings of self-esteem are related to public self-presentations.

Sociometer Theory

In particular, sociometer theory (Leary, 1999; Leary & Baumeister, 2000; Leary & Downs, 1995) provides a framework for thinking about the nature of private and public self-enhancement. According to sociometer theory, human beings possess a psychological mechanism – a *sociometer* – that monitors the quality of their interpersonal relationships, specifically the degree to which other people value having relationships with them. As a gauge of relational evaluation – the degree to which other people regard their relationship with the individual to be important, close, or valuable – the sociometer operates more or less continuously outside of focal awareness, alerting the individual through affective signals when cues indicating possible relational devaluation are detected. Thus, people do not devote constant attention to the task of monitoring other people's responses, yet they become quickly attuned to indications that others may be feeling negatively about them.

Although one may accept the existence of such a monitor without adopting any particular perspective on where such a mechanism might have come from, I personally favor an evolutionary perspective on this question. Although being accepted by other people remains important for our well-being today, in the ancestral environment in which human evolution occurred, social acceptance would have been literally vital (Baumeister & Leary, 1995). Individuals who, for whatever reason, did not develop mutually supportive relationships with other people and who were not valued as members of the social group would have found themselves in dire straits. In extreme cases, they might have been ostracized or abandoned on the African plains, likely to fall victim to predators, injury, or starvation. In less extreme cases, they would have been relegated to the social periphery of the group, with limited access to mates, food, childcare, and other types of assistance. Thus, it was essential that each individual behave in ways that found favor with others in the group and that led others to value having relationships with them. In light of the importance of being accepted, it was also essential for them to keep track of how well they were doing in terms of social acceptance by other individuals.

Tooby and Cosmides (1996) made a very similar point. They suggested that a primary task faced by our prehistoric ancestors was to insure that they had relationships with those who would help them when they needed it. As Tooby and Cosmides observed, "if you are a hunter-gatherer with few or no individuals who are deeply engaged in your welfare, then you are extremely vulnerable to the volatility of events – a hostage to fortune" (p. 135). Thus, natural selection would have favored adaptations that kept individuals attuned to their social value and motivated them to be valued and accepted by others.

Two features of the sociometer are particularly relevant to the present discussion. First, as noted, when cues that are relevant to low relational evaluation are detected, the person is alerted by negative affect (Leary, Tambor, Terdal, & Downs, 1995; Leary, Haupt, Strausser, & Chokel, 1998). Thus, the sociometer resembles other systems that alert individuals when events threaten their well-being through unpleasant feelings, thereby prompting a conscious appraisal of the event's meaning. In the case of threats to relational value, the appraisal will focus on one's social acceptability. According to sociometer theory, this affect-tinged self-appraisal is what we typically call self-esteem. One might imagine that other social animals also have a mechanism for detecting social threats, but for an organism without the capacity for self-relevant thought, the affective warnings would not be accompanied by a self-relevant appraisal. Thus, although the affective aspect of the process may be present, the animal could not be said to have self-esteem per se.

Second, when activated by cues that connote that one is not being adequately valued as a social participant or relational partner, the sociometer prompts the individual to behave in ways that will restore his or her relational value in other people's eyes (Leary & Downs, 1995). In large part, the resulting behaviors are self-presentational efforts to show other people that the individual possesses characteristics, beliefs, motives, and abilities that are valued by others. Thus, in addition to signaling low relational evaluation through lowered self-esteem, the sociometer motivates self-presentational behavior when decrements in relational evaluation are detected. The sociometer/self-esteem system monitors relational value and motivates remedial behavior when needed, and self-presentation is the behavioral means of enhancing the person's relational value in others' eyes.

Sociometer theory provides a very different perspective on the nature of self-enhancement than the view that has prevailed for over 100 years. As noted, most theorists have assumed that people need self-esteem because it is important for its own sake or because it somehow enhances psychological well-being. From the standpoint of sociometer theory, self-esteem is important because it serves as a gauge of relational evaluation – or, more concretely, acceptance and rejection. People do not seek self-esteem for its own sake but rather use feelings of self-esteem as an indicator of the degree to which they are valued (Leary &: Baumeister, 2000).

State and Trait Self-esteem

People's evaluations of themselves fluctuate over time as the sociometer detects changes in relational evaluation. Researchers use the term *state self-esteem* to refer to an individual's feelings about him- or herself at a particular moment in time. Consistent with sociometer theory, research shows that state self-esteem is strongly tied to how valued and accepted the individual feels at a given moment (Haupt & Leary, 1997; Leary et al., 1998; Leary, Tambor, et al., 1995).

However, these changes in state self-esteem occur against a backdrop of *trait self-esteem* – the person's general or average level of self-esteem across situations and time. From the standpoint of sociometer theory, trait self-esteem may be regarded as the resting point of the sociometer's gauge in the absence of incoming social information relevant to relational evaluation. Trait self-esteem is the result of the person's assumptions (most of which are implicit) regarding the degree to which he or she possesses characteristics that other people value and, thus, the extent to which other people tend to regard their relationships with him or her as important, close, or valuable. Research supports the idea that trait self-esteem reflects people's general beliefs about their relational value, social desirability, and includability (Leary, Tambor et al., 1995, Study 5).

The question then arises of whether people are motivated to maintain their state self-esteem, their trait self-esteem, or both. From the standpoint of sociometer theory, the answer is either "neither" or "both," depending on how one views the question. The answer is "neither" in the sense that, as we have seen, people are not actually motivated to maintain their self-esteem at all. Rather, they are motivated to be valued and accepted, and self-esteem is simply the psychological gauge that they use to monitor their social inclusion.

However, if we concede that people may be said, in a loose sense, to want to keep their self-esteem high (in the same way that a driver does not want a car's fuel gauge to fall to Empty), the answer is that people seek both state and trait self-esteem. That is, they desire for others to value them in the present context (state self-esteem) as well as in the long run (trait self-esteem). Just as financial investors monitor both the daily fluctuations in the stock market and long-term trends, the sociometer monitors momentary changes in relational evaluation as well as one's ongoing potential for social acceptance and rejection.

Incidentally, sociometer theory helps to explain why most people who are classified as "low," in trait self-esteem (by virtue of having a score in the lower third or lower half of the distribution of self-esteem scores) do not actually have low self-esteem in an objective sense. When their responses are examined closely, one finds that most people at the lower end of the distributions of self-esteem scores do not endorse highly negative self-statements. Rather, they express neutral, ambivalent, or mixed opinions about themselves. (Put differently, the statistical median of all self-esteem scales is always above the conceptual midpoint [i.e., neutral feelings about oneself], and often far above it; Baumeister, Tice, & Hutton, 1989). Presumably, people who are high in trait self-esteem experience a greater proportion of experiences that connote high relational evaluation than people with low trait self-esteem. However, lows are not necessarily rejected by other people; rather, they simply perceive a lower degree of relational appreciation than highs. Given that most people are valued by at least some individuals, we should rarely find people with bona fide low self-esteem, and those whose self-esteem is truly low should show psychopathological symptoms consistent with widespread rejection (Leary, Schreindorfer, & Haupt, 1995).

Moderating Effects of Self-esteem on Self-presentation

Sociometer theory provides an overarching framework for thinking about private and public self-enhancement and helps to explain why self-esteem and self-presentation are reciprocally related. Self-esteem – as a indicator of relational evaluation – is associated both with the degree to which people are motivated to obtain acceptance and the ways in which they try to do so. At the same time, by affecting real and anticipated relational evaluation, self-presentation feeds back to affect subjective self-esteem. After first examining the role of self-esteem in self-presentation, I will turn to the effects of self-presentation on self-esteem.

Self-esteem, need for approval and impression-motivation

A consistent finding is that self-esteem – whether measured as a state or a trait – is inversely related to the degree to which people are concerned about others' impressions of them. Compared to people who score high on measures of trait self-esteem, people who are low in trait self-esteem are more concerned with how they are viewed by others, have a stronger desire to obtain approval and to avoid disapproval, and are more motivated to be perceived favorably (S. C. Jones, 1973; Shrauger, 1975; Watson & Friend, 1969). Furthermore, people whose state self-esteem is lowered by failure, rejection, or other events become more highly motivated to obtain others' approval and will engage in self-presentational behaviors that will attain it (Apsler, 1975; Baumeister & Jones, 1978; Miller & Schlenker, 1978; Modigliani, 1971; Schneider, 1969; Walster, 1965).

 Sociometer theory provides a clear explanation for the inverse relationship between self-esteem and approval motivation. Given that self-esteem reflects perceived relational evaluation, lower self-esteem is associated with feeling insufficiently valued, thereby naturally inducing a desire to increase one's relational value. Along these lines, Tooby and Cosmides (1996) suggested that evolutionary adaptations may be designed "to respond to signs of waning affection by increasing the desire to be liked, and mobilizing changes that will bring it about"

(p. 139). Whether one accepts the evolutionary underpinnings, it is clear that lowered self-esteem is associated with an increased desire for approval and acceptance.

One exception to this general pattern involves the fact that, although their overall desire for approval increases after rejection, people are sometimes less interested in being accepted by those who have rejected them than they were previously, and they may even retrospectively minimize the degree to which they say that they wanted the rejector to accept them in the first place (Leary, Tambor, et al., 1995). On the surface, this sour grapes rationalization may seem to work against the person being socially accepted. However, such a tactic may be functional in disengaging rejected individuals from pursuing acceptance by those who do not adequately value them, thereby freeing them to seek relational appreciation in more promising places.

Along these lines, evidence suggests that events that cause people to feel inadequately valued in one interpersonal context increase their motivation to pursue acceptance in other, unrelated contexts and relationships. For example, people who embarrass themselves in front of one audience may subsequently go out of their way to project a more favorable image of themselves to other audiences (Apsler, 1975).

Self-presentational strategies

As we have seen, low self-esteem is related to the motivation to seek approval through impression-management, presumably because low self-esteem signals low relational evaluation. In addition, once people are motivated to manage their impressions, self-esteem is related to the self-presentational strategies they prefer. Although everyone desires both to make favorable impressions and to avoid making unfavorable impressions, the relative strength of these self-presentational orientations differs across situations and among individuals. Based on a comprehensive review of the empirical evidence, Baumeister et al. (1989) concluded that low- and high-self-esteem people tend to adopt different self-presentational styles. Specifically, people with high self-esteem tend to strive to make a positive impression (what Arkin, 1981, labeled acquisitive self-presentation), whereas those with low self-esteem try to prevent others from developing negative impressions of them (protective self-presentation).[3]

In line with Baumeister et al.'s (1989) conclusions, Schlenker, Weigold, and Hallam (1990) found that participants with high self-esteem were more egotistical (i.e., acquisitive) when they were particularly concerned about another person's evaluations, whereas participants with low self-esteem were less egotistical. Along the same lines, Tice (1991; Tice & Baumeister, 1990) found evidence that trait self-esteem moderates the use of enhancing and protective self-handicapping strategies. Her studies showed that people with high self-esteem self-handicap when doing so allows them to make favorable impressions, whereas people with low self-esteem are prone to self-handicap to avoid making negative impressions. Furthermore, she found that participants who were low vs. high in self-esteem explicitly reported having different reasons for self-handicapping. Low-self-esteem people indicated that they self-handicapped to diffuse the implications of failure, whereas high-self-esteem people indicated that they self-handicapped when it allowed them to look better following success. Similarly, when enhancing and protective self-presentational styles were measured as individual difference variables, trait self-esteem correlated positively with the self-enhancing style but negatively with self-protection (Wolfe, Lennox, & Cutler, 1986).

The fact that people with lower self-esteem are not as self-enhancing as those with higher self-esteem does not reflect the fact that people who have low self-esteem do not desire approval or want other people to evaluate them negatively, as was once assumed (e.g., Aronson & Mettee, 1968; Maracek & Mettee, 1972). As noted earlier, they desire approval and acceptance as much as, if not more than people with high self-esteem (S. C. Jones, 1973; Shrauger, 1975; Swann, Griffin, Predmore, & Gaines, 1987). Nonetheless, their efforts to impression-manage tend to be cautious, prudent, noncommital, or evasive, particularly when self-presentational failure may have negative repercussions (Baumeister et al., 1989; Tice, 1993).

Sociometer theory provides a straightforward interpretation of this pattern. People who believe that others do not habitually value them – people who score low in trait self-esteem – feel less secure in their relationships and experience their social bonds as more tenuous. As a result, they believe that they cannot afford to take self-presentational risks that, if unsuccessful, will leave them with lower relational value than before. Thus, they may settle for a neutral or minimally acceptable image that will at least insure that they will not be rejected and that might even promote acceptance (although perhaps not as much as if they successfully self-aggrandized). Just as a person with little money cannot afford to lose it in risky investments (no matter how large the potential payoff), people with low self-esteem seem unwilling to risk whatever relational value they have by trying to be perceived more positively. On top of that, a history of low relational evaluation leads people with low self-esteem to believe that they do not possess characteristics that readily draw other people to them. As a result, they are less likely than high-self-esteem people to believe that they can successfully present themselves in highly positive ways (Baumeister, 1982b).

In contrast, people with high self-esteem already feel accepted and, certain that they are the kind of people whom others value, are not greatly concerned about being rejected in the long run. However, they often seek the benefits of even greater acceptance and are willing to invest some of their interpersonal capital in seeking it. Thus, people with high self-esteem are particularly self-aggrandizing when they have something to gain by being egotistical (Schlenker et al., 1990; Schneider & Turkat, 1975).

One empirical finding that is particularly relevant to sociometer theory involves the fact that the relationship between behavior and self-esteem is moderated by the degree to which the situation is public (i.e., open to observation by other people) or private (Archibald & Cohen, 1971; Baumeister, 1982a; Schlenker et al., 1990; Tice & Baumeister, 1990). The general pattern is that people with high self-esteem are more self-enhancing in public than their private self-reports suggest they really see themselves, whereas people with low self-esteem are more self-effacing in public than they are in private (see Baumeister et al., 1989 for a review).

If self-esteem were only a private, intrapsychic self-evaluation – as has typically been assumed – there is no clear reason why it should typically moderate behavior differently in public than in private (see, however, Tetlock & Manstead, 1985). However, if one accepts the premise that self-esteem reflects something about the perceived security of one's inter-personal relationships, the effects of publicness are easily explained. This is not to say that self-serving biases never occur in private; they sometimes do. However, the frequency and intensity of self-serving responses are clearly lower in private than in public.

Effects of Self-presentation on Self-esteem

As noted, much self-presentation is in the service of enhancing one's relational value in other people's eyes. To the extent that people are successful in projecting images that increase their relational value, their self-esteem should increase correspondingly. Under some circumstances, self-presentational behaviors may influence self-esteem even in the absence of interpersonal feedback if the person believes that his or her relational value will be enhanced.

Little research has been conducted on the effects of self-presentation on people's private thoughts and feelings about themselves, but the available evidence clearly shows that presenting images of oneself to other people affects the presenter's self-perceptions and self-esteem. Most relevant to the present chapter, presenting oneself in a positive fashion generally leads to changes in state self-esteem. In a series of studies, Jones, Rhodewalt, Berglas, and Skelton (1981) found that participants who were induced to present themselves positively to another person – either because they were explicitly instructed to do so or because they observed other self-enhancing people (people tend to match the positivity of others' self-presentations) – subsequently showed higher state self-esteem than participants who were induced to be less self-enhancing. Similar effects of self-presentation on self-esteem have been found by Schlenker and Trudeau (1990) and McKillop, Berzonsky, and Schlenker (1992).

Kowalski and Leary (1990) found that the effects of self-presentation on state self-esteem were more pronounced for participants who were low than high in trait self-esteem. Not only did presenting themselves positively (presenting images of being psychologically adjusted) raise the self-esteem of participants who were low in trait self-esteem, but after presenting themselves favorably, the state self-esteem of participants low in trait self-esteem was as high as that of participants high in trait self-esteem. One explanation of this finding is that the inducement to present themselves positively may have overridden low-self-esteem participants' cautious, protective self-presentational style (Arkin, 1981; Baumeister et al., 1989). By eliciting more favorable self-presentations, the experiment may have led low-self-esteem participants to perceive an increase in their relational value, thereby raising their state self-esteem. Participants who were high in trait self-esteem were accustomed to conveying positive impressions of themselves, so being induced to project a positive image in the context of the study had no notable effect on their subsequent self-esteem.

This explanation may help to account for why low self-esteem is chronic and difficult for people to change. Perceiving low relational value lowers self-esteem and leads to a cautious, protective self-presentational style. Protective self-presentations rarely make a truly positive impression (although they may stave off a negative one), so perceived relational value and self-esteem remain low. If people who are low in trait self-esteem rarely take the self-presentational risks that will lead others to value them more highly, their self-esteem is unlikely to increase. Incidentally, many clinical interventions that have been designed to increase self-esteem include features that indirectly enhance the positivity of the individual's public image, such as social skills training and help with physical appearance (Leary, 1999; Mruk, 1995).

In an important contribution to our understanding of the effects of self-presentation on the private self, Tice (1992) found that participants' private self-views were affected more strongly when they engaged in identity-relevant behaviors in public than in private. In fact, Tice concluded that her results "cast doubt on whether people will internalize their behavior (i.e., alter their self-concepts to fit their recent behavior) in the absence of an interpersonal context and self-presentational concerns" (p. 449). Although her studies did not measure self-esteem per se, one might expect – both on the basis of Tice's research and sociometer theory – that public self-presentations would likewise affect self-esteem more strongly than either private self-thoughts or behaviors that are performed when one is alone. Consistent with this reasoning, McKillop et al. (1992) found that participants who described themselves positively subsequently showed an increase in state self-esteem when they presented themselves in a face-to-face interview, but not when they described themselves in a written interview or on an anonymous questionnaire. Importantly, this effect was obtained only for participants whose identities were based heavily on their social roles and relationships (i.e., those who were high in social identity).

The effects of self-presentation on state self-esteem appear to occur via at least three routes. First, to the extent that the person's self-presentational behavior actually affects the degree to which other people value and accept him or her – for better or for worse – state self-esteem should change accordingly. Conveying images that lead to approval, approbation, and acceptance will raise state self-esteem, and conveying images that lead to disapproval, ridicule, and rejection will lower it. Given that people typically try to be regarded positively, most successful self-presentations will be accompanied by increased relational evaluation and state self-esteem. Along these lines, Gergen (1965) showed that, when another person explicitly agreed with participants' favorable self-presentations, participants showed an increase in state self-esteem over the course of the experiment.

Second, even without receiving feedback from others, people can anticipate the effects of their self-presentations on others' reactions and experience corresponding changes in state self-esteem. Thus, knowing that we made a good impression makes us feel better about ourselves without anyone having to indicate their approval or acceptance explicitly. Likewise, embarrassments and other self-presentational predicaments lower state self-esteem even if we only imagine other people's reactions (Miller, 1996).

The notion that *imagined* social reactions affect self-esteem may seem to run counter to sociometer theory. If self-esteem is an internal gauge of others' feelings about the individual, why should it be affected by how the person imagines others will react? The answer is that, in order to prevent the individual from jeopardizing his or her relational ties, the self-esteem/sociometer system must alert the individual whenever he or she behaves in ways that may lower relational evaluation or even when he or she contemplates such actions, whether or not explicit social feedback is received. As the symbolic interactionists noted, one function of the self is to allow people to think about themselves from the perspectives of other people (Cooley, 1902; Mead, 1934). This ability to take the role of other people in thinking about ourselves allows us to imagine how they are feeling about us and helps us behave accordingly, and the sociometer must be responsive to these imaginings.

A third process by which self-presentation may affect self-esteem involves what Jones et al. (1981) called biased scanning. Presenting oneself in a particular way may prime thoughts about oneself that are associated with the projected image, temporarily changing how the individual feels about him- or herself. According to this explanation, which was first used to explain the effects of role-playing on attitude change (Janis & Gilmore, 1965), behaving in a particular way leads certain aspects of the self to become more or less salient. Because people typically try to present positive rather than negative images of themselves, self-presentations usually make people think about their desirable attributes, thereby moving people's self-esteem upward.

Although positive self-presentations generally raise self-esteem, a reversal of this effect may occur under special circumstances. The person who is trying to make a favorable impression is faced with two tasks: conveying positive self-relevant information and concealing (or at least downplaying) negative information. According to ironic processes theory (Wegner, 1994), trying to suppress an undesired thought sometimes makes that thought more cognitively accessible. Thus, when people wish to conceal unflattering information about themselves, negatively-tainted self-thoughts become cognitively available, which may lead to diminished self-esteem in spite of a positive projected impression under certain conditions.

To test this hypothesis, Smart and Wegner (1994) asked participants to make either a good or a bad impression, or gave participants no self-presentational instructions. Before publicly answering each of a series of questions about themselves, participants were asked to memorize either a one-digit number (low cognitive load) or a five-digit number (high cognitive load). After completing the self-presentation task, participants' state self-esteem was measured. For participants who were under low cognitive load, self-esteem was higher when they presented themselves positively rather than negatively, replicating previous research (Jones et al., 1981; Kowalski & Leary, 1990). However, participants who were under a high cognitive load showed an inverse relationship between the positivity of their impressions and their subsequent self-esteem. Apparently, presenting a positive impression of oneself under high cognitive load makes information relevant to one's negative characteristics more salient and lowers self-esteem.

Private Self-enhancement and Self-deception

Our discussion of self-esteem and self-presentation motives would not be complete without considering the question of whether people are "taken in" by their own overly positive self-beliefs and self-presentational behaviors. The topic of self-deception has fueled much controversy within psychology for many years, and I make no pretense at resolving the issues here. Rather, I simply wish to raise several questions about the nature of self-deception and offer some thoughts.

The concept of self-deception presents a paradox because it implies that the private self is split into a part that knows the truth about oneself and a part that does not know, and that the knowing part actively misleads the other one. Disassociation of this nature undoubtedly occurs in certain cases of psychopathology, but whether it is a normal component of psychological functioning is unclear.

The prevailing view, both in psychology and the popular culture, seems to be that a certain degree of self-deception is normal, if not psychologically beneficial. Many writers have touted the advantages of self-deception, suggesting that self-enhancing illusions enhance behavioral efficacy and psychological well-being (see Martin, 1985; Taylor & Brown, 1988). However, whatever its occasional benefits, self-deception would seem to be generally malad-aptive. Effective coping requires a reasonably accurate assessment of one's personal capabil-ities and characteristics relative to the challenges one confronts (Bandura, 1997). A pervasive self-enhancing bias that exaggerates one's physical, intellectual, or interpersonal abilities would appear to be a recipe for chronic disaster, and it is difficult to understand how an ostensibly universal motive for deceptive self-enhancement could have arisen as a fundamental feature of human nature. Without denying occasional advantages of mild self-deception (Baumeister, 1989), I find it difficult to reconcile the general disadvantages of self-deception with the pervasive idea that people are inherently disposed to privately self-enhance.

These arguments notwithstanding, empirical research does seem to demonstrate a wide array of self-serving biases in how people perceive themselves, make attributions about their good and bad behaviors, compare themselves to others, evaluate the groups to which they belong, and so on (e.g., Blaine & Crocker, 1993; Greenwald, 1980). These biases have typically been interpreted as efforts to maintain private self-esteem and as evidence for a certain degree of self-deception. After all, if the self-enhancing person does not *believe* his or her self-serving judgments – that is, if he or she is not truly self-deceived – those egotistical beliefs would not maintain self-esteem.

However, three issues call into question the idea that people are as self-aggrandizingly deluded as they often appear in psychological research. First, although most psychologists have emphasized the human tendency toward private self-enhancement and self-serving illu-sions, a moment's thought will reveal that people are as often as self-deprecating as they are self-aggrandizing. People often underestimate their abilities and other desirable characteris-tics, expect the worst in situations in which they will be evaluated, and react strongly to seemingly trivial failures, slights, and personal shortcomings. Whatever self-enhancing biases people exhibit are counterbalanced by equally self-deprecating ones, yet we do not view these negative biases as examples of "unflattering self-deception."

Second, in most studies of self-serving biases, participants' responses are not fully private, opening the possibility that their self-enhancing reactions reflect public self-presentations rather than privately-held self-beliefs. Some studies make no effort to convince participants that their answers are anonymous, and in others, participants may well have doubted the researcher's claim that no one – the researcher included – would be able to identify their answers. As a result, participants have a clear self-presentational stake in conveying certain impressions of themselves, and whatever self-enhancing biases their responses show may well be self-presentational rather than self-deceptive. This is a difficult, though not insurmount-able methodological problem that limits our ability to infer that experimental results are due to self-deception rather than self-presentation (Leary, 1993; Tetlock & Manstead, 1985).

Third, as noted above, self-enhancing reactions are highly dependent upon the social context, and particularly on who will ostensibly see participants' responses (Kolditz & Arkin, 1982; Leary, Barnes, Griebel, Mason, & McCormack, 1987; Schlenker et al., 1990). This fact alone argues against true self-deception which, with a few exceptions (Aronson, 1968; Tetlock & Manstead, 1985), should occur regardless of who else might see a person's answers. Even more convincing is the fact that self-serving biases often disappear or reverse

when participants assume that the others will disapprove of self-enhancing claims (Miller &
Schlenker, 1985).

I am not suggesting that self-deception never occurs. However, conceptual, logical, and
empirical considerations strongly suggest that much of what has been interpreted as private
self-enhancement for the purpose of preserving self-esteem is better interpreted as public self-
enhancement for the purpose of presenting desired images. These self-serving behaviors
undoubtedly affect self-esteem, but they do so by affecting real, imagined, or anticipated
relational evaluation rather than through private self-delusion.[4]

Conclusions

Self-esteem and self-presentation have been studied by psychologists and other behavioral
scientists for many years. As a result, we know a great deal about these constructs, and both
have been used to explain a wide array of cognitive, affective, and behavioral phenomena.
For both, the fundamental process of interest involves a strong proclivity toward self-
enhancement. In the case of self-esteem, people seem strongly motivated to maintain favorable images of and to feel good about themselves; in the case of self-presentation, people
are pervasively motivated to make good impressions on other people. The central thesis
of this chapter is that underlying superficial differences between private and public self-
enhancement is a common process that helps the individual monitor and respond to interpersonal events that have implications for the degree to which he or she is valued and
accepted vs. devalued and rejected by other people. Private self-esteem lies at the heart of the
system that monitors relational value (i.e., the sociometer), and public self-presentation
serves as a primary means of maintaining and enhancing one's relational value to other people.

Having examined the connections between self-esteem and self-presentation, and their
joint role in maintaining one's relational value, a reasonable question is whether this is all
there is to self-esteem and self-presentation. Is self-esteem only part of an interpersonal
monitoring system, or does it do other things? Is self-presentation only a means of maintaining relational value, or does it have other functions?

The second question is the easier of the two to answer. People clearly engage in self-
presentational behaviors for many reasons other than to be accepted. Although people engage
in self-presentation to increase their relational value and promote social acceptance, they also
impression-manage to influence other people for many other reasons. By conveying particular images of themselves, people can obtain assistance from other people, induce others'
compliance, improve their financial well-being, avoid unpleasant tasks, perform social roles
more effectively, inflict distress on others, and achieve other personal and interpersonal goals
(Baumeister, 1982a; Jones & Pittman, 1982; Leary, 1995; Leary & Kowalski, 1990; Schlenker,
1980). So, although self-presentation is centrally involved in maintaining one's connections
with other people, it serves other goals as well.

The first question – whether self-esteem involves more than the subjective output from the
sociometer – is less easy to answer. A strong case can be made that most documented
antecedents, consequences, and concomitants of self-esteem can be explained in terms of
their role in the maintenance of relational value (Leary & Baumeister, 2000; Leary &

Downs, 1995; Leary, Schreindorfer, & Haupt, 1995; Leary, Tambor et al., 1995). Virtually all events that affect self-esteem have potential implications for the degree to which people are socially valued and accepted, and their effects can be explained by sociometer theory. However, the fact that these events have implications for relational evaluation does not imply that their effects on self-esteem are necessarily mediated by perceived relational value nor that they owe their effects to processes associated with the sociometer. Perhaps the safest conclusion at present is that much of what we know about self-esteem and about the self-esteem motive can be explained in terms of sociometer theory, but whether the theory can account for all features of self-esteem remains an open question.

Much early theorizing about self-esteem and self-presentation explicitly considered how they relate to the give-and-take of social life. In particular, the symbolic interactionists tied both the private self and public self-presentation directly to people's relationships with one another (Cooley, 1902; Goffman, 1959; Mead, 1934). Yet, until recently, psychologists have tended to regard self-esteem and self-presentation as independent constructs, treating self-esteem purely as an intrapsychic entity and self-presentation solely as a means of projecting impressions in social interactions. As we have seen, however, both the self we know and the self we show are involved in perhaps the most important interpersonal task that a social species must face – insuring acceptance by other members of its own kind.

NOTES

1   Schlenker's (1985, 1986) self-identification theory perhaps comes closest. This theory subsumes both private self-thoughts and public self-presentations within the broader construct of "self-identification" – the process of showing oneself to be a particular type of person. Schlenker proposed that self-identification may occur with respect to three kinds of audiences: other people with whom we interact, imagined audiences, and ourselves. He discussed similarities and differences in the ways in which people identify themselves to these three audiences, but did not explicitly address the relationship between self-esteem and self-presentation that is our focus in this chapter.

2   I am not arguing here against the distinction between private and public *self-consciousness* proposed by Fenigstein, Scheier, and Buss (1975). When they are self-aware, people may focus their attention on either private, unobservable aspects of themselves (e.g., sensations, thoughts, motives, emotions) or on public, observable aspects (e.g., their physical appearance, overt behavior, or speech), and focusing attention on private versus public aspects of oneself moderates how people respond to events (Carver & Scheier, 1987; Fenigstein, 1987). However, whether people are focused on private or on public aspects of themselves, the processes involved in both private and public self-awareness occur in the private self.

3   Baumeister et al. (1989) took the argument a step further to suggest that self-report measures of self-esteem are, at least in part, measuring people's willingness to make enhancing claims about themselves. People who are willing to present themselves very positively will endorse "high self-esteem" items on such scales and, thus, score higher in self-esteem than those who are reluctant to self-enhance. Accordingly, scores on commonly used self-esteem scales may reflect, in part, individual differences in self-presentation.

4   Trivers (1985) suggested another benefit of self-deception with direct implications for self-presentation. People will be more convincing in projecting highly favorable impressions of themselves if they believe that their self-presentations are accurate and honest than if they know they are

contrived. Thus, self-deception may enhance people's ability to make positive impressions. Trivers may be correct, but his view seems to argue for a very selective form of self-deception that is engaged primarily when the individual is making impressions but disengaged when the individual needs to know the truth about his or her characteristics in order to respond effectively to the environment.

REFERENCES

Apsler, R. (1975). Effects of embarrassment on behavior toward others. *Journal of Personality and Social Psychology, 32,* 145–153.

Archibald, W. R., & Cohen, R. L. (1971). Self-presentation, embarrassment, and face-work as a function of self-evaluation, conditions of self-presentation, and feedback from others. *Journal of Personality and Social Psychology, 29,* 287–297.

Arkin, R. M. (1981). Self-presentational styles. In J. T. Tedeschi (Ed.), *Impression management theory and social psychological research* (pp. 311–323). New York: Academic Press.

Aronson, E. (1968). Dissonance theory: Progress and problems. In R. P. Abelson, E. Aronson, W. J. McGuire, T. M. Newcomb, M. J. Rosenberg, & P. H. Tannenbaum (Eds.), *Cognitive consistency theories: A sourcebook* (pp. 5–27). Skokie, IL: Rand McNally.

Aronson, E., & Mettee, D. (1968). Dishonest behavior as a function of differential levels of induced self-esteem. *Journal of Personality and Social Psychology, 9,* 121–127.

Asendorpf, J. B., & Ostendorf, F. (1998). Is self-enhancement healthy? Conceptual, psychometric, and empirical analysis. *Journal of Personality and Social Psychology, 74,* 955–966.

Bandura, A. (1997). *Self-efficacy: The exercise of control.* New York: Freeman.

Barkow, J. H. (1980). Prestige and self-esteem: A biosocial interpretation. In D. R. Omark, F. F. Strayer, & D. G. Freedman (Eds.), *Dominance relations: An ethological view of human conflict and social interaction* (pp. 319–332). New York: Garland STPM Press.

Baumeister, R. F. (1982a). A self-presentational view of social phenomena. *Psychological Bulletin, 91,* 3–26.

Baumeister, R. F. (1982b). Self-esteem, self-presentation, and future interaction: A dilemma of reputation. *Journal of Personality, 50,* 29–45.

Baumeister, R. F. (Ed.). (1986). *Public self and private self.* New York: Springer-Verlag.

Baumeister, R. F. (1989). The optimal margin of illusion. *Journal of Social and Clinical Psychology, 8,* 176–189.

Baumeister, R. F., Heatherton, T. F., & Tice, D. M. (1993). When ego threats lead to self-regulation failure: The negative consequences of high self-esteem. *Journal of Personality and Social Psychology, 64,* 141–156.

Baumeister, R. F., & Jones, E. E. (1978). When self-presentation is constrained by the target's knowledge: Consistency and compensation. *Journal of Personality and Social Psychology, 36,* 608–618.

Baumeister, R. F., & Leary, M. R. (1995). The need to belong: Desire for interpersonal attachments as a fundamental human motivation. *Psychological Bulletin, 17,* 497–529.

Baumeister, R. F., Smart, L., & Boden, J. M. (1996). Relation of threatened egotism to violence and aggression: The dark side of high self-esteem. *Psychological Review, 103,* 5–33.

Baumeister, R. F., & Tice, D. M. (1986). Four selves, two motives, and a substitute process self-regulation model. In R. F. Baumeister (Ed.), *Public self and private self* (pp. 63–74). New York: Springer-Verlag.

Baumeister, R. F., Tice, D. M., & Hutton, D. G. (1989). Self-presentational motivations and personality differences in self-esteem. *Journal of Personality, 57,* 547–579.

Bednar, R. L., Wells, M. G., & Peterson, S. R. (1989). *Self-esteem: Paradoxes and innovations in clinical theory and practice*. Washington, DC: American Psychological Association.

Blaine, B., & Crocker, J. (1993). Self-esteem and self-serving biases in reactions to positive and negative events: An integrative review. In R. F. Baumeister (Ed.), *Self-esteem: The puzzle of low self-regard* (pp. 55–85). New York: Plenum.

Branden, N. (1994). *The six pillars of self-esteem*. New York: Bantam.

Carver, C. S., & Scheier, M. F. (1981). *Attention and self-regulation: A control-theory approach to human behavior*. New York: Springer-Verlag.

Carver, C. S., & Scheier, M. F. (1987). The blind men and the elephant: Examination of the public-private literature gives rise to a faulty perception. *Journal of Personality, 55*, 525–541.

Colvin, C. R., & Block, J. (1994). Do positive illusions foster mental health? An examination of the Taylor and Brown formulation. *Psychological Bulletin, 116*, 3–20.

Colvin, C. R., Block, J., & Funder, D. C. (1995). Overly positive self-evaluations and personality: Negative implications for mental health. *Journal of Personality and Social Psychology, 68*, 1152–1162.

Cooley, C. H. (1902). *Human nature and the social order*. New York: Scribner's.

Dawes, R. (1994). *House of cards: Psychology and psychotherapy built on myth*. New York: Free Press.

Deci, E. L., & Ryan, R. M. (1995). Human autonomy: The basis for true self-esteem. In M. H. Kernis (Ed.), *Efficacy, agency, and self-esteem* (pp. 31–71). New York: Plenum.

de Waal, F. B. M. (1986). Deception in the natural communication of chimpanzees. In R. W. Mitchell & N. S. Thompson (Eds.), *Deception: Perspectives on human and nonhuman deceit* (pp. 221–266). Albany: State University of New York Press.

Fenigstein, A. (1987). On the nature of public and private self-consciousness. *Journal of Personality, 55*, 543–554.

Fenigstein, A., Scheier, M. F., & Buss, A. H. (1975). Public and private self-consciousness: Assessment and theory. *Journal of Consulting and Clinical Psychology, 43*, 522–527.

Gallup, G. G., Jr. (1977). Self-recognition in primates: A comparative approach to the bidirectional properties of consciousness. *American Psychologist, 32*, 329–338.

Gallup, G. G., Jr., & Suarez, S. D. (1986). Self-awareness and the emergence of mind in humans and other primates. In J. Suls & A. G. Greenwald (Eds.), *Psychological perspectives on the self* (Vol. 3, pp. 3–26). Hillsdade, NJ: Erlbaum.

Gergen, K. J. (1965). The effects of interaction goals and personalistic feedback on the presentation of self. *Journal of Personality and Social Psychology, 1*, 413–424.

Goffman, E. (1959). *The presentation of self in everyday life*. Garden City, NY: Doubleday Anchor.

Greenberg, J., Pyszcynski, T., Solomon, S., Rosenblatt, A., Burling, J., Lyon, D., Simon, L., & Pinel, E. (1992). Why do people need self-esteem? Converging evidence that self-esteem serves an anxiety-buffering function. *Journal of Personality and Social Psychology, 63*, 913–922.

Greenwald, A. G. (1980). The totalitarian ego: Fabrication and revision of personal history. *American Psychologist, 35*, 603–613.

Greenwald, A. G. (1982). Ego task analysis: An integration of research on ego-involvement and awareness. In A. H. Hastorf & A. M. Isen (Eds.), *Cognitive social psychology* (pp. 109–147). New York: Elsevier North Holland.

Greenwald, A. G., & Breckler, S. (1985). To whom is the self presented? In B. R. Schlenker (Ed.), *The self and social life* (pp. 126–145). New York: McGraw-Hill.

Haupt, A., & Leary, M. R. (1997). The appeal of worthless groups: Moderating effects of trait self-esteem. *Group Dynamics: Theory, Research, and Practice, 1*, 124–132.

Hoyle, R. H., Kernis, M. H., Leary, M. R., & Baldwin, M. W. (1999). *Selfhood: Identity, esteem, regulation*. Boulder, CO: Westview Press.

James, W. (1890). *The principles of psychology*. New York: Holt.

Janis, I. L., & Gilmore, J. B. (1965). The influence of incentive conditions on the success of role playing in modifying attitudes. *Journal of Personality and Social Psychology, 1,* 17–27.

Jones, E. E. (1964). *Ingratiation.* New York: Appleton-Century-Crofts.

Jones, E. E., Gergen, K. J., & Jones, R. G. (1963). Tactics of ingratiation among leaders and subordinates in a status hierarchy. *Psychological Monographs, 77* (Whole No. 566).

Jones, E. E., & Pittman, T. (1982). Toward a general theory of strategic self-presentation. In J. Suls (Ed.), *Psychological perspectives on the self* (Vol. 1, pp. 231–262). Hillsdale, NJ: Erlbaum.

Jones, E. E., Rhodewalt, F., Berglas, S., & Skelton, J. A. (1981). Effects of strategic self-presentation on subsequent self-esteem. *Journal of Personality and Social Psychology, 41,* 407–421.

Jones, S. C. (1973). Self- and interpersonal evaluations: Esteem theories vs. consistency theories. *Psychological Bulletin, 79,* 185–199.

Kolditz, T. A., & Arkin, R. M. (1982). An impression management interpretation of the self-handicapping strategy. *Journal of Personality and Social Psychology, 43,* 492–502.

Kowalski, R. M., & Leary, M. R. (1990). Strategic self-presentation and the avoidance of aversive events. Antecedents and consequences of self-enhancement and self-depreciation. *Journal of Experimental Social Psychology, 26,* 322–336.

Leary, M. R. (1993). The interplay of private self-processes and interpersonal factors in self-presentation. In J. Suls (Ed.), *Psychological perspectives on the self* (Vol. 4, pp. 127–155). Hillsdale, NJ: Erlbaum.

Leary, M. R. (1995). *Self-presentation: Impression management and interpersonal behavior.* Boulder, CO: Westview Press.

Leary, M. R. (1999). The social and psychological importance of self-esteem. In R. M. Kowalski & M. R. Leary (Eds.), *The social psychology of emotional and behavioral problems: Interfaces of social and clinical psychology* (pp. 197–221). Washington, DC: American Psychological Association.

Leary, M. R., Barnes, B. D., Griebel, C., Mason, E., & McCormack, D., Jr. (1987). The impact of conjoint threats to social- and self-esteem on evaluation apprehension. *Social Psychology Quarterly, 50,* 304–311.

Leary, M. R., & Baumeister, R. F. (2000). The nature and function of self-esteem: Sociometer theory. *Advances in Experimental Social Psychology, 32,* 1–62.

Leary, M. R., & Downs, D. L. (1995). Interpersonal functions of the self-esteem motive: The self-esteem system as a sociometer. In M. Kernis (Ed.), *Efficacy, agency, and self-esteem* (pp. 123–144). New York: Plenum.

Leary, M. R., Haupt, A., Strausser, K., & Chokel, J. (1998). Calibrating the sociometer: The relationship between interpersonal appraisals and state self-esteem. *Journal of Personality and Social Psychology, 74,* 1290–1299.

Leary, M. R., & Kowalski, R. M. (1990). Impression management: A literature review and two-factor model. *Psychological Bulletin, 107,* 34–47.

Leary, M. R., Schreindorfer, L. S., & Haupt, A. L. (1995). The role of self-esteem in emotional and behavioral problems: Why is low self-esteem dysfunctional? *Journal of Social and Clinical Psychology, 14,* 297–314.

Leary, M. R., Tambor, E. S., Terdal, S. K., & Downs, D. L. (1995). Self-esteem as an interpersonal monitor: The sociometer hypothesis. *Journal of Personality and Social Psychology, 68,* 518–530.

Lecky, P. (1945). *Self-consistency: A theory of personality.* New York: Island Press.

Maracek, J., & Mettee, D. (1972). Avoidance of continued success as a function of self-esteem, level of esteem certainty, and responsibility for success. *Journal of Personality and Social Psychology, 22,* 98–107.

Martin, M. W. (1985). General introduction. In M. W. Martin (Ed.), *Self-deception and self-understanding* (pp. 1–27). Lawrence: University of Kansas Press.

McKillop, K. J., Jr., Berzonsky, M. D., & Schlenker, B. R. (1992). The impact of self-presentation on self-beliefs: Effects of social identity and self-presentational context. *Journal of Personality, 60*, 789–808.

Mead, G. H. (1934). *Mind, self, and society*. Chicago: University of Chicago Press.

Mecca, A. M., Smelser, N. J., & Vasconcellos, J. (Eds.). (1989). *The social importance of self-esteem*. Berkeley: University of California Press.

Miller, R. S. (1996). *Embarrassment Poise and peril in everyday life*. New York: Guilford.

Miller, R. S., & Schlenker, B. R. (1978). *Self-presentation as affected by a valid or invalid past performance*. Paper presented at the meeting of the American Psychological Association, Toronto.

Miller, R. S., & Schlenker, B. R. (1985). Egotism in group members: Public and private attributions of responsibility for group performance. *Social Psychology Quarterly, 48*, 85–89.

Modigliani, A. (1971). Embarrassment, facework, and eye contact: Testing a theory of embarrassment. *Journal of Personality and Social Psychology, 17*, 15–24.

Mruk, C. (1995). *Self-esteem: Research, theory, and practice*. New York: Springer.

Rogers, C. (1959). A theory of therapy, personality, and interpersonal relationships, as developed in the client-centered framework. In S. Koch (Ed.), *Psychology: A study of a science* (Vol. 3, pp. 184–256). New York: McGraw-Hill.

Rosenberg, M. (1965). *Society and the adolescent self image*. Princeton, NJ: Princeton University Press.

Scheier, M. F., & Carver, C. S. (1983). Two sides of the self: One for you and one for me. In J. Suls (Ed.), *Psychological perspectives on the self* (Vol. 1, pp. 123–157). Hillsdale: Erlbaum.

Schlenker, B. R. (1980). *Impression management: The self-concept, social identity, and interpersonal relations*. Monterey, CA: Brooks/Cole.

Schlenker, B. R. (1985). Identity and self-identification. In B. R. Schlenker (Ed.), *The self and social life* (pp. 65–99). New York: McGraw-Hill.

Schlenker, B. R. (1986). Self-identification: Toward an integration of the private and public self. In R. F. Baumeister (Ed.), *Public self and private self* (pp. 21–62). New York: Springer-Verlag.

Schlenker, B. R., & Trudeau, J. V. (1990). Impact of self-presentation on private self-beliefs: Effects of prior self-beliefs and misattribution. *Journal of Personality and Social Psychology, 58*, 22–32.

Schlenker, B. R., Weigold, M. F., & Hallam, J. R. (1990). Self-serving attributions in social context: Effects of self-esteem and social pressure. *Journal of Personality and Social Psychology, 58*, 855–863.

Schneider, D. J. (1969). Tactical self-presentation after success and failure. *Journal of Personality and Social Psychology, 13*, 262–268.

Schneider, D. J., & Turkat, D. (1975). Self-presentation following success or failure: Defensive self-esteem models. *Journal of Personality, 43*, 127–135.

Sedikides, C. (1993). Assessment, enhancement, and verification determinants of the self-evaluation process. *Journal of Personality and Social Psychology, 65*, 317–338.

Shepperd, J. A., & Kwavnick, K. D. (1999). Maladaptive image maintenance. In R. M. Kowalski & M. R. Leary (Eds.), *The social psychology of emotional and behavioral problems* (pp. 249–277). Washington, DC: American Psychological Association.

Shrauger, J. (1975). Responses to evaluation as a function of initial self-perceptions. *Psychological Bulletin, 82*, 581–596.

Smart, L., & Wegner, D. M. (1994, July). *The ironic effects of self-presentation on self-esteem*. Paper presented at the meeting of the American Psychological Society, Washington, DC.

Spencer, S. J., Josephs, R. A., & Steele, C. M. (1993). Low self-esteem: The uphill struggle for self-integrity. In R. F. Baumeister (Ed.), *Self-esteem: The puzzle of low self-regard*. New York: Plenum.

Steele, C. M. (1988). The psychology of self-affirmation: Sustaining the integrity of the self. In L. Berkowitz (Ed.), *Advances in experimental social psychology* (Vol. 21, pp. 261–302). San Diego, CA: Academic Press.

Steele, C. M., Spencer, S. J., & Lynch, M. (1993). Self-image resilience and dissonance: The role of affirmation processes. *Journal of Personality and Social Psychology, 64,* 885–896.

Swann, W. B., Jr., Griffin, J. J., Predmore, S. C., & Gaines, B. (1987). The cognitive affective crossfire: When self-consistency confronts self-enhancement. *Journal of Personality and Social Psychology, 52,* 881–889.

Taylor, S. E., & Brown, J. D. (1988). Illusion and well-being: A social psychological perspective on mental health. *Psychological Bulletin, 103,* 193–210.

Tetlock, P. E., & Manstead, A. S. R. (1985). Impression management vs. intrapsychic explanations in social psychology: A useful dichotomy? *Psychological Review, 92,* 59–77.

Tice, D. M. (1991). Esteem protection or enhancement? Self-handicapping motives and attributions differ by trait self-esteem. *Journal of Personality and Social Psychology, 60,* 711–725.

Tice, D. M. (1992). Self-concept change and self-presentation: The looking glass self is also a magnifying glass. *Journal of Personality and Social Psychology, 63,* 435–451.

Tice, D. M. (1993). The social motivations of people with low self-esteem. In R. F. Baumeister (Ed.), *Self-esteem: The puzzle of low self-regard* (pp. 37–53). New York: Plenum.

Tice, D. M., & Baumeister, R. F. (1990). Self-esteem, self-handicapping, and self-presentation: The strategy of inadequate practice. *Journal of Personality, 58,* 443–464.

Tooby, J., & Cosmides, L. (1996). Friendship and the banker's paradox: Other pathways to the evolution of adaptations for altruism. *Proceedings of the British Academy, 88,* 119–143.

Trivers, R. (1985). *Social evolution.* Menlo Park, CA: Benjamin/Cummings.

Walster, E. (1965). The effect of self-esteem on romantic liking. *Journal of Personality and Social Psychology, 1,* 184–197.

Watson, D., & Friend, R. (1969). Measurement of social-evaluative anxiety. *Journal of Consulting and Clinical Psychology, 33,* 448–457.

Wegner, D. M. (1994). Ironic processes of mental control. *Psychological Review, 101,* 34–52.

Wolfe, R. N., Lennox, R. D., & Cutler, B. L. (1986). Getting along and getting ahead: Empirical support for a theory of protective and acquisitive self-presentation. *Journal of Personality and Social Psychology, 50,* 356–361.

Wylie, R. C. (1961). *The self-concept: A critical review of pertinent research literature.* Lincoln: University of Nebraska Press.

CHAPTER ELEVEN

Motivational Aspects of Empathic Accuracy

William Ickes and Jeffry A. Simpson

"I want the truth!"
"You can't handle the truth!!"
Dialogue from the film *A Few Good Men*

As desirable as the truth may be as a theoretical ideal, the hard reality is that sometimes the truth hurts. Sometimes we just can't handle the truth. Sometimes we are even motivated to avoid it. But sometimes, knowing that the truth will hurt, we are motivated to seek it out anyway – even if we have to pay a very painful price for this knowledge.

These abstract propositions have a special force and immediacy when they are viewed within the context of close relationships. With regard to the first proposition, achieving a true understanding of a relationship partner is not only a theoretical ideal; it has considerable practical value as well. To ensure that their close relationship will continue to "work" over any extended period of time, partners must effectively coordinate their individual and shared motives and actions. Such coordination requires that they must be relatively accurate, much of the time, when inferring the specific content of each other's thoughts and feelings. As a general rule, then, partners who can accurately infer each other's thoughts and feelings should be more successful in maintaining satisfying and stable relationships than partners who cannot.

There are times, however, when relationship partners suspect – or even know for certain – that understanding the truth about the other's thoughts and feelings could have a devastating impact on their relationship. Rather than confront the truth about the other's thoughts and feelings in these relationship-threatening situations, one or both partners may avoid this knowledge and thereby attempt to spare themselves and their relationship the pain and injury that might otherwise occur. In such cases, the partners' motivated inaccuracy may provide an important exception to the more general rule that partners seek an accurate understanding of each other in order to make their relationship work. In the short run at least, the use of motivated inaccuracy in relationship-threatening situations may actually be an effective strategy for protecting the partners and their relationship from the threat of impending pain and injury.

However, for some partners, and in some circumstances, even the threat of impending pain and injury may not be a sufficient deterrent. There are cases in which a person's need to confront the truth is so strong that an accurate knowledge of the partner's thoughts and feelings is sought even when this knowledge comes at a very high cost – a cost that can include damage to self-esteem, to esteem for the partner, and to the strength and stability of the relationship. Such cases constitute another important exception to the rule that relationship partners will typically seek to make accurate, rather than inaccurate, inferences about each other's thoughts and feelings in order to help the relationship "work" more effectively. Although perceivers do seek to be accurate in such cases, their accuracy is sought at the expense of – rather than in the service of – relational stability and satisfaction.

In this chapter we consider the motivational implications of empathic accuracy in terms of the general rule and the two important exceptions described above. We first summarize the findings from studies that are consistent with the general rule that motivated accuracy usually helps close relationships to work effectively, resulting in moderate to high levels of relationship satisfaction and stability. We next examine the findings from a recent study that provides preliminary support for the first exception to the rule, i.e., that there are cases in which partners will use motivated inaccuracy to protect themselves and their relationships from personal and relational distress (Simpson, Ickes, & Blackstone, 1995). We then consider findings from a follow-up study that provides preliminary support for the second exception to the rule, i.e., that there are cases in which partners are motivated to "read" each other accurately even though they are likely to pay a high price for this knowledge in both personal and relational terms (Simpson, Ickes, & Grich, 1999). Finally, we integrate these sets of findings within our developing theoretical model (Ickes & Simpson, 1997) of how empathic accuracy might be "managed" in close relationships.

The Rule: Motivated Accuracy Helps Relationships

Many studies in the *marital adjustment literature* have documented a positive association between marital adjustment and understanding of the attitudes, role expectations, and self-perceptions of one's spouse (see Sillars & Scott, 1983, for a review). This claim is based on the results of studies by Dymond (1954), Corsini (1956), Luckey (1960), Stuckert (1963), Laing, Phillipson, and Lee (1966), Taylor (1967), Murstein and Beck (1972), Christensen and Wallace (1976), Newmark, Woody, and Ziff (1977), Ferguson and Allen (1978), Noller (1980, 1981), Noller and Venardos (1986), and Guthrie and Noller (1988). Additional evidence for a positive association between marital adjustment and understanding has been reported by Katz (1965), Navran (1967), Kahn (1970), Gottman et al. (1976), Knudson, Sommers, and Golding (1980), Gottman and Porterfield (1981), Madden and Janoff-Bulman (1981), and Neimeyer and Banikiotes (1981).

Collectively, these studies support the view that, as a rule, more understanding (i.e., greater empathic accuracy) is good for relationships. The generality of this rule has recently been questioned, however, in articles by Noller (Noller, 1984; Noller & Ruzzene, 1991) and by Sillars (Sillars & Scott, 1983; Sillars, Pike, Jones, and Murphy, 1984; Sillars, 1985). For example, in some of the early studies that focused on judgments of spouses' self-rated traits, attitudes, and role expectations, the relationship between understanding and marital adjustment held only when the wife was the respondent and the husband's perceptions were being predicted (Stuckert, 1963; Murstein & Beck, 1972; Corsini, 1956; Kotlar, 1965; see also Barry, 1970). Similarly, research examining the judgments of spouses' intentions has found evidence that distressed wives may display less understanding than nondistressed wives and husbands (Noller & Ruzzene, 1991). Such findings suggest that the association between understanding and marital adjustment is more complicated than earlier theorists and researchers supposed.

Although there are fewer relevant studies available in the recent *empathic accuracy literature*, the results of these studies also suggest that, as a general rule, the partners' accuracy in inferring each other's thoughts and feelings is associated with positive relationship outcomes. For example, in their study of empathic accuracy in a sample of newly married couples, Kilpatrick, Bissonnette, and Rusbult (1999) reported that empathic accuracy was significantly correlated at the couple level with such variables as commitment to the relationship (.42), willingness to accommodate the partner's bad behavior (.60), and dyadic adjustment (.58). These effects, which were found when the couples were in the first 12–18 months of their marriages, generally declined in strength across time, so that only the couple-level correlation between empathic accuracy and dyadic adjustment was still significant (.35) two years later.

Kilpatrick and her colleagues speculated that empathic accuracy might have its greatest effect on positive relationship outcomes early in the course of close relationships because this is a time when the partners' attitudes, values, and behaviors are still relatively unpredictable and difficult to anticipate and accommodate. Accordingly, partners who can successfully infer each other's thoughts and feelings will achieve better relational outcomes during this early period of adjustment than will couples who cannot. With the passage of time, the positive effects of empathic accuracy on relational outcomes may decrease for couples who, having learned each other's idiosyncratic cognitive, emotional, and behavioral predilections, have developed habits that automatically accommodate them. On the other hand, for the (presumably smaller) subset of couples who do not develop such habits – either because of a continuing ignorance of each other's predilections or an unwillingness to accommodate them – empathic accuracy may continue to play an important role in promoting positive relationship outcomes.

A complementary interpretation was proposed in an earlier study by Thomas, Fletcher, and Lange (1997), who studied a larger sample of New Zealand couples who had been married for an average of over 15 years. Thomas and his colleagues also found that couple-level empathic accuracy decreased as the length of the marriage increased (−.31), but discovered that this relationship was mediated by the extent to which the content of the individual partners' thoughts and feelings was divergent. In other words, couples who had been married for longer periods of time tended to have fewer shared thoughts and feelings (and, by implication, more idiosyncratic ones) during their interactions than did more recently married couples; and it was this difference in the level of "shared cognitive focus" that accounted for the lower levels of empathic accuracy attained by couples married for longer periods of time. Thomas and his colleagues suggested that "partners in long-standing relationships become complacent and overly familiar with each other" (p. 840). They therefore lack the motivation to actively monitor each other's words and actions and attain the kind of common, intersubjective focus in their thoughts and feelings that facilitates empathic accuracy.

If the link between empathic accuracy and positive relationship outcomes is likely to be most evident in the earlier stages of a relationship, it makes sense that empathic accuracy was significantly related to marital adjustment in Kilpatrick et al.'s (1999) newlywed sample but was not significantly related to marital satisfaction in Thomas et al.'s (1997) sample of longer-married couples. It may not be surprising, therefore, that Ickes, Stinson, Bissonnette, and Garcia (1990) found that opposite-sex strangers were more accurate in inferring each other's thoughts and feelings to the extent they found each other physically attractive, because – like the recently married couples in the Kilpatrick et al. (1999) and Thomas et al. (1997) studies – they were presumably highly motivated to monitor each other closely and to try to achieve a "shared cognitive focus." In general, then, the available studies suggest that motivated accuracy can contribute to positive relationship outcomes, particularly during the formative stages of close relationships.

The First Exception: Sometimes Motivated Inaccuracy Helps Relationships

As we have just seen, there is support for the commonsense belief that, as a general rule, greater understanding is associated with greater stability and satisfaction in close relationships. It would be a serious mistake, however, not to recognize that there are important exceptions to this rule.

The first exception occurs whenever relationship partners suspect (or know for certain) that their partner harbors thoughts and feelings that they might be better off *not* knowing – thoughts and feelings that, if accurately inferred, could have a devastating effect on their relationship. Rather than confront the painful knowledge of what the other person thinks and feels, one or both partners may be motivated to *mis*infer this knowledge and thereby spare themselves and their relationship the pain and injury that might otherwise occur. In such cases, the partners' *motivated inaccuracy* may provide an important exception to the more general rule that partners seek an accurate understanding of each other in order to keep their relationship happy and stable.

In a recent study (Simpson et al., 1995), we found some preliminary evidence that partners may indeed use motivated inaccuracy to ward off an impending threat to their relationship. The participants in this study were 82 heterosexual dating couples. In each other's presence, the members of each couple took turns rating and discussing with their partner the physical and sexual attractiveness of a set of opposite-sex persons as "potential dating partners." About half of the couples were randomly assigned to view and rate slides of highly attractive people, whereas the remaining couples viewed and rated slides of less attractive people. After the male (or the female) partner rated aloud on a 10-point scale the attractiveness and sexual appeal of each opposite-sex stimulus person, both partners discussed what they liked or disliked about each person for 30 seconds.

Each couple's interaction during this rating-and-discussion task was covertly videotaped. Immediately afterwards, we informed the partners about the taping and obtained their written consent to let us code the videotapes for subsequent analysis. We also asked them to participate in the next phase of the study – a phase in which the actual thoughts and feelings they had experienced during the rating-and-discussion task were assessed.

The partners were seated in different rooms, where each partner viewed a copy of the videotape of the couples' interaction over the entire course of the rating-and-discussion task. Consistent with the experimenter's instructions, each partner made a written record of each of his or her thoughts and feelings as well as the "tape stops" (i.e., the specific times during the interaction) at which each thought or feeling occurred. Each partner then viewed the tape again, this time with the assigned task of attempting to accurately infer the specific content of each of their *partner's* thoughts and feelings at their respective "tape stops" (for additional methodological details, see Ickes, Bissonnette, Garcia, & Stinson, 1990; and Simpson et al., 1995). Four months later, both partners were telephoned to determine whether or not they were still dating.

The purpose of this study was to see if we could identify conditions in which relationship partners would exhibit motivated *in*accuracy and thereby minimize the relational instability and dissatisfaction that might otherwise result. As we predicted, we found that the *least* empathic accuracy during the rating-and-discussion task was displayed by dating partners who were closer (i.e., more interdependent), who were less certain about the stability of their relationship, and who rated attractive (vs. less attractive) "potential dating partners" in each other's presence. We also found that the relation between these last three variables and empathic accuracy was mediated by the perceiver's level of self-reported threat. That is, the partners who were the most interdependent, the least certain about the stability of their relationship, and who rated highly attractive others reported feeling the most threatened, and these high levels of threat in turn predicted their lower (near-chance) levels of empathic accuracy. Even more impressive, the partners in this category were all still dating at the four-month follow-up, whereas the remaining couples in the study had a significantly higher breakup rate of 28 percent.

In general, the pattern of behavior displayed by these close-but-uncertain partners who rated and discussed attractive others provides good preliminary evidence for what we have termed "the first exception to the rule" – that *sometimes motivated inaccuracy helps relationships.* Apparently, there are cases in which partners use motivated inaccuracy in relationship-threatening situations to protect themselves and their relationship from the pain and injury that might result from a more accurate understanding of what the other is thinking or feeling. That such a strategy might help to protect relationships is suggested by Simpson et al.'s finding that the least accurate couples were the most likely to still be together four months later. For a review of the evidence that supports our "motivated inaccuracy" interpretation of this effect, see Simpson et al. (1995).

The Second Exception: Sometimes Motivated Accuracy Hurts Relationships

Within the ranks of relationship researchers, Alan Sillars and his colleagues were among the first to note that an accurate understanding of a partner's thoughts and feelings is not always associated with positive outcomes. After reviewing the literature that was available in the early 1980s, Sillars and his colleagues concluded that there are conditions in which greater understanding is associated with greater personal and relational distress (Sillars, 1981, 1985; Sillars & Parry, 1982; Sillars, Pike, Jones, & Murphy, 1984; Sillars, Pike, Jones, & Redmon, 1983; Sillars & Scott, 1983).

In general, these conditions were found in *conflict paradigms* – experimental situations in which married or dating couples were required to discuss one or more issues that had previously been a source of major conflict in their relationships (Sillars & Parry, 1982; Sillars et al., 1984; Sillars, et al., 1983). Ideally, the partners' successive goals in such discussions should be (1) to identify their respective differences in opinions, values, motives, etc., (2) to clarify the reasons for these differences, and (3) to successfully resolve them. Surprisingly, however, the more successful the partners were in understanding each other's respective positions, the *less* satisfied they felt with the outcome of their attempted conflict-resolution and with the current state of their relationship. Ironically, the more the couples succeeded in achieving their first two goals, the less they succeeded in achieving the third. How could this seemingly paradoxical outcome have occurred?

Sillars (1985) proposed a partial answer to this question by suggesting that when couples attempt to identify and clarify the reasons for their differences, they often wind up making some unpleasant discoveries. In some cases, they discover that their differences are apparently irreconcilable, so that extended discussion and clarification of their respective viewpoints does not improve the relationship but only seems to make things worse (Aldous, 1977; Kursh 1971). In other cases, they discover that "benevolent misconceptions" which they have previously held about each other's viewpoints are false and can no longer be sustained (Levinger & Breedlove, 1966). And, in still other cases, they uncover blunt, unpleasant truths about each other's private thoughts and feelings that could undermine their views of each other and of their relationship (Aldous, 1977; Rausch, Berry, Hertel, & Swain, 1974; Watzlawick, Weakland, & Fisch, 1974).

Granting the importance of all of those processes, we think another important factor is that the partners in such studies do not choose to initiate their conflict discussions but are instead *required* to initiate them. In their daily lives, many of these couples would probably avoid, or at least repeatedly postpone, major confrontations over such high-conflict issues, recognizing them as potential "danger-zone topics" and doing their best to steer clear of them. However, in the special context of laboratory conflict paradigms, couples are essentially compelled to express and defend their respective points of view, and to do so publicly and "for the record" (because their interactions are recorded in some form). Even if their assigned goal is to resolve the conflict(s) in some way, individual face-saving should be an important motive as well – one that could plausibly promote both increased understanding (through the forceful presentation and defense of the partners' respective viewpoints) and decreased satisfaction with the current state of the relationship. Thus, although requiring couples to argue might increase their understanding of each other by making their individual perspectives more explicit (Sillars, 1998), the understanding they gain may be of a type that they find aversive – and therefore usually seek to avoid in the absence of any strong situational constraints (Berger, 1993).

The conflict paradigm studies reported by Sillars and his colleagues provide examples of cases in which increased empathic accuracy can hurt relationships. However, because these studies imposed strong situational constraints, they cannot be regarded as clear-cut examples of cases in which *motivated* accuracy hurts relationships. This observation raises an important question: If relationship partners tend to avoid confronting the more unpleasant truths to be found in each other's thoughts and feelings, would there ever be cases in which *motivated* accuracy hurts relationships, as our second proposed exception to the rule suggests? When, if ever, would partners be motivated to gain such painful knowledge, if the consequences are so predictably aversive?

Perhaps the most obvious answer is that they would do so whenever the alternative (i.e., *not* knowing their partner's actual thoughts and feelings) is perceived as even *more* aversive. Thus, given a choice between learning that a partner does not really love you or spending the rest of your life in an "empty shell" marriage in which you suspect that to be true, you might be motivated to more accurately infer your partner's thoughts and feelings, despite the potential damage to your relationship. Similarly, if you have any reason to believe that your engagement-partner might be less in love with you than with the concept of a quick divorce and a healthy share of your inherited fortune, you might also be motivated to achieve greater empathic accuracy in the face of potential relationship loss. Perceivers in such cases are, in the final analysis, acting rationally; their motive to be accurate derives from a calculated decision to risk an immediate relationship loss in order to avoid a potentially greater one in the future.

A less rational basis for such behavior might also exist, however, in the form of a strong and enduring dispositional motive to accurately infer a partner's private thoughts and feelings. We (Simpson et al., 1999) recently found some preliminary evidence for such a dispositionally-based *accuracy motive* when we re-analyzed the data from our original dating couples study (Simpson et al., 1995) with respect to the partners' scores on the anxiety and avoidance attachment dimensions (see Simpson, Rholes, & Phillips, 1996). Highly anxious partners (particularly highly anxious women) did not display the motivated inaccuracy that we observed in partners with other attachment orientations in the relationship-threatening situation we created. On the contrary, the more anxious they were, the more accurate they were at inferring their partners' relationship-threatening thoughts and feelings. At the same time, however, the more anxious they were, the more they also felt distressed, threatened, and jealous, and the more they displayed other signs of relationship dissatisfaction and instability. In its overall pattern, the behavior of these highly anxious individuals provides intriguing evidence for what we have termed "the second exception to the rule" – that *sometimes motivated accuracy hurts relationships.*

Complementing this evidence that highly anxious partners have a strong "accuracy motive," we also found evidence of what appears to be a contrasting motive in highly avoidant partners. In this case, the more avoidant the partners were, the more likely they were to leave slots on the empathic inference form blank, thereby declining to make certain inferences about their dating partner's potentially threatening thoughts and feelings at certain "tape stops." Taken together, these findings for the anxiety and avoidance attachment dimensions suggest that there may be substantial individual differences in the motive to accurately infer one's partner's thoughts and feelings in relationship-threatening situations, and that this motive may be especially pronounced in highly anxious individuals.

A Theoretical Integration of the Rule and Its Exceptions

Conventional wisdom suggests that understanding a relationship partner's thoughts and feelings should be good for relationships. As we have just seen, however, this widely held belief is overly simplistic and does not account for the entire pattern of available findings. Although greater empathic accuracy tends to be associated with more relationship satisfaction and greater stability in situations that pose little or no threat to relationships (e.g., Kahn, 1970; Noller, 1980; Noller & Ruzzene, 1991), it is associated with *less* satisfaction and *less* stability in relationship-threatening situations (e.g., Sillars et al., 1984; Simpson et al., 1995). At first glance, the findings from the studies involving relationship-threatening situations seem counterintuitive, if not completely paradoxical, in light of the widely held assumption that threats to relationships are more easily defused if partners can gain a greater understanding of each other's respective thoughts and feelings.

To help resolve this apparent paradox, we have proposed a theoretical model of how partners might "manage" their levels of empathic accuracy in relationship-threatening versus nonthreatening situations (Ickes & Simpson, 1997). A description of this model, elaborated in certain respects from its original presentation, is provided below. The goal of the model is to specify the conditions in which (1) empathic accuracy should help relationships (the general rule); (2) empathic *in*accuracy should help relationships (the first exception to the rule); and (3) empathic accuracy should hurt relationships (the second exception to the rule).

The empathic accuracy model

Our model starts by assuming that the range of empathic accuracy (the upper and lower boundaries) that can be attained in a given interaction is set by (1) the partners' respective levels of "readability" (the degree to which each partner conveys cues that reflect his or her true internal states), and (2) the partners' respective levels of empathic ability (the degree to which each partner can accurately decipher the other's valid behavioral cues). Within these broad constraints, however, the model presumes that empathic accuracy should be "managed" very differently depending on a number of factors. The factors we regard as most fundamental are represented in the portion of our model that is depicted in figure 11.1.

It is important to note that figure 11.1 characterizes behavior at the individual, rather than the dyadic, level of analysis. According to this model, each partner makes his or her own preliminary assessment of whether or not the current situation is likely to lead to a *danger zone* in the partners' relationship. As we define it, the term "danger zone" is a convenient shorthand. It denotes having to confront an issue that could potentially threaten the relationship by revealing thoughts and feelings harbored by one's partner that one might personally find distressing and upsetting.

Of course, what one partner might find distressing and upsetting might not be viewed in a similar way by the other partner (for example, male partners might find a revelation of sexual infidelity more threatening than a revelation of emotional infidelity, whereas the reverse might be true for female partners; cf. Buss et al., 1999). A broader and more detailed

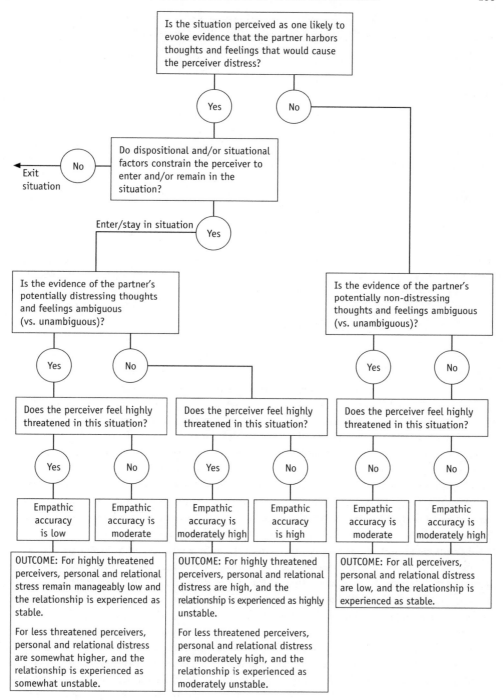

Figure 11.1 The empathic accuracy model

version of our model would therefore begin by acknowledging that individual relationship partners could assign themselves to different "paths" or trajectories if one partner anticipated a danger zone in the current situation whereas the other partner did not. Although developing the various theoretical implications of this broader, more complex "dyadic" model is beyond the scope of the present chapter, we will consider a few of these implications below. In addition, we encourage researchers who are interested in this topic to routinely assess both partners' danger zones (the specific forms they take and how threatening they are perceived to be) at both the individual and the dyadic levels of analysis.

At the first branching point in our model, each individual anticipates either a situation in which a danger-zone issue is likely to present itself or one in which no danger-zone issue is likely to emerge. To "walk through" the possible subsequent outcomes, let us first consider the part of the model that applies when an individual perceives that a situation is nonthreatening (i.e., that no danger-zone issue is likely to emerge that might force the partners to confront each other's relationship-threatening thoughts and feelings).

Empathic accuracy in nonthreatening contexts.   When perceivers expect to deal with issues that do not have threatening implications for their relationship (see the right-hand portion of figure 11.1), the model predicts that they should be at least somewhat motivated to accurately infer their partners' thoughts and feelings. Because experience should have taught them that mutual understanding often facilitates their ability to coordinate their actions and thereby pursue both individual and common goals more effectively, and because the behaviors needed to attain such understanding typically become habitual through repeated reinforcement (Bissonnette, Rusbult, & Kilpatrick, 1997), perceivers should be motivated to attain at least minimal levels of accuracy when inferring their partners' thoughts and feelings.

Accordingly, in nonthreatening situations in which no danger zones are perceived (e.g., everyday conversations concerning trivial or mundane issues), perceivers should display a habit-based "accuracy" orientation. This orientation should help them to clarify misunderstandings over nonthreatening issues, keep minor conflicts from escalating into major ones, and gain a deeper understanding of their partner, all of which should enhance feelings of satisfaction and closeness in the relationship over time. Thus, as long as the situation does not lead the perceiver to anticipate the emergence of issues that could evoke and potentially reveal a partner's relationship-threatening thoughts and feelings, the perceiver should be motivated to attain at least a moderate level of empathic accuracy.

On the other hand, the perceiver's motivation to be accurate should be attenuated to some degree by the routine, taken-for-granted nature of such mundane, nonthreatening interactions (cf. Thomas & Fletcher, 1997; Thomas, Fletcher, & Lange, 1997). The level of empathic accuracy displayed by perceivers in nonthreatening interactions should therefore be moderate to moderately high rather than high (see the lower right portion of figure 11.1). Finally, the levels of relationship satisfaction and stability should correlate positively with the level of empathic accuracy in these nonthreatening situations, consistent with the rule that, in general, *motivated accuracy is good for relationships*. These positive correlations may be small, however, because they are likely to be attenuated by the truncated ranges of both the empathic accuracy and the relationship-outcome variables in most nonthreatening interaction contexts.

Empathic accuracy in threatening contexts. Inevitably, perceivers will at times encounter situations in which "danger zones" are anticipated – situations that might destabilize their close relationships (see the left-hand portion of figure 11.1). When these situations arise, the model predicts that the perceiver's first impulse should be to avoid or escape from them if it is possible to do so. The strategy of avoiding or escaping from danger-zone situations is the first "line of defense" that perceivers can use to manage their empathic accuracy and keep themselves from having to confront their partners' relationship-threatening thoughts and feelings.

The use of this strategy presumes, of course, that perceivers can recognize – and even anticipate – potential "danger zone" areas in their relationships, that is, the areas in which painful insights or revelations about their partners' private thoughts and feelings might occur (e.g., positive feelings about old flames or lustful thoughts about other attractive people). Over time, perceivers in most (but not all) relationships should learn to identify and avoid such danger-zone areas in order to protect their own self-esteem, their partners' self-esteem, and their positive views of the relationship. In doing so, perceivers can avoid dealing with danger-zone topics directly, acting as if it is better (and easier) to avoid confronting one's worst fears than it is to have one's worst fears confirmed and then be forced to deal with them.

Avoiding or escaping danger-zone issues is not always possible, however, and the section of our model that is relevant to these cases is depicted in the left and middle portions of figure 11.1. When perceivers feel obliged to remain in a relationship-threatening situation, the model predicts that their second "line of defense" should be *motivated inaccuracy* – a conscious or unconscious failure to accurately infer the specific content of their partner's potentially hurtful thoughts and feelings. The success of this strategy should vary, however, depending on the degree to which the inferred content of the partner's potentially distressing thoughts and feelings is perceived to be ambiguous versus unambiguous.

If the content of the partners' potentially threatening thoughts and feelings is perceived as ambiguous (see the left-hand portion of figure 11.1), perceivers should be free to use motivated inaccuracy as a defense. By using subception and other defense mechanisms (e.g., denial, repression, rationalization) to avoid having to deal with the most threatening implications of their partners' potentially destructive thoughts and feelings, perceivers should display low levels of empathic accuracy. Their perceptual-inferential defenses should provide them with an important payoff, however, in helping to minimize their personal and relational distress, and in helping to keep their relationship stable. Thus, the left-hand portion of our model illustrates the "first exception to the rule" – that *sometimes motivated inaccuracy helps relationships.*

What happens when perceivers feel obliged to remain in a relationship-threatening situation but are precluded from using motivated inaccuracy as a secondary strategy for warding off relationship threat? The middle portion of figure 11.1 depicts one case of this type. In this case, the relationship-threatening content of the partner's thoughts and feelings is perceived to be clear and unambiguous (e.g., the partner openly admits that s/he loves someone else). The sheer clarity of this information should force the perceiver to achieve at least moderately high levels of empathic accuracy, accompanied by very low relationship satisfaction and stability. Obviously, this case is one in which increased empathic accuracy hurts relationships. However, because the perceiver is forced to be accurate by virtue of the clarity of the available information, it does not illustrate a case in which true *motivated accuracy* hurts relationships.

Such a case should occur, however, if the perceiver has a strong personal need to confront the truth about the partner's relationship-relevant thoughts and feelings. We were first alerted to such a case when we discovered that the more anxiously attached dating partners in the Simpson et al. (1995) study displayed motivated accuracy, rather than motivated *in*accuracy, in response to relationship threat (Simpson et al., 1999). This finding suggests that a strong, dispositionally based accuracy motive can override such tendencies as avoiding danger-zone situations or using motivated inaccuracy to ward off their threatening implications. Preliminary evidence that motivated accuracy can hurt relationships in cases like this has already been presented in our review of the findings of Simpson et al. (1999). These findings can be used to illustrate the second exception to the rule, i.e., that *sometimes motivated accuracy hurts relationships*.

Toward a revised empathic accuracy model

How should our empathic accuracy model be revised to take such individual differences in accuracy motives into account? We think that, at each level of the model, two individual difference factors should be considered. The first factor concerns how much threat each partner experiences in the situation at hand. To some extent, this factor is already represented explicitly in the figure 11.1 version of the model, although it is treated as a within-individual variable rather than as a within-dyad variable.

The second factor, yet to be included in the model, concerns the strength of each partner's accuracy motive. If figure 11.1 were revised to include only this second factor (ignoring the first factor for the moment to simplify things), the resulting predictions would reflect an overall main effect of the within-dyad difference in the partners' accuracy motives on their ability to accurately read each other's thoughts and feelings (that is, in general, the partner with the stronger accuracy motive should display the higher level of empathic accuracy).

With regard to the right-hand portion of the figure 11.1 model, we would predict that, in mundane, nonthreatening situations, the partner with the stronger accuracy motive should be more empathically accurate than the partner with the weaker accuracy motive. Moreover, because greater accuracy should enhance relationship quality in such situations, strong accuracy motives exhibited by one or both partners should generally lead to greater relationship stability and satisfaction. We should note, however, that as partners become increasingly "mismatched" in their accuracy motives (i.e., when one partner's accuracy motive is very high and the other's is very low), additional dynamics may emerge that complicate the prediction of individual and relational outcomes in this case (for evidence suggesting such dynamics, see Ickes, 1993; Simpson et al., 1995; Stinson & Ickes, 1992).

With regard to the left and middle portions of figure 11.1, differences in the strength of the partners' accuracy motives should lead them down different "paths" in the model. At the second branching point near the top of the model, the partner with the weaker accuracy motive should be more likely to avoid or escape the relationship-threatening situation, whereas the partner with the stronger accuracy motive should be more likely to confront it directly.

If escape/avoidance is either not possible or not chosen (see the next level of the figure 11.1 model), the partner with the weaker accuracy motive should be more likely to use motivated inaccuracy to evade the impending threat when the partner's thoughts and feelings are perceived to be ambiguous, but should be forced to make at least moderately accurate inferences when they are perceived to be clear and unambiguous. In contrast, the other partner's stronger accuracy motive should be more likely to counter or even override the tendency to use motivated inaccuracy, resulting in relatively higher levels of empathic accuracy in both the ambiguous and the unambiguous conditions.

Given these predictions, it should be evident that partners with weak accuracy motives can minimize the threat to their relationships by taking either of the two paths in the model (avoidance/escape or motivated inaccuracy) that are not available to partners with strong accuracy motives. In contrast, partners with strong accuracy motives must directly confront these threats, which they should find difficult to avoid or escape.

Let us now summarize the implications of *both* of the within-dyad differences that we have just considered (i.e., level of perceived threat and accuracy motivation) for the processes depicted in the left and middle portions of the model in figure 11.1. Occasionally, a situation will arise that evokes an initial feeling of threat in the perceiver. This feeling should be based on the conscious or unconscious perception that the unfolding situation might present a danger-zone issue that could potentially threaten the relationship. The strength of this initial feeling should vary substantially, however, depending on (1) the degree to which the perceiver is anxious (i.e., easily threatened) in a dispositional sense, and (2) the strength of the perceiver's accuracy motivation.

Highly threatened perceivers with weak accuracy motives should be the most likely to avoid or exit potentially relationship-threatening situations. In contrast, highly threatened perceivers with strong accuracy motives (e.g., the highly anxious women in the Simpson et al., 1999, study) should be highly *ambivalent*. On the one hand, they should find these situations so threatening that they would ideally prefer to leave them, if they could; on the other hand, their level of accuracy motivation is so high that it tends to override their anxiety and compels them to remain in the situation and confront their "worst fears." Weakly threatened perceivers, regardless of whether their accuracy motives are weak or strong, should also be inclined to stay in relationship-threatening situations. Their responses are likely to diverge not at this point but at the *next* branching point of the model, as we shall see below.

As the situation unfolds, the perceiver's feeling of threat should increasingly reflect the degree to which the developing situation has either clarified the presence of a danger-zone issue (in the unambiguous case) or has failed to clarify its presence (in the ambiguous case). If highly threatened perceivers with weak accuracy motives have not already avoided or escaped from the situation, but have remained in it instead (perhaps because of strong situational constraints), they should follow the path of motivated inaccuracy in the ambiguous case and display only moderate accuracy in the unambiguous case. In contrast, highly threatened perceivers with strong accuracy motives should eschew the path of motivated inaccuracy and display higher levels of empathic accuracy in both cases, but particularly when the potential for threat is unambiguous.

How should weakly threatened perceivers react at this "level" of the model? Weakly threatened perceivers with weak accuracy motives should be more likely to follow the path of motivated accuracy than should weakly threatened perceivers with strong accuracy motives. However, this difference should be less extreme than that observed in these perceivers' more highly threatened counterparts.

Assessing the strength of perceivers' accuracy motives

If perceivers' levels of threat can be measured by a self-report index such as that used by Simpson et al. (1995), how might the strength of their accuracy motives be assessed? To some extent, perceived threat and accuracy motivation may be naturally confounded in relationship-threatening situations, according to the findings of Simpson et al. (1999). Their data suggest that such confounding might be particularly evident in highly anxious women, who appeared to have an exceptionally strong need to accurately infer their partner's thoughts and feelings in the relationship-threatening situation that Simpson et al. (1995) created.

From the standpoint of attachment theory (Bowlby, 1973; Cassidy & Berlin, 1994), this confounding of perceived threat and accuracy motivation makes sense in the case of anxiously attached individuals. Attachment theory proposes that highly anxious individuals are chronically uncertain about the availability and dependability of their relationship partners (Bowlby, 1973). They are chronically worried about the possibility of losing their partners/relationships, and are therefore motivated to monitor their partners closely – a phenomenon that Cassidy and Berlin (1994) have characterized as *hypervigilance* (see also Kobak & Sceery, 1988; Mikulincer, Florian, & Weller, 1993).

These considerations suggest that, to the extent that perceived threat and accuracy motivation are naturally confounded for anxiously attached individuals, perceivers' scores on the anxiety attachment dimension might be used as a single proxy measure that captures the combined influence of both variables. On the other hand, because the natural confounding of perceived threat and accuracy motivation might prove to be relatively limited (e.g., applying primarily to anxiously attached women in relationship-threatening situations), it might be a serious conceptual mistake to assume any general tendency for these two factors to covary. The best strategy, therefore, would be to obtain separate measures of perceived threat and accuracy motivation so that predictions of the type we have outlined above could be tested more impartially.

This strategy would require us to complement our existing measure of perceived threat with one or more new measures specifically designed to assess the strength of individuals' accuracy motives. We are currently pursuing this strategy, which has forced us to confront an important question: Should the accuracy motive be measured at a global level (i.e., generalizing across all types of relationship partners and all categories of their thought/feeling content), or should it be measured in a more differentiated way (i.e., assessing the strength of the accuracy motive for specific categories of relationship partners and/or their thought/feeling content)?

We would expect, for example, that the strength of the motive to accurately infer a partner's *relationship-threatening* thoughts and feelings would be especially relevant to the paths in the left and center portions of the model depicted in figure 11.1. This expectation has led us to develop the MARTI (*Motive to Acquire/Avoid Relationship-Threatening Information*) scale – a self-report measure that assesses the strength of perceivers' motives to apprehend versus avoid their partners' relationship-threatening thoughts and feelings in dating or marital relationships. Two research investigations using the MARTI scale with samples of dating couples are currently in progress.

Managing Empathic Accuracy in Close Relationships

Given the importance of controlling what one knows and does *not* know about a partner's thoughts and feelings, how should individuals deal with the delicate problem of "managing" their level of empathic accuracy in their close relationships? Any attempt to answer this question must begin by acknowledging that relationship partners have multiple – and sometimes competing – goals in their interactions (Sillars, 1998). When the goal of achieving a good understanding of a partner's thoughts and feelings does not compromise the goal of protecting the relationship from threatening information, empathic understanding should remain relatively high. However, when these goals clash, the first goal (achieving better understanding) may often be sacrificed for the sake of the second one (sheltering relationship partners from painful insights or revelations that could damage their relationship).

Because the relative strength of these two goals cannot be assessed at each branching point in our model without interfering with the very processes we are attempting to predict, our model relies on the use of less proximal predictors. We assume that perceivers' strategies for dealing with both relationship-threatening and nonthreatening situations are guided by the combined influences of relevant situational factors (e.g., whether perceivers think their partner may be having relationship-threatening thoughts or feelings and the ambiguity of the evidence on which this belief is based), and relevant dispositional factors (i.e., their level of relational anxiety and their accuracy motivation).

We suggest that the dispositional factors will influence partners' perceptions at each of the branching points in our model – affecting, for example, the degree to which certain people (e.g., anxiously attached individuals) are prone to infer that their partner might be having damaging thoughts or feelings, "find" evidence supporting these concerns, and therefore feel threatened. Because such dispositions can color and constrain individuals' perceptions through the entire course of a given interaction, it may often be unclear whether the management of empathic accuracy is more strongly governed by situational or by dispositional influences. This blurring of situational and dispositional influences should be especially characteristic of highly anxious individuals, who are chronically predisposed to expect and find the worst in relationship-threatening settings (Bowlby, 1973; Simpson & Rholes, 1994). It may also characterize individuals who are more emotionally invested in their relationship than their partners are (i.e., the "strong-link" partner in each relationship: see Ickes & Simpson, 1997).

Relational implications of motivated inaccuracy and motivated accuracy

Our model has several implications for how the management of empathic accuracy should affect the quality and functioning of relationships, both in the short term and over a longer period of time. In this section, we speculate about how the two "exceptions" to the general rule should affect both short-term and long-term relationship outcomes. We further suggest how certain dyad-level effects (such as the degree of discrepancy between partners' levels of empathic accuracy) may also effect their long-term relational outcomes. Finally, we consider the possible consequences for the partners' relationship of (1) treating "exception-to-the-rule" situations as if they were "general rule" cases and (2) treating "general rule" situations as if they were "exception-to-the-rule" cases.

Implications of motivated inaccuracy. For individuals who "turn a blind eye" to their partners' potentially distressing thoughts and feelings in relationship-threatening situations, motivated inaccuracy should help to maintain the stability of their relationships in the short term, especially if the threats they "ignore" are temporary, beyond their control, or not likely to reoccur. However, when the threats they ignore involve important, recurrent problems in the relationship, motivated inaccuracy should become an increasingly less effective strategy, particularly if problems that could be resolved are allowed to grow or worsen. Over time, partners who fail to address and solve their chronic problems should experience increased personal and relational distress, ultimately resulting in greater relationship instability.

From this perspective, motivated inaccuracy is best employed as a "stopgap" defensive strategy, freeing individuals from having to ponder and worry about the implications of relational threats that are temporary or largely beyond their control. But when motivated inaccuracy is repeatedly used to avoid or circumvent recurrent, solvable problems, it should have pernicious and damaging long-term effects on most relationships.

Implications of motivated accuracy. For individuals who cannot "turn a blind eye" to what their partners might be thinking and feeling in relationship-threatening situations, the heightened empathic accuracy they experience should have destabilizing effects on their relationships, particularly in the short term. Acute empathic accuracy in these situations may reflect the operation of substantive information processing (Forgas, 1995), which occurs when individuals are motivated to engage in active, on-line processing in order to observe and interpret the behavior of others very carefully. Substantive processing tends to be elicited when interactions are personally relevant or ambiguous, and when individuals have a strong need to understand what is happening at the moment (see Forgas, 1995). Persons engaged in substantive processing typically think about both new (current) and old (former) information relevant to their interaction partners, and their current emotional states (either positive or negative) are more likely to infuse the judgments and inferences they make about their partners and related events.

Highly anxious individuals may automatically shift to this mode of information processing in relationship-threatening situations, particularly those that might portend relationship loss. This would explain why, in many relationship-threatening contexts, highly anxious individuals (1) become hypervigilant (Mikulincer et al., 1993; Simpson et al., 1999), (2) allow old and often irrelevant relationship issues to invade current discussions with their partners (Simpson et al., 1996), and (3) base their judgments of their partners and relationships on their current emotional states (Tidwell, Reis, & Shaver, 1996). Over time, the tendency to "infer the worst" about what one's partner might be thinking or feeling should produce distrust and suspicion in relationships. This process could explain why highly anxious individuals experience higher rates of relationship dissolution than less anxious individuals do (Kirkpatrick & Davis, 1994; Simpson et al., 1999).

Empathic accuracy over time within relationships

Recent research using conflict resolution tasks indicates that empathic accuracy decreases over the first few years of marriage (e.g., Thomas & Fletcher, 1997; Thomas, Fletcher, & Lange, 1997). A number of factors might help to explain this trend. First, partners in newly formed relationships are probably more motivated to track each other's changing thoughts and feelings by listening to each other carefully, making frequent eye contact, and monitoring the changes in each other's facial expressions and body language. This motivation could reflect the newlyweds' tendency to dote on each other, their desire to get to know each other as well as possible, or their desire to avoid offending each other during the early stages of adjusting to their new life together (Bissonnette et al., 1997; Thomas & Fletcher, 1997). Second, because they have probably not yet settled into familiar interdependent routines (Kelley & Thibaut, 1978), partners in newly formed relationships should approach many recurring interactions as if they were novel ones, at least until they discover ways to maximize their joint reward/cost outcomes (Rusbult & Arriaga, 1997). Third, because they are less certain about how their partners are likely to think, feel, and react in various situations, newlywed partners may be more careful to avoid using premature stereotypes of what their partner is "like" to guide their empathic inferences.

As time passes, the degree of disparity in the partners' general levels of empathic accuracy should play an increasingly important role in their relationship. If one partner consistently understands the other partner well but feels poorly understood in return, the relationship should have a greater potential to become unstable than if both partners are evenly matched in their levels of empathic accuracy (see Ickes, 1993; Simpson et al., 1995; Stinson & Ickes, 1992, for supportive evidence). Glaring, persistent inequities in feeling understood by one's partner could generate increasing feelings of resentment in the more accurate (i.e., the more misunderstood) partner, whereas feeling vulnerable to exploitation by the more accurate partner could generate increasing feelings of resentment in the less accurate (i.e., the better understood) partner. Pronounced asymmetries in the partners' levels of understanding may also signify a flawed intersubjectivity in their relationship – an inability of the partners to bring their individual understandings into synchrony with each other in their day-to-day interactions. For all of these reasons, partners who have "mismatched" levels of empathic accuracy may be at higher risk than more "evenly matched" partners of experiencing greater relational instability over time.

Misapplications of the general rule and its exceptions

In this chapter, we have reviewed the research evidence relevant to a general rule (that motivated accuracy helps relationships) and its two exceptions (that motivated *in*accuracy sometimes helps relationships, and that motivated accuracy sometimes hurts them). What happens when individuals "misapply" either the general rule or its two major exceptions? More specifically, what happens when individuals apply the general rule in situations in which invoking one of the exceptions would be more appropriate? And what happens when individuals apply one of the exceptions when subscribing to the general rule would be more appropriate?

Misapplying the general rule when motivated inaccuracy is the more appropriate response can have potentially devastating consequences for close relationships. Partners who, out of misplaced idealism or naïveté, believe that they should always have free and total access to each other's thoughts and feelings may repeatedly insist on knowing things about each other's private experiences that they might be better off not knowing. By failing to overlook danger-zone issues that are temporary, uncontrollable, and otherwise inconsequential, perceivers may repeatedly make mountains out of molehills, and thereby experience considerable personal and relational distress. On the other hand, if the danger-zone topics involve long-standing, recurrent, and potentially resolvable issues, misapplying the general rule could yield positive long-term outcomes. By providing opportunities for perceivers to finally understand how their partners *really* think and feel about such issues, individuals may come to realize – perhaps for the very first time – that these issues can indeed be resolved. This understanding may, in turn, motivate them to address such issues directly and eventually solve the underlying problems, thereby eliminating the need for motivated inaccuracy to "contain" the danger-zone topic in future interactions.

Mistakenly employing a motivated inaccuracy strategy (the first exception to the rule) in cases when the general rule ought to be followed can also have negative consequences for relationships, particularly if danger-zone issues are recurrent and can be resolved. Besides failing to see and potentially solve these chronic problems, individuals who display motivated inaccuracy when general accuracy should prevail are likely to (1) experience larger disparities in empathic accuracy relative to their partners, and (2) offend or upset their partners by not showing proper empathy and understanding in situations that the partner correctly views as mundane and nonthreatening. These deleterious effects have their origin in dyad-level processes that are triggered by the negative attributions that a perceiver's *partner* makes for the perceiver's apparent lack of empathy and understanding in situations in which the partner justifiably expects more of both.

At first glance, it might appear that adopting a motivated accuracy orientation when the general rule should be applied can never be an inappropriate response, because the consequence in both cases is apparently the same – enhanced empathic accuracy. An excessively high level of empathic accuracy that is motivated by anxiety can be problematic and inappropriate, however, when hypervigilance leads individuals to focus narrowly on, ruminate about, and reach exaggerated, overly generalized conclusions about the nature of their partner's relationship-threatening thoughts and feelings. By basing their subsequent behaviors on such exaggerated and overly generalized inferences, hypervigilant perceivers might engender negative relationship outcomes that would *not* have occurred if the more general "mundane accuracy" rule had governed their behavior. If hyperviligance leads perceivers to search for evidence that might validate their "worst case" fears and concerns each time a danger-zone issue arises, their resulting suspicion – and their partners' awareness of it – could engender a pattern of reciprocated suspicion and hypervigilance laden with strong negative affect (cf. Forgas, 1995). As this process escalates in its intensity, it should amplify both partners' personal and relational distress, lead them to seriously question the quality and viability of their relationship, and engender increased relational instability. Ironically, then, "too much" accuracy can create problems in situations in which a more mundane level of accuracy is appropriate.

Final note

There is an old bromide which holds that greater understanding is a sovereign cure for the various ills that plague close relationships. As we have seen, however, this bromide is not – as it purports to be – an all-purpose panacea. In fact, in some circumstances it is a prescription for disaster.

In this chapter, we have tried to specify the general conditions in which motivated accuracy can help relationships and the exception-to-the rule conditions in which motivated *in*accuracy can help relationships and in which excessive (hypervigilant) accuracy can hurt them. Although relationship partners typically seek to understand the "truth" about each other's thoughts and feelings, there are occasions when the truth can carry a very big price. Knowing when to pay this price, and when to avoid paying it, may be the beginning of wisdom for the partners in close relationships.

ACKNOWLEDGMENT

The preparation of this chapter was supported in part by National Science Foundation grant no. SBR 9732476 to the authors.

REFERENCES

Aldous, J. (1977). Family interaction patterns. *Annual Review of Sociology, 3*, 105–135.

Barry, W. A. (1970). Marriage research and conflict: An integrative review. *Psychological Bulletin, 73*, 41–54.

Berger, C. R. (1993). Goals, plans, and mutual understanding in relationships. In S. Duck (Ed.), *Individuals in relationships* (pp. 30–59). Newbury Park, CA: Sage.

Bissonnette, V., Rusbult, C., & Kilpatrick, S. D. (1997). Empathic accuracy and marital conflict resolution. In W. Ickes (Ed.), *Empathic accuracy* (pp. 251–281). New York: Guilford Press.

Bowlby, J. (1973). *Attachment and loss*, vol. 2: *Separation: Anxiety and anger.* New York: Basic Books.

Buss, D. M., Shackelford, T. K., Kirkpatrick, L. A., Choe, J. C., Lim, H. K., Hasegawa, M., Hasegawa, T., & Bennett, K. (1999). Jealousy and the nature of beliefs about infidelity: Tests of competing hypotheses about sex differences in the United States, Korea, and Japan. *Personal Relationships, 6*, 125–150.

Cassidy, J., & Berlin, L. J. (1994). The insecure/ambivalent pattern of attachment: Theory and research. *Child Development, 65*, 971–991.

Christensen, L., & Wallace, L. (1976). Perceptual accuracy as a variable in marital adjustment. *Journal of Sex and Marital Therapy, 2*, 130–136.

Corsini, R. J. (1956). Understanding and similarity in marriage. *Journal of Abnormal and Social Psychology, 52*, 327–332.

Dymond, R. (1954). Interpersonal perception and marital happiness. *Canadian Journal of Psychology*, 8, 164–171.

Ferguson, L. R., & Allen, D. R. (1978). Congruence of parental perception, marital satisfaction, and child adjustment. *Journal of Consulting and Clinical Psychology*, 46, 345–346.

Forgas, J. (1995). Mood and judgment: The affect infusion model (AIM). *Psychological Bulletin*, 116, 39–66.

Gottman, J. M., Notarius, C., Markman, H., Bank, S., Yoppi, B., & Rubin, M. E. (1976). Behavior exchange theory and marital decision making. *Journal of Personality and Social Psychology*, 34, 14–23.

Gottman, J. M., & Porterfield, A. L. (1981). Communicative competence in the nonverbal behavior of married couples. *Journal of Marriage and the Family*, 43, 817–824.

Guthrie, D. M., & Noller, P. (1988). Married couples' perceptions of one another in emotional situations. In P. Noller & M. A. Fitzpatrick (Eds.), *Perspectives on marital interaction* (pp. 153–181). Cleveland, OH: Multilingual Matters.

Ickes, W. (1993). Empathic accuracy. *Journal of Personality*, 61, 587–610.

Ickes, W., Bissonnette, V., Garcia, S., & Stinson, L. (1990). Implementing and using the dyadic interaction paradigm. In C. Hendrick & M. Clark (Eds.), *Review of personality and social psychology: Research methods in personality and social psychology* (Vol. 11, pp. 16–44). Newbury Park, CA: Sage.

Ickes, W., & Simpson, J. A. (1997). Managing empathic accuracy in close relationships. In W. Ickes (Ed.), *Empathic accuracy* (pp. 218–250). New York: Guilford Press.

Ickes, W., Stinson, L., Bissonnette, V., & Garcia, S. (1990). Naturalistic social cognition: Empathic accuracy in mixed-sex dyads. *Journal of Personality and Social Psychology*, 59, 730–742.

Kahn, M. (1970). Nonverbal communication and marital satisfaction. *Family Process*, 9, 449–456.

Katz, M. (1965). Agreement on connotative meaning in marriage. *Family Process*, 5, 64–74.

Kelley, H. H., & Thibaut, J. W. (1978). Interpersonal relations: A theory of interdependence. New York: Wiley.

Kilpatrick, S. D., Bissonnette, V. L., & Rusbult, C. E. (1999). *Empathic accuracy among newly married couples*. Manuscript submitted for publication.

Kirkpatrick, L. A., & Davis, K. E. (1994). Attachment style, gender, and relationship stability: A longitudinal analysis. *Journal of Personality and Social Psychology*, 66, 502–512.

Knudson, R. A., Sommers, A. A., & Golding, S. L. (1980). Interpersonal perception and mode of resolution in marital conflict. *Journal of Personality and Social Psychology*, 38, 251–263.

Kobak, R. R., & Sceery, A. (1988). Attachment in late adolescence: Working models, affect regulation, and representations of self and others. *Child Development*, 59, 135–146.

Kotlar, S. L. (1965). Middle-class marital role perceptions and marital adjustment. *Sociology and Social Research*, 49, 284–291.

Kursh, C. O. (1971). The benefits of poor communication. *Psychoanalytic Review*, 58, 189–208.

Laing, R. D., Phillipson, H., & Lee, A. R. (1966). *Interpersonal perception: A theory and a method of research*. New York: Springer.

Levinger, G., & Breedlove, J. (1966). Interpersonal attraction and agreement. *Journal of Personality and Social Psychology*, 3, 367–372.

Luckey, E. B. (1960). Number of years married as related to personality perception and marital satisfaction. *Journal of Marriage and the Family*, 28, 44–48.

Madden, M. E., & Janoff-Bulman, R. (1981). Blame, control, and marital satisfaction: Wives' attributions for conflict in marriage. *Journal of Marriage and the Family*, 43, 663–674.

Mikulincer, M., Florian, V., & Weller, A. (1993). Attachment styles, coping strategies, and posttraumatic psychological distress: The impact of the Gulf War in Israel. *Journal of Personality and Social Psychology*, 64, 817–826.

Murstein, B. I., & Beck, G. D. (1972). Person perception, marriage adjustment, and social desirability. *Journal of Consulting and Clinical Psychology, 39*, 396–403.

Navran, L. (1967). Communication and adjustment in marriage. *Family Process, 6*, 173–184.

Neimeyer, G. J., & Banikiotes, P. G. (1981). Self-disclosure flexibility, empathy, and perceptions of adjustment and attraction. *Journal of Counseling Psychology, 28*, 272–275.

Newmark, C. S., Woody, G., & Ziff, D. (1977). Understanding and similarity in relation to marital satisfaction. *Journal of Clinical Psychology, 33*, 83–86.

Noller, P. (1980). Misunderstandings in marital communication: A study of couples' nonverbal communication. *Journal of Personality and Social Psychology, 39*, 1135–1148.

Noller, P. (1981). Gender and marital adjustment level differences in decoding messages from spouses and strangers. *Journal of Personality and Social Psychology, 41*, 272–278.

Noller, P. (1984). *Nonverbal communication and marital interaction.* Oxford: Pergamon.

Noller, P., & Ruzzene, M. (1991). Communication in marriage: The influence of affect and cognition. In G. J. O. Fletcher & F. D. Fincham (Eds.), *Cognition in close relationships* (pp. 203–233). Hillsdale, NJ: Erlbaum.

Noller, P., & Venardos, C. (1986). Communication awareness in married couples. *Journal of Social and Personal Relationships, 3*, 31–42.

Rausch, H. L., Barry, W. A., Hertel, R. K., & Swain, M. A. (1974). *Communication conflict and marriage.* San Francisco: Jossey-Bass.

Rusbult, C. E., & Arriaga, X. B. (1997). Interdependence processes in close relationships. In S. Duck et al. (Eds.), *Handbook of personal relationships: Theory, research, and interventions.* (2nd ed., pp. 221–250). Chichester, UK: Wiley.

Sillars, A. L. (1981). Attributions and interpersonal conflict resolution. In J. H. Harvey, W. J. Ickes, & R. F. Kidd (Eds.), *New directions in attribution research* (Vol. 3). Hillsdale, NJ: Erlbaum.

Sillars, A. L. (1985). Interpersonal perception in relationships. In W. Ickes (Ed.), *Compatible and incompatible relationships.* (pp. 277–305). New York: Springer-Verlag.

Sillars, A. L. (1998). (Mis)understanding. In B. H. Spitzberg and W. R. Cupach (Eds.), *The dark side of close relationships* (pp. 73–102). Mahwah, NJ: Erlbaum.

Sillars, A. L., & Parry, D. (1982). Stress, cognition, and communication in interpersonal conflicts. *Communication Research, 9*, 201–226.

Sillars, A. L., Pike, G. R., Jones, T. S., & Murphy, M. A. (1984). Communication and understanding in marriage. *Human Communication Research, 10*, 317–350.

Sillars, A. L., Pike, G. R., Jones, T. J., & Redmon, K. (1983). Communication and conflict in marriage. In K. Bostrom (Ed.), *Communication yearbook* (Vol. 7). Beverly Hills, CA: Sage.

Sillars, A. L., & Scott, M. D. (1983). Interpersonal perception between intimates: An integrative review. *Human Communication Research, 10*, 153–176.

Simpson, J. A., Ickes, W., & Blackstone, T. (1995). When the head protects the heart: Empathic accuracy in dating relationships. *Journal of Personality and Social Psychology, 69*, 629–641.

Simpson, J. A., Ickes, W., & Grich, J. (1999). When accuracy hurts: Reactions of anxiously-attached dating partners to a relationship-threatening situation. *Journal of Personality and Social Psychology, 76*, 754–769.

Simpson, J. A., & Rholes, W. S. (1994). Stress and secure base relationships in adulthood. In K. Bartholomew & D. Perlman (Eds.), *Advances in personal relationships: Vol. 5. Attachment processes in adulthood* (pp. 181–204). London: Kingsley.

Simpson, J. A., Rholes, W. S., & Phillips, D. (1996). Conflict in close relationships: An attachment perspective. *Journal of Personality and Social Psychology, 71*, 899–914.

Stinson, L., & Ickes, W. (1992). Empathic accuracy in the interactions of male friends versus male strangers. *Journal of Personality and Social Psychology, 62*, 787–797.

Stuckert, R. (1963). Role perception and marital satisfaction: A configuration approach. *Marriage and Family Living, 25,* 415–419.

Taylor, B. A. (1967). Role perception, empathy, and marriage adjustment. *Sociology and Social Research, 52,* 22–34.

Thomas, G., & Fletcher, G. J. O. (1997). Empathic accuracy in close relationships. In W. Ickes (Ed.), *Empathic accuracy* (pp. 194–217). New York: Guilford Press.

Thomas, G., Fletcher, G. J. O., & Lange, C. (1997). On-line empathic accuracy in marital interaction. *Journal of Personality and Social Psychology, 72,* 839–850.

Tidwell, M. O., Reis, H. T., & Shaver, P. R. (1996). Attachment, attractiveness, and social interaction: A diary study. *Journal of Personality and Social Psychology, 71,* 729–745.

Watzlawick, P., Weakland, J., & Fisch, R. (1974). *Principles of problem formation and problem resolution.* New York: Norton.

CHAPTER TWELVE

Helping and Altruism

John F. Dovidio and Louis A. Penner

Introduction

Prosocial behavior represents a broad category of actions that are "defined by society as generally beneficial to other people and to the ongoing political system" (Piliavin, Dovidio, Gaertner, & Clark, 1981, p. 4). This category includes a range of behaviors that are intended to benefit others, such as helping, sharing, cooperating, comforting, and donating to charity. The present chapter focuses on two subcategories of prosocial behavior: helping and altruism. We examine the nature of these concepts and review the current state of research on these topics. Specifically, we address three questions: When do people help? Why do people help? Who helps? (see also Batson, 1998; Piliavin & Charng, 1990; Schroeder, Penner, Dovidio, & Piliavin, 1995).

Helping and altruism defined

Helping and altruism are two fundamental types of prosocial behavior. *Helping* represents an intentional action that has the outcome of benefiting another person. Attempts to identify essential characteristics of helping have suggested several key dimensions involving, for example, the type of assistance needed and the potential consequences of helping and of not helping (McGuire, 1994; Pearce & Amato, 1980; Shotland & Huston, 1979).

Whereas the concept of helping concerns the outcomes of an action, the concept of *altruism* concerns the motivation underlying the behavior. Classic definitions in psychology (cf. Sober, 1988, 1992) have included internal motivation as a defining feature of altruistic helping. For example, altruism was defined as a special type of helping in which the benefactor provides aid to another person *without anticipation of rewards from external sources for providing assistance* (Macaulay & Berkowitz, 1970) while incurring some personal costs for taking this action (Krebs, 1982; Wispé, 1978). More recent perspectives have emphasized the importance of further distinguishing the different types of internal motivations involved in helping. For Batson (1991, 1998), altruism refers not to the prosocial act *per se* but to the underlying goal of the act: "Altruism is a motivational state with the ultimate goal of increasing another's welfare" (Batson, 1991, p. 6). In contrast, egoistic helping is motivated by the ultimate goal of improving one's own welfare.

When Do People Help?

Many of the earlier studies of when people help focused on nonemergency situations and thus considered helping to be guided by many of the same external factors (e.g., norms of reciprocity) and internal influences (e.g., need for social approval) as other forms of socially valued behaviors. By the mid-1960s, stimulated by dramatic incidents in the news about failures of bystanders to intervene to save the lives of others, empirical attention turned to emergency situations and to the relatively unique nature of helping behavior. Much of this research was shaped by the pioneering ideas reflected in Latané and Darley's (1970) decision model of bystander intervention.

A decision model of intervention

The Latané and Darley (1970) decision model of bystander intervention proposes that whether or not a person helps depends upon the outcomes of a series of prior decisions. Although the model was initially developed to understand how people respond in emergencies that require immediate assistance, aspects of the model have been successfully applied to many other situations, ranging from preventing someone from driving drunk to making a decision about whether to donate a kidney to a relative (Borgida, Conner, & Manteufel, 1992; Rabow, Newcomb, Monto, & Hernandez, 1990).

According to Latané and Darley, before a person initiates a helping response, that person goes through five decision-making steps. The person must: (1) notice that something is wrong, (2) define it as a situation that requires some sort of intervention, (3) decide whether to take personal responsibility, (4) decide what kind of help to give, and (5) decide to implement the chosen course of action. The decision made at any one step has important implications for the bystander's ultimate response – a "no" response at *any* step means the victim will not be helped.

With respect to the first step of the model, noticing the event, bystanders are more likely to notice events that are inherently more vivid and attention-getting. As a consequence, they are more likely to intervene. Beyond the characteristics of the potential helping situations themselves, aspects of the physical environment (e.g., noise; Mathews & Canon, 1975) and the social environment (e.g., population density; Levine, Martinez, Brase, & Sorenson, 1994) may influence whether people notice an event and respond in helpful ways. For example, in studies conducted in several different countries (e.g., the United States, the United Kingdom, Saudi Arabia, and Sudan) people in urban environments tend to be less helpful than residents in rural settings (Hedge & Yousif, 1992; Yousif & Korte, 1995). One explanation of this rural–urban difference is that in order to cope with stimulus overload (Milgram,

1970) urban residents restrict their attention mainly to personally relevant events. Strangers, and thus their situations of need, may therefore go unnoticed.

Another factor that may influence whether or not people notice that something is wrong is their mood or other transitory feelings or states. There is considerable evidence that when individuals are in a good mood, they are more likely to help (Salovey, Mayer, & Rosenhan, 1991) due, at least in part, to increased attentiveness to others (McMillen, Sanders, & Solomon, 1977). Pleasant environments, such as those with appealing aromas, also facilitate helping (Baron, 1997), mediated in part by positive mood. Conversely, environmental stressors usually have a negative impact on people's moods (Bell, Fisher, Baum, & Greene, 1996).

In terms of the second step of the model, one basic factor that can influence whether a situation, once noticed, is interpreted as a situation requiring assistance is the nature of the event itself. Across a range of studies, bystanders are more inclined to help victims who make their need clear with overt distress cues (e.g., screams) than victims in similar situations who do not scream (Piliavin et al., 1981). The social environment can also influence whether an event is interpreted as requiring help. When bystanders notice an event but the nature of the event is unclear, the reactions of other witnesses may shape their assessment of the situation. Thus, although the presence of others typically inhibits intervention (Latané, Nida, & Wilson, 1981), others' expressions of concern or alarm can facilitate helping (Wilson, 1976).

In the third step of Latané and Darley's model, once the need for assistance is determined, bystanders must decide who is responsible for helping. When a person is the only potential helper, the decision is obvious. In contrast, when a bystander believes that other people are also witnessing the event and that these other people can help, *diffusion of responsibility* may occur. That is, the belief that others will take action can relieve a bystander from assuming personal responsibility for intervention, because it can be reasoned that assistance is no longer necessary (Darley & Latané, 1968; Otten, Penner, & Waugh, 1988). Diffusion of responsibility thus does not occur when the other bystanders are believed to be incapable of intervening (Korte, 1969). It is more likely to occur when personal danger is involved in helping, when other witnesses are perceived as better able to help, and when norms permit or support it (Dovidio, Piliavin, Gaertner, Schroeder, & Clark, 1991; Piliavin et al., 1981).

Whereas the first three steps of the Latané and Darley model have received careful empirical scrutiny and support, the fourth and fifth steps, deciding what to do and implementing the chosen course of action have not been the focus of substantial research. Nevertheless, the work that does exist is generally supportive. People with first aid training, for instance, offer more medically effective help than do people without relevant training (Shotland & Heinold, 1985).

Overall, the Latané and Darley decision model of intervention provides a valuable broad framework for understanding when bystanders will or will not help others in need. The next model to be considered allows a more detailed analysis of how the nature of the situation and characteristics of the victim influence helping.

A cost–reward framework

A cost–reward analysis of helping assumes an economic view of human behavior – people are motivated to maximize their rewards and to minimize their costs (Piliavin et al., 1981). From this perspective, people are relatively rational and mainly concerned about their self-interest. In a potential helping situation, a person analyzes the circumstances, weighs the probable costs and rewards of alternative courses of action and then arrives at a decision that will result in the best personal outcome. There are two categories of costs and rewards: those for helping, and those for *not* helping. Costs for helping can involve effort and time, danger, embarrassment, and disruption of ongoing activities. Costs for not helping include feelings of guilt or shame and public censure. Rewards for helping may include money, fame, self-praise, avoidance of guilt, thanks from the victim, and the intrinsic pleasure derived from having helped. Current research is consistent with the central tenet of the cost–reward approach. Situational factors that decrease the net costs (costs minus rewards) for helping or increase the costs for not helping facilitate intervention (Dovidio et al., 1991).

The cost–reward perspective also assumes that both the negative values attached to costs and the positive values associated with rewards are subjective ones. They are influenced by factors such as characteristics of the person in need, the nature of the relationship between that person and a potential benefactor, and the personal attributes of a potential benefactor. For example, costs for not helping are perceived as lower when the person is seen as responsible for his or her plight (e.g., due to immoral actions) than when the cause is beyond the person's control (e.g., illness; Otten et al., 1988). Physical attractiveness and interpersonal attraction may promote helping because they increase potential rewards associated with opportunities to initiate a relationship. More positive attitudes towards and feelings for a person in need also may increase costs for not helping (e.g., stronger feelings of guilt), decrease costs for helping (e.g., less anxiety about how the person will respond to help), or increase rewards for helping (e.g., more value associated with the recipient's gratitude) – and thereby increase helping. For instance, people who desire a communal relationship with another person experience elevated positive affect when they choose or even are required to help that person. In contrast, those who do not desire a relationship react with negative affect when they are required to help (Williamson & Clark, 1992). Finally, studies of individuals dispositionally inclined to act prosocially provide indirect and direct evidence that these people estimate the costs of such interventions as lower than do individuals not so inclined (Colby & Damon, 1992; Oliner & Oliner, 1992; Penner & Fritzsche, 1993; also see the later section of this chapter, Who Helps? Dispositional Variables).

Similarity, in terms of dress style, nationality, personality, attitudes, and shared group membership or social identity is also positively associated with helping (Dovidio, 1984; Dovidio et al., 1997). Although the general tendency to help members of one's own group more than members of other groups occurs cross-culturally, the effect is stronger in collectivist societies (e.g., Japan and China) than in individualistic cultures (e.g., the United States; see Moghaddam, Taylor, & Wright, 1993). One reason that similarity promotes helping in general is that it leads to interpersonal attraction (Byrne, 1971), which can increase costs for not helping and rewards for helping (Williamson & Clark, 1992). In addition, people who are seen as dissimilar are typically perceived as unpredictable, holding different beliefs and values, and threatening. From a cost-reward perspective, therefore, the benefits for helping a similar other are higher and the costs are lower.

Whereas positive attitudes promote helping, negative attitudes can decrease it. Stigmatized persons are typically less likely to receive help than non-stigmatized persons (Edelmann,

Evans, Pegg, & Tremain, 1983; Walton et al., 1988). However, because negative social attitudes, such as racial prejudice, are themselves sanctioned and stigmatized, the effects of race on helping can be complex (Gaertner & Dovidio, 1986). Indeed, whereas some studies show that Whites are less likely to help African Americans than Whites, other studies demonstrate that Whites are as likely or are even more likely to help African Americans than Whites. Gaertner and Dovidio offered a framework to account for these seemingly contradictory results. Because discrimination violates current social norms and may violate most people's self-image of being fair, there are special costs associated with Whites discriminating against African Americans. As a consequence of these costs, Whites may help African Americans as often, and sometimes more often (Dutton & Lennox, 1974), than they help Whites in situations in which a failure to help could be interpreted as bias. However, when Whites can rationalize not helping on the basis of some factor *other* than race (as in the belief that someone else will help), their self-image is no longer threatened, these costs do not apply, and they are then less likely to help African Americans than Whites (e.g., Gaertner & Dovidio, 1977).

In general, then, helping is more likely to occur when the rewards for helping outweigh the costs. Nevertheless, because costs and rewards are subjectively determined, there is considerable individual variation in response to similar situations. In addition, costs and rewards are not necessarily weighed equivalently: costs are normally weighed more heavily (Dovidio et al., 1991). Under highly arousing conditions, because of a more narrow focus of attention, not all costs and rewards may be considered (Piliavin et al., 1981). In the next section, we examine the underlying psychological processes that can shape perceptions of costs and rewards and produce different motivations for helping.

Why Do People Help?

Approaches to the question of why people help have focused on three types of mechanisms: (1) learning, (2) arousal and affect, and (3) social and personal standards. The learning explanation applies general principles from learning theories to the acquisition of helping skills and of beliefs about why these skills should be used to benefit others. Arousal and affect theories focus on emotionally based motivations but generally share a guiding principle with learning theory that people are motivated to behave in ways that bring them some kind of reward – in this case, feeling better. However, there are some theorists who argue that under some very special circumstances people may be motivated by the primary goal of making another person feel better, by true altruism. Finally, there is the social and personal standards approach that considers how people's personal values can motivate helping by affecting both cognitive and affective processes.

Learned helpfulness

Two basic processes have been implicated in the application of learning theory to helping behavior: operant conditioning and social learning. Consistent with the principles of operant learning, people are more likely to help others when their previous helping responses have been positively reinforced (see Staub, 1979). Conversely, people may learn *not* to help others because helping has led to negative consequences (see Grusec, 1991; Staub, 1978).

Social learning, either through modeling or direct instruction, can also be an effective way to facilitate helping. Consistent with more general research on attitudes and behavior, the effectiveness of persuasion is related to the nature of the message and characteristics of the audience and the persuader. Social learning through observing models has both immediate and long-term effects on helping (see Grusec, 1981). Again consistent with general principles, the consequences to the model (e.g., positive, neutral, negative), characteristics of the model (e.g., status, attractiveness, similarity), and relationship between the observer and the model (e.g., attachment between a child and parent) mediate the influence of prosocial models. Furthermore, temporary states or moods, such as positive affect, that may increase the salience of positive, previously learned behaviors can increase the likelihood of helping (Isen, 1993; Salovey et al., 1991).

Parental models can have a strong and prolonged impact on helping. Fabes, Eisenberg, and Miller (1990) found that primary school girls who were sympathetic to children in distress had mothers who also were sympathetic in such situations, suggesting that the children were in part modeling their mothers' reactions. There is also an association between prosocial parental models and the behavior of their children in adulthood (Clary & Miller, 1986; Oliner & Oliner, 1988; Piliavin & Callero, 1991; Rosenhan, 1969).

The relationship between the nature of rewards and helpfulness, however, varies developmentally. According to Bar-Tal and Raviv's (1982) cognitive learning model, very young children are usually motivated by specific material rewards and punishments, older children are motivated by social approval, and adolescents are motivated by self-satisfaction and personal conviction. Similarly, the work of Eisenberg and her colleagues (Eisenberg et al., 1987; Eisenberg, Miller, Shell, McNalley, & Shea, 1991) suggests that prosocial moral reasoning proceeds developmentally. Preschool children engage mainly in hedonistic and self-centered moral reasoning, whereas older children demonstrate more sophisticated and other-oriented kinds of reasoning – and generally more helpfulness. Furthermore, Grusec (1991) suggests that reliance on direct or material rewards may undermine the internalization of helping tendencies for older children. Children who help in order to receive material rewards may be less likely to assist others when these rewards are unlikely (e.g., for anonymous help) and may be less likely to develop intrinsic motivations for helping (Fabes, Fultz, Eisenberg, May-Plumlee, & Christopher, 1989).

Arousal and affect

In addition to the cognitive processes involved in direct and vicarious learning, arousal and affect play important roles in helping and altruism. People are aroused by the distress of others (see Eisenberg & Fabes, 1991). This reaction appears even among very young children and occurs across cultures. In fact, this phenomenon is so strong and universal some researchers have proposed that empathic arousal, arousal generated vicariously by another person's distress, has a biological and evolutionary basis (Cunningham, 1985/6; Hoffman, 1990).

Empathy and emotion. Although most researchers agree that empathic arousal is important and fundamental in helping (see Dovidio, 1984), there is much less agreement about the nature of this emotion and how it actually motivates people to help. Empathic arousal may produce different emotions. In severe emergency situations, bystanders may become upset and distressed; in less critical, less intense problem situations, observers may feel sad (Cialdini, Schaller, et al., 1987), tense (Hornstein, 1982), or concerned and compassionate (Batson, 1991). How arousal is interpreted can shape the nature of prosocial motivation.

What determines the specific emotion that a person experiences in response to another's problem? Weiner (1980, 1986) suggests that another's need for help stimulates a search for causes by the observer. People seek to understand why the person needs assistance. The perceived causes are then analyzed (with attribution of responsibility and controllability being particularly important dimensions). These attributions, in turn, create an affective experience that motivates action. Weiner suggests, for example, that attribution to uncontrollable causes produces sympathy that motivates helping. Attribution to controllable causes may generate anger, which may inhibit helping. Thus, "attributions guide our feelings, but emotional reactions provide the motor and direction for behavior" (Weiner, 1980, p. 186).

The roles of empathy and emotional experience in prosocial motivation are the focus of several models of helping that rely on arousal and affect as primary motivational constructs underlying helping and altruism. Negative emotions, such as guilt, can be powerful motivators of helping. People are more likely to help others when they feel they have harmed these individuals in some way (Salovey et al., 1991). One explanation is that when people feel that they have unfairly harmed others, their self-esteem suffers. Therefore, they try to make amends. This image-reparation hypothesis suggests that by making a positive social response, people's self-esteem is restored and their self-image is repaired. It is also possible that simply anticipating guilt can motivate helping. That is, within relationships where help is normative – such as parent–child, romantic, or other types of communal relationships – people may offer assistance because they believe, probably through past experience, that they will feel guilty if they do not help. Such guilt is most strongly and commonly experienced in communal relationships (Baumeister, Stillwell, & Heatherton, 1994).

The notion that people are motivated to repair their self-images and avoid feelings of guilt for not helping when it is expected explains some but not all of the data on negative affect and helping. They cannot explain why people who simply witness a transgression against someone else also become more helpful. Cialdini and his colleagues have proposed a broader model, the *negative state relief model* (Cialdini, Kenrick, & Baumann, 1982; Cialdini et al., 1987) to explain such reactions.

Negative state relief model. According to the negative state relief model, harming another person or witnessing another person being harmed can produce negative feelings such as guilt or sadness. People who experience these negative states are then motivated to reduce them. Through socialization and experience, people learn that helping can serve as a secondary reinforcer (Williamson & Clark, 1989; Yinon & Landau, 1987); the good feelings derived from helping may therefore relieve their negative mood. Thus, negative moods such as guilt and sadness may motivate people to help because helping produces the reward of making them feel better. In contrast to the image-reparation hypothesis, the negative state relief model proposes that people are motivated primarily to feel good rather than to look good. In both theories, however, the motivation for helping is essentially egoistic. That is, the primary motive for helping another person is that helping improves the helper's own situation.

Three fundamental assumptions of the negative state relief model have received some support. The first assumption is that the negative state that motivates a person to help can originate from a variety of sources. Guilt from having personally harmed a person and sadness from simply observing another person's unfortunate situation, because they are negative experiences, can both motivate helping (Cialdini, Darby, & Vincent, 1973). More-over, these effects seem to motivate *helping* in response to requests in particular; negative moods do not increase compliance in general (Forgas, 1998). The second assumption is that other events besides helping may just as effectively make the person feel better, and exposure to these events can relieve the motivation to help caused by negative states. Consistent with this aspect of the model, if some other event that improves the potential helper's mood precedes the opportunity to help (e.g., receiving praise; Cialdini et al., 1973) or if the person anticipates a less costly way of improving their mood (e.g., listening to a comedy tape; Schaller & Cialdini, 1988), the potential helper is no longer particularly motivated to pro-vide assistance. A third assumption of this model is that negative moods motivate helping only if people believe that their moods can be improved by helping. Negative feelings will *not* promote helping if people are led to believe that these feelings cannot be relieved (Manucia, Baumann, & Cialdini, 1984) or if, as with younger children, the self-rewarding properties have not yet developed (Cialdini & Kenrick, 1976; Cialdini et al., 1982). (For a critique of the negative state relief model as an explanation of helping see Carlson & Miller, 1987.)

Arousal: cost–reward model.   Whereas the negative state relief model is based directly on principles of operant conditioning and on virtually the sole concern with one's own well-being, other affective models focus more on the assessment of and reaction to another person's problem, plight, or distress. Arousal is a central motivational concept in the Piliavin et al. (1981) *arousal: cost–reward model* (see also Dovidio et al., 1991). Arousal motivates a bystander to take action, and the cost–reward analysis shapes the direction that this action will take. Specifically, this model proposes that empathic arousal is generated by witnessing the distress of another person. When the bystander's empathic arousal is attributed to the other person's distress, it is emotionally experienced by the observer as unpleasant and the bystander is therefore motivated to reduce it. One normally efficient way of reducing this arousal is by helping to relieve the other's distress.

There is substantial evidence for the fundamental proposition of this model that people are emotionally responsive to the distress of others (see Fabes, Eisenberg, & Eisenbud, 1993). Adults and children not only report feeling empathy, but they also become physiologically aroused by the pain and suffering of others. Moreover, observers may not just feel bad about the pain or distress of another person, but they may also begin to experience what the other person is feeling (Vaughan & Lanzetta, 1980). Preschool children also spontaneously show signs of facial concern and physiological arousal at the distress of others (Fabes et al., 1993), and there is evidence that even one- and two-day-old infants will respond with crying to the distress of another infant (Sagi & Hoffman, 1976).

Also supportive of the arousal: cost–reward model, empathic arousal attributed to the other person's situation motivates helping. Facial, gestural, and vocal indications of empathically induced arousal, as well as self-reports of empathically induced anxiety, are consistently positively related to helping (see Dovidio et al., 1991; Eisenberg & Miller, 1987; Marks, Penner, & Stone, 1982). Consistent with the hypothesized importance of attributing this arousal to the other's situation, people are more likely to help when arousal from extraneous sources such as exercise (Sterling & Gaertner, 1984), erotic films (Mueller & Donnerstein, 1981), and aggressive films (Mueller, Donnerstein, & Hallam, 1983) are attributed to the immediate need of another person. People are less likely to help when arousal generated by witnessing another person's distress is associated with a different cause (e.g., misattributed to a pill; Gaertner & Dovidio, 1977). In addition, work by Eisenberg and her associates (e.g., Eisenberg & Fabes, 1998; Fabes et al., 1993) suggests that extreme empathic overarousal or the inability to regulate empathic arousal, which may interfere with the attribution process, can also reduce helpfulness.

Although the arousal: cost–reward model and the negative state relief model both posit egoistic motivations for helping, there are at least two important differences between them. First, attribution of arousal plays a central role in the arousal: cost–reward model; only arousal attributed to the plight of the other person will motivate helping. In contrast, the negative state relief model posits that, regardless of their attributed source, negative states (particularly guilt and sadness; see Cialdini et al., 1987) can motivate helping. The second major distinction between the two models concerns the goal of the help that is given. The arousal: cost–reward model is a tension-reduction model that assumes that the victim's need produces an arousal state in the potential benefactor and that the goal of the benefactor's intervention is to alleviate his or her own aversive state by eliminating the distress of the victim. According to the negative state relief model, however, people in negative moods are looking for ways to eliminate or neutralize their negative mood. Thus, any event that might improve the emotional state of the observer, including events that have nothing whatsoever to do with benefiting the person in distress, may serve this purpose equally well.

Empathy-altruism hypothesis. In contrast to egoistic models of helping, Batson and his colleagues (see Batson, 1991) present an *empathy-altruism hypothesis.* Although they acknowledge that egoistically motivated helping occurs, Batson and his colleagues argue that true altruism also exists. Altruism is defined as helping with the primary goal of improving the other person's welfare. Specifically, according to the empathy-altruism hypothesis, witnessing another person in need can produce a range of emotional experiences, such as sadness, personal distress (e.g., upset, worry), and empathic concern (e.g., sympathy, compassion). Whereas sadness and personal distress produce egoistic motivations to help, empathic concern creates altruistic motivation.

The primary mechanism in Batson's empathy-model is the emotional reaction to another person's problem. Batson suggests that under some circumstances, for example if there is a special bond between the potential helper and the person in need, it can elicit empathy or empathic concern, which he defines as "an other-oriented emotional response (e.g., sympathy, compassion) congruent with the . . . welfare of another person" (Batson & Oleson, 1991, p. 63). In contrast to sadness and personal distress which, as noted above, generate an egoistic desire to reduce one's own distress, Batson (1987, 1991) proposes that empathic concern produces an altruistic motivation to reduce the other person's distress. The altruistically motivated person will then help if (a) helping is possible, (b) helping is perceived to be ultimately beneficial to the person in need, and (c) helping personally will provide greater benefit to the person in need than would assistance from another person also able to offer it. Thus, empathic concern is hypothesized to produce greater concern for the welfare of the other person.

In numerous experiments, conducted over a 20-year period, Batson and his colleagues have produced impressive empirical support for the empathy-altruism hypothesis (Batson, 1991, 1998). Participants who experience relatively high levels of empathic concern (and who presumably are altruistically motivated) show high levels of helpfulness even when it is easy to avoid the other person's distress, when they can readily justify not helping, when helping is not apparently instrumental to improving the benefactor's own mood, and when mood-improving events occur prior to the helping opportunity (see Batson, 1991, 1998; Batson & Oleson, 1991). However, several researchers have proposed alternative explanations that challenge Batson's contention that helping may be altruistically motivated. The controversy surrounding the empathy-altruism hypothesis centers on *why* these effects occur.

The *empathy-specific punishment* explanation suggests that feeling empathic concern may generate additional costs for not helping that make these people likely to help even when helping requires moderate effort. From this perspective, the motivation that Batson and his colleagues described as altruistic may represent a subtle form of egoism based on the social costs associated with what *other* people's negative evaluations might be (Archer, 1984; Archer, Diaz-Loving, Gollwitzer, Davis, & Foushee, 1981) or *self-imposed* costs for violating one's personal standards (Schaller & Cialdini, 1988). However, inconsistent with these egoistic interpretations, evidence of altruistic motivation has been obtained even when social evaluation is not possible (Fultz, Batson, Fortenbach, McCarthy, & Varney, 1986); and when information is provided that gives them a reason for not helping that preserves their personal standards of behavior. For example, people who experience empathic concern still help after being told about the inaction of previous potential helpers or about people's general preference for a less helpful option (Batson, Dyck, et al., 1988, Study 2 & 3).

The *empathy-specific reward* interpretation, another alternative explanation for evidence of altruistic motivation, is closely related to the punishment explanations. It proposes that people help others because they expect a reward from the recipient, from others who observe the act, or from themselves. Several specific versions of this alternative egoistic explanation have been proposed and tested. One involves the desire to share in the other's joy – "empathic joy." Another concerns the helper's reactions to the relief of the other person's need.

The evidence with respect to empathic joy is mixed. In support of the egoistic perspective, Smith, Keating, and Stotland (1989) found that participants who were high in empathy helped more when they believed that they would learn of the consequences for helping than when they believed they would not. But in a subsequent study, Batson and his colleagues also varied the likelihood of learning about the consequences of helping and produced support for the empathy-altruism hypothesis (Batson, Batson, Slingsby, et al., 1991). Participants who experienced low levels of empathic concern and were presumably egoistically motivated were more likely to help when they believed they would learn of the benefits of their intervention, particularly when there was a high likelihood it would improve the other person's situation (and thus produce "empathic joy"). In contrast, those who reported high levels of empathic concern and were presumably altruistically motivated exhibited high levels of helping regardless of whether they would have the opportunity to experience "empathic joy." The desire to share in the other's joy, therefore, does not account for helping by these empathically-aroused participants. Overall, this version of the empathy-specific reward explanation, although still possible, does not definitely disprove the existence of altruism.

The other explanation concerns how people respond to the person in need being helped. If empathically concerned people are primarily motivated by a personal desire for reward, they should feel better if *they* help the person in need (and earn the reward) than if someone else does it. In contrast, if people are altruistically motivated, they should feel better just knowing that the person in need is helped, regardless of who the helper is. Empathically concerned people seem to care for others in this latter way. Their moods improve when they learn that the other person's need has been relieved, regardless of the source of relief (Batson, Dyck, et al., 1988). In addition, people experiencing empathic concern respond in ways that maximally benefit the other person's long-term welfare more than their own immediate needs, for example by withholding assistance when it will undermine the other person's subsequent performance and ultimate well-being. Sibicky, Schroeder, and Dovidio (1995), for example, found that participants experiencing higher levels of empathic concern gave fewer hints to help a partner with a problem-solving task when they were led to believe that providing hints would impair the person's performance on a subsequent task with aversive consequences (greater likelihood of being shocked). When they were not informed of these subsequent negative consequences of providing hints, participants experiencing higher levels of empathic concern offered more hints. In general, then, the weight of the evidence is on the side of the empathy-altruism hypothesis. The behavior that Batson and his colleagues identify as altruistic cannot fully be explained by a desire to obtain personal rewards.

Another egoistic interpretation for findings that support the empathy-altruism hypothesis was proposed by Cialdini and his colleagues (Cialdini et al., 1987; Schaller & Cialdini, 1988). They have argued that empathic people may have a greater motivation to help because empathy has aroused sadness as well as empathic concern, and it is the egoistic need to relieve this sadness that is really motivating helping. The data relevant to this argument are inconsistent and controversial. Indicative of egoistic motivation, Cialdini and his colleagues found that empathy produced high levels of sadness as well as empathic concern (Cialdini et al., 1987, Study 1) and that empathically concerned people showed high levels of helpfulness *only* when they believed that their sad mood could be improved by helping (Cialdini et al., 1987, Study 2). In contrast, in two subsequent studies, Batson et al. (1989) demonstrated, consistent with altruistic motivation, that anticipating a mood-enhancing event did *not* lead people high in empathic concern to be less helpful. Other studies have revealed that empathically aroused participants exhibit a high level of helping even when they are led to believe that helping could not improve their mood (Schroeder, Dovidio, Sibicky, Matthews, & Allen, 1988) and that their motivation is directed at helping the particular person for whom they feel empathy, not helping just anyone (which would also presumably improve their mood; Dovidio, Allen, & Schroeder, 1990). Apparently, these individuals' primary goal was not to make themselves feel better; regardless of whether their own moods would soon be improved, they were highly motivated to help the other person.

The most recent egoistic challenge of results that apparently show an altruistic motivation for helping also comes from Cialdini and his associates. Cialdini, Brown, Lewis, Luce, and Neuberg (1997) have argued that the manipulation typically used to induce empathic concern for another person may also create a greater sense of self–other overlap, or "oneness" between the potential helper and the recipient of the help. This raises the possibility that empathy-related helping may not be selfless, because helping would also indirectly improve at least the psychological well-being of the helper. In support of this contention, Cialdini et al. carried out path analyses of participants' responses to helping requests from different individuals and found that empathic concern did not directly lead to helping; rather, it was correlated with "oneness" between the helper and the victim, which did directly affect helping. In response to this challenge, Batson et al. (1997) conducted a series of studies in which they directly manipulated empathy and shared group membership (which presumably affects self–other overlap). Contrary to Cialdini's argument, Batson et al. reported that the empathy helping relationship was "unqualified by group membership" (p. 495). (For further discussion of these studies see also Batson, 1997; Neuberg et al., 1997.)

The extremely large number of conflicting experimental results regarding the question of altruism versus egoism as the motivational basis for prosocial actions makes it quite difficult to draw any firm conclusions about any specific motive responsible for any particular set of results. Certainly, some behaviors labeled as "altruistic" by one researcher may, in fact, be motivated by egoistic concerns and vice versa. However, the preponderance of evidence from the 20 or so years of experimentation on this question strongly suggests that truly altruistic motivation may exist and all helping is not necessarily egoistically motivated.

Social norms and personal standards

Both cognitive (learning) and affective factors are likely involved in the third motivational perspective, social norms and personal standards. Normative theories of helping emphasize that people help others because they have expectations based on previous social learning or the current behavior of others that it is the socially appropriate response. That is, helping is viewed as "a function of the pressure to comply with shared group expectations about appropriate behavior that are backed by social sanctions and rewards" (Schwartz & Howard, 1982, p. 346). For example, one of the most common reasons people give for becoming involved in volunteer work is to satisfy others' expectations of them (Reddy, 1980). Researchers have identified two classes of social norms involving in helping. One class relates to feelings of fairness and involves perceptions of reciprocity (Gouldner, 1960), equity (Walster, Walster, & Berscheid, 1978), and social justice (Lerner, 1980). The other class of norms relates to very general norms of aiding, such as the social responsibility norm (Berkowitz, 1972). Because it is often difficult to identify all of the relevant social norms in a situation and assess their relative salience, research has also focused on the role of personal standards in helping.

Social responsibility.   According to the *norm of social responsibility*, people are expected to help others who are dependent on them, even when there is no tangible gain for the benefactor (Berkowitz & Daniels, 1963). In general, the greater the need, the more likely people are to help (Piliavin et al., 1981), and, as the research on physical attraction suggests (Dovidio, 1984), this effect may be particularly pronounced when helping increases the likelihood of a desired long-term interdependent relationship, such as a romantic one. There are, however, exceptions and limits to this rule. People are less obligated to adhere to the social responsibility norm if the interdependent relationship is unwanted or threatens feelings of personal freedom and choice (Berkowitz, 1973). This norm also exerts less influence if the person in need is responsible for creating his or her own plight through a lack of effort (Frey & Gaertner, 1986) or through immoral conduct (Weiner, Perry, & Magnusson, 1988). There are also cultural differences, with individualistic cultures having weaker social responsibility norms than collectivistic cultures (Ma, 1985).

Personal norms, goals, and self-concept.   Whereas general norms of social responsibility may provide only a vague guide for behavior in concrete situations, the use of personal norms and standards is valuable for accounting how a particular person will behave in a specific situation. Internalized moral values and personal norms can motivate helping both cognitively and affectively. The cognitive component involves expectations of behavior that are based on personal standards; the affective component concerns the emotional reaction (e.g., pride, guilt) associated with meeting or not meeting one's standards. Personal norms typically predict helping better than general social norms (Schwartz & Howard, 1982), particularly when attention is focused inward on these personal standards (Hoover, Wood, & Knowles, 1983).

Perhaps because of similar cognitive and affective mechanisms, people who are led to make dispositional self-attributions for their helpfulness and to develop the self-concept that they are helpful people subsequently show relatively high levels of helpful behavior (Grusec, 1991; Swinyard & Ray, 1979). In contrast, those who are offered money to help or are pressured externally to help perceive themselves to have helped less altruistically than if they helped without such inducements (Batson, Fultz, Schoenrade, & Paduano, 1987; Thomas & Batson, 1981; Thomas, Batson, & Coke, 1981), which may make them less helpful in the future.

Similarly, with respect to nonspontaneous helping such as volunteering (see Piliavin & Charng, 1990), helping may be functional in fulfilling personal needs and motives (Clary & Snyder, 1991). For example, the most frequent reasons cited for donating blood are humanitarian or altruistic concerns (Piliavin & Callero, 1991). As with spontaneous helping, external pressure to volunteer, such as mandatory volunteer programs within colleges, can undermine these motives and make previously committed volunteers less likely to give their time freely in the future (Stukas, Snyder, & Clary, 1999).

Also like spontaneous helping, self-interest can be directly involved in volunteer activities. People may donate money to achieve personal recognition, to get ahead in their careers, to gain the respect of others, or even because they may expect some financial reward for their "charity" (e.g., tax benefits). Two in-depth studies of volunteerism conducted over 30 years apart (Daniels, 1988; Sills, 1957) both found that concern for others co-occurred with personal interest, a feeling of power, feelings of obligation, identification with the goals of the organization, the desire for social contact, and other self-centered motives (see also Chambre, 1987; Pearce, 1983). Thus, although people often report "altruistic" reasons for helping, personal needs and goals also appear to be very important. (The issue of people's specific motives for helping will be addressed in greater detail in the next major section of this chapter, Who Helps? Dispositional Variables.)

The consequences of action or inaction for one's self-concept, values, and needs may be directly related to cost–reward considerations and affective reactions to opportunities to help. Thus, the issues of when people help and why they help may be closely interrelated.

Regular and public commitments to helping, such as donating blood or volunteering for charities, can lead to the development of a role-identity consistent with those behaviors (Grube & Piliavin, in press; Penner & Finkelstein, 1998; Stryker, 1980). For example, not only are one's own feelings of moral obligation and personal identity important in deciding whether to donate blood, but also the perceived expectations of significant others (e.g., friends, family) are critical. Students who believe that others expect them to continue giving blood express stronger intentions to give blood in the future, and as a consequence, they are more likely to donate blood (Callero, 1985/6; Charng, Piliavin, & Callero, 1988; Piliavin & Callero, 1991). Thus, one's self-identity, which can itself motivate people to donate blood, can become more publicly formalized in terms of social roles and others' expectations. Similarly, people may perform volunteer work in hospitals or for charity because it has become a part of their own identity and what others expect of them (Deaux & Stark, 1996). These influences continue to develop across an entire lifetime. Older volunteers who help others, for example, report that they are motivated to fulfill a "meaningful role" (Bengtson, 1985; Midlarsky & Hannah, 1989).

Fairness.   The second class of norms for helping relates to issues of perceived fairness. One facet is the norm of reciprocity. According to this norm, people should help those who have helped them, and they should not help those who have denied them help for no legitimate reason (Gouldner, 1960). Consistent with this proposition, people normally reciprocate assistance to others who have helped them. This is particularly true when the person expects to see the helper again (Carnevale, Pruitt, & Carrington, 1982), although it can also occur when there is no expectation of future interaction (Goranson & Berkowitz, 1966). Also, the more assistance a person receives, the more help he or she subsequently gives (Kahn & Tice, 1973). Reciprocity involving the repayment of specific benefits is particularly strong for most casual relationships, but may be weaker in more intimate communal relationships (Clark & Mills, 1993). In communal relationships, however, a broader type of reciprocity may be involved in which people are generally mutually responsive to the needs of the other person, if needs arise. People involved in such relationships are primarily concerned about the welfare of their partner and anticipate that kindnesses will be reciprocated if such actions are ever needed (Webley & Lea, 1993). Consequently, they monitor the needs of their partner more closely than the immediate exchange of assistance, and thus helping is tied more directly to responsiveness to these needs than to a desire to repay specific assistance previously received. However, these circumstances notwithstanding, the norm of reciprocity appears to be a basic and fundamental aspect of human social exchanges. However, the work of Miller and her colleagues (e.g., Miller & Bersoff, 1994) does suggest that in different cultures there may be different reasons why people feel obligated to return favors.

The concern for fairness and balance that underlies the reciprocity norm also relates to the principle of *equity*. Equity exists when people in a relationship believe that their input and output – what they contribute to and what they get out of the relationship – are balanced (Walster et al., 1978). When people perceive an imbalance, they are motivated to restore equity. There is considerable evidence of equity motives in helping. People who have unfairly received benefits – for example, those who receive too much reward based on their contribution to the group activity – often freely choose to give up some of their reward (Schmitt & Marwell, 1972). Conversely, if people feel that they have been undercompensated, they will be less helpful to coworkers or the company for which they work (Organ & Ryan, 1995). In addition, when people have transgressed they are less likely to help others if equity has been restored by retribution, and they are more likely to help others if they are simply forgiven, which increases feelings of indebtedness (Kelln & Ellard, 1999). Helping or withholding assistance is therefore instrumental in restoring balance and achieving equity.

The need to see the world as fair and just is also central to the *just-world hypothesis* (Lerner, 1980). Like equity theory, the just-world hypothesis suggests that people will be motivated to help others who have been treated unfairly – to make the world fair and just again. For instance, people are more likely to support federal disaster assistance for people and communities that take appropriate precautions against flood damage than for those that do not take responsibility for preparing for a flood (Skitka, 1999). People who have stronger beliefs in a just-world are also more strongly motivated to achieve positions of power that will enable them to share resources to help compensate others for perceived injustices (Foster & Rusbult, 1999). However, if a person cannot be helped, the just-world hypothesis suggests that people will disparage the victim, thus making the world right again but decreasing the likelihood of helping that person in the future, as well (Lerner & Simmons, 1966).

Biological "motives" for helping and altruism.   Although biologists and ethologists have long argued for a biological basis of helping and altruism, the extension of these arguments to prosocial actions among humans is a relatively recent development. Three things seem responsible for the greater acceptance of a biological view of helping and altruism. First, in general, explanations of human social behaviors that rely on evolutionary theory have become more socially and scientifically acceptable in recent years (see Buss & Kenrick, 1998). Second, it is generally agreed that empathy plays a critical role in helping and altruism and it appears that there is a specific part of the human brain – the limbic system – that gives humans the capacity to empathize with other people (Carlson, 1998). Moreover, this brain structure was present very early in human evolutionary history (MacLean, 1985). Indeed, it may have been present in the earliest mammals, over 180 million years ago. Further, studies of identical twins have consistently suggested the heritability of empathy (Davis, Luce, & Kraus, 1994; Rushton, Fulker, Neale, Nias, & Eysenck, 1986; Zahn-Waxler, Robinson, & Emde, 1992). Thus, although there may be individual differences, people appear to be generally inherently empathic. Finally, there is the fact that in all known cultures the principle of reciprocity exists in some form (Moghaddam et al., 1993), suggesting to some researchers that there is a biological basis for this behavior (Sober & Wilson, 1998).

Trivers (1971), for example, used the term *reciprocal altruism* to refer to a genetic tendency for mutual helping that increases inclusive fitness, the likelihood that one's genes will be transmitted to future generations. One important component of inclusive fitness is a form of helping known as kin selection. A well-documented phenomenon among animals, *kin selection* refers to the strong positive association between biological (i.e., genetic) relatedness and the incidence of mutual helping (Alcock, 1989). Kin selection makes evolutionary sense because saving the lives of relatives (sometimes even at the sacrifice of one's own life) can increase the incidence of one's own genes in subsequent generations (Buss & Kenrick, 1998). Cunningham (1985/6) reviewed the research on kin selection and reciprocal altruism in humans and found, supportive of the biological perspective, that the closer the kinship relationship the greater the expectations that help would be given to them, the greater the resentment if help were withheld, the greater the willingness to provide aid to the other person, and the more they expected that help would be reciprocated. More recently, Burnstein, Crandall, and Kitayama (1994) found that, consistent with the notion of kin selection, biological relatedness has a much greater impact on life-saving help than on mundane helping. Moreover, the impact of relatedness on life-saving help (but not mundane helping) was substantially reduced or eliminated if the recipient relative was unlikely to produce offspring.

Simon (1990) has used the literatures from evolutionary theory, behavioral genetics, and economic theory to develop a model that accounts for both kin selection and reciprocal altruism. In essence, Simon argues that because "altruistic" individuals contribute more to the common good than do "selfish" individuals, they are more valued by and receive more benefits from other members of their group. As a result, they are more likely to survive and to pass their altruistic genetic predispositions on to their offspring.

Comparisons between fraternal and identical twins also point to a genetic basis for altruism. Specifically, there is evidence of greater cooperation among identical than fraternal twins (Segal, 1993). For example, Segal (1984) presented identical and fraternal twins with a joint completion puzzle task. Relative to fraternal twins, identical twins demonstrated much greater cooperation on this task, as shown by measures such as a higher proportion of successful puzzle completions and more equidistant placement of the puzzle pieces between the twins. And in a later study, Segal (1991) found that in a Prisoners' Dilemma game, identical twins chose cooperative strategies more often than did fraternal twins.

On the other side of this issue, Batson (1998) has provided perhaps the most cogent criticism of the evolutionary approach to helping and altruism. It is the absence of any hard or direct information on the mechanisms that mediate the relationship between genes and behavior. That is, it is unlikely that humans are genetically "hardwired" to help others, as is almost certainly the case with insects and other "lower" animals. Thus, in humans certain genes (or gene combinations) must make certain affective and cognitive processes more likely, and these processes are the proximal and direct causes of helping and altruism. At present, however, we can only speculate as to how genetics might make these processes more or less likely to occur by genetic factors.

In summary, the reasons why people help involve both cognitive and affective influences. Cognitively, people learn that helping is a positively valued social behavior and learn when it is appropriate to help. Affectively, the distress of another person can elicit empathic arousal.

Depending on how this arousal is interpreted, it can inhibit intervention, facilitate egoistic helping, or produce altruistic motivation. As many models emphasize (e.g., Piliavin et al., 1981), the affective and cognitive processes are not independent. Moreover, individual, developmental, and cultural differences can occur for both the cognitive and affective processes (Fiske, 1991). The next section examines how individual differences moderate the effects of these processes on helping.

Who Helps? Dispositional Variables

Dispositions, situations, and helping

Prosocial dispositional variables are enduring personal attributes that are, across time and situations, associated with consistencies in the tendency to engage in helpful or altruistic acts. The dispositional variables we will consider include demographic characteristics, personal motives, and personality traits.

Over 70 years ago, Hartshorne and May (1928) concluded that prosocial actions are largely situationally determined rather than the result of enduring personal characteristics. This led to the conventional wisdom that dispositional variables are weak and unreliable predictors of helping and altruism. Further, when interest in helping was rekindled in the late 1960s and early 1970s (Dovidio, 1984), the research findings were consistent with the situationist perspective – the notion that social actions such as helping are primarily determined by the characteristics of the situation in which the action occurred (Mischel, 1973). Gergen, Gergen, and Meter (1972) succinctly described the data on the personality correlates of helpful or altruistic actions as a "quagmire of evanescent relations among variables, conflicting findings, and low order correlations" (p. 113). In the same vein, Piliavin et al. (1981) concluded that "[t]he search for the 'generalized helping personality' has been futile" (p. 184).

One likely reason for the absence of strong or consistent relationships between personality measures and measures of prosocial actions was the context in which the dispositional correlates of helping were studied. A substantial portion of the research on helping in the 1960s and 1970s used some variant of the bystander intervention paradigm, measuring a single decision to help or not help in a situation in which strong situational variables had been effectively manipulated (e.g., the severity or clarity of the emergency). However, the impact of traits (or any other dispositional variable) on behavior is most likely to be observed in behavioral consistencies across time and situations rather than in one specific situation. Also, the greater the strength of situational cues or demands, the less likely it is that dispositional variables will influence a person's behavior in that situation. Thus, the failure of dispositional variables to account for meaningful amounts of variance in the bystander intervention experiments is not surprising, and may say as much about the characteristics of the research paradigms employed as about the relationship between dispositional variables and helping (Penner, Escarrez, & Ellis, 1983).

In recent years there has been somewhat of a resurgence of interest in dispositional correlates of helping and altruism. The more recent research generally supports the interactionist perspective on social behavior – situational and dispositional variables jointly explain more of the variance in a measure of interest than either class of variable does individually. However, within this context empirical findings indicate a much more important role for dispositional variables than was suggested by the earlier studies. We now turn to some of dispositional variables that are related to helping and altruism.

Demographic characteristics

Demographic variables are background characteristics related to a person's physical or social status. Among the demographic characteristics that have been studied in relation to prosocial actions are age, ethnicity, socioeconomic status, religion, and gender. Most studies of the demographic correlates of helping have been surveys of the incidence of financial donations to and volunteering for service organizations, including religious, educational, and health organizations. While strong with regard to external validity, surveys, of course, are limited in their capacity to identify causal relationships. Another limitation of these data is that they come almost exclusively from the United States; some of the relationships reported might vary across different countries and cultures. Nonetheless, the results of these studies are informative and useful.

In the United States, at least, there is a curvilinear relationship between age and charitable contributions and volunteering. People in their late fifties and early sixties donate more than other age groups (Independent Sector, 1997). This pattern likely reflects the greater resources available to people at this time in their lives than to people who are younger or older. Indeed, there is generally a positive association between socioeconomic status and charitable actions (Independent Sector, 1997; Weismann & Galper, 1998). The same process may explain why, in the United States, the percentage of African Americans and Hispanic Americans who report engaging in volunteer activities is lower than the percentage of European Americans (Independent Sector, 1997). That is, because members of these ethnic minorities are overrepresented in lower socioeconomic classes, they may have less time and money to give to charities (Schroeder et al., 1995).

However, these associations may not be solely due to wealth. Education relates to charitable actions in ways that cannot be simply explained by greater resources. For example, in the United States blood donors are most likely to be people with at least some college education and who hold professional jobs (Piliavin & Callero, 1991). Bellah and his colleagues (1985) concluded that among wealthy, well-educated people, prosocial actions may also serve personal growth needs. That is, having attained many of their material goals, these people may turn to goals that give more meaning to their lives.

There is also a strong association between religiosity and both donations and volunteerism. People who report a religious affiliation contribute a greater percentage of their household income than people with no religious affiliation (Independent Sector, 1997). It is likely that part of the reason for this is that in the United States religious institutions are the most frequent recipients of donations of time and money (Galper, 1998).

Turning to gender, although national surveys consistently show that a larger percentage of women than men serve as volunteers (Independent Sector, 1997), early laboratory research on gender differences in helping indicated that men were more likely to help than women. Reconciling these apparently conflicting findings, Eagly and Crowley (1986) concluded from their review of the literature that men and women do not differ in *how much* they help but rather in the *kinds of help* they offer. Moreover, the kinds of help men and women will provide is largely determined by whether the helping action is consistent or inconsistent with the actor's gender role, a set of norms about how people should behave based on their biological sex.

Gender-role expectations relate to both cognitive and affective factors in helping. The female gender role is often associated with the trait of "communion" – being caring, emotionally expressive, and responsive to others (Ashmore, Del Boca, & Wohlers, 1986), and being supportive and nurturant, especially to their friends and family (Eagly & Crowley, 1986). In addition, although both men and women experience physiological arousal when they observe distress in others, women are more likely to interpret this arousal as a positive empathic response to the other person's needs (Eisenberg & Lennon, 1983). In accord with these findings, women are more likely than men to provide their friends with personal favors, emotional support, and informal counseling about personal or psychological problems (Eagly & Crowley, 1986; Eisenberg & Fabes, 1991).

The male gender role is more consistent with the trait of "agency" – being independent and assertive (Ashmore et al., 1986). Perhaps because of this, there is a greater expectation that men will engage in *heroic* helping, in which they risk their own well-being in order to help others, even strangers; and *chivalrous* helping, in which they protect individuals who are less able and powerful than them. Systematic reviews of the literature (Eagly & Crowley, 1986; Piliavin & Unger, 1985) strongly support this gender-role explanation of male–female differences in helping. That is, people tend to offer the kinds of help that are most consistent with and appropriate for their gender roles. And the more salient the person's gender role, the stronger is this relationship (Eagly & Crowley, 1986).

It is also likely that gender roles affect perceptions of the costs and rewards associated with various kinds of helping. In particular, women, because of how they have been socialized, may find the rewards associated with nurturant forms of helping and the costs for not helping to be greater, and the costs for helping to be lower, than do men. Otten et al. (1988), for example, demonstrated that in response to a friend's request for psychological support, women reported that they would feel worse than men for not visiting the friend (a higher cost for not helping) and perceived the visit to be less of an imposition on their time (a lower cost for helping). Analogous socialization processes may cause men to see the costs of failing to act "heroically" as greater than women would and the cost for intervening (e.g., personal harm) to be lower (Eagly & Crowley, 1986).

Motives and helping

People may also systematically differ in their personal goals that underlie helping. Snyder, Clary, and their associates (e.g., Clary & Snyder, 1991; Clary et al., 1998; Omoto & Snyder, 1990) have made this idea the cornerstone of their approach to helping and altruism. More specifically, they have employed a "functional analysis" to explain long-term, sustained prosocial actions, such as volunteering. This approach attempts to identify the "personal and social needs, plans, goals, and functions that are being served by . . . [these] actions" (Clary & Snyder, 1991, p. 123).

According to these researchers, there are six primary needs or motives that may be served by volunteering (Clary et al., 1998; Clary & Snyder, 1991). They are: (1) value-expressive – expressing values related to altruistic and humanitarian concerns; (2) understanding – gaining knowledge or exercising existing knowledge, skills, and abilities; (3) social – being among friends and engaging in activities that might win their approval; (4) career – pursuing activities that might directly or indirectly benefit one's career; (5) protective – protecting one's ego from negative features of the self and helping to address personal problems; and (6) enhancement – enhancing positive feelings about oneself and furthering personal growth and development.

Consistent with this functional analysis, surveys of volunteers (e.g., Allen & Rushton, 1983; Anderson & Moore, 1978; Independent Sector, 1997) suggest that different people have different reasons for engaging in this activity. For example, national surveys in the United States find that the most common reason for volunteering seems to be value-expressive – volunteers are concerned about the welfare of other people – but respondents report other, more self-centered motives, as well. For example, in one survey 33 percent of the people who reported making charitable contributions said that keeping their taxes down was one of the reasons for their charitable contributions; and 14 percent of the volunteers said that they did this for career-related reasons (Independent Sector, 1997; see also Anderson & Moore, 1978; Frisch & Gerard, 1981; Jenner, 1982).

Omoto and Snyder (1995; see also Snyder & Omoto, 1992) have conducted longitudinal studies of the motives of volunteers at organizations that serve people with the HIV infection or AIDS. Omoto and Snyder (1995) found that three self-serving motives – understanding, personal development, and esteem enhancement – were all positively associated with tenure as a volunteer, but the value-expressive motive was not. These findings were consistent with earlier findings by Snyder and Omoto (1992), and led Omoto and Snyder (1995) to conclude: "it appears that the opportunity to have personal, self-serving, and perhaps even selfish functions served by volunteering was what kept volunteers actively involved" (p. 683).

Other studies have also found that personal motives play a significant role in volunteerism, but sometimes these are not the same motives identified by Omoto and Snyder. For example, Penner and Finkelstein (1998) also studied AIDS volunteers but did not find any significant relationships involving the self-serving or selfish motives. However, among male volunteers they did find significant positive correlations between the value-expressive motive and level of commitment to the organization, and willingness to directly help a person with HIV and/or AIDS. Similarly, Clary and Orenstein (1991) found a positive association between altruistic motives and the length of service of crisis counseling volunteers. And Deaux and Stark (1996) found a positive correlation between the value-expressive motive and intention to donate time to a conflict resolution program for prisoners, as well as a positive correlation with an egoistic motive. More recent research suggests that motives, including value-expressive ones, may also play a role in sustained prosocial activities ("Organizational Citizenship Behavior") within private, for-profit organizations (Rioux & Penner, 1999; Tillman, 1998).

Overall, although the primary motives for helping appear to vary across situations and studies, there is consistent evident that helping serves many important functions and that different people have different motives for helping.

Personality correlates of helping and altruism

Graziano and Eisenberg (1997) have identified three kinds of evidence supporting the conclusion that personality traits can account for significant amounts of variance in prosocial actions. The first is that, as noted earlier, differences in empathy, a characteristic that is strongly linked with helping and altruism, may be at least in part inherited (Davis et al., 1994). The second kind of evidence is consistency of prosocial actions across situations and across time. For instance, Oliner and Oliner (1988) found that 40 years after World War II ended, people who had risked their lives to save Jews from the Nazis were still more helpful than people with comparable demographic characteristics (e.g., age, nationality) who had not rescued Jews (see also Colby & Damon, 1992; Marwell, Aiken, & Demerath, 1987; Reddy, 1980; Savin-Williams, Small & Zeldin, 1981). The third kind of evidence relates to replicable associations between "prosocial behavior and those personality characteristics conceptually linked to (helping and) altruism" (Graziano & Eisenberg, 1997, p. 813). We briefly consider some of these personality characteristics; and consistent with the approach we have taken in this chapter, focus on how these personality variables relate to the cognitive and affective processes that generally underlie helping.

Personality characteristics associated primarily with cognitive processes may relate to individual differences in how people perceive and weigh the various costs and rewards for helping and to the steps involved in making a decision to help. For instance, individual differences in the propensity to accept responsibility for helping have been identified as an important personality characteristic (Schwartz & Howard, 1982). In their work with the rescuers, the Oliners also found that this trait also distinguished rescuers from nonrescuers. Studies of other kinds of helping, including medical donations and short-term interventions on behalf of a person in trouble, also find a positive association between ascription of responsibility and helping (Schwartz & Howard, 1982; Staub, 1986, 1996).

A sense of self-efficacy and feelings of confidence, which also relate to the subjective assessment of costs and rewards and perceptions of the ability to help successfully, are also consistent personality correlates of helpful and altruistic actions (see Graziano & Eisenberg, 1997). For example, the Oliners identified self-efficacy as an important attribute of the rescuers. And according to Colby and Damon (1992), one of the most salient attributes of the 22 life-long altruists they interviewed was that the altruists welcomed the challenges to achieving their goals and were unlikely to be discouraged by the obstacles that stood in the way of helping others – they were individuals with a strong sense of their own self-efficacy. More direct evidence for the impact of personality traits on cost assessments comes from Penner and his associates (Penner, Fritzsche, Craiger, & Freifeld, 1995). They developed a measure of prosocial personality characteristics, the Prosocial Personality Battery. One of the two factors on this measure is called Helpfulness (a self-reported history of being helpful and an absence of egocentric responses to distress in others). Helpfulness is correlated with a broad range of helpful actions, including emergency intervention, helping peers and friends in nonemergency situations, sustained volunteering, and informal prosocial activities among employees within a large organization (Penner & Finkelstein, 1998; Penner et al., 1995; Penner, Midili, & Kegelmeyer, 1997). And it also is negatively correlated with estimates of the costs of helping distressed others (Penner et al., 1995).

Other personality characteristics that are consistently associated with helping relate directly or indirectly to arousal. Dispositional empathy is one of the most important of these characteristics. Affective empathy involves the tendency to experience affect or emotion in response to others' emotional experiences. Cognitive empathy relates to the tendency or ability to see things from another person's perspective (Davis, 1994). There is substantial consistency in the literature regarding the positive association between dispositional empathy and a broad range of prosocial actions. For example, Oliner and Oliner (1988) identified empathy as one of the personality characteristics that differentiated people who rescued the Jews from those who did not. Turning to less dramatic forms of helping, Davis (1983) found that empathy was correlated with the amount of money donated to a charity telethon, and Rushton (1984) reported that community volunteers were more empathic than nonvolunteers. Otten, Penner, and Altabe (1991) found that even among a group of professional helpers (psychotherapists), helping (in this case, allowing a person to interview them about their work) was positively associated with self-reports of dispositional empathy.

Personality measures also represent characteristics that reflect closely intertwined configurations of both cognitive and affective factors. Penner and his associates (Penner & Craiger, 1991; Penner et al., 1995) have found that empathy, social responsibility, and concern for the welfare of others are all strongly related to one another. Indeed, they form the other factor of their prosocial personality measure, which is called Other-Oriented Empathy – the tendency to experience empathy for, and to feel responsibility and concern about, the well-being of others; in other words, prosocial thoughts and feelings. Scores on this factor correlate with cost estimates and affective reaction to distress in others.

The Other-Oriented Empathy factor is associated with a rather broad range of prosocial actions in emergency and nonemergency situations and involves formal and informal forms of helping. The measures of helping have included the likelihood a person will intervene in an emergency and the speed with which the intervention occurs (Harter, personal communication, April 8, 1997; also see Carlo, Eisenberg, Troyer, Switzer, & Speer, 1991), intention to volunteer (Sibicky, Mader, Redshaw, & Cheadle, 1994), actually volunteering (Penner & Fritzsche, 1993), length of service as a volunteer (Penner & Fritzsche, 1993; Penner & Finkelstein, 1998), the amount of direct contact that male (but not female) volunteers had with people who were HIV positive or who had AIDS (Penner & Finkelstein, 1998), and self-reports and peer reports of informal prosocial activity among retail store workers, municipal employees, and college students who worked in a wide variety of different jobs (Midili & Penner, 1995; Negrao, 1997; Rioux & Penner, 1999; Tillman, 1998).

Personality and helping: some caveats

Before concluding the discussion of dispositional factors and helping and altruism, several caveats must be offered. First, a comprehensive understanding of helping involves an appreciation not only of personality (and situational) factors separately but how they interact to produce helping. Second, although personality is now recognized as an important factor in helping, personality traits typically play a less substantial role in helping than do situational factors (e.g., Oliner & Oliner, 1988; see also Piliavin & Charng, 1990). Third, in many of the studies on personality and helping causal inference is difficult. For instance, sustained volunteering may shape one's self-concept as an empathic, responsible, and efficacious person rather than these characteristics be the causes of helping. Finally, personality studies need to speak even more directly to the mechanisms that mediate the relationship between a particular personality trait and a helpful or altruistic act. That is, people do not help because they score high on, say, a measure of empathy, but rather because their empathic tendencies elicit some sort of affective or cognitive reaction, which, in turn, leads to a certain behavior. Further consideration of these processes may not only help to answer the question about who helps more definitively but also contribute to an understanding of when people help and why.

Integration and Conclusions

In this chapter, we have reviewed a range of causes, moderating influences, and mediating mechanisms involved in helping and altruism. We conclude with a brief, integrative discussion of the processes relating to the answers to the three fundamental questions we posed: When do people help? Why do people help? Who helps? A conceptual model of these processes and how they affect helping and altruism is presented in figure 12.1.

At the model's base are the most distal causes of a prosocial action; the causes become progressively more proximal as we move toward the top. Thus, the model begins with the evolutionary processes associated with natural selection and inclusive fitness. Among humans' ancestors, helping was a behavior that, under many circumstances, served to increase inclusiveness fitness, and thus it is a characteristic that is likely to be reflected in prosocial genetic predispositions among contemporary humans. This should be especially likely for helping biological relatives because this action directly increases the likelihood that one's own genes will be transmitted to future generations. But, in addition, even helping others who are unrelated may ultimately be beneficial to one's own survival or the survival of relatives through processes of reciprocity.

Humans are both feeling and thinking organisms. Thus, the model suggests that affective and cognitive processes provide mechanisms for translating genetic predispositions into prosocial actions. With respect to affect, Zajonc (1980) proposed, "Affect is the first link in the evolution of complex adaptive functions" (p. 156). As we noted earlier in this chapter, the capacity to experience empathy and empathic arousal is universal. The neurological structures that are responsible for feelings and emotions (i.e., the limbic system) are among the oldest in the human brain. Moreover, consistent with an evolutionary perspective, empathy is a highly heritable characteristic and empathic arousal increases with closeness to the person in need. From a cognitive perspective, people learn about helping and how to be helpful in the same ways that they learn other social behaviors, through direct or vicarious rewards and punishments. Socialization experiences and culture also affect the way they think about helping (Miller & Bersoff, 1994). Affect and cognitive processes are, of course,

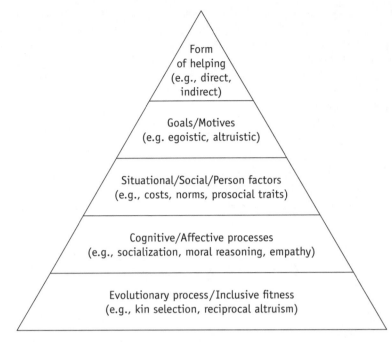

Figure 12.1 Conceptual processes in helping and altruism

reciprocally intertwined. For example, recognition of a discrepancy between one's self-concept and actions may generate unpleasant emotional arousal. In addition, arousal may influence how different costs and rewards for helping are attended to and ultimately how they are weighed in decisions to help.

Reflecting plasticity, and thus adaptiveness, in response, the characteristics of the situation, the victim, and the potential helper may cause particular affective and cognitive mechanisms to be activated selectively and to varying degrees. For example, situations of greater clarity and severity produce higher levels of empathic arousal and are associated with stronger norms supporting intervention and greater guilt for not helping. People have higher levels of cognitive and affective empathy with others who are similar to them, with whom they share group membership, and with whom they are closer. Personal dispositions may also affect affective and cognitive factors and thus produce individual differences in helpfulness. For example, people who are higher in traits such as Other-Oriented Empathy and who are more confident and higher in self-efficacy display affective and cognitive responses that typically produce helpful actions.

How affective and cognitive processes operate as a function of the situational, personal, and interpersonal context determines the nature of the motivation for helping and the ultimate objectives of the action. Helping can be egoistically motivated. In such instances, the primary objective with respect to affect might be to improve one's mood or relieve one's own empathic distress. With regard to cognition, egoistically-motivated helping may reaffirm one's positive self-image or satisfy a wide range of personal goals (e.g., job advancement, distraction from personal problems). Helping may even be used strategically to gain advantage over another person by making them dependent on assistance, by undermining their self-confidence, or by shaping more negative impressions of them by others (Gilbert & Silvera, 1996). However, helping can also be altruistically motivated, with the ultimate goal of improving the other person's welfare. As Batson (1991) has argued, demonstration of truly altruistic motivation provides a broader and different perspective on behavior for a discipline that has been traditionally considered virtually exclusively the effect of personal consequences for behavior (e.g., the Law of Effect or drive reduction models).

Finally, we note that the behavioral outcome of these processes can come in various forms. Helping may be direct or indirect (e.g., calling the police). It may be short-term or involve long-term commitments. Helping may also be reflected in inaction when helping has negative social consequences (e.g., stigmatization for providing academic assistance; Major & Crocker, 1993) or personal consequences (e.g., the failure to develop important skills; Sibicky et al., 1995) that outweigh the immediate benefits of intervention or in the refusal to acquiesce to a request for assistance that might ultimately cause another harm (e.g., an alcoholic's request for a drink).

In conclusion, although many manifestations of helping, particularly those that are commonly studied in the laboratory, appear simple and straightforward, helping is a complex, multidetermined behavior. Whether it is spontaneous and short-term or planned and sustained, helping is an evolutionarily important behavior that is shaped by fundamental cognitive and affective processes, involves self- and other-directed motives, and has consequences that are central to one's self-image and social relationships. Thus, an understanding of the processes underlying helping can illuminate a wide range of other behaviors while offering genuinely unique insights to human motivation.

REFERENCES

Alcock, J. (1989). *Animal behavior* (4th ed.). Sunderland, MA: Sinauer Press.

Allen, N., & Rushton, J. P. (1983). The personality of community volunteers. *Journal of Voluntary Action Research, 9,* 1183–1196.

Anderson, J. C., & Moore, L. (1978). The motivation to volunteer. *Journal of Voluntary Action Research, 7,* 232–252.

Archer, R. L. (1984). The farmer and the cowman should be friends: An attempt at reconciliation with Batson, Coke, and Pych. *Journal of Personality and Social Psychology, 46,* 709–711.

Archer, R. L., Diaz-Loving, R., Gollwitzer, P. M., Davis, M. H., & Foushee, H. C. (1981). The role of dispositional empathy and social evaluation in the empathic mediation of helping. *Journal of Personality and Social Psychology, 46,* 786–796.

Ashmore, R., Del Boca, F., & Wohlers, A. J. (1986). Gender stereotypes. In R. Ashmore & F. L. Del Boca (Eds.), *The social psychology of female–male relations* (pp. 69–119). Orlando, FL: Academic Press.

Bar-Tal, D., & Raviv, A. (1982). A cognitive-learning model of helping behavior development: Possible implications and applications. In N. Eisenberg (Ed.), *The development of prosocial behavior* (pp. 199–217). New York: Academic Press.

Baron, R. A. (1997). The sweet smell of . . . helping: Effects of pleasant ambient fragrance on prosocial behavior in shopping malls. *Personality and Social Psychology Bulletin, 23,* 498–503.

Batson, C. D. (1987). Prosocial motivation: Is it ever truly altruistic? In L. Berkowitz (Ed.), *Advances in experimental social psychology* (Vol. 20, pp. 65–122). New York: Academic Press.

Batson, C. D. (1991). *The altruism question: Toward a social-psychological answer.* Hillsdale, NJ: Erlbaum.

Batson, C. D. (1997). Self–other merging and the empathy–altruism hypothesis: Reply to Neuberg et al. (1997). *Journal of Personality and Social Psychology, 73*, 517–522.

Batson, C. D. (1998). Altruism and prosocial behavior. In D. T. Gilbert, S. T. Fiske, & G. Lindzey (Eds.), *The handbook of social psychology* (4th ed., Vol. 2, pp. 282–315). New York: McGraw-Hill.

Batson, C. D., Batson, J. G., Griffitt, C. A., Barrientos, S., Brandt, J. R., Sprengelmeyer, P., & Bayly, M. J. (1989). Negative-state relief and the empathy-altruism hypothesis. *Journal of Personality and Social Psychology, 56*, 922–933.

Batson, C. D., Batson, J. G., Slingsby, J. K., Harrell, K. L., Peekna, H. M., & Todd, R. M. (1991). Empathic joy and the empathy-altruism hypothesis. *Journal of Personality and Social Psychology, 61*, 413–426.

Batson, C. D., Dyck, J. L., Brandt, J. R., Batson, J. G., Powell, A. L., McMaster, M. R., & Griffitt, C. (1988). Five studies testing two new egoistic alternatives to the empathy-altruism hypothesis. *Journal of Personality and Social Psychology, 55*, 52–77.

Batson, C. D., Fultz, J., Schoenrade P. A., & Paduano, A. (1987). Critical self-reflection and self-perceived altruism: When self-reward fails. *Journal of Personality and Social Psychology, 53*, 594–602.

Batson, C. D., & Oleson, K. C. (1991). Current status of the empathy-altruism hypothesis. In M. S. Clark (Ed.), *Review of personality and social psychology: Vol. 12. Prosocial behavior* (pp. 62–85). Newbury Park, CA: Sage.

Batson, C. D., Sager, K., Garst, E., Kang, M., Rubchinsky, K., & Dawson, K. (1997). Is empathy-induced helping due to self-other merging? *Journal of Personality and Social Psychology, 73*, 495–509.

Baumeister, F. F., Stillwell, A. M., & Heatherton, T. F. (1994). Guilt: An interpersonal approach. *Psychological Bulletin, 115*, 243–267.

Bell, F. A., Fisher, J. D., Baum, A., & Greene, T. (1996). *Environmental psychology.* (4th ed.). New York: Harcourt.

Bellah, R. N., Madsen, R., Sullivan, W. M., Swidler, A., & Tipton, S. M. (1985). *Habits of the heart: Individualism and commitment in American life.* Berkeley: University of California Press.

Bengtson, V. (1985). Diversity and symbolism in grandparental roles. In V. Bengtson & J. Robertson (Eds.), *Grandparenthood* (pp. 11–25). Beverly Hills, CA: Sage.

Berkowitz, L. (1972). Social norms, feelings, and other factors affecting helping behavior and altruism. In L. Berkowitz (Ed.), *Advances in experimental social psychology* (Vol. 6, pp. 63–108). New York: Academic Press.

Berkowitz, L. (1973). Reactance and the unwillingness to help others. *Psychological Bulletin, 79*, 310–317.

Berkowitz, L., & Daniels, L. R. (1963). Responsibility and dependency. *Journal of Abnormal and Social Psychology, 66*, 429–436.

Borgida, E., Conner, C., & Manteufel, L. (1992). Understanding living kidney donation: A behavioral decision-making perspective. In S. Spacapan & S. Oskamp (Eds.), *Helping and being helped* (pp. 183–212). Newbury Park, CA: Sage.

Burnstein, E., Crandall, C., & Kitayama, S. (1994). Some neo-Darwinian decision rules for altruism: Weighing cues for inclusive fitness as a function of the biological importance of the decision. *Journal of Personality & Social Psychology, 67*, 773–789.

Buss, D. M., & Kenrick, D. T. (1998). Evolutionary social psychology. In D. T. Gilbert, S. T. Fiske, & G. Lindzey (Eds.), *Handbook of social psychology.* (4th ed., Vol 2, pp. 982–1026). Boston: McGraw-Hill.

Byrne, D. (1971). *The attraction paradigm.* New York: Academic Press.

Callero, P. L. (1985/6). Putting the social in prosocial behavior: An interactionist approach to altruism. *Humboldt Journal of Social Relations, 13*, 15–34.

Carlo, G., Eisenberg, N., Troyer, D., Switzer, G., & Speer, A. L. (1991). The altruistic personality: In what contexts is it apparent? *Journal of Personality and Social Psychology, 61*, 450–458.

Carlson, N. R. (1998). *Physiology of behavior*. Boston: Allyn Bacon.

Carlson, M., & Miller, N. (1987). Explanation of the relation between negative mood and helping. *Psychological Bulletin, 102*, 91–108.

Carnevale, P. J. D., Pruitt, D. G., & Carrington, P. I. (1982). Effects of future dependence, liking, and repeated requests for help on helping behavior. *Social Psychology Quarterly, 45*, 9–14.

Chambre, S. M. (1987). *Good deeds in old age: Volunteering by the new leisure class*. Lexington, MA: Lexington Books.

Charng, H. W., Piliavin, J. A., & Callero, P. L. (1988). Role-identity and reasoned action in the prediction of repeated behavior. *Social Psychology Quarterly, 51*, 303–317.

Cialdini, R. B., Brown, S. L., Lewis, B. P., Luce, C., & Neuberg, S. L. (1997). Reinterpreting the empathy-altruism relationship: When one into one equals oneness. *Journal of Personality and Social Psychology, 73*, 481–494.

Cialdini, R. B., Darby, B. K., & Vincent, J. E. (1973). Transgression and altruism: A case for hedonism. *Journal of Experimental Social Psychology, 9*, 502–516.

Cialdini, R. B., & Kenrick, D. T. (1976). Altruism as hedonism: A social development perspective on the relationship of negative mood state and helping. *Journal of Personality and Social Psychology, 34*, 907–914.

Cialdini, R. B., Kenrick, D. T., & Baumann, D. J. (1982). Effects of mood on prosocial behavior in children and adults. In N. Eisenberg (Ed.), *The development of prosocial behavior* (pp. 339–359). New York: Academic Press.

Cialdini, R. B., Schaller, M., Houlihan, D., Arps, K., Fultz, J., & Beamen, A. L. (1987). Empathy-based helping: Is it selflessly or selfishly motivated? *Journal of Personality and Social Psychology, 52*, 749–758.

Clark, M. S., & Mills, J. (1993). The difference between communal and exchange relationships: What is and what is not. *Personality and Social Psychology Bulletin, 19*, 684–691.

Clary, E. G., & Miller, J. (1986). Socialization and situational influences on sustained altruism. *Child Development, 57*, 1358–1369.

Clary, E. G., & Orenstein, L. (1991). The amount and effectiveness of help: The relationship of motives and abilities to helping behavior. *Personality and Social Psychology Bulletin, 17*, 58–64.

Clary, E. G., & Snyder, M. (1991). A functional analysis of altruism and prosocial behavior: The case of volunteerism. In M. Clark (Ed.), *Review of personality and social psychology: Vol. 12. Prosocial behavior* (pp. 119–148). Knobbier Park, CA: Sage.

Clary, E. G., Snyder, M., Ridge, R., Copeland, J., Haugen, J., & Miene, P. (1998). Understanding and assessing the motivations of volunteers: A functional approach. *Journal of Personality and Social Psychology, 74*, 1516–1530.

Colby, A., & Damon, W. (1992). *Some do care*. New York: Free Press.

Cunningham, M. R. (1985/6). Levites and brother's keepers: A sociobiological perspective on prosocial behavior. *Humboldt Journal of Social Relations, 13*, 35–67.

Daniels, A. K. (1988). *Invisible careers: Women civic leaders from the volunteer world*. Chicago: University of Chicago Press.

Darley, J. M., & Latané, B. (1968). Bystander intervention in emergencies: Diffusion of responsibility. *Journal of Personality and Social Psychology, 8*, 377–383.

Davis, M. H. (1983). Empathic concern and muscular dystrophy telethon: Empathy as a multidimensional construct. *Personality and Social Psychology Bulletin, 9*, 223–229.

Davis, M. H. (1994). *Empathy: A social psychological approach.* Madison, WI: Brown & Benchmark.

Davis, M. H., Luce, C., & Kraus, S. J. (1994). The heritability of characteristics associated with dispositional empathy. *Journal of Personality, 62,* 369–391.

Deaux, K., & Stark, B. E. (1996, May). *Identity and motive: An integrated theory of volunterism.* Ann Arbor, MI: Society for the Psychological Study of Social Issues.

Dovidio, J. F. (1984). Helping behavior and altruism: An empirical and conceptual overview. In L. Berkowitz (Ed.), *Advances in experimental social psychology* (Vol. 17, pp. 361–427). New York: Academic Press.

Dovidio, J. F., Allen, J., & Schroeder, D. A. (1990). The specificity of empathy-induced helping: Evidence for altruism. *Journal of Personality and Social Psychology, 59,* 249–260.

Dovidio, J. F., Gaertner, S. L., Validzic, A., Matoka, A., Johnson, B., & Frazier, S. (1997). Extending the benefits of recategorization: Evaluations, self-disclosure, and helping. *Journal of Experimental Social Psychology, 33,* 401–420.

Dovidio, J. F., Piliavin, J. A., Gaertner, S. L., Schroeder, D. A., & Clark, R. D., III (1991). The Arousal: Cost-Reward Model and the process of intervention: A review of the evidence. In M. S. Clark (Ed.), *Review of personality and social psychology: Vol. 12. Prosocial behavior* (pp. 86–118). Newbury Park, CA: Sage.

Dutton, D. G., & Lennox, V. L. (1974). Effect of prior "token" compliance on subsequent interracial behavior. *Journal of Personality and Social Psychology, 29,* 65–71.

Eagly, A. H., & Crowley, M. (1986). Gender and helping behavior: A meta-analytic view of the social psychological literature. *Psychological Bulletin, 100,* 283–308.

Edelmann, R. J., Evans, G., Pegg, I., & Tremain, M. (1983). Responses to physical stigma. *Perceptual and Motor Skills, 57,* 294.

Eisenberg, N., & Fabes, R. A. (1991). Prosocial behavior and empathy: A multimethod developmental perspective. In M. S. Clark (Ed.), *Review of personality and social psychology: Vol. 12. Prosocial behavior* (pp. 34–61). Newbury Park, CA: Sage.

Eisenberg, N., & Fabes, R. (1998). Prosocial development. In W. Colby (Ed.), *Handbook of child psychology* (5th ed., Vol. 3, pp. 701–798). New York: Wiley.

Eisenberg, N., & Lennon, R. (1983). Sex differences in empathy and related capacities. *Psychological Bulletin, 94,* 100–131.

Eisenberg, N., & Miller, P. (1987). The relation of empathy to prosocial and related behaviors. *Psychological Bulletin, 101,* 91–119.

Eisenberg, N., Miller, P., Shell, P., McNalley, S., & Shea, C. (1991). Prosocial development in adolescence: A longitudinal study. *Developmental Psychology, 27,* 849–857.

Eisenberg, N., Shell, R., Pasternack, J., Lennon, R., Beller, R., & Mathy, R. M. (1987). Prosocial development in middle childhood: A longitudinal study. *Developmental Psychology, 23,* 712–718.

Fabes, R. A., Eisenberg, N., & Eisenbud, L. (1993). Behavioral and physiological correlates of children's reactions to others in distress. *Developmental Psychology, 29,* 655–664.

Fabes, R. A., Eisenberg, N., & Miller, P. A. (1990). Maternal correlates of children's vicarious emotional responsiveness. *Developmental Psychology, 26,* 639–648.

Fabes, R. A., Fultz. J., Eisenberg, N., May-Plumlee, T., & Christopher, F. S. (1989). Effects of rewards on children's prosocial motivation: A socialization study. *Developmental Psychology, 25,* 509–515.

Fiske, A. (1991). The cultural relativity of selfish individualism: Anthropological evidence that humans are inherently sociable. In M. S. Clark (Ed.), *Review of personality and social psychology: Vol. 12. Prosocial behavior* (pp. 176–214). Newbury Park, CA: Sage.

Forgas, J. P. (1998). Asking nicely? The effects of mood on responding to more or less polite requests. *Personality and Social Psychology Bulletin, 24,* 173–185.

Foster, C. A., & Rusbult, C. E. (1999). Injustice and powerseeking. *Personality and Social Psychology Bulletin, 25*, 834–849.

Frey, D. L., & Gaertner, S. L. (1986). Helping and the avoidance of inappropriate interracial behavior: A strategy that perpetuates a nonprejudiced self-image. *Journal of Personality and Social Psychology, 50*, 1083–1090.

Frisch, M. B., & Gerard, M. (1981). Natural helping systems: A survey of Red Cross volunteers. *American Journal of Community Psychology, 9*, 567–579.

Fultz, J., Batson, C. D., Fortenbach, V. A., McCarthy, P. M., & Varney, L. L. (1986). Social evaluation and the empathy-altruism hypothesis. *Journal of Personality and Social Psychology, 50*, 761–769.

Gaertner, S. L., & Dovidio, J. F. (1977). The subtlety of white racism, arousal, and helping behavior. *Journal of Personality and Social Psychology, 35*, 691–707.

Gaertner, S. L., & Dovidio, J. F. (1986). The aversive form of racism. In J. F. Dovidio & S. L. Gaertner (Eds.), *Prejudice, discrimination, and racism* (pp. 61–90). Orlando, FL: Academic Press.

Galper, J. (1998). *An exploration of social capital, giving and volunteering at the United States county level.* (Working paper). Washington, DC: Urban Institute.

Gergen, K. J., Gergen, M. M., & Meter, K. (1972). Individual orientations to prosocial behavior. *Journal of Social Issues, 8*, 105–130.

Gilbert, D. T., & Silvera, D. H. (1996). Overhelping. *Journal of Personality and Social Psychology, 70*, 678–690.

Goranson, R., & Berkowitz, L. (1966). Reciprocity and responsibility reactions to prior help. *Journal of Personality and Social Psychology, 3*, 227–232.

Gouldner, A. (1960). The norm of reciprocity: A preliminary statement. *American Sociological Review, 25*, 161–178.

Graziano, W. G., & Eisenberg, N. (1997). Agreeableness: A dimension of personality. In R. Hogan, J. A. Johnson, & S. Briggs (Eds.), *Handbook of personality* (pp. 795–825). San Diego, CA: Academic Press.

Grube, J. A., & Piliavin, J. A. (in press). Role-identity, organizational commitment, and volunteer performance. *Personality and Social Psychology Bulletin.*

Grusec, J. E. (1981). Socialization processes and the development of altruism. In J. P. Rushton & R. M. Sorrentino (Eds.), *Altruism and helping behavior: Social, personality, and developmental perspectives* (pp. 65–90). Hillsdale, NJ: Erlbaum.

Grusec, J. E. (1991). The socialization of empathy. In M. S. Clark (Ed.), *Review of personality and social psychology: Vol. 12. Prosocial behavior* (pp. 9–33). Newbury Park, CA: Sage.

Hartshorne, H., & May, M. A. (1928). *Studies in the nature of character: Vol. I. Studies in deceit.* New York: Macmillan.

Hedge, A., & Yousif, Y. H. (1992). Effects of urban size, urgency, and cost of helpfulness: A cross-cultural comparison between the United Kingdom and the Sudan. *Journal of Cross-Cultural Psychology, 23*, 107–115.

Hoffman, M. L. (1990). Empathy and justice motivation. *Motivation and Emotion, 14*, 151–172.

Hoover, C. W., Wood, E. E., & Knowles, E. S. (1983). Forms of social awareness and helping. *Journal of Experimental Social Psychology, 18*, 577–590.

Hornstein, H. A. (1982). Promotive tension: Theory and research. In V. J. Derlega & J. Grezlak (Eds.), *Cooperation and helping behavior: Theories and research* (pp. 229–248). New York: Academic Press.

Independent Sector (1997). *The American volunteer.* Washington, DC: Author.

Isen, A. M. (1993). Positive affect and decision making. In M. Lewis & J. M. Haviland (Eds.), *Handbook of emotion* (pp. 261–277). New York: Guilford Press.

Jenner, J. R. (1982). Participation, leadership, and the role of volunteerism among selected women volunteers. *Journal of Voluntary Action Research, 11*, 27–38.

Kahn, A., & Tice, T. (1973). Returning a favor and retaliating harm: The effects of stated intention and actual behavior. *Journal of Experimental Social Psychology, 9*, 43–56.

Kelln, B. R. C., & Ellard, J. H. (1999). An equity theory analysis of the impact of forgiveness and retribution on transgressor compliance. *Personality and Social Psychology Bulletin, 25*, 864–872.

Korte, C. (1969). Group effects on help-giving in an emergency. *Proceedings of the 77th Annual Convention of the American Psychological Association, 4*, 383–384.

Krebs, D. (1982). Psychological approaches to altruism: An evaluation. *Ethics, 92*, 447–458.

Latané, B., & Darley, J. M. (1970). *The unresponsive bystander: Why doesn't he help?* New York: Appleton-Century-Crofts.

Latané, B., Nida, S. A., & Wilson, D. W. (1981). The effects of group size on helping behavior. In J. P. Rushton & R. M. Sorrentino (Eds.), *Altruism and helping behavior: Social, personality, and developmental perspectives* (pp. 287–313). Hillsdale, NJ: Erlbaum.

Lerner, M. J. (1980). *The belief in a just world: A fundamental delusion.* New York: Plenum.

Lerner, M. J., & Simmons, C. H. (1966). Observers' reactions to the "innocent victim." *Journal of Personality and Social Psychology, 4*, 203–210.

Levine, R. V., Martinez, T. S., Brase, G., & Sorenson, K. (1994). Helping in 36 U. S. cities. *Journal of Personality and Social Psychology, 67*, 69–82.

Ma, H. (1985). Cross-cultural study of altruism. *Psychological Reports, 57*, 337–338.

Macaulay, J. R., & Berkowitz, L. (Eds.). (1970). *Altruism and helping behavior.* New York: Academic Press.

MacLean, P. D. (1985). Evolutionary psychiatry and the triune brain. *Psychological Medicine, 15*, 219–221.

Major, B., & Crocker, J. (1993). Social stigma: The consequences of attributional ambiguity. In D. M. Mackie & D. L. Hamilton (Eds.), *Affect, cognition, and stereotyping: Interactive processes in group perception* (pp. 345–370). San Diego, CA: Academic Press.

Manucia, G. K., Baumann, D. J., & Cialdini, R. B. (1984). Mood influences in helping: Direct effects or side effects? *Journal of Personality and Social Psychology, 46*, 357–364.

Marks, E., Penner, L. A., & Stone, A. V. (1982). Helping as a function of empathic responses and sociopathy. *Journal of Research in Personality, 16*, 1–20.

Marwell, G., Aiken, M. T., & Demerath, N. J., III. (1987). The persistence of political attitudes among 1960s civil rights activists. *Public Opinion Quarterly, 51*, 359–375.

Mathews, K. E., & Canon, L. K. (1975). Environmental noise level as a determinant of helping behavior. *Journal of Personality and Social Psychology, 32*, 571–577.

McGuire, A. M. (1994). Helping behaviors in the natural environment: Dimensions and correlates of helping. *Personality and Social Psychology Bulletin, 20*, 45–56.

McMillen, D. L., Sanders, D. Y., & Solomon, G. S. (1977). Self-esteem, attentiveness, and helping behavior. *Personality and Social Psychology Bulletin, 3*, 257–261.

Midili, A. R., & Penner, L. A. (1995, August). *Dispositional and environmental influences on Organizational Citizenship Behavior.* Annual meeting of the American Psychological Association, New York.

Midlarsky, E., & Hannah, M. E. (1989). The generous elderly. *Psychology and Aging, 4*, 346–351.

Milgram, S. (1970). The experience of living in cities. *Science, 167*, 1461–1468.

Miller, J. G., & Bersoff, D. M. (1994). Cultural influences on the moral status of reciprocity and the discounting of endogenous motivation. *Personality and Social Psychology Bulletin, 20*, 592–602.

Mischel, W. (1973). Toward a cognitive social learning reconceptualization of personality. *Psychological Review, 80*, 252–283.

Moghaddam, F. M., Taylor, D. M., & Wright, S. C. (1993). *Social psychology in cross-cultural perspective.* New York: W. H. Freeman.

Mueller, C. W., & Donnerstein, E. (1981). Film-facilitated arousal and prosocial behavior. *Journal of Experimental Social Psychology, 17*, 31–41.

Mueller, C. W., Donnerstein, E., & Hallam, J. (1983). Violent films and prosocial behavior. *Personality and Social Psychology Bulletin, 9*, 83–89.

Negrao, M. (1997). *On good Samaritans and villains: An investigation of the bright and dark side of altruism in organizations.* Unpublished manuscript, University of South Florida, Tampa, Florida.

Neuberg, S. L., Cialdini, R. B., Brown, S. L., Luce, C., Sagarin, B. J., & Lewis, B. P. (1997). Does empathy lead to anything more than superficial helping? Comment on Batson et al. (1997). *Journal of Personality and Social Psychology, 73*, 510–516.

Oliner, S., & Oliner, P. (1988). *The altruistic personality: Rescuers of Jews in Nazi Europe.* New York: Free Press.

Oliner, P. M., & Oliner, S. P. (1992). Promoting extensive altruistic bonds: A conceptual elaboration and some pragmatic implications. In P. M. Oliner & S. P. Oliner (Eds.), *Embracing the Other: Philosophical, psychological, and historical perspectives on altruism* (pp. 369–389). New York: New York University Press.

Omoto, A. M., & Snyder, M. (1990). Basic research in action: Volunteerism and society's response to AIDS. *Personality and Social Psychology Bulletin, 16*, 152–166.

Omoto, A., & Snyder, M. (1995). Sustained helping without obligation: Motivation, longevity of service, and perceived attitude change among AIDS volunteers. *Journal of Personality and Social Psychology, 68*, 671–687.

Organ, D. W., & Ryan, K. (1995). A meta-analytic review of attitudinal and dispositional predictors of organizational citizenship behavior. *Personnel Psychology, 48*, 775–802.

Otten, C. A., Penner, L. A., & Altabe, M. N. (1991). An examination of therapists' and college students' willingness to help a psychologically distressed person. *Journal of Social and Clinical Psychology, 10*, 102–120.

Otten, C. A., Penner, L. A., & Waugh, G. (1988). That's what friends are for: The determinants of psychological helping. *Journal of Social and Clinical Psychology, 7*, 34–41.

Pearce, J. L. (1983). Participation in voluntary associations: How membership in a formal organization changes the rewards of participation. In D. H. Smith (Ed.), *International perspectives on voluntary action research* (pp. 148–156). Washington, DC: University Press of America.

Pearce, P. L., & Amato, P. R. (1980). A taxonomy of helping: A multidimensional scaling analysis. *Social Psychology Quarterly, 43*, 363–371.

Penner, L. A., & Craiger, J. P. (1991, August). *The altruistic personality.* Paper presented at the annual meeting of the American Psychological Association, San Francisco, CA.

Penner, L. A., Escarrez, J., & Ellis, B. (1983). Sociopathy and helping: Looking out for number one. *Academic Psychology Bulletin, 5*, 209–220.

Penner, L. A., & Finkelstein, M. A. (1998). Dispositional and structural determinants of volunteerism. *Journal of Personality and Social Psychology, 74*, 525–537.

Penner, L. A., & Fritzsche, B. A. (1993, August). *Measuring the prosocial personality: Four construct validity studies.* Paper presented at the annual meeting of the American Psychological Association. Toronto, Canada.

Penner, L. A., Fritzsche, B. A., Craiger, J. P., & Freifeld, T. R. (1995). Measuring the prosocial personality. In J. Butcher & C. D. Spielberger (Eds.), *Advances in personality assessment* (Vol. 10, pp. 147–163). Hillsdale, NJ: Erlbaum.

Penner, L. A., Midili, A. R., & Kegelmeyer, J. (1997). Beyond job attitudes: A personality and social psychology perspective on the causes of Organizational Citizenship Behavior. *Human Performance, 10*, 111–131.

Piliavin, J. A., & Callero, P. (1991). *Giving blood: The development of an altruistic identity*. Baltimore: Johns Hopkins University Press.

Piliavin, J. A., & Charng, H. W. (1990). Altruism: A review of recent theory and research. *Annual Review of Sociology, 16*, 27–65.

Piliavin, J. A., Dovidio, J. F., Gaertner, S. L., & Clark, R. D., III. (1981). *Emergency intervention*. New York: Academic Press.

Piliavin, J. A., & Unger, R. K. (1985). The helpful but helpless female: Myth or reality? In V. O'Leary, R. K. Unger, & B. S. Wallston (Eds.), *Women, gender and social psychology* (pp. 149–186). Hillsdale, NJ: Erlbaum.

Rabow, J., Newcomb, M. D., Monto, M. A., & Hernandez, A. C. R. (1990). Altruism in drunk driving situations: Personal and situational factors in helping. *Social Psychology Quarterly, 53*, 199–213.

Reddy, R. D. (1980). Individual philanthropy and giving behavior. In D. H. Smith & J. Macaulay (Eds.), *Participation in social and political activities* (pp. 370–399). San Francisco: Jossey-Bass.

Rioux, S., & Penner, L. A. (1999, April). *Assessing personal motives for engaging in Organizational Citizenship Behavior: A field study*. Paper presented at the Annual Meeting of the Society for Industrial and Organizational Psychology, Atlanta, GA.

Rosenhan, D. (1969). The kindnesses of children. *Young Children, 25*, 30–44.

Rushton, J. P. (1984). The altruistic personality: Evidence from laboratory, naturalistic and self-report perspectives. In E. Staub, D. Bar-Tal, J. Karylowski, & J. Reykowski (Eds.), *Development and maintenance of prosocial behavior*. New York: Plenum.

Rushton, J. P., Fulker, D. W., Neale, M. C., Nias, D. K. B., & Esyenck, H. J. (1986). Altruism and aggression: The heritability of individual differences. *Journal of Personality and Social Psychology, 50*, 1192–1198.

Sagi, A., & Hoffman, M. L. (1976). Empathic distress in the newborn. *Developmental Psychology, 12*, 175–176.

Salovey, P., Mayer, J. D., & Rosenhan, D. L. (1991). Mood and helping: Mood as a motivator of helping and helping as a regulator of mood. In M. S. Clark (Ed.), *Review of personality and social psychology: Vol. 12. Prosocial behavior* (pp. 215–237). Newbury Park, CA: Sage.

Savin-Williams, R. C., Small, S., & Zeldin, R. S. (1981). Dominance and altruism among adolescent males: A comparison of ethological and psychological methods. *Ethology and Sociobiology, 2*, 167–176.

Schaller, M., & Cialdini, R. B. (1988). The economics of empathic helping: Support for a mood management motive. *Journal of Experimental Social Psychology, 24*, 163–181.

Schmitt, D. R., & Marwell, G. (1972). Withdrawal and reward reallocation as responses to inequity. *Journal of Experimental Social Psychology, 8*, 207–221.

Schroeder, D. A., Dovidio, J. F., Sibicky, M. E., Matthews, L. L., & Allen, J. L. (1988). Empathy and helping behavior: Egoism or altruism. *Journal of Experimental Social Psychology, 24*, 333–353.

Schroeder, D. A., Penner, L. A., Dovidio, J. F., & Piliavin, J. A. (1995). *The psychology of helping and altruism: Problems and puzzles*. New York: McGraw-Hill.

Schwartz, S. H., & Howard, J. A. (1982). Helping and cooperation: A self-based motivational model. In V. J. Derlega & J. Grzelak (Eds.), *Cooperation and helping behavior: Theories and Research* (pp. 327–353). New York: Academic Press.

Segal, N. L. (1984). Cooperation, competition, and altruism within twin sets: A reappraisal. *Ethology and Sociobiology, 5*, 163–177.

Segal, N. L. (1991, April). *Cooperation and competition in adolescent MZ and DZ twins during the Prisoners' Dilemma Game*. Paper presented at meeting of Society for Research in Child Development, Seattle, WA.

Segal, N. L. (1993). Twin sibling, and adoption methods: Test of evolutionary hypotheses. *American Psychologist, 48*, 943–956.

Shotland, R. L., & Heinold, W. D. (1985). Bystander response to arterial bleeding: Helping skills, the decision-making process, and differentiating the helping response. *Journal of Personality and Social Psychology, 49*, 347–356.

Shotland, R. L., & Huston, T. L. (1979). Emergencies: What are they and how do they influence bystanders to intervene? *Journal of Personality and Social Psychology, 37*, 1822–1834.

Sibicky, M., Mader, D., Redshaw, I., & Cheadle, B. (1994, May). *Measuring the motivation to volunteer.* Paper presented at the annual meeting of the Midwestern Psychological Association, Chicago, IL.

Sibicky, M. E., Schroeder, D. A., & Dovidio, J. F. (1995). Empathy and helping: Considering the consequences of intervention. *Basic and Applied Social Psychology, 16*, 435–453.

Sills, D. L. (1957). *The volunteers.* Glencoe, IL: Free Press.

Simon, H. A. (1990, December 21). A mechanism for social selection and successful altruism. *Science, 250*, 1665–1668.

Skitka, L. J. (1999). Ideological and attributional boundaries on public compassion: Reactions to individuals and communities affected by a natural disaster. *Personality and Social Psychology Bulletin* (in press).

Smith, K. D., Keating, J. P., & Stotland, E. (1989). Altruism reconsidered: The effect of denying feedback on a victim's status to empathic witnesses. *Journal of Personality and Social Psychology, 57*, 641–650.

Snyder, M., & Omoto, A. M. (1992). Who helps and why? In S. Spacapan & S. Oskamp (Eds.), *Helping and being helped* (pp. 213–239). Newbury Park, CA: Sage.

Sober, E. (1988). What is evolutionary altruism? [Special Issue] *Journal of Philosophy* [M. Matthen & B. Linsky (Eds.), Philosophy and biology], *14*, 75–100.

Sober, E. (1992). The evolution of altruism: Correlation, cost and benefit. *Biology and Philosophy, 7*, 177–188.

Sober, E., & Wilson, D. S. (1998). *Unto others: The evolution and psychology of unselfish behavior.* Cambridge, MA: Harvard University Press.

Staub, E. (1978). *Positive social behavior and morality: Vol. 1. Social and personal influences.* New York: Academic Press.

Staub, E. (1979). *Positive social behavior and morality: Vol. 2. Socialization and development.* New York: Academic Press.

Staub, E. (1986). A conception of the determinants and development of altruism and aggression: Motives, the self, and the environment. In C. Zahn-Waxler, E. M. Cummings, & R. Ianotti (Eds.), *Altruism and aggression: Biological and social origins* (pp. 135–164). Cambridge, England: Cambridge University Press.

Staub, E. (1996). Responsibility, helping, aggression, and evil: Comment. *Psychological Inquiry, 7*, 252–254.

Sterling, B., & Gaertner, S. L. (1984). The attribution of arousal and emergency helping: A bidirectional process. *Journal of Experimental Social Psychology, 20*, 286–296.

Stryker, S. (1980). *Symbolic interactionalism: A social structural version.* Menlo Park, CA: Benjamin/Cummings.

Stukas, A. A., Snyder, M., & Clary, E. G. (1999). The effects of "mandatory volunteerism" on intentions to volunteer. *Psychological Science, 10*, 59–64.

Swinyard, W. R., & Ray, M. L. (1979). Effects of praise and small requests on receptivity to direct-mail appeals. *Journal of Social Psychology, 108*, 177–184.

Thomas, G., & Batson, C. D. (1981). Effect of helping under normative pressure on self-perceived altruism. *Social Psychology Quarterly, 44*, 127–131.

Thomas, G. C., Batson, C. D., & Coke, J. S. (1981). Do Good Samaritans discourage helpfulness? Self-perceived altruism after exposure to highly helpful others. *Journal of Personality and Social Psychology, 40,* 194–200.

Tillman, P. (1998). *In search of moderators of the relationship between antecedents of Organizational Citizenship Behavior and Organizational Citizenship Behavior: The case of motives.* Unpublished master's thesis. University of South Florida.

Trivers, R. L. (1971). The evolution of reciprocal altruism. *Quarterly Review of Biology, 46,* 35–37.

Vaughan, K. B., & Lanzetta, J. T. (1980). Vicarious instigation and conditioning of facial expressive and autonomic responses to a model's expressive display of pain. *Journal of Personality and Social Psychology, 38,* 909–923.

Walster, E., Walster, G. W., & Berscheid, E. (1978). *Equity: Theory and research.* Boston: Allyn & Bacon.

Walton, M. D., Sachs, D., Ellington, R., Hazlewood, A., Griffin, S., & Bass, D. (1988). Physical stigma and the pregnancy role: Receiving help from strangers. *Sex Roles, 18,* 323–331.

Webley, P., & Lea, S. E. G. (1993). The partial unacceptability of money in repayment for neighborly help. *Human Relations, 46,* 65–76.

Weiner, B. (1980). A cognitive (attribution)-emotion-action model of motivated behavior: An analysis of judgments of help-giving. *Journal of Personality and Social Psychology, 39,* 186–200.

Weiner, B. (1986). *An attributional theory of motivation and emotion.* New York: Springer-Verlag.

Weiner, B., Perry, R. P., & Magnusson, J. (1988). An attributional analysis of reactions to stigmas. *Journal of Personality and Social Psychology, 55,* 738–748.

Weismann, R. X., & Galper, J. (1998). The grid. *American Demographics, December,* 46–47.

Williamson, G. M., & Clark, M. S. (1989). Effects of providing help to another and of relationship type on the provider's mood and self-evaluation. *Journal of Personality and Social Psychology, 56,* 722–734.

Williamson, G. M., & Clark, M. S. (1992). Impact of desired relationship type on affective reactions to choosing and being required to help. *Personality and Social Psychology Bulletin, 18,* 10–18.

Wilson, J. P. (1976). Motivation, modeling, and altruism: A person x situation analysis. *Journal of Personality and Social Psychology, 34,* 1078–1086.

Wispé, L. (Ed.). (1978). *Altruism, sympathy, and helping.* New York: Academic Press.

Yinon, Y., & Landau, M. O. (1987). On the reinforcing value of helping behavior in a positive mood. *Motivation and Emotion, 11,* 83–93.

Yousif, Y., & Korte, C. (1995). Urbanization, culture, and helpfulness: Cross-cultural studies in England and the Sudan. *Journal of Cross-Cultural Psychology, 26,* 474–489.

Zahn-Waxler, C., Robinson, J. L., & Emde, R. N. (1992). The development of empathy in twins. *Developmental Psychology, 28,* 1038–1047.

Zajonc, R. B. (1980). Feeling and thinking: Preferences need no inferences. *American Psychologist, 35,* 151–175.

CHAPTER THIRTEEN

Social Comparison Motives in Ongoing Groups

John Darley

The concern in this chapter is with the workings of social comparison motives and processes in ongoing groups. What historically have been the concerns of "social comparison theory?" What we might call the "standard" social comparison theory about individuals (Festinger, 1954; Goethals & Darley, 1977; Suls & Miller, 1977; for recent developments see Suls & Wheeler, in press) has addressed how a person evaluates his/her own opinions and abilities by comparison with others who are voicing opinions or performing similar ability-linked tasks around him/her. This needs more explanation. In its original statement, by Leon Festinger (1954), social comparison theory addressed how an individual determined the correctness of the opinions that he/she tentatively held, or whether a certain ability was high or low. This determination was made by comparing one's own abilities and opinions with what could be observed from the ability and opinion-linked performances of others. Further postulates of the theory addressed how these inferences would be affected by the similarity or dissimilarity of the comparison others to the person doing the comparing. Social comparison theory, then, concerned itself with two problems: how persons use information from others to learn about the physical or social world around them, and also to learn important things about their own abilities. The original formulation of the theory drew on Lewinian concepts. Since that formulation, the theory has been recast in attributional terms (Goethals & Darley, 1977) and its implications for various aspects of self-presentation (Darley & Goethals, 1980) have been recognized.

The present chapter addresses a somewhat different set of questions than does the standard social comparison theory, and it is useful to begin by spelling out those differences. The present chapter attempts to articulate a social comparison theory that addresses social comparison processes in ongoing groups. We will be concerned with extending social comparison notions to groups that exist within social and organizational domains, and have been formed to carry out certain tasks or to fill certain needs. On examination, classical social comparison theory has not paid a great deal of attention to the origins of the set of individuals that forms the set of comparison others for an individual. Sometimes the standard theory has conceptualized those others to be individuals recruited in the imagination of the individual rather than the individuals actually present. At other times the theory has conceptualized the comparison others as a present collection of individuals, such as fellow students in an elementary school classroom, or the other sprinters gathered for a track meet. Thus, there is a sense in which classic social comparison theory has not been about social comparison with groups of persons. The comparison others are not necessarily in the same group as the comparing individual in any psychologically meaningful sense.

A second set of social comparison theories focuses on comparisons between groups. Social identity theory (Abrams, 1992; Hogg & Abrams, 1988; Tajfel & Turner, 1986; see Hogg, 2001, for a perspective on social identity theory that takes into account the recent inclusion of self-categorization considerations) asserts that the individual finds self-esteem in belonging to a favorably regarded ingroup, an assertion documented by research that demonstrates that individuals can and do "bask in reflected glory" by brandishing their group membership when that group has, for example, won a sporting event. Hogg (in press) examines the historical and current role of social comparison processes in the social identity perspective. Relative deprivation theory (Runciman, 1966; Walker & Pettigrew, 1984) would make a similar assertion, although its focus is characteristically on the loss of status or esteem that an individual feels when that individual is a member of a poorly regarded group. A group that is disrespected by other groups is social comparison-deprived, for instance, and develops some explanation of that relative deprivation that leads it to acquiesce in or rebel against its deprivation.

Our concern in this chapter is rather different. We focus on the individual within a group that has been formed for other purposes than social comparison, and the social comparison processes that take place for that individual with other members of that group. (This is not to deny that a person extracts self-esteem from the standing of his or her group vis-à-vis other groups. Since this is so, the person will work hard to contribute to the product of the group so that this group will excel. The increase in self-esteem that is gained by the rise in prestige of the ingroup is a force that motivates each individual's contributions to the group efforts.) In our theory the group in which the individual belongs "comes first" as it were and it is with others in that group that the individual compares. Paradigmatically, the group is a sports team, a work group in a factory, a group of computer programmers working together on creating a computer application, or a set of sorority sisters living together in a sorority house on a college campus. The comparisons that take place, obviously, can he on abilities and skills that are central to the group's existence, or ones that are largely irrelevant to the group's purposes. Given the fact that the group is often a task-driven group, it will frequently be the case that the comparisons are on the tasks that are central to the group's purposes.

We begin by assuming that a person is a member of a group and that membership in that group is "psychologically significant" to the person. If a group is "psychologically significant" to a group member, then the group will exert influence on the behaviors, thoughts, and emotions of that group member. This, of course, is the standard definition of "social influence" and we need to restrict the domain further to limit the scope of this chapter. The limit is easily arrived at. Social comparison theorists have suggested three basic motives that the individual brings to the group. The first is one of accurate self-perceptions of one's skills and talents (Festinger, 1954). In a world in which one is often offered the possibility to attempt tasks, it is useful to know the level of one's various abilities in order to determine the probabilities of success at these tasks. Second, since William James (1890) we have recognized that people not only want to know how well they can perform a task, but also that they can "perform it well" (Goethals & Darley, 1977). For many, perhaps most of the tasks that we are called on to perform, to do them well is to increase our self-esteem, and to do them poorly is to lower it. Third, and closely connected to the second motive, a person wants to do well at a task in order that the others in the group will increase their esteem for her, or at least avoid failure so that others will not decrease their esteem for her.

It is the last two motives that we focus on in this chapter. Since Mead (1934) and Cooley (1902), psychologists have recognized that the two are inextricably linked. Since we all learn through socialization to take the role of the other, and to see ourselves from the perspective of a generalized other, we apply to ourselves the standards of normal members of our culture. Therefore, a poor performance that causes others to regard me in negative ways lowers my self-esteem. Self-esteem is to some considerable extent driven by the regard of others.

This can easily be applied to performances on tasks that are necessary for group functioning. The more the group values the task, the more doing well on this task matters; the more one's esteem in the group depends on succeeding at that task. It is how the group manages these issues of esteem they grant to others within the group, and the effects that has on the individual's self-esteem, that we will find are central to this chapter's considerations.

This is generally consistent with the thrust of classic social comparison theory. It has historically concentrated on the influence of others on the self-relevant thoughts and feelings of a group member, with particular attention focused on the evaluations that persons within groups make of their own achievements, abilities, moral worth, and social competencies. The suggestion, confirmed in a number of studies, is that these self-evaluations are heavily comparative in nature. My evaluation of my own performance depends on its standing vis-à-vis the performances of others in my group. It is these self-evaluations and my evaluations of what others "think of me" that we will be concerned with in this chapter.

In the real world, groups are formed for a number of purposes. Thus "the group" can be created for a number of functions: a work group in an organizational setting, a baseball team, an affinity group such as a sorority or a set of model train hobbyists, a combat platoon, or a committee of faculty.

These groups exist in the world in the standard ways that groups exist, and generally the new member can be said to have "joined" the group at a fairly well-defined moment in time. But psychological research has taught us that the propensity of an individual to regard himself as a member of a psychologically meaningful group extends beyond existing groups joined in a standard manner. Recall from research using the minimal group paradigm (Diehl, 1990) that people are quick to identify with "groups" by discovering similarities on quite minor and fleeting shared characteristics, so almost every characteristic that can be made salient to an individual can create an ingroup that shares that characteristic, and an outgroup that does not. In other words, "group membership" created on the basis of quite minor characteristics can be psychologically significant to the individual. Relatedly, social identity theory, particularly in its self-categorization mode, makes clear that a person's identification with a particular classification that forms a group depends on the surrounding social context (Hogg & Abrams, 1990). Three or four women executives at a convention, surrounded by a sea of men, will feel a common shared identity that may drive them to get in contact with each other, and form an interacting group.

What we can do, in the present chapter, is analyze comparison processes in interacting groups. These other "proto-groups" will figure in our analyses if they become interacting groups, with a set of purposes for interacting, which implies a set of skills and efforts on which the members can be evaluated.

We can now summarize the argument this chapter will make. Groups come together for a number of reasons. The functions that the group takes on, or are assigned, determine the tasks the groups must perform, and thus the abilities that are central to its mission. The central point of this chapter is that the group's purposes will determine the dimensions along which members compare their performances to one another, and social comparison of these group-relevant performances will determine the esteem in which the group holds the individual, and thus the esteem the individuals have for themselves. As a group's purposes emerge, develop, or are changed by changing demands on its functioning, social comparison processes can lead to an individual's standing rising and falling in the group. Next we turn to a taxonomy of groups, in terms of the functions the groups are expected to fulfill.

A Taxonomy of Groups

Any number of social scientists have made interesting conceptual distinctions between kinds of groups. Here we can only address the distinctions that are most germane to the social comparison considerations that we address in this chapter. Before we examine these distinctions, we will illustrate the sorts of groups that we intend to consider. Some groups have relatively well-defined production tasks. An army platoon is to capture a hill, a work group is to assemble a certain number of parts into an array of functioning machines, and a faculty committee is to design an undergraduate curriculum. For other groups, the commodity to be produced is the training of the group members. Boy scout patrols and high school study groups are examples of this sort of group. For still other groups, it is not at all easy to specify what they are to produce, and it may even be the case that thinking of them as groups assembled for the purposes of production is wrong. A group of people who get together to discuss a book gather together partially to inform each other, but partly to have a good time together. Hobby groups share knowledge with each other, but mainly share the social validation of the legitimacy of the excitement of the hobby.

A rough division of groups is possible, and will be useful for this chapter. Some groups are task groups, in that their major purpose is to perform certain tasks. Work groups in organizations are paradigmatic examples of this, and we would also include the combat platoon, and the faculty committee. Other groups might be called affinity groups; for them the major purpose of getting together in the group is to affiliate with like-minded others. A group of hobbyists would fit this definition, as would a sorority.

Typologies oversimplify. Obviously affinity groups have tasks to do, and the members of task groups often feel strong affinities for each other. The model railroad hobbyists plan eagerly for their pre-Christmas model train show, and the sorority sisters run their sorority house, budget their expenses, and generally carry out the tasks necessary for their continuing existence. The affinity bonding in military service is often the strongest bond those people form in life, and work groups often draw very close to each other. (See Prentice, Miller, &

Lightdale, 1994, for a discussion of how groups that begin as having only bonds to each other develop into valuing the group's identity, over and above those bonds.)

McGrath and his colleagues (Arrow, McGrath, & Berdahl, in press) have made a useful distinction that illuminates but does not exactly map the distinction that we are making. They distinguish between groups that interact and who have some relationships of inter-dependence, and categories of people who come to mind because they share one or more attributes. It is this second term of the distinction, a category of people that share attributes, that we think is often imaginatively called into mind when standard social comparison processes are at issue. I run the 100 m dash and call to mind the category of Olympic-class dash runners (or aging, out-of-condition professors) and Olympic dash records, and compare my performance with those records. But it is important to say that the affinity groups that we have described are not just people who share an interest and therefore are just a categorical and imagined collection of individuals. Our affinity groups meet face to face, and the time they spend together they would describe as some of the most important time they have. Individuals in these affinity groups may begin by focusing on the bonds they feel to other group members, beginning (Prentice, Miller, & Lightdale, 1994) as a "common-bond" group. However, over time they are likely to form an identification with the group over and above their bonds to individual other group members. Further, since they need to carry out the various chores required in order that the group continue to exist, and even to expand and take on more activities for its members, there is a need for multiple skills and talents, and group members who have those skills are thus useful to the group.

What Characteristics and Abilities does the Group Value?

As we suggested above, task groups are likely to value the characteristics and talents of individuals that contribute to the success of the central group tasks. Stereotypically, when we think of task groups, we tend to imagine groups such as football teams or combat platoons in which it seems to the outsider that one essential skill is required – in the case of the team, the ability to smash the opponent; in the case of the platoon the ability to kill the enemy. Actually, the notion that a person is valued by the group in proportion to her contribution to the group's central tasks requires some amendment. Expectation states theory (Ridgeway, 2001) points out that status within a group, which is generally equivalent to our notion of the group's valuation of the individual, is produced in not one but two ways. First, how good you are at the group-defining tasks, but second, by your more diffuse and general status characteristics. Being the best trumpet player in the football marching band gains one status because of its central utility to the band, but having a high general status in the larger world of status via socio-demographic considerations also makes a difference in the way that the group regards you and treats you. For instance, a brain surgeon and a janitor may be equally poor musicians, but the band is going to grant the brain surgeon higher status. This strikes me as true but it might be useful to distinguish exactly what sort of standing these two considerations gives one, rather than lumping them together as "status." The poorly playing janitor has few other useful functions to perform for the band, and thus could be expected to see this and quietly exit. The poorly playing brain surgeon can, for instance, help the band gain audiences, and perhaps stage fund raisers among his fellow brain surgeons. To the extent that he whole-heartedly throws himself into these supporting role considerations, and to the extent that he recognizes his poor musical skills and plays very softly, the band may have a complex but positive regard for him that will allow him to remain.

As this hints, the notion that a person is valued by the group in proportion to her contribution to the group's central tasks is usefully amended by a second realization. In fact, in most task and affinity groups, not one but a number of skills, abilities, and expenditures of efforts are required for success. Even in those relatively "one-central-skill-homogeneous" groups, having different people with differing talent profiles is useful. It is useful to realize that, for any moderately complex task, a number of different skills and talents will be necessary for the group's success. If the group task is putting out a newspaper, for instance, then good writers and photographers are needed, but also good manuscript editors and layout artists. Those who knew about printing presses used to be required, now skills with computer pagemaking programs are necessary.

For present purposes, I want to focus on the self-esteem that an individual feels because of the weight and value of his contributions to the group as compared to the contributions of others in the group, and on the signals he receives from other group members about the value of these contributions. (This is thus separate from Crocker & Luhtanen's (1990) concept of collective self-esteem that springs from the esteem in which the group is held. However, desire for collective self-esteem will motivate group members to work for the success and glory of their groups.) At first glance, the fact that groups generally require a multiplicity of talents seems to create a solution to the problem of each member gaining self-esteem in the group. Each member simply values most heavily those talents he or she is in a position to contribute. There is probably some of this (Ross & Sicoly, 1979) but the process has a limit: each individual who is a group member is psychologically likely to value those characteristics and talents that seem most central to the group's essential purposes. Concretely, the newspaper delivery boy is not going to get the status that the newspaper reporters get. This is so for reasons pointed out to us by an expanded social identity theory (Hogg, in press: Turner, Hogg, Oakes, Reicher, & Wetherell, 1987). The addition of self-categorization theory to social identity theorizing stresses the fact that an existing and salient group identity causes the group member to depersonalize his or her normal self-identity, and to "shift toward the perception of self as an interchangeable exemplar of some social category and away from the perception of self as a unique person defined by individual differences from others" (Turner et al., 1987, pp. 50–51). Deaux (1996) has written extensively on the relationships between a person's own view of his/her identity and the transformations that this view goes through when the person is a member of a group (Deaux, Read, Mizhari, & Cutting, 1999; Deaux, Read, Mizhari, & Ethier, 1995; Reid & Deaux, 1996).

The general point we want to extract is that there is a trend here. Social identity theory will cause all group members to most value the display of those traits or skills that are central to the group's tasks, but for reasons we point out, the group member who is not skilled at those central tasks may still contribute to the group's purposes by taking on non-central but essential tasks. What we will discover is that it is in an important sense the choice of the group whether the person who fulfils those tasks is granted esteem from the group.

How does the Group Convey Self-esteem to its Members?

Equity theory (Adams, 1965) points out that the group frequently has tangible benefits to convey to its members, often in the form of the distribution of valued material commodities earned by its joint activities. Since groups often have resources to share out among their members, the sharing strategies will be interpreted as giving the group members clues about their differential worth and the comparative value of their skills, performances, and efforts. The standard assumption in a group, equity theory suggests, is that one's outcomes are proportional to one's contributions to fulfilling the group's tasks. Any individual can use this assumption to reason backward from the share of the benefits offered her to the group's valuation of her contributions. Relative deprivation theory has a similar postulate about entitlements to resources generated by contributions to group efforts that allows for a similar decoding of one's value to the group.

The point here, drawn both from equity and relative deprivation theory, is that for a group that as a group earns resources, the decisions of the group or those authorities granted power to make those decisions about the distribution of those resources among the group members is what reveals the collective agreement on the "real" value of each of the group members to the group.

As we have said, sometimes the resources earned are straightforwardly monetary or involve some other commodity that is limited and so creates a zero-sum allocation problem. When that is so, the "bottom line" is the bottom line, and it is the distribution of the fixed resource that reveals member standing. Other times the resources earned by the group are less zero sum in character; perhaps they involve the prestige of a win or a job well done, or generalized good regard from other groups. These other kinds of "earnings" have more expandable possibilities. In the dialogues that occur after a baseball team wins its game, the members create stories about how one fielder made a catch that prevented a large number of runs being scored by the other team, about how a pitcher performed well in relief, and even about how a first-base coach alertly held up a runner who otherwise would have been thrown out at second. These stories allocate credit for the group success to various members; importantly, the stories are told by other than the subject of the story. In a well-working group, the story about how Dave made a great contribution is told by anyone other than Dave. The individuals who made the most contributions to the success of the group have the gracious possibility of telling stories that cede some of their glory for having produced the victory to the efforts of others, making them also entitled recipients of the now shared glory, which is expanded by being shared.

What we see here is something that we all understand intuitively, and its existence is one of the most interesting consequences of considering social comparison processes in groups when those group's exist for reasons other than social comparison. These groups generally need to continue to exist. They will sometimes facilitate their continuing existence by blunting or moderating the workings of social comparison processes. They do so because they cannot tolerate the negative consequences that follow from the free workings of social comparison processes, with the attendant possibilities of lowering the self-esteem of certain of the group's members. They therefore "downkey' interpretations that limit credit for success to those whom stereotypic analysis would code as most responsible for a task, and develop narratives that distribute the credits more evenly among the group members.

This "downkeying" is easiest when the resources being distributed are symbolic and un-limited rather than financial and limited. As we said, when a work setting group receives a bonus for over-achieving their production quota, its choices about the allocation of that bonus among the workers tells each member how that member "really" is valued by the group. But even then, it is possible for the system to use allocation mechanisms for limited resources that do not single out certain members as central contributors and deny group esteem to the others. Wise groups, therefore, know how to choose an allocation mechanism that does not attempt to put a precise valuation onto each member's contribution. They divide it "equally" or according to individual need. Best of all, they allocate it to some joint group purpose like a banquet, thus celebrating the fact that it was the group effort that earned the bonus.

But we shouldn't spend too much time in this comparison-benign world without remem-bering that sometimes groups do distribute their rewards according to the differential value they place on different members' contributions to the group efforts, and they do not attempt to develop narratives that will bolster the self-esteem of the less-valued group members. In fact, they will sometimes sharpen the contrasts between the differential value of the different group members by criticizing or otherwise denigrating the lower status individuals.

When does a group take one or the other of these alternatives? The answer to this is provided by a consideration of the ecological conditions that surround the group, par-ticularly the possibilities that the group has to replace its members.

Groups Exist in Ecological Settings

Groups exist in ecological settings, and some aspects of these contexts are important to social comparison processes in groups. Along one dimension, a group may have an open character such that it can theoretically recruit new members from large pools of available people, or it may be "closed" in that its membership is for all intents and purposes fixed, in the sense that no new members are feasible. A professional basketball team is an example of the former case, while a faculty basketball team from a department of five souls is the latter case. On a related dimension, a group may have the power to expel existing members (and recruit new ones) or it may exist in a social context in which every member is precious and cannot be replaced. As we will see, the social context surrounding the group will have quite important consequences for the group's regard for various of its members, and thus for the self-esteem of each individual.

Predicting when group members will be motivated to be tactful or ruthless in their distribution of material rewards and prestige requires us to draw on another psychological theory that is rarely mentioned in the social comparison literature. The ecological setting of the group sharply affects the rules that are likely to be used for the distribution of the group-earned resource. The examples given above implicitly assumed a group that needed to retain the committed loyalties of its members. This occurs in groups in which there are few or no possible replacements for the existing members. This may emerge for any number of groups, but is particularly likely to emerge for groups that exist in what are called "understaffed" settings. Groups, that is, that need every member in order to fulfill their essential tasks. These are the predictions drawn from what is now called "staffing" theory, formerly called "manning" theory, which is a contribution of the ecological psychologists (Barker & Gump, 1964; Schoggen & Barker, 1974; Wicker, 1968). An "understaffed" or underpopulated setting is one in which there are metaphorically fewer hands than are needed to do all that is necessary. An example would be a high school with so few students that it couldn't have a football team, cheerleaders, and a marching band, unless everybody who could remotely fill one of those roles did so (and the football team still didn't have many substitutes, the cheerleaders were few, and the band was small).

Theory and research suggest (Willems, 1967) that in understaffed settings, individuals "have less sensitivity to and are less evaluative of individual differences in behavior," "see themselves as having greater functional importance," and have "more responsibility." This turns out to work to the advantage of the group, as it seeks to retain the participation of those members who have less to contribute to the group enterprises, but whose retention is none the less necessary. We argue that for the group to survive, it must arrange for a reasonable amount of gratification of the social comparison motives for group members. How this is arranged involves the occasional muting of social comparative information, and the exercise of tact and "downkeying" of the inadequacy of occasional performances by weak performers on the part of those at the top of the performance ladder. We suggest that in understaffed settings, the group members recognize the utility – the necessity – of eliciting contributions from all group members, and also recognize that this almost dictates a reasonably egalitarian distribution of rewards and esteem. This is not to say that there are not differences in an individual's regard for different group members; but it is to say that the regard that is expressed for even the lowest ranked members does not fall into a negative zone. Further, candid assessments of the inadequacies in the performances of the less-qualified group members are stifled rather than expressed, at least in the presence of these less-qualified group members.

Think next of overstaffed settings; ones in which the group would be able to recruit skill-qualified replacements for group members; or for affinity groups, highly prestigious fraternities and clubs that have far more applicants than they can or will admit. There a group member who does not perform tasks with adequate skill will not damage the group by his departure, in fact may improve the group performance if his replacement is more skilled. In the affinity group, a member who does not participate fully in the group, or who withholds voluntary energy, is one who is taking the place of a better group member. In these situations, the group members do not feel a mutual obligation for the egalitarian distribution of resources among members, or an easygoing willingness to share in the glory of the group successes. On the contrary, these groups are likely to be quite willing to signal low regard for marginal group members, on the theory that they can easily replace these members and the replacements will be more valuable to the group. In these groups, social comparison is a mechanism that can be used to create psychologically untenable positions for a group member, causing that member to exit the group. This, of course, reminds us of Marques' "black sheep" effect (Marques, Abrams, Páez, & Hogg, this volume, chapter 17; Marques & Páez, 1994; see Marques, Páez, & Abrams, 1998 for a discussion that examines a notion of intragroup differentiation similar to the one developed here). The black sheep in a group is one who is marginal on one or more of the group's prototypical attributes. Other group members conveying low regard for the black sheep's contributions to the group's efforts is an effective mechanism for the expulsion of the black sheep. The present point is that this will happen only when the group has the option of expelling the black sheep. Moreland and Levine's (Levine & Moreland, 1994; Moreland & Levine, 1982; Moreland, Levine, & Cini, 1993; Levine, Moreland, & Choi, 2001) model of group socialization is illuminating here. The group does a cost/benefit analysis of the value of the member in question to the group and withdraws commitment to that member if the calculations come out unfavorably for the retention of that individual. Relatedly, the group will not allow entry to potential new group members if the calculations are similarly low. The point developed here is that whether or not the calculations are favorable for the retention of an individual depends on what other individuals are potentially recruitable.

Returning to the question of how an understaffed group can create a climate in which, metaphorically, a black sheep can gently be painted at least gray if not white. Assume an individual who is performing poorly on the central group tasks, and is at least occasionally required to perform. Another research literature becomes relevant here, and it is the literature on excuses and self-handicapping (Jones, Rhodewalt, Berglas, & Skelton, 1981; Rhodewalt, Morf, Hazlett, & Fairfield, 1991; Snyder & Higgins, 1988; Snyder, Higgins, & Stucky, 1983). For a group seeking to retain its members, and to retain their willingness to contribute what efforts they can to the group tasks, those members need to be allowed to create "excusing conditions" for their less than stellar past performances. When those performances are of the sort thought to be linked to underlying abilities, the excuses given highlight the non-ability determinants of past poor performances. A tragic event in one's personal life temporarily destroys motivation and the ability to concentrate, for instance.

Not only do the members need to be allowed to put forward these excuses, but also the group needs to honor and validate them. This may take quite a good deal of face-saving ingenuity on the part of the group members. But if this ingenuity is not mustered, the danger is that the poorly performing individual feels a contempt stemming from the other group members that is destructive to his self-esteem.

This, of course, is the mechanism that can lead to voluntary departures from groups that have the possibilities of recruiting replacement members. Depending on the choices made by the poorly performing member, this can be a more or less esteem-damaging process. If the exiting member is willing to exit early and signals that, then she may offer an excuse that attributes poor past performance to lack of motivation rather than ability. The member choosing that option will need to create a story to tell to herself and others that makes her exit as non-stigmatizing as possible. Given that she has encased the excuse in a narrative that announces her exit, the group will not be motivated to contradict the truth of the excuse. In affinity groups, similar stories can be told. It is not, for instance, that one does not value the fraternity's activities, it is just that "time demand" do not allow full participation. If this announcement is coupled with the member's resignation, the other group members will not find it necessary to point out to the exiting member that they all face and cope with similar time demands on their activities.

The interaction can get nastier. If the group member is continuing to perform poorly, or failing to keep work commitments, and if the group has the possibility of replacing that group member with a more productive new recruit, then the group may force that member to exit by explicitly contradicting the excuses the member offers for poor performance. This essentially forces the person to face the contempt in which his low abilities or failed commitments have led the group to regard him. By this manipulation of social comparison information, the failing member is generally led to exit the group.

Emergent Functions in Group Settings

There is an undeniable bleakness to the above account of social comparison's role that the group can mobilize to cause non-performing members to exit if their replacement is possible. But that bleakness can be at least ameliorated if one examines the full range of activities that groups need in order to function successfully. The fact is this: When individuals act within groups, more functions are necessary than when those individuals function as individuals. Putting this another way, any group requires certain functions to continue its existence as a group, with coordination and control functions being the most obvious examples. "Leadership" is another function thought of in this context. This creates a wider set of possibilities for group members to find ways to be useful to their group, and persons who take on these functions are valuable to the group. For instance, a group certainly will require communication between members for task coordination, and those who take on this communication and coordination function are valuable to the group. In fact, in the famous Bavalas studies, people at the center of communication hubs often are chosen as leaders by their groups. Other functions are often necessary: record keeping and other forms of institutional memory are examples of this. Many other functions are necessary, depending on the composition and the task of the group. This creates a number of "behavioral niches" into which people can insert themselves to facilitate the group's progress. Further, successful performance in many of these niches may rely more on a willingness to expend effort rather than on abilities. As Daubenmier, Smith, and Tyler (1997) have shown, the willingness to engage in what they call "extra-role" behaviors is linked to being viewed by others as a valuable group member. (An example of extra-role behavior might be the web-page designer who during the all-nighter gets coffee for the programmers while waiting for their markups of her designs.) As this indicates, a generalized alertness to what the group needs, and a willingness to "go beyond the call of duty" in providing what the group needs, is a valued stance for a group member. While it is probably true that those who are best regarded in a group are those who have the most to contribute to the central tasks of the group, these niches can create the possibility of an individual finding value in the eyes of the other group members by performing some essential but not central task for the success of the joint effort.

The Consequences of Giving or Denying Individuals Self-esteem within Groups

Respectful treatment enhances self-esteem

We have seen how a group can use social comparison information to cause less valued members to exit from the group if replacement is possible. A closely related idea is that the desire for esteem from the group can motivate group members to expend effort on tasks that will benefit the group. This is so both because esteem matters and what goes along with esteem matters.

First, consider what goes along with the distribution of esteem within a group. If, as is often the case, the group has material rewards to distribute to members, then we can expect group members to expend effort for the group because the esteem in which the group holds different members is generally linked to the differential distribution of these material rewards. Social exchange theory (Thibaut & Kelley, 1959) suggests that people interact with each other to gain material resources. Extending this to the functioning of people within groups, the degree to which the person contributes to the group is a reflection first of the past rewards and resources the person has received for past contributions, and second, the person's expectations about the contingencies between future contributions and future rewards.

This is the analysis that flows tautologically from one powerful and prevalent theory of human nature, the theory that holds that people are motivated primarily by material self-interest. But recent work (Tyler, 2000) suggests that our culture's tendency to focus on self-interest and material rewards for individual efforts, may not be the true central motivator of the individual group member who contributes time, energy, effort, and abilities to the group. What Tyler, Lind (Tyler & Lind, 1992), and their colleagues have shown, at its most general level, is the consequences that follow when a group gives a person "standing" within that group. An individual who feels that a group he is in gives him "standing" or "respect" is a person who is willing to sacrifice his own interests to the interests of the group, and to voluntarily pitch in to help the group fulfill its purposes. Importantly, there is a non-calculational component to this response. The person will often voluntarily comply with a decision a group makes, even when the decision goes directly counter to her self-interests. For instance (Tyler & Degoey, 1995), citizens who feel that they are granted standing by the relevant authorities, and that the relevant authorities make decisions in a fair way, voluntarily reduce their water consumption during droughts when asked to do so by the authorities, even though their consumption is not monitored. In other words, they voluntarily exercise restraint in a social dilemma situation. The group-value theorists (for a recent review, see Tyler & Blader, 2000) have collected an impressive set of results showing that an individual who perceives that a group he is in treats him in ways that signal that he is a respected member of that group feels an enhanced self-esteem and will be a loyal and hard-working member of that group.

What does it mean for a group to give a group member "standing?" What are the actions by means of which the actions of the group convey "standing" or "respect" to the individual? On our terms, granting a person "respect" involves treating that person in ways that convey that the group values his membership in the group. The group-value theorists raise an interesting question. What classes of actions can the group, or the authorities of the group, take to convey that self-esteem enhancing message? Essentially (Tyler, 1999), the task is to convey messages of "respect," which tell the recipient how he or she is evaluated by others in that group. To tie the group-value model to the social comparison considerations discussed here, it is useful to mark these researchers' (Smith, Tyler, Huo, Ortiz, & Lind, 1998) demonstration that treatment quality works through perceptions that the group respects the individual, which enhances self-esteem.

Respect, the group-value theorists suggest, is conveyed to an individual in three ways: first by indicators of status recognition, second by signals that the group and its authorities have a benevolent stance toward the individual, and third by signals that the group will make decisions about the person that begin with a neutral stance, and are fair-minded, rather than playing favorites within the group. Evidence (Tyler, Degoey, & Smith, 1996) shows that an individual's perception that a group treats her favorably on these three dimensions enhances self-esteem.

Disrespectful treatment

Respectful treatment increases self-esteem and brings the group member to be a loyal contributor to the group's needs. What are the consequences of a group or organization treating an individual in ways that signal disrespect? Some we have already dealt with; the individual will desire to exit the group. But suppose that exit is somehow blocked, either because the material resources the individual gains from group membership are too high to forego, or for some other reason. The psychological considerations we have developed here suggest that is a highly volatile situation. Basically, to preserve some self-esteem the disrespectfully treated individual must cease to grant any validity to those signals of disrespect and to the individuals from which they come. The group-value theory helps us understand how this is done: the individual decides that the group is malevolent toward him, and gives unfairly favorable treatment to others. In social identity theory terms, the person psychologically exits the group, and no longer derives elements of his identity from group membership. His contributions to the group, if he makes any, are only due to compliance to power, enforced by surveillance.

It can get worse. If the group or organization is perceived as hostile toward one, then acts of hostility toward the group are retaliatory and appropriate. A recent book (Kramer & Tyler, 1996) contains a good many chapters by social and organizational psychologists showing the consequences that occur when individuals mistrust the groups or organizations in which they are situated, and they are about what the current perspective would lead us to expect. In a chapter entitled "The road to hell," Sitkin and Stickel (1996) demonstrate the demoralization of a research team when management inflicts what they perceive to be demeaning performance requirements on them. Kramer (1996) demonstrates the development of "paranoid cognition" in workers who are made to feel insecure about their status or standing within an organization. Bies and Tripp (1996) document acts of revenge taken by organizational members who were mistreated by their organizations. Two findings emerge. First, demeaned individuals felt it morally appropriate to retaliate against the offending institution, and second, they bided their time in order to retaliate when it would be maximally harmful to the organization.

It is hard to escape the conclusion that an individual who is disrespected by a group in which he retains membership, although he may initially strive to gain respect, will later cease to be a productive member of that group, and will eventually be a destructive member. Applying psychological theories to self-esteem gained by social comparison processes explains many phenomena of productive and loyal behavior on the part of group members. Applying the same theories to situations of self-esteem destruction by social comparison processes illuminates the origins of destructive behavior by group members.

Chapter Overview

This chapter has considered a specific, perhaps unusual, and narrow set of issues concerning social comparison. The orienting question concerned the operation of social comparison processes in groups that exist to fulfill certain tasks or to share certain interests. Social comparison here is taken to mean the reflected information that individuals receive about their own abilities and skills by engaging in comparison processing of the information provided by the performances of the other group members. The information is processed, as Festinger suggested, to reveal to individuals the level of their abilities. But a second motive, other than learning the level of one's abilities, is more important. Since "abilities" are qualities that the culture values possessing, and since the individual is generally a well-socialized member of the culture, the self-esteem of the individual is dependent on doing well at the ability tasks, and thus being seen by others and by oneself as having high abilities. The tendency for one's own self-esteem to depend on one's performances on the ability-linked tasks that are central to the group's functioning is increased by social identity considerations. As a member of the group, the individual adopts the group's view of what abilities are important, and these abilities will be the ones that are important to the group's success.

This means that the self-esteem of an individual work group member is heavily dependent on the signals that the individual gets from the group about the adequacy of his or her performance. If the individual's performances are poor on the group's core tasks, the group has a choice to make about the signals it sends to the individual about the adequacy of those performances. Here we suggested that the signals depend on estimates of whether the potential exit of the marginally performing individual will benefit or harm the group in the long run. Staffing theory, growing out of the work of Barker and other ecological psychologists, was drawn on to determine the relative costs and benefits of the exit of the marginal individual. Essentially, if the marginal individual can be replaced with a much better-performing substitute, then the marginal individual's exit is desired; if replacement is impossible, or all potential replacements will be more marginal in their ability-linked performances, then the group must engage in the complex task of maintaining and even bolstering the self-esteem of the marginally performing individual.

There is a bleak side to this. For groups that have the possibility of replacing marginal members, this analysis suggests that the processes by which the marginal member is led to exit will involve considerable self-esteem damage to that individual. However, there is an alternate path available to the marginal individual that may retain his or her membership in the group, and his or her self-esteem. The individual who is less skilled on the tasks that are central to the group's identity has a second path to demonstrating some utility to the group. This involves finding or creating some activities that facilitate and support the group's performance on its core tasks, and diligently and assiduously contributing to the group's functioning in this way. The greater the ingenuity involved in the discovery of these secondary but useful roles, and the greater the effort and talent demonstrated in carrying out the role-related tasks, the more esteem the role player can earn from the more central group members.

REFERENCES

Abrams, D. (1992). Social identity. In D. Abrams & M. Hogg (Eds.) (1999). *Social identity and social cognition*. Oxford, UK: Blackwell.

Adams, J. S. (1965). Inequity in social exchange. In L. Berkowitz (Ed.), *Advances in experimental social psychology* (Vol. 2, pp. 267–299). New York: Academic Press.

Arrow, H., McGrath, J. E., & Berdahl, J. L. (in press). *A theory of groups as complex systems*. Thousand Oaks, CA: Sage.

Barker, R. G., & Gump, P. V. (Eds.) (1964). *Big school, small school: High school size and student behavior*. Stanford, CA: Stanford University Press.

Bies, R. J., & Tripp, T. M. (1996). Beyond distrust: "Getting even" and the need for revenge. In R. M. Kramer & T. R. Tyler (Eds.), *Trust in organizations: Frontiers of theory and research* (pp. 246–260). Thousand Oaks, CA: Sage.

Cooley, C. H. (1902). *Human nature and the social order*. New York: Scribner's.

Crocker, J., & Luhtanen, R. (1990). Collective self-esteem and in-group bias. *Journal of Personality and Social Psychology, 58*, 60–67.

Darley, J., & Goethals, G. (1980). People's analyses of the causes of ability linked performances. In L. Berkowitz (Ed.), *Advances in experimental social psychology*, (Vol. 13, pp. 1–37). New York: Academic Press.

Daubenmier, J. J., Smith, H. J., & Tyler, T. R. (1997). *Group status, self-esteem, and group-oriented behavior*. Unpublished manuscript. University of California, Berkeley.

Deaux, K. (1996). Social identification. In E. T. Higgins & W. A. Kruglanski (Eds.), *Social psychology: Handbook of basic principles* (pp. 777–798). New York: Guilford Press.

Deaux, K., Reid, A., Mizrahi, K., & Cotting, D. (1999). Connecting the person to the social: The functions of social identification. In T. R. Tyler & R. M. Kramer (Eds.), *The psychology of the social self: Applied social research* (pp. 91–113). Mahwah, NJ: Erllbaum.

Deaux, K., Reid, A., Mizrahi, K., & Ethier, K. A. (1995). Parameters of social identity. *Journal of Personality and Social Psychology, 68*, 280–291.

Diehl, M. (1990). The minimal group paradigm: Theoretical explanations and empirical findings. *European Review of Social Psychology, 1*, 263–292.

Festinger, L. (1954). A theory of social comparison processes. *Human Relations, 7*, 117–140.

Goethals, G., & Darley, J. (1977). *Social comparison theory: An attributional approach*. In J. M. Suls & R. L. Miller (Eds.), *Social comparison processes: Theoretical and empirical perspectives* (pp. 259–278). Washington, DC: Hemisphere.

Hogg, M. A. (2001). Social categorization, depersonalization and group behavior. In M. A. Hogg & S. Tindale (Eds.), *Blackwell handbook of social psychology: Group processes* (pp. 56–85). Oxford: Blackwell Publishing.

Hogg, M. A. (in press). Social identity and social comparison. In J. Suls & L. Wheeler, (Eds.), *Handbook of social comparison: Theory and research*. New York: Plenum.

Hogg, M. A., & Abrams, D. (1988). *Social identifications*. New York: Routledge.

Hogg, M. A., & Abrams, D. (1990). Social motivation, self-esteem, and social identity. In D. Abrams & M. Hogg (Eds.), *Social identity theory: Constructive and critical advances* (pp. 28–47). New York: Springer-Verlag.

James, W. (1890). *Principles of psychology* (2 Vols.). New York: Holt.

Jones, E. E., Rhodewalt, F., Berglas, S., & Skelton, J. A. (1981). Effects of strategic self-presentation on subsequent self-esteem. *Journal of Personality and Social Psychology, 41*, 407–421.

Kramer, R. M. (1996). Divergent realities and convergent disappointments in the hierarchic relation: Trust and the intuitive auditor at work. In R. M. Kramer & T. R. Tyler (Eds.), *Trust in organizations: Frontiers of theory and research* (pp. 216–245). Thousand Oaks, CA: Sage.

Kramer, R. M., & Tyler, T. R. (1996). *Trust in organizations: Frontiers of theory and research*. Thousand Oaks, CA: Sage.

Levine, J. M., & Moreland, R. L. (1994). Group socialization: Theory and research. *European Review of Social Psychology, 5*, 305–336.

Levine, J. L., Moreland, R. L., & Choi, H. -S. (2001). Group socialization and newcomer innovation. In M. A. Hogg & S. Tindale (Eds.), *Blackwell handbook of social psychology: Group processes* (pp. 86–106). Oxford: Blackwell Publishing.

Marques, J. M. (1990). The black-sheep effect: Out-group homogeneity in social comparison settings. In D. Marques, J. M., & Páez, D. (1994). The "black sheep effect": Social categorization, rejection of ingroup deviates and perception of group variability. *European Review of Social Psychology, 5*, 37–68.

Marques, J. M., Páez, D., & Abrams, D. (1998). Social identity and intragroup differentiation as subjective social control. In S. Worchel, J. F. Morales, D. Páez, & J.-C. Deschamps (Eds.), *Social identity: International perspectives* (pp. 124–141). London: Sage.

Mead, G. H. (1934). *Mind, self, and society* (posthumous; C. M. Morris (Ed.). Chicago, IL: University of Chicago Press.

Moreland, R. L., & Levine, J. M. (1982). Socialization in small groups: Temporal changes in individual-group relations. In L. Berkowitz (Ed.), *Advances in experimental social psychology* (Vol. 15, pp. 137–192). New York: Academic Press.

Moreland, R., L., Levine, J. M., & Cini, M. (1993). Group socialization: The role of commitment. In M. A. Hogg & D. Abrams (Eds.), *Group motivation: Social psychological perspective* (pp. 105–129). London: Harvester Wheatsheaf.

Prentice, D., Miller, D., & Lightdale, J. (1994). Asymmetries in attachments to groups and to their members: Distinguishing between common-identity and common-bond groups. *Personality and Social Psychological Bulletin, 20*, 484–493.

Reid, A., & Deaux, K. (1996). Relationship between social and personal identities: Segregation or integration. *Journal of Personality and Social Psychology, 71*, 1084–1091.

Rhodewalt, F., Morf, C., Hazlett, S., & Fairfield, M. (1991). Self-handicapping: The role of discounting and augmentation in the preservation of self-esteem. *Journal of Personality and Social Psychology, 61*, 122–131.

Ridgeway, C. L. (2001). Social status and group structure. In M. A. Hogg & S. Tindale (Eds.), *Blackwell handbook of social psychology: Group processes* (pp. 357–375). Oxford: Blackwell Publishing.

Ross, M., & Sicoly, F. (1979). Egocentric biases in availability and attribution. *Journal of Personality and Social Psychology, 37*, 322–336.

Runciman, W. G. (1966). *Relative deprivation and social justice: A study of attitudes to social inequality in twentieth-century England*. Berkeley: University of California Press.

Schoggen, P., & Barker, R. G. (1974). The ecological psychology of adolescents in an American and an English town. *Contributions to Human Development, 1*, 12–23.

Sitkin, S. B., & Stickel, D. (1996). The road to hell: The dynamics of distrust in an era of quality. In R. M. Kramer & T. R. Tyler (Eds.), *Trust in organizations: Frontiers of theory and research* (pp. 196–215). Thousand Oaks, CA: Sage.

Smith, H. J., Tyler, T. R., Huo, Y. J., Ortiz, D., & Lind, E. A. (1998). The self-relevant implications of the group-value model: Group membership, self-worth, and treatment quality. *Journal of Experimental Social Psychology, 34*, 470–493.

Snyder, C. R., & Higgins, R. L. (1988). Excuses: Their effective role in the negotiation of reality. *Psychological Bulletin, 104*, 23–35.

Snyder, C. R., Higgins, R. L., & Stucky, R. J. (1983). *Excuses: Masquerades in search of grace.* New York: Wiley.

Suls, J. M., & Miller, R. L. (Eds.) (1977). *Social comparison processes: Theoretical and empirical perspectives.* Washington, DC: Hemisphere.

Suls, J. M., & Wheeler, L. (Eds.) (in press). *Handbook of social comparison: Theory and research.* New York: Plenum.

Tajfel, H., & Turner, J. C. (1986). The social identity theory of intergroup behavior. In S. Worchel (Ed.), *The psychology of intergroup relations.* Chicago, IL: Nelson Hall.

Thibaut, J., & Kelley, H. (1959). *The social psychology of groups.* New York: Wiley.

Turner, J. C. (1987). *Rediscovering the social group: A self-categorization theory.* Oxford, UK: Blackwell.

Turner, J. C., Hogg, M. A., Oakes, P. J., Reicher, S. D., & Wetherell, M. S. (1987). *Rediscovering the social group: A self-categorization theory.* Oxford, UK: Blackwell.

Tyler, T. R. (1999). Why people cooperate with organizations. *Research in Organizational Behavior, 21*, 201–246.

Tyler, T R., & Degoey, P. (1996). Trust in organizational authorities: The influence of motive attributions on willingness to accept decisions. In R. M. Kramer & T. R. Tyler (Eds.), *Trust in organizations: Frontiers of theory and research* (pp. 331–350). Thousand Oaks, CA: Sage.

Tyler, T. R., & Blader, S. (2000). *Cooperation in groups: Procedural justice, social identity, and behavioral engagement.* Philadelphia, PA: Psychology Press.

Tyler, T. R., Degoey, P., & Smith, H. J. (1996). Understanding why the justice of group procedures matters. *Journal of Personality and Social Psychology, 70*, 913–930.

Tyler, T. R., & Lind, E. A. (1992). A relational model of authority in groups. In M. Zanna (Ed.), *Advances in experimental social psychology* (Vol. 25, pp. 115–191). New York: Academic Press.

Walker, I., & Pettigrew, T. F. (1984). Relative deprivation theory: An overview and conceptual critique. *British Journal of Social Psychology, 23*, 301–310.

Wicker, A. W. (1968). Undermanning, performances, and students' subjective experiences in behavior settings of large and small high schools. *Journal of Personality and Social Psychology, 10*, 255–261.

Willems, E. P. (1967). Sense of obligation to high school activities as related to school size and marginality of student. *Child Development, 38*, 1247–1260.

CHAPTER FOURTEEN

Aversive Discrimination

Amélie Mummendey and Sabine Otten

Introduction

"I don't want my grave blasted in the air – like Heinz Calinski's grave. Regrettably, the danger that the dignity of the dead is violated is still serious in this country." Ignaz Bubis, the president of the Central Council of Jews in Germany uttered this sentence in July 1999, in an interview where he came up with the resigned conclusion that more than half a century after the defeat of Nazi Germany, Jews, although German citizens, remain foreigners in Germany, and Jewish graveyards are still targets of destruction. Of course, in today's Germany, these attacks are prosecuted as criminal acts and there is a high sensitvity with regards to the explicit expression of negative attitudes toward Jewish people. However, in Germany as in other societies, there are plenty of other groups whose differentiation and exclusion are much more deliberate or even accepted: Ethnicity, religion, gender, sexual orientation, age, disabilities, and regional or national origin are all wellknown criteria for social differentiation. Besides, social psychological research provides ample evidence that even arbitrary categorizations can elicit ingroup–outgroup differentiation effects (e.g., Brewer, 1979; Brown, 1999; Messick & Mackie, 1989).

The questions we want to deal with in this chapter are twofold: (1) Why do particular categorizations become relevant for differentiation between ingroup and outgroup, and when does social differentiation lead to discrimination? (2) What are the determinants of derogation, hostility, and antagonism against outgroups? Dealing with these issues, we will not emphasize instances of mild ingroup favoritism, but will focus on negative treatments, that is, on derogation, hostility, and dehumanization based on social category membership. However, first, we will analyze the psychological definition of social discrimination and its crucial constituents: Social categorization, normative context, position-specific perspectives, and the quality of behavior manifesting intergroup discrimination.

Discrimination as Social Interaction

Most of the theoretical and empirical work on social discrimination refers to Gordon Allport (1954), who defines discrimination as behavior that ". . . comes about only when we deny to individuals or groups of people equality of treatment which they may wish" (p. 51). This definition comprises two crucial aspects: First, social discrimination necessitates social categorization; and second, it involves not only an actor, that is, somebody deciding about and realizing an intergroup treatment, but also a recipient, who *disagrees* with this treatment.

A more recent definition by Dovidio and collaborators describes social discrimination as "inappropriate treatment to individuals due to their group membership" (Dovidio, Brigham, Johnson, & Gaertner, 1996, p. 279). By reference to the issue of inappropriateness, this statement illustrates a further decisive aspect: Processes of judgment and interpretation, not just clear-cut, "objective" characteristics of the intergroup treatment determine what we conceive of as social discrimination (Otten & Mummendey, 1999a). Correspondingly, Graumann and Wintermantel (1989) state that "the concept of social discrimination is inextricably connected to notions of justice and equ(al) ity . . ." (p. 183).

Instances of discrimination are not only restricted to category-based transgressions of the equality-norm, but can also imply transgressions of the equity-norm. Neither do equal distributions of resources guarantee that there is *no* discrimination, nor is unequal intergroup allocation a reliable criterion to identify instances of bias, favoritism, and derogation. A key criterion is some *dissent* between allocating group (member) and targeted group (member) about the appropriateness of their relative treatment. Accordingly, the subsequent analysis will focus upon the different facets that might determine such dissent.

Differentiation versus discrimination

Social differentiation does not necessarily imply social discrimination, but forms the basis for both consensual and conflictual forms of unequal intergroup treatment. Thus, it is a necessary, but not a sufficient condition for social discrimination. As such, it can take different forms: First, it can refer to a *quantitative* dimension – for example, those who work longer get more salary. Second, category-based treatment can follow a *qualitative* differentiation – for instance, more money for those with better qualifications. Third, social differentiation can determine the access to opportunities and rights by reference to *descriptive*, inherited characteristics – for example, giving the right to vote only to citizens of 18 years and above. In all of these cases the parties involved can be demarcated into those who get more and those who get less, into those who have access to a certain resource and those who do not. None the less, for the examples given, we can also assume a shared consensus about the adequacy of the criteria applied or the dimension underlying differentiation. However, if there is dissent about the categorization that has been applied, or about the consequences derived from the categorical distinction, then social differentiation will turn into social discrimination.

Historical and cultural differences.   Depending on the social context, the identical differentiation might be perceived as adequate and functional or as illegitimate and aversive. Such contextual differences can be due to historical change. For example, the changed ideas on gender equality demonstrate the *inter-time perspective* on the (in)appropriateness of social differentiation: Until the 20th century women were typically conceived of as predisposed to raise children, keep the house, feed their family, while men were obliged to provide for their families materially. Gender-specific roles were assumed to fit gender-specific abilities (see Eagly, 1987). Even in democratic systems, it took a long time until the claim "Women and men are equal!" was heard and translated into social reality. For example, not until the 1960s were women accepted as students at prestigious American universities such as Princeton. Today, however, the same universities would be sued if they rejected a student based on gender. In addition to such variations over time, there are also examples of diverging *inter-cultural perspectives* on certain categorical distinctions (see Triandis & Trafimow, 2001, for a discussion of cultural differences).

Discrimination and social categorization

Social discrimination can involve individual group members or groups as a whole. What makes it a *social* phenomenon is not the number of persons involved but the fact that it presupposes social identities and is based upon categorical distinctions among groups of individuals. As outlined in the previous sections, the distinction of individuals in terms of social categories is not problematic per se, but its application as a basis of resource allocations might cause conflict and dissent. Accordingly, a crucial question for the social psychological analysis of social discrimination is: Why does a certain categorization of persons into members of ingroup and outgroup become the adequate basis for their differential treatment? Mere category salience does not necessarily imply a differential treatment according to the lines of this categorization. For example, article 3, 3 of the German constitution explicitly says: Nobody should be (dis)advantaged because of gender, descent, race, language, origin, faith, religious or political beliefs. Although these are highly accessible, frequently applied social categories, their members have to be treated equally before the law, and are guaranteed equal opportunities.

Mere categorization effects.   Although salient social categories *must* not imply unequal treatment based on this distinction, a huge body of research on so-called minimal groups (Rabbie & Horwitz, 1969; Tajfel, Billig, Bundy, & Flament, 1971) documents that simply by introducing a categorization into "we" and "they," even when based on fully arbitrary criteria and without directly serving realistic self-interest, ingroup bias and intergroup discrimination occur (e.g., Brewer, 1979; Brown, 1999). "Social identity theory" (Tajfel & Turner, 1986) offered an account for this "mere categorization effect" by emphasizing the motivational functions of social categorization. People's desire to see themselves positively can partly be derived from their membership of social groups (Tajfel, 1981); by perceiving and treating own groups in a way that distinguishes them positively from other groups, individuals can enhance or ensure their positive social identity. Thus, even positive differentiation of a minimal ingroup can serve an overall positive self-concept.

Social categorization and identification.   According to Tajfel and Turner (1986), identification with the ingroup is necessary for the assumed sequence from categorization via social comparison to positive ingroup distinctiveness. Research showed, however, that when measuring ingroup identification and intergroup bias, especially under minimal conditions, correlations are often only weak (see Hinkle & Brown, 1990). More recently, ingroup identification has been manipulated as an independent variable (Perreault & Bourhis, 1999). Here, the relation between identification and favoritism turned out to be straightforward: Under conditions increasing ingroup-identification (chosen group membership) discriminatory behavior was significantly stronger than under conditions with lower identification (assigned minimal group membership). Other studies manipulating or measuring ingroup identification independently of the intergroup treatment similarly reveal that ingroup-identification can be understood as a key variable of discriminatory behavior (e.g., Branscombe & Wann, 1994; Ellemers, Van Rijswijk, Roefs, & Simons, 1997).

Police officers and police dogs: Defining adequate levels of categorization.   It is beyond the scope of this chapter to deal with empirical and theoretical work criticizing and extending the theoretical explanation of the "mere categorization effect" as provided by social identity theory (e.g., Diehl, 1989; Mummendey, 1995). In the present chapter we can state that understanding social discrimination as a result of positive distinctiveness striving cannot suffice to explain why certain category distinctions are taken as rationales for (unequal) distributions of resources while others are not. Here, self-categorization theory (Turner, Hogg, Oakes, Reicher, & Wetherell, 1987) allows more precise predictions: An individual will apply a certain social categorization, if it subjectively gives meaning to the given situation. Such meaning and, thus, category salience is determined by three aspects: accessibility, structural fit, and normative fit (Oakes, 1987). Accessibility refers to the perceiver's readiness to apply a certain categorization, which is due to prior experiences or to situational goals. Structural fit is defined by the meta-contrast ratio, the proportion of perceived intra-category differences and inter-category differences; the more the latter outscore the former, the higher is the structural fit (Turner et al., 1987). Finally, normative fit refers to the match between category and the content properties of its stimuli (cf. Oakes, 1996), that is, it indicates whether in a given situation a categorization in fact allows appropriate behavioral predictions (e.g., in a decision about building of a new atomic reactor, the members of the Christian Democrats might predominantly stress economic interests while members of the Green Party will mainly focus on environmental risks).

The notion of fit, however, presupposes a general comparability of the two categories. In order to guide intergroup treatment a social categorization must be linked to a superordinate, inclusive category defining a frame for the comparison. Consider a member of the police wondering whether his salary is fair. He might compare salaries of members of the secret service with those from the mounted police, but not consider relevant what the State spends for its human police members compared to its police dogs. A dissent about the intergroup treatment necessitates that there is an inclusive category (e.g., human police members) within which ingroup (e.g., secret service) and outgroup (e.g., mounted police) can compete for their entitlements in a certain allocation decision.

Categorization and justice.   We have argued that discrimination is inextricably linked to both justice and social categorization (see also Tyler, 2001). Both aspects are taken into account in an approach by Wenzel (1997; 2000) who combined self-categorization theory (Turner et al., 1987) with theories of distributive justice. According to self-categorization theory, ingroup favoritism implies that the own group is seen as more prototypically representing dimensions that are defined as crucial for the superordinate category including both ingroup and outgroup (Turner et al., 1987; Mummendey & Wenzel, 2000). For example, a male employer could argue: Jobs in business necessitate advanced skills in math. Males are better at math than females; thus, male applicants should be preferred. Wenzel (1997; in press) argues and provides evidence that perceptions of social justice follow the same logic: Perceived entitlements are bound to the positive or negative evaluation of the own subcategory compared to the corresponding other subcategory in terms of relevant dimensions of the *primary category*, which includes all potential recipients in the given allocation situation.

Crucial is the social categorization of the target entity: As one possibility, the target may be categorized as a member of the category that includes the potential recipients in a certain allocation situation. In this case, the target is perceived to be equal to the other members of the primary category and, consequently, entitled to the same treatment. If, however, the primary category is further divided into subcategories (e.g., gender), then the subgroups' prototypicality in terms of comparison dimensions relevant for the primary category (e.g., math skills) will determine perceived entitlement. Thus, we can conclude that salience and abstraction level of a certain categorization crucially determine whether social inequality will be perceived, accepted, neglected, questioned, or protested against (see also Major, 1994).

Discrimination as perspective-specific

As mentioned above, Allport's (1954) definition of the term "social discrimination" involves the issue of perspective. None the less, until recently, the overwhelming body of social-psychological theorizing and research on social discrimination has focused on the agents of social discrimination. Such one-sided focus on an *interactional* phenomenon is not a deficiency unique to the domain of intergroup research, but has also been criticized in traditional aggression research (e.g., Mummendey, Linneweber, & Löschper, 1984; Mummendey & Otten, 1993; Tedeschi, 1984). While recently there has been a growing interest in the consequences of social inequality and social discrimination on the targets' side (see Crocker & Quinn and Ellemers & Barreto, this volume, chapters 12 and 16, respectively), the *relation* between target and actor still lacks a thorough theoretical empirical investigation.

Specific to the perspectives of either allocating/privileged group (member) or receiving/disadvantaged group (member) the single groups' entitlement to the resources in question will be estimated. As outlined in the previous section, social categorization provides a basis for judging this entitlement: Those who are categorized as equal or prototypical within the primary category of recipients deserve equal treatment, while those who are categorized as unequal may legitimately be treated unequally (Wenzel, 1997). Accordingly, a perspective-specific dissent can involve three aspects: (1) Is the division of the primary category into subcategories appropriate (e.g., should job candidates be distinguished in terms of gender)? (2) Is the value differentiation linked to the categorization appropriate (e.g., is it true that women are worse in math than men)? (3) Are the decisions about intergroup treatment derived from categorization and value differentiation appropriate (e.g., does the job require high proficiency in math)? In other words, social discrimination as an interactional phenomenon is characterized by a lack of consensus about the fit (Oakes, 1987) of the given social categorization in the respective social context.

As outlined above, an unequal or negative treatment of a group per se does not yet define an instance of social discrimination, but it might be accepted as finally functional, or as legitimized by different needs or different inputs on behalf of the differentiated groups. Groups might be willing to take serious burdens without complaint. Relative deprivation theories (see Taylor & Moghaddam, 1994) state that it is not hardship and negative living conditions per se, which make people feel unjustly treated: The key point is the experience that there are others who are better off, although they are perceived as equal in terms of entitlement or deservingness (see Mikula, 1994 for a respective analysis in interpersonal relations).

However, acknowledging perspectivity in social discrimination and defining a judgmental dissent as its manifesting characteristic might provoke a serious misunderstanding. Our position does not imply that we do not have to care about the exploitation of groups so long as they do not complain about their fate. First, the dissent may not only be located between target and allocating party, but also between an outside observer and the allocating party. Second, such conclusion would imply a confound between the analysis of social discrimination from a political point of view with our attempt to clarify the *psychological processes* that are at stake for the individuals involved in specific instances of implementing or receiving socially discriminating intergroup treatment. Only by analyzing how *both* allocators and recipients differ in their understanding of the appropriateness of certain categorizations, value differentiations and, finally, intergroup allocations, can social discrimination as an interactional phenomenon be fully understood and convincingly dealt with.

Valence, behavioral mode, and discriminating behavior

The reflection on the distinction between differentiation and discrimination already implied that the quality of the "treatment" which might be perceived as discrimination needs a careful analysis. It is not sufficient to take into account whether a certain evaluation or allocation violates norms of equality or equity; in addition its specific characteristics and the dimension to which it refers have to be considered.

A taxonomy of social discrimination. Mummendey and Simon (1991) have offered a taxonomy of social discrimination, which distinguishes two aspects: (a) the valence of resources (positive or negative) that are distributed between groups; and (b) the type of behavioral mode (direct/inflicting or indirect/withdrawing) by which this distribution is established. In each of the resulting four cells, ingroup favoritism or outgroup antagonism can be realized: One might opt for the own professional group getting a higher salary than another professional group, but expect the latter to pay more money when taxes are increased (direct and indirect discrimination in the positive domain); one might vote for another rather than the own home town as a place for an additional large garbage dump, but claim that the own community should be first in line when the township starts the re-naturation of areas that have been destroyed by the coal-mining industry (direct and indirect discrimination in the negative domain).

This variety of possibilities for differentiation and discrimination between groups is not reflected in the empirical work in this domain: Although everyday life provides many examples of a category-based infliction of burdens or costs in ways that the outgroup suffers relatively more than the ingroup, research has overwhelmingly dealt with differential positive treatments.

Positive–negative asymmetry in social discrimination.   Findings by Mummendey and collaborators about the so-called positive–negative asymmetry in social discrimination (for a survey, see Mummendey & Otten, 1998; Otten & Mummendey, 2000) indicate that – at least for direct forms of discrimination – results obtained in the domain of positive resources should not be simply extrapolated to the negative area. The experiments mostly followed a typical minimal categorization procedure, but varied the valence of resources that were distributed between groups: On matrices like the ones in the original study by Tajfel and collaborators (1971) participants either allocated points that were allegedly to be transferred either into money, or into the duration of unpleasant noise or the number of unpleasant tasks (see Mummendey et al., 1992; Otten, Mummendey & Blanz, 1996). In other studies, the manipulation of valence was realized by asking participants to evaluate the novel ingroup and outgroup on either positive or negative trait dimensions (Blanz, Mummendey, & Otten, 1995). These and a number of subsequent experiments consistently showed that for both intergroup allocations and evaluations there were no favoritism effects if negative resources or evaluation dimensions were involved. In the positive domain, however, the typical "mere categorization effect" was replicated: The (minimal) ingroup was significantly and positively differentiated from the respective outgroup.

Integrating the empirical evidence from their studies, Mummendey and Otten (1998) propose the following explanation: Social categories that are minimal do not offer a legitimate rationale for unequal intergroup treatment. Accordingly, in the negative domain a more elaborate cognitive processing (Otten, Mummendey, & Buhl, 1998) and a stronger concern about normative inhibitions (Blanz, Mummendey, & Otten 1997; Otten & Mummendey, 1999b) will raise the probability that the minimal categorization will be considered irrelevant. Thus, group members will re-categorize as a common ingroup (Gaertner, Dovidio, Anastasio, Bachman, & Rust, 1993) and refrain from differential intergroup treatment (Mummendey, Otten, Berger, & Kessler, in press). These findings were further corroborated in a recent study by Gardham and Brown (in press), demonstrating that subgroup and superordinate group identification were crucial for the effects of stimulus valence on intergroup treatment. Besides, this study is noteworthy as it manipulated not only valence but also behavioral mode (allocation, withdrawal). In fact, only for instances of beneficiary decisions (i.e., allocating positive stimuli and withdrawing negative stimuli) was there significant ingroup favoritism. Finally, the importance of category salience in understanding the differential effects of stimulus valence on category salience was underlined in recent studies by Reynolds, Turner, and Haslam (2000), who argue that the positive-negative asymmetry might rely on valence-specific differences in the normative fit of the social categorization and the intergroup comparison dimension.

However, when testing the explanations for the potential explanations of the positive–negative asymmetry effect, Mummendey and collaborators also documented that there are conditions, where ingroup favoritism and outgroup derogation were shown irrespective of valence. Introducing so-called "aggravating conditions" (Blanz, Mummendey, & Otten, 1995; Otten, Mummendey, & Blanz, 1996), such as inferior status and/or minority status, which increased the salience of the intergroup distinction and – possibly – elicited a threat towards positive social identity, resulted in significant favoritism effects in both valence conditions.

We can conclude from the above that negative forms of social discrimination can be demonstrated in the laboratory and in fairly reduced forms of intergroup settings. However, when we turn from allocating minutes of unpleasant noise or samples of boring experimental tasks to much more dramatic negative treatments, then these effects necessitate a salient, subjectively meaningful social categorization that provides even greater legitimization for a category-based intergroup treatment. In the following, we will analyze what such legitimizing rationales might look like, and how an allocating party might come up with the decision that it is appropriate or even inevitable to treat another group negatively.

Determinants of Social Discrimination

Collective beliefs and social norms

Ordinary people typically perceive and describe themselves as friendly, and will claim that their normal everyday activities are primarily motivated to gradually improve their and their families' living conditions, to live in good relations with friends, to be fair to other people, and to achieve further positive goals. Hardly anybody would perceive him- or herself as primarily and explicitly aiming at excluding, insulting, injuring, or even killing somebody else. Nevertheless, aversive discrimination is undoubtedly a social reality. Social norms as part of the belief systems prevailing in a society can – at least partly – account for this apparent paradox.

Norms tell people which kind of differentiation is normal or even necessary, and which differentiation is unacceptable or even sanctioned by authorities. They may dictate against which groups (e.g., Jews, African Americans) public expressions of prejudice are unacceptable, and against which groups (e.g., overweight, asylum seekers) such prejudice may be tolerated or even positively sanctioned. Beyond a simple dichotomous differentiation between own and other groups, norms may prescribe a further differentiation between different outgroups. Pettigrew (1998) differentiates seven different types of minorities in Western Europe according to their status, ranging from the most favored national migrants (e.g., "Aussiedler" "returning home" from Romania after eight centuries) to rejected illegal immigrants. Depending on their respective status assigned by authorities and legislation, members of these groups are treated more or less negatively. Often, illegal immigrants are officially expelled by the host country's police, who will apply severe physical coercion "if necessary." These events are not kept secret from ordinary citizens, but are occasionally shown in TV programs or reported in the newspapers. Little protest is heard on these occasions: Coercion and violence against such groups maybe seem regrettable, but can be normatively justified.

With minority groups holding a higher status, negative treatment is not accepted officially, but since these groups are not viewed as belonging to the host nationalities, differentiation in terms of employment, public accommodation, housing, insurance, banks, etc. is still widespread.

Moral exclusion and delegitimization. A remote observer would notice an inconsistency between a country's constitution and its fundamental paragraphs against any discrimination and the apparently accepted and legitimate differential treatment of people in terms of their group membership. Members of the society itself won't necessarily recognize it because of the consensual acceptance of the normative beliefs. Opotow (1990, 1995) has coined the term "scope of justice" as a fundamental psycho-social orientation toward others. It refers to the fact that people have psychological boundaries of fairness or form a defined and limited moral community. For members of social categories inside this community and within the scope of justice, rules of justice and morality apply. For members of categories outside this scope, the same rules don't apply or seem irrelevant. Thus, members of other social categories might be excluded from the moral community, ". . . permitting justifications – even jubilation – for harm that befall outsiders" (Opotow, 1995, p. 348). In a similar way, Bar-Tal (1989) sees "delegitimization" as categorization of groups into extreme negative social categories which are excluded from human groups that are considered as acting within limits of acceptable norms and/or values (p. 170). Ways to delegitimize outgroups are to dehumanize them, to attribute negative personality traits generalized to the group, to use political labels and associations with consensually despised groups. Delegitimization functions as justification for extreme negative behavior against the dehumanized outgroup.

Social norms, the scope of justice, and moral exclusion lead to differential awareness of legitimate differentiation, on the one hand, or discrimination as illegitimate differentiation, on the other hand. Societal beliefs and norms provide not only the frame for consensual differentiation, but also for dissent and conflicts about the appropriateness of a category to serve as a differentiation basis.

Violence against minorities. Analyses of anti-minority violence in various European countries committed since the beginning of the 1990s showed that the perpetrators were not predominantly from the far right. Moreover, a mixed group of people, adolescents, young adults, and large crowds of ordinary people actively committed, applauded, or refrained from interfering against violence and brutality against foreigners and other minorities. These incidents were often paralleled by the political elite legitimizing the view of foreigners as unbearable burdens or, as the political scientist Thränhardt (1995) puts it, by "playing the race card." Supported by a social climate of intergroup tension, in which outgroups are declared as cause of unsatisfying life conditions, some people might feel legitimized actively to attack outgroups in order to solve social problems (see Pettigrew, 1998, for further discussion of this point). Group members might mutually reinforce each other in their view that they are all behaving appropriately (Mummendey & Otten, 1993; Otten, Mummendey, & Wenzel, 1995; Postmes & Spears, 1998).

The most extreme case of moral exclusion and violence against outgroups is *genocide.* Again, the smaller group of active perpetrators as well as the large majority of bystanders act with support and justification of the dominant ideology. Following Staub (1989), in situations where societies are unstable and provide difficult living conditions, where citizens are unable to improve by individual effort, simple ideological solutions become attractive: "The Jews are our evil." Here, from the perspective of perpetrators, "ethnic cleansing" fulfils social functions; the expulsion of the minority is assumed to solve social problems. The severity of atrocities develops gradually. The society and its authorities provide norms and laws which successively justify more and more extreme actions against the minority. By this stepwise adaptation to severe derogation and harm as normality, perpetrators, bystanders but also victims gradually undergo changes. Increasing levels of harm can be inflicted together with an increasingly firm sense of "justification." Repression, expulsion, and finally extermination are done to protect the own group. This protection is needed not against threat from attacks by enemies from outside, as in wartime; rather, attacks are perceived from within, threatening "essence purity" of the own group, be that essence defined in terms of biology such as race, or in terms of political or religious beliefs.

Intragroup deviance and group threat.   In the incidents outlined above, the majority agrees that certain minorities are threatening the ingroup's identity. There are other cases where there is dissent within the majority itself about which of two conflicting views or beliefs would contradict the essence of group identity. Following these lines, Sani and Reicher (1998, 1999) provide an explanatory approach toward the process of group-schism. Schism of a group stands for collective agreement about the essence of group identity being ruptured: Two opposing fractions mutually claim that the other fraction is negating the group's identity. The perspective-specific divergence about who is supporting and who is negating group identity becomes crucial. Some group members put forward beliefs or values which are viewed by other group members as "destroying" their identity. Sani and Reicher propose that in such situation, intergroup differences become non-negotiable, dissent will be exacerbated, and schism as the state of conflict and incompatibility arises. Convincing evidence for their model is presented by their analysis of two political incidents, namely the split in the Italian Communist Party into two new fractional parties (Sani & Reicher, 1998) and the split in the Church of England following the decision to ordain women to priesthood (Sani & Reicher, 1999).

The actor's perspective

Looking from the actor's perspective, we can see basically three types of differentiation between ingroup and outgroup, differing in terms of the intentionality of outgroup derogation and rejection, and, correspondingly, differing in terms of the (in)consistency between evaluative attitude and behavior toward own and other group.

Mindless ingroup favoritism. An ingroup might be evaluated positively simply due to its automatic association with the typically positive self, without explicit social comparison between ingroup and outgroup. In line with this assumption, Perdue, Dovidio, Gurtman, and Tyler (1990) documented that ingroup or outgroup designators (like "us"and "them") can produce affective congruency effects when combined with previously neutral verbal material, or when presented subliminally in masked affective priming tasks. Recently, such intergroup bias on the implicit level could be shown in three studies even with minimal groups (Otten & Moskowitz, 2000; Otten & Wentura, 1999). Thus, positive ingroup evaluation might result from mindless intergroup differentiation. However, as soon as the individual reflects on the rationale for this differentiation more consciously or is asked to account for it, the differentiation is likely to be given up (Dobbs & Crano, in prep.; Otten et al., 1998).

Ambivalent discrimination. Second, and in line with the "aversive racism" approach (Dovidio, Mann, & Gaertner, 1989; Gaertner & Dovidio, 1986), many actors endorse principles of egalitarianism and fairness, and want to avoid discrimination. Simultaneously, they possess negative beliefs and affect about outgroups, just because they grew up in a society in which stereotypes and prejudice against certain groups still prevail. Differentiation in favor of the own group might be shown only if it can be rationalized by reasons independent of prejudice and without deliberate intention to disadvantage the outgroup. Aversive racists avoid overt displays of intergroup distinctions when the normative structure of a situation is clear, but when the situation is normatively ambiguous, intergroup distinction may occur.

Intentional discrimination. Finally, actors might differentiate deliberately and be able to account for it. They may apply criteria for distinction which they consider justified and based on social norms. In this case, actors perceive outgroups as being distinct and as deserving less positive or even negative treatment. Consistently, they will behave negatively toward these groups or will support others in doing so. Realistic conflict between groups (Sherif, 1966), delegitimization (Bar-Tal, 1989), and moral exclusion (Opotow, 1995) or non-negotiable differences about ingroup identity essence (Sani & Reicher, 1999) provide rationales for deliberately downgrading a particular outgroup.

Accounting for social discrimination.   It is the intentional, fully reflected decision to treat ingroup and outgroup differently that is of particular interest when looking for antecedents of explicit derogation, rejection, and aversive treatment of outgroups. If actors can refer to social justifications for their behavior toward outgroups, the question is how these justifications are provided or developed.

Traditional beliefs. First, justifications might be a feature of traditional beliefs and thus a facet of normality in a stable society. In Germany, for example, until 1994, the constitutional right for equal opportunities did not encompass disabled people. It was taken for granted and adequate to keep them separated from non-disabled people in schools, housing facilities, and at the workplace, where they still get only minimum salary for their work. In the German courts, tourists successfully sued travel agents for damage, because they felt disturbed while on their holidays by a group of disabled people in their hotel and restaurants. People maintaining this situation won't have recognized that they were blocking an outgroup from resources it was entitled to.

Threat. Second, in situations of instability and major social change, people might experience threat to their group status, economically and with respect to their values and belief systems. Macro-social studies show a clear coincidence of high percentages of immigrant minorities and low gross national product, on the one hand, and pronounced xenophobic attitudes, on the other hand (Quillian, 1995). Besides, laboratory experiments provide evidence for the crucial function of perceived threat to positive ingroup identity. In line with social identity theory, Branscombe and Wann (1994) showed that for individuals identifying highly with their threatened ingroup, derogating the threatening outgroup apparently serves motivational functions. Only if an outgroup is threatening the status of the own group, and if positive identity is based upon membership in that group, then positive collective self-esteem is negatively affected, and is re-established by actively derogating the outgroup.

Individual differences.   Beyond situation-specific experiences, people differ individually with respect to a generalized experience of negative interdependence and threat from outgroups leading to a disposition to react against these outgroups in a hostile manner. Several personality constructs have been proposed to explain interindividual variance of outgroup hostility and rejection. In response to the authoritarian-personality-approach (Adorno, Frenkel-Brunswik, Lewinson, & Sanford, 1950), Rokeach (1960) created the politically "neutral" concept of *dogmatism* which stresses the importance of value-differences: dogmatic people with a "closed mind" will conceive value-differences as incompatibility and therefore feel threat to their own values and beliefs by those held by outgroups. *Right-wing authoritarianism* (Altemeyer, 1988, 1994) implies submission to established authorities, aggression directed at targets sanctioned by established authorities, and adherence to traditional social conventions. Like nationalistic orientations (Eckhardt, 1991) it is related to both evaluative bias in favor of ingroup and to the perception of outgroups as inferior to the own group. A related concept to authoritarianism is the concept of *social dominance orientation* as the basic desire to have one's own primary ingroup considered to be superior to and dominant over relevant outgroups (Sidanius, 1993).

Batson and Burris (1994) provide evidence for a close relationship between *prejudice and religion*. Based upon their three-dimensional model of personal religion, they see especially their "religion as quest" dimension associated with outgroup rejection. Individuals whose religious beliefs face the complexity of the human condition, who accept doubts and open questions, show much less inclination toward prejudice than those whose religious beliefs predominantly comprise clear-cut answers and simplistic views of the world as either good or bad.

From a survey of seven representative samples drawn from four European countries, Wagner and Zick (1995) report strong evidence for a positive correlation between level of formal education and outgroup rejection, a correlation which, however, is mediated by social psychological variables such as perceived fraternal relative deprivation (Runciman, 1966; Vanneman & Pettigrew, 1972), or political conservatism and conventional values (Crandall & Cohen, 1994).

In their distinction between blatant and subtle prejudice as two types of intergroup prejudice, Pettigrew and Meertens (1995) take into account the possible effect of societal norms and social desirability striving on individuals' expressing negative attitudes toward outgroups. Subtle prejudice stands for defense of traditional values, exaggeration of cultural differences, and denial of positive emotions; as such, it is in line with today's socially accepted forms of rejecting minorities. Blatant prejudice stands for direct rejection of minorities on the basis of perceived threat from outgroups. Blatant prejudice sees inferior positions of outgroups as biologically or naturally given; hence, differential treatment is justified. From the perspective of a blatant racist, discrimination against ethnic minorities does not exist.

Social emotion and discrimination.   Experience of category-based threat, either induced by a particular intergroup conflict situation, or by a generalized expectation of an outgroup's intentions and actions, refers to an aversive event, which evokes emotions associated with motivations to fight or flight. Emotions such as hostility, but also anger and contempt, are connected to behavioral tendencies to attack, to aggress, or to retaliate against the source of aversion. Fear or disgust accompany avoidance tendencies. Ample evidence in aggression research shows that anger arousal and feelings of provocation on the actor's side are instigated when the opponent's behavior is perceived as illegitimate and norm-violating (Averill, 1982; Tedeschi & Felson, 1994). The actor's subsequent reaction will aim at a subjectively justified payback to the aggressor. Feelings of hostility and anger against outgroups, therefore, can be expected by those people holding a prejudice which explicitly represents such an "offense-retaliation" scheme. In this vein, Smith (1993) stresses the important function of emotion for explaining discrimination. He defines prejudice as "a social emotion experienced with respect to one's social identity as a group member, with an outgroup as a target" (p. 304). Discrimination is seen as the behavior consistent with and driven by emotional action tendencies. Evidence from relative deprivation research supports Smith's predictions: Beyond social categorization in ingroup and outgroups, effects of fraternal relative deprivation on outgroup discrimination require an affective reaction (Pettigrew, 1998).

The target's perspective

As outlined in previous sections of this chapter, we think that an appropriate approach to social discrimination as social interaction necessitates reference to both the actor's and the target's perspective. In addition to the aspects dealt with below, we would like to refer to two other contributions: Crocker and Quinn (2001), for the issue of social stigmatization and stereotype threat, and Ellemers and Barreto (2001), for more details on strategies to cope with negative social identity.

The experience of relative deprivation.   Similar to actors differing in terms of the intentionality of social differentiation, targets either may not realize unequal treatment, or accept it as normatively adequate, or, on the contrary, feel discriminated against. Relative deprivation theory (Crosby, 1982; Folger, 1986) offers concepts about how these diverging views between targets evaluating group-based social inequality may be explained. There is little relationship between objective standard of living and personal dissatisfaction with own income. In order to know whether their own situation is adequate and satisfying, people need an acceptable standard of reference. In addition, the perception of personal entitlement within a context of social inequality is determined by legitimizing beliefs and attributions of the causes for the status quo (see Major, 1994, for an extended discussion of this issue). For example, the more people believe in a just world, the more they feel that they are in personal control of their own outcomes, and the more they believe that their outcomes are deserved (Crocker & Major, 1994).

If people perceive a gap between their expectations and their outcomes, then feelings of relative deprivation such as hostility, grievance, moral outrage, or resentment will arise. The concept of relative deprivation encompasses a cognitive component, the perceived is-ought discrepancy, and an affective component, the feeling of resentment. Egoistical deprivation refers to a person's position within his or her ingroup, while fraternal deprivation refers to an ingroup's status compared to other groups in society (Runciman, 1966). Fraternal rather than egoistic deprivation is expected to affect intergroup behavior (Dion, 1986): Feelings of group-level dissatisfaction have been found to be correlated with negative attitudes toward ethnic outgroups (Applegryen & Nieuwoudt, 1988), with support for nationalist movements (Guimond & Dubé-Simard, 1983), and with a desire for social change and militancy (Koomen & Fränkel, 1992).

The personal/group discrepancy of social discrimination. Often, when describing their present status quo, members of underprivileged minorities clearly perceive their group as a target of discrimination, but claim they personally would experience little if any discrimination. This meanwhile often-replicated "personal/group discrimination discrepancy" (Taylor, Wright, Moghaddam, & Lalonde, 1990), originally regarded as a phenomenon restricted to minorities and negative evaluations, was recently generalized to majorities and positive evaluations (Moghaddam, Stolkin, & Hutcheson, 1997).

There have been several attempts to explain this seemingly irrational effect. One category of explanations refers to motivational processes. First, denying personal discrimination might protect the self from negative emotional consequences and threat (Crosby, 1984). Second, exaggerating the amount of group discrimination might be functional, as it raises feelings of fraternal relative deprivation and increases the probability of actions to improve the group's status (Taylor, Wright, & Porter, 1994). In contrast to motivated reasoning assumptions, Moghaddam et al. (1997) conceive of the effect as result of the differential availability of incidents of discrimination on the personal and the group level. In a recent longitudinal study, Kessler, Mummendey, and Leiße (in press) showed that the person/group discrepancy might stem from the integration of separate non-overlapping sets of comparative information which are derived from different levels of self-categorization. Depending on the salient level of self-categorization different comparison referents, either persons or groups are selected and provide different comparison outcomes.

Strategies to cope with group-based inequality. According to social identity theory, a positive social identity is to a large extent based on favorable comparisons of the ingroup with some relevant outgroup on salient comparison dimensions (Turner, 1975). Belonging to a less privileged group results in an unsatisfactory or negative social identity (Tajfel & Turner, 1986). Individuals therefore are expected to engage in "identity management strategies" (Van Knippenberg, 1989). Tajfel and Turner (1986) distinguish three classes of strategies, namely individual mobility, social creativity, and social competition. These strategies can be categorized further as individualistic versus collectivistic and as behavioral versus cognitive. Beliefs about the socio-structural characteristics of the intergroup relations are expected to influence the choice of coping strategies. Principally important is the question whether individuals can conceive of an alternative intergroup situation to the status quo. This manifests itself in the perceived stability and legitimacy of status differences, as well as in the perceived permeability of intergroup boundaries. Besides sociostructural variables, the extent to which individuals identify with their ingroup constitutes an important determinant of whether individual or collective strategies are chosen (see Ellemers & Barreto, this volume, chapter 16).

Typically, experimental studies in this field referred to an intergroup situation where the continuous existence of the two groups was beyond doubt. This is different in a merger situation, where two groups axe expected to exchange their previous identity against a broader, common ingroup identity (Gaertner et al., 1993). Such a situation was examined in a field study on the relation between East and West Germans after the unification and hence after the merger into the inclusive group of Germans. Here the typically reported effect of perceived stability of status differences was reversed: The pessimistic alternative to the promised change and to the extinction of obvious (material) status differences between East and West was the stability and endurance of the status quo. Consequently, perception of stability rather than instability strengthened East Germans' identification as well as their preferences for collective strategies (Mummendey, Klink, Mielke, Wenzel, & Blanz, 1999).

The prediction of preferences for identity management strategies can be significantly improved by combining assumptions of social identity theory and relative deprivation theory into an integrative model: Individual strategies such as actual or cognitive individual mobility are directly and negatively related to ingroup identification. Collective strategies such as social competition or readiness to participate in social protest are directly connected to negative feelings of resentment and deprivation (Mummendey, Kessler, Klink, & Mielke, 1999).

Conclusions

Differentiation between people because of their group membership is a *necessity* because it is needed by individuals as a basis for orientations and decisions in their everyday life. *Discrimination* between people is a *problem* because it is an inappropriate and unjustified differentiation between people because of their group membership. It is judgment and interpretation and not clear-cut "objective" characteristics of the intergroup treatment itself which define instances of social discrimination. Differentiation changes into discrimination when two parties disagree about the appropriateness and justifiability of a respective distribution and of the underlying categorization. Dissent results from perspective-specific evaluations of a group's entitlement to certain shares of resources derived from the categorization which provided the basis of judging this entitlement. The dissent may be located between actors and targets, or it may exist between actors and targets on the one hand and external observers on the other. With this conception of social discrimination as social interaction we obviously do not intend to "define away" the social problem but to clarify the psychological processes breeding it.

As evidence on the positive–negative asymmetry in social discrimination exemplifies, in the negative more than in the positive domain, differential treatment of own group and outgroup in the negative domain requires elaborate and substantial justifications on behalf of the actor. The abundance of incidents of derogation, rejection, and hostility against outgroups across time and societies demonstrates that ample justifications must be available. Strong ingroup identification and beliefs which interpret unstable or insecure situations as threat from outgroups seem to be key candidates to provide these types of justification. Some approaches see the roots of these social and political beliefs in personality variables such as right-wing authoritarianism, social dominance orientation, or dogmatism. Personality differences, however, cannot account for the homogeneity of people belonging to dominant groups which is necessary for a broad consensus either actively or, in most cases, passively, to support disadvantageous treatment of minorities. As Staub (1989) convincingly demonstrates, even "the roots of evil" could not generate such extreme cases as dehumanization or genocide in a society, if a vast majority would not yield more or less direct support to the whole elimination machinery.

Moreover, it is the interplay between ethnocentric and other discrimination-legitimizing ideologies, created and defended by political and religious elites, gradually coagulated in collective beliefs and social norms and, finally, the sometimes blind, often utilitarian conformity with these norms, which account for the obvious homogeneity in dominant group members' aversive behavior toward minorities. It would be naive to think that a tolerant society would ever be constituted of solely tolerant, non-authoritarian, individual citizens. Rather, a society is tolerant because people conform to norms prescribing tolerance (Kinder, 1998; Pettigrew, 1991). Unfortunately, after a major political change, these people would not have much difficulty in gradually conforming to very different norms. This is exactly the sad lesson that the Kosovo conflict recently taught us: Victims can easily turn into perpetrators as soon as political power changes, and their retaliatory violence is in no way less dehumanizing and cruel than what they have suffered before.

REFERENCES

Adorno, T. W., Frenkel-Brunswik, E., Lewinson, D., & Sanford, R. N. (1950). *The authoritarian personality*. New York: Harper.

Allport, G. W. (1954). *The nature of prejudice*. Reading, MA: Addison-Wesley.

Altemeyer, B. (1988). *Enemies of freedom: Understanding right-wing authoritarianism*. San Francisco, CA: Jossey-Bass.

Altemeyer, B. (1994). Reducing prejudice in right-wing authoritarians. In M. P. Zanna & J. M. Olson (Eds.), *The psychology of prejudice: The Ontario symposium* (Vol. 7, pp. 131–148). Hillsdale, NJ: Erlbaum.

Appelgryen, A. E., & Nieuwoudt, J. M. (1988). Relative deprivation and the ethnic attitudes of Blacks and Afrikaans-speaking Whites in South Africa. *Journal of Social Psychology, 128*, 311–323.

Averill, J. R. (1982). *Anger and aggression. An essay on emotion*. New York: Springer.

Bar-Tal, D. (1989). Delegitimization: The extreme case of stereotyping and prejudice. In D. Bar-Tal, C. F. Graumann, A. W. Kruglanski, & W. Stroebe (Eds.), *Stereotyping and prejudice* (pp. 169–182). Berlin: Springer.

Batson, C. D., & Burris, C. T. (1994). Personal religion: Depressant or stimulant of prejudice and discrimination? In M. P. Zanna & J. M. Olson (Eds.), *The psychology of prejudice: The Ontario symposium* (Vol. 7, pp. 149–170). Hillsdale, NJ: Erlbaum.

Blanz, M., Mummendey, A., & Otten, S. (1995). Positive-negative asymmetry in social discrimination: The impact of stimulus-valence, size- and status-differentials in intergroup evaluations. *British Journal of Social Psychology, 34*(4), 409–419.

Blanz, M., Mummendey, A., & Otten, S. (1997). Normative evaluations and frequency expectations regarding positive versus negative outcome allocations between groups. *European Journal of Social Psychology, 27*, 165–176.

Branscombe, N. R., & Wann, D. L. (1994). Collective self-esteem consequences of outgroup derogation when a valued social identity is on trial. *European Journal of Social Psychology, 24*, 641–657.

Brewer, M. B. (1979). In-group bias in the minimal intergroup situation: A cognitive-motivational analysis. *Psychological Bulletin, 86*(2), 307–324.

Brown, R. J. (1999). *Group processes: Dynamics within and between groups.* Oxford, UK: Blackwell.

Crandall, C. S., & Cohen, C. (1994). The personality of the stigmatizer: Cultural world view, conventionalism, and self-esteem. *Journal of Research in Personality, 28*, 461–480.

Crocker, J., & Major, B. (1994). Reactions to stigma: The moderating role of jusifications. In M. P. Zanna & J. M. Olson (Eds.), *The psychology of prejudice: The Ontario symposium* (Vol. 7, pp. 289–314). Hillsdale, NJ: Erlbaum.

Crocker, J., & Quinn, D. M. (2001). Psychological consequences of devalued identities. In R. Brown & S. Gaertner (Eds.), *Blackwell handbook of social psychology: Intergroup processes* (pp. 238–257. Oxford: Blackwell Publishing.

Crosby, F. (1982). *Relative deprivation and working women.* New York: Oxford University Press.

Crosby, F. (1984). The denial of personal discrimination. *American Behavioral Scientist, 27*, 371–386.

Diehl, M. (1989). Justice and discrimination between minimal groups: The limits of equity. *British Journal of Social Psychology, 28*, 227–238.

Dion, K. L. (1986). Responses to perceived discrimination and relative deprivation. In J. M. Olson, C. P. Herman, & M. P. Zanna (Eds.), *Relative deprivation and social comparison: The Ontario symposium* (Vol. 5, pp. 159–179). Hillsdale, NJ: Erlbaum.

Dobbs, M., & Crano, W. D. (in prep.). *Accountability in the Minimal Group Paradigm: Implications for aversive discrimination and social identity theory.*

Dovidio, J. F., Brigham, J. C., Johnson, B. T., & Gaertner, S. L. (1996). Stereotyping, prejudice, and discrimination: Another look. In C. N. Macrae, C. Stangor, & M. Hewstone (Eds.), *Stereotypes and stereotyping* (pp. 276–319). New York: Guilford Press.

Dovidio, J. F., Mann, J., & Gaertner, S. L. (1989). Resistance to affirmative action: The implications of aversive racism. In F. A. Blanchard & F. J. Crosby (Eds.), *Affirmative action in perspective* (pp. 85–102). New York: Springer.

Eagly, A. H. (1987). *Sex differences in social behavior: A social-role interpretation.* Hillsdale, NJ: Erlbaum.

Eckhardt, W. (1991). Authoritarianism. *Political Psychology, 12*, 97–124.

Ellemers, N., & Barreto, M. (2001). The impact of relative group status: Affective, perceptual, and behavioral consequences. In R. Brown & S. Gaertner (Eds.), *Blackwell handbook of social psychology: Intergroup processes* (pp. 324–343). Oxford: Blackwell Publishing.

Ellemers, N., Van Rijswijk, W., Roefs, M., & Simons, C. (1997). Bias in intergroup perceptions: Balancing group identity with social reality. *Personality and Social Psychology Bulletin, 23*, 186–198.

Folger, R. (1986). A referent cognition theory of relative deprivation. In J. M. Olson, C. P. Herman, & M. P. Zanna (Eds.), *Relative deprivation and social comparison: The Ontario symposium* (Vol. 4, pp. 33–55). Hillsdale, NJ: Erlbaum.

Gaertner, S. L., & Dovidio, J. F. (1986). The aversive form of racism. In J. F. Dovidio & S. L. Gaertner (Eds.), *Prejudice, discrimination, and racism* (pp. 61–90). San Diego, CA: Academic Press.

Gaertner, S. L., Dovidio, J. F., Anastasio, P. A., Bachman, B. A., & Rust, M. C. (1993). The common ingroup identity model: Recategorization and the reduction of intergroup bias. In W. Stroebe & M. Hewstone (Eds.), *European review of social psychology* (Vol. 4, pp. 1–26). Chichester, UK: Wiley.

Gardham, K., & Brown, R. J. (in press). Two forms of intergroup discrimination with positive and negative outcomes: Explaining the positive-negative asymmetry effect. *British Journal of Social Psychology.*

Graumann, C. F., & Wintermantel, M. (1989). Discriminatory speech acts. A functional approach. In D. Bar-Tal, C. F. Graumann, A. W. Kruglanski, & W. Stroebe (Eds.), *Stereotyping and prejudice* (pp. 183–204). New York: Springer.

Guimond, S., & Dubé-Simard, L. (1983). Relative deprivation theory and the Québec nationalist movement: The cognition-emotion distinction and the personal-group deprivation issue. *Journal of Personality and Social Psychology, 44,* 526–535.

Kessler, T., Mummendey, A., & Leiße, U. K. (in press). The personal/group discrepancy: Is there a common information basis?

Hinkle, S., & Brown, R. J. (1990). Intergroup comparisons and social identity: Some links and lacunae. In D. Abrams & M. Hogg (Eds.), *Social identity theory: Constructive and critical advances.* Hemel Hempstead, UK: Wheatsheaf.

Kinder, D. R. (1998). Opinion and action in the realm of politics. In D. T. Gilbert, S. T. Fiske, & G. Lindzey (Eds.), *The handbook of social psychology* (Vol. 2, pp. 778–867). Boston, MA: McGraw-Hill.

Koomen, W., & Fränkel, E. G. (1992). Effects of experienced discrimination and different forms of relative deprivation among Surinamese, a Dutch ethnic minority group. *Journal of Community and Applied Social Psychology, 2,* 63–71.

Major, B. (1994). From social inequality to personal entitlement: The role of social comparisons, legitimacy appraisals, and group membership. In M. P. Zanna (Ed.), *Advances in experimental social psychology* (Vol. 26, pp. 293–355). San Diego, CA: Academic Press.

Messick, D. M., & Mackie, D. M. (1989). Intergroup relations. *Annual Review of Psychology, 40,* 45–81.

Mikula, G. (1994). Perspective-related differences in interpretations of injustice by victims and victimizers: A test with close relationships. In M. J. Lerner & G. Mikula (Eds.), *Injustice in close relationships: Entitlement and the affectional bond* (pp. 175–203). New York: Plenum.

Moghaddam, F. M., Stolkin, H. J., & Hutcheson, L. S. (1997). A generalized personal/group discrepancy: Testing the domain specificity of a perceived higher effect of events on one's group than on one's self. *Personality and Social Psychology Bulletin, 23,* 724–750.

Mummendey, A. (1995). Positive distinctiveness and intergroup discrimination: An old couple living in divorce. *European Journal of Social Psychology, 25,* 657–670.

Mummendey, A., Kessler, T., Klink, A., & Mielke, R. (1999). Strategies to cope with negative social identity: Predictions by Social Identity Theory and Relative Deprivation Theory. *Journal of Personality and Social Psychology, 76,* 229–245.

Mummendey, A., Klink, A., Mielke, R., Wenzel, M., & Blanz, M. (1999). Socio-structural relations and identity management strategies: Results from a field study in East Germany. *European Journal of Social Psychology, 29,* 259–285.

Mummendey, A., Linneweber, V., & Löschper, G. (1984). Aggression: From act to interaction. In A. Mummendey (Ed.), *Social psychology of aggression: From individual behavior to social interaction* (pp. 69–106). New York: Springer.

Mummendey, A., & Otten, S. (1993). Aggression: Interaction between individuals and social groups. In R. B. Felson & J. T. Tedeschi (Eds.), *Aggression and violence. Social interactionist perspectives* (pp. 145–167). Washington, DC: American Psychological Association.

Mummendey, A., & Otten, S. (1998). Positive-negative asymmetry in social discrimination. In W. Stroebe & M. Hewstone (Eds.), *European review of social psychology* (Vol. 9, pp. 107–143). New York: John Wiley & Sons Ltd.

Mummendey, A., Otten, S., Berger, U., & Kessler, T. (in press). Positive-negative asymmetry in social discrimination: Valence of evaluation and salience of categorization. *Personality and Social Psychology Bulletin.*

Mummendey, A., & Simon, B. (1991). Diskriminierung von Fremdgruppen: Zur Asymmetrie im Umgang mit positiven und negativen Bewertungen und Ressourcen. In D. Frey (Ed.), *Berichte über den 37. Kongreß der Deutschen Gesellschaft für Psychologie in Kiel 1990* (Vol. 2, pp. 359–365). Göttingen, Germany: Hogrefe.

Mummendey, A., Simon, B., Dietze, C., Grünert, M., Haeger, G., Kessler, S., Lettgen, S., & Schäferhoff, S. (1992). Categorization is not enough: Intergroup discrimination in negative outcome allocations. *Journal of Experimental Social Psychology, 28,* 125–144.

Mummendey, A., & Wenzel, M. (1999). Social discrimination and tolerance: Reactions to intergroup difference. *Personality and Social Psychology Review, 3,* 158–174.

Oakes, P. J. (1987). The salience of social categories. In J. C. Turner, M. A. Hogg, P. J. Oakes, S. Reicher, & M. Wetherell (Eds.), *Rediscovering the social group: A self-categorization theory* (pp. 117–141). Oxford, UK: Blackwell.

Oakes, P. J. (1996). The categorization process: Cognition and the group in the social psychology of stereotyping. In W. P. Robinson (Ed.), *Social groups and identities* (pp. 95–119). Oxford, UK: Butterworth.

Opotow, S. (1990). Moral exclusion and injustice: An introduction. *Journal of Social Issues, 46,* 1–20.

Opotow, S. (1995). Drawing the line. Social categorization, moral exclusion, and the scope of justice. In B. B. Bunker & J. Z. Rubin (Eds.), *Conflict, cooperation, and justice: Essays inspired by the work of Morton Deutsch* (pp. 347–369). San Francisco, CA: Jossey-Bass.

Otten, S., & Moskowitz, G. B. (2000). Evidence for implicit evaluative ingroup bias: Affect-biased spontaneous trait inference in a minimal group paradigm. *Journal of Experimental Social Psychology, 36,* 77–89.

Otten, S., & Mummendey, A. (1999a). Aggressive Interaktionen und soziale Diskriminierung: Zur Rolle perspektiven – und kontextspezifischer Legitimationsprozesse. *Zeitschrift für Sozialpsychologie, 30,* 126–138.

Otten, S., & Mummendey, A. (1999b). To our benefit or at your expense? Justice considerations in intergroup allocations of positive and negative resources. *Social Justice Research, 12,* 19–38.

Otten, S., & Mummendey, A. (2000). Valence-dependent probability of ingroup-favoritism between minimal groups: An integrative view on the positive-negative asymmetry in social discrimination. In D. Capozza & R. Brown (Eds.), *Social identity processes* (pp. 33–48). London: Sage.

Otten, S., Mummendey, A., & Blanz, M. (1996). Intergroup discrimination in positive and negative outcome allocations: The impact of stimulus valence, relative group status, and relative group size. *Personality and Social Psychology Bulletin, 22,* 568–581.

Otten, S., Mummendey, A., & Buhl, T. (1998). Accuracy in information processing and the positive-negative asymmetry in social discrimination. *Revue Internationale de Psychologie Sociale, 11,* 69–96.

Otten, S., Mummendey, A., & Wenzel, M. (1995). Evaluation of aggressive interactions in inter-personal and intergroup contexts. *Aggressive Behavior, 21,* 205–224.

Otten, S., & Wentura, D. (1999). About the impact of automaticity in the Minimal Group Paradigm: Evidence from affective priming tasks. *European Journal of Social Psychology, 29,* 1049–1071.

Perdue, C. W., Dovidio, J. F., Gurtman M. B., & Tyler, R. B. (1990). Us and them: Social categorization and the process of intergroup bias. *Journal of Personality and Social Psychology, 59,* 475–486.

Perreault, S., & Bourhis, R. Y. (1999). Ethnocentrism, social identification, and discrimination. *Personality and Social Psychology Bulletin, 25,* 92–103.

Pettigrew, T. F. (1991). Normative theory in intergroup relations: Explaining both harmony and conflict. *Psychology and developing societies, 3,* 3–16.

Pettigrew, T. F. (1998). Reactions toward the new minorities of Western Europe. *Annual Review of Sociology, 24,* 77–103.

Pettigrew, T. F., & Meertens, R. W. (1995). Subtle and blatant prejudice in Western Europe. *European Journal of Social Psychology, 25,* 57–75.

Postmes, T., & Spears, R. (1998). Deindividuation and anti-normative behavior: A meta-analysis. *Psychological Bulletin, 123,* 1–21.

Quillian, L. (1995). Prejudice as a response to perceived group threat: Population composition and anti-immigrant and racial prejudice in Europe. *American Sociology Review, 60,* 586–611.

Rabbie, J. M., & Horwitz, M. (1969). Arousal of ingroup–outgroup bias by a chance win or loss. *Journal of Personality and Social Psychology, 13,* 269–277.

Reynolds, K., Turner, J. C., & Haslam, A. (2000). When are we better than them and they worse than us? A closer look at social discrimination in positive and negative domains. *Journal of Personality and Social Psychology, 78,* 64–80.

Rokeach, M. (Ed.). (1960). *The open and closed mind.* New York: Basic Books.

Runciman, W. G. (1966). *Relative deprivation and social justice.* London: Routledge & Kegan Paul.

Sani, F., & Reicher, S. (1998). When consensus fails: An analysis of the schism within the Italian Communist Party (1991). *European Journal of Social Psychology, 28,* 623–645.

Sani, F., & Reicher, S. (1999). Identity, argument, and schism: Two longitudinal studies of the split in the Church of England over the ordination of women to the priesthood. *Group Processes and Intergroup Relations, 2,* 279–300.

Sidanius, J. (1993). The psychology of group conflict and the dynamics of oppression: A social dominance perspective. In S. Iyngar & W. McGuire (Eds.), *Current approaches to political psychology* (pp. 173–211). Durham, NC: Duke University Press.

Sherif, M. (1966). *Group conflict and cooperation.* London: Routledge & Kegan Paul.

Smith, E. R. (1993). Social identity and social emotions: Toward new conceptualizations of prejudice. In D. M. Mackie & D. L. Hamilton (Eds.), *Affect, cognition, and stereotyping* (pp. 297–315). San Diego, CA: Academic Press.

Staub, E. (1989). *The roots of evil. The origins of genocide and other group violence.* Cambridge, UK: Cambridge University Press.

Tajfel, H. (1981). *Human groups and social categories: Studies in social psychology.* Cambridge, UK: Cambridge University Press.

Tajfel, H., Billig, M. G., Bundy, R. P., & Flament, C. (1971). Social categorization and intergroup behaviour. *European Journal of Social Psychology, 1,* 149–178.

Tajfel, H., & Turner, J. C. (1986). The social identity theory of intergroup behavior. In S. Worchel & W. G. Austin (Eds.), *Psychology of intergroup relations* (pp. 7–24). Chicago, IL: Nelson-Hall Publishers.

Taylor, D., & Moghaddam, F. M. (1994). *Theories of intergroup relations.* New York: Praeger.

Taylor, D. M., Wright, S. C., Moghaddam, F. M., & Lalonde, R. N. (1990). The personal/group discrimination discrepancy: Perceiving my group, but not myself, to be a target for discrimination. *Personality and Social Psychology Bulletin, 16,* 254–262.

Taylor, D. M., Wright, S. C., & Porter, L. E. (1994). Dimensions of perceived discrimination: The personal/group discrimination discrepancy. In M. P. Zanna & J. M. Olson (Eds.), *The psychology of prejudice: The Ontario symposium* (Vol. 7, pp. 233–255). Hillsdale, NJ: Erlhaum.

Tedeschi, J. T. (1984). A social psychological interpretation of human aggression. In A. Mummendey (Ed.), *Social psychology of aggression: From individual behavior to social interaction* (pp. 5–20). Berlin: Springer.

Tedeschi, J. T., & Felson, R. B. (1994). *Aggression and coercive actions: A social interactionist perspective.* Washington, DC: American Psychological Association.

Thränhardt, D. (1995). The political uses of xenophobia in England, France, and Germany. *Party Politics, 1*, 323–345.

Triandis, H. C., & Trafimow, D. (2001). Culture and its implications for intergroup behavior. In R. Brown & S. Gaertner (Eds.), *Blackwell handbook of social psychology: Intergroup processes* (pp. 367–385). Oxford: Blackwell Publishing.

Turner, J. C. (1975). Social comparison and social identity: Some prospects for intergroup behaviour. *European Journal of Social Psychology, 5*, 5–35.

Turner, J. C., Hogg, M. A., Oakes, P. J., Reicher, S. D., & Wetherell, M. S. (1987). *Rediscovering the social group. A self-categorization theory.* Oxford, UK: Blackwell.

Tyler, T. R. (2001). Social justice. In R. Brown & S. Gaertner (Eds.), *Blackwell handbook of social psychology: Intergroup processes* (pp. 344–364). Oxford: Blackwell Publishing.

Van Knippenberg, A. (1989). Strategies of identity management. In J. P. Oudenhoven & T. M. Willemsen (Eds.), *Ethnic minorities: Social-psychological perspectives* (pp. 59–76). Amsterdam: Swets & Zeitlinger.

Vanneman, R. D., & Pettigrew, T. F. (1972). Race and relative deprivation in the urban United States. *Race, 13*(4), 461–486.

Wagner, U., & Zick, A. (1995). Formal education and ethnic prejudice. *European Journal of Social Psychology, 25*, 41–56.

Wenzel, M. (1997). *Soziale Kategorisierungen im Bereich distributiver Gerechtigkeit.* Münster, Germany: Waxmann.

Wenzel, M. (2000). Justice and identity: The significance of inclusion for perceptions of entitlement and the justice motive. *Personality and Social Psychology Bulletin, 26*, 157–176.

Author Index

Subject Index